Profiting from Intellectual Capital

INTELLECTUAL PROPERTY SERIES

Trademark Valuation by Gordon V. Smith

How to License Technology by Robert C. Megantz

Intellectual Property Infringement Damages: A Litigation Support Handbook by Russell L. Parr

Intellectual Property: Licensing and Joint Venture Profit Strategies, Second Edition by Gordon V. Smith and Russell L. Parr

Law and the Information Superhighway: Privacy, Access, Intellectual Property, Commerce, Liability by Henry H. Perritt, Jr.

Licensing Intellectual Property Rights by John W. Schlicher

Managing Intellectual Property Rights by Lewis C. Lee and J. Scott Davidson

Multimedia Legal Handbook: A Guide From the Software Publisher's Association by Thomas J. Smedinghoff

The New Role of Intellectual Property in Commercial Transactions by Melvin Simensky and Lanning G. Bryer

Protecting Trade Dress by Robert C. Dorr and Christopher H. Munch

Protecting Trade Secrets, Patents, Copyrights, and Trademarks by Robert C. Dorr and Christopher H. Munch

Software Patents by Gregory A. Stobbs

Technology Licensing: Corporate Strategies for Maximizing Value by Russell L. Parr and Patrick H. Sullivan

Valuation of Intellectual Property and Intangible Assets, Second Edition by Gordon V. Smith and Russell L. Parr

Electronic Contracting, Publishing, and EDI Law by Michael S. Baum and Henry H. Perritt, Jr.

Intellectual Property for the Internet edited by Lewis C. Lee and J. Scott Davidson

Intellectual Property Litigation: Pretrial Practice Guide by Eric M. Dobrusin

1997 Wiley Intellectual Property Law Update edited by Anthony B. Askew and Elizabeth C. Jacobs

Profiting from Intellectual Capital

Extracting Value from Innovation

Patrick H. Sullivan

John Wiley & Sons, Inc.

New York • Chichester • Weinheim • Brisbane • Singapore • Toronto

To Patsy for our yesterdays,
To Christine, Suzanne, and Patrick for our tomorrows

This book is printed on acid-free paper. ♾

Published simultaneously in Canada.

Library of Congress Cataloging-in-Publication Data:

Profiting from intellectual capital : extracting value from innovation / Patrick H. Sullivan.
p. cm. — (Intellectual property series)
Includes bibliographical references and index.
ISBN 0-471-19302-X (cloth : alk. paper) ISBN 0-471-41747-5 (paper: alk. paper)
1. Technological innovations—Management. 2. Intellectual property. I. Sullivan, Patrick H. II. Series.
HD45.P763 1998
658.5'77—dc21

97-34975
CIP

Printed in the United States of America.

10 9 8 7 6 5 4 3 2 1

About the Author

Patrick H. Sullivan, DBA, MS, BS, is an expert at developing profits from intellectual assets. He is a founding partner of the ICM Group, LLC, a consulting company focused on extracting value from intellectual capital. His consulting practice involves assessing the value extraction capabilities and needs of corporations, developing IC strategies that enhance and enable corporate strategy, assessing the IC management needs of corporations, and designing and implementing decision processes and management systems for extracting value.

Dr. Sullivan has worked as an engineer on the launch team of the Saturn/Apollo moon project at Cape Kennedy and, following graduate school, as the chief financial officer at two research universities. He has been a Vice President of the MAC Group and a Principal Consultant at SRI International, where he managed the firm's general consulting practice in Europe. A sampling of his clients include Dow Chemical, Xerox, Bofors, Canon, General Motors, Rockwell, Eastman Chemical, Air Liquide, and NASA.

Dr. Sullivan is a frequent speaker, giving talks on a range of intellectual capital management issues, including strategy, stock value, licensing, and developing profits from IC. He is a Fellow of the American Council on Education, a member of the Licensing Executives Society (where he is currently chairman of the Intellectual Capital Management Committee), the WIPO Trade Forum, and the American Bar Association Intellectual Property Section. He is a regular contributor of articles to the LES Journal, *les Nouvelles.*

About the Contributors

Joseph J. Daniele, Ph.D., is Corporate Manager of Intellectual Properties and heads the Corporate MIP Office at Xerox Corporation. He is responsible for senior management review, revision, and approval of all Xerox intellectual property transfers worldwide, as well as corporate IP strategy and product infringement analyses and follow-up.

Leif Edvinsson is the world's leading expert on intellectual capital (IC). As Vice President and newly named Corporate Director of Intellectual Capital at Skandia AFS of Stockholm, Sweden, he has been a key contributor to the theory of IC and oversaw the creation of the world's first corporate intellectual capital annual report.

Stephen P. Fox is Associate General Counsel and Director of Intellectual Property at Hewlett-Packard Company, headquartered in Palo Alto, California. He has overall responsibility for the Intellectual Property Section of the Legal Department comprising 90 professionals in Europe, Asia and the United States. He received a bachelor's degree in electrical engineering from Northwestern University and a Juris Doctorate from George Washington University Law School. Mr. Fox has been with Hewlett-Packard Company for 30 years.

Paul B. Germeraad, JD, Ph.D., is Vice President and Director, Research and Development at Avery Dennison. Dr. Germeraad has formerly worked at both James River Corporation and Raychem in senior technical management positions.

Peter C. Grindley, Ph.D., is a Senior Economist at the Law and Economics Group, Inc. He has been both a Visiting Professor of Economics at the University of California, Berkeley, and an Assistant Professor of Economics at London Business School. Dr. Grindley has authored numerous publications in the area of technology and has broad experience in economic consulting in the areas of intellectual property and licensing, competitive strategy, and regulation, especially in high technology industries.

Harry J. Gwinnell, JD, is Assistant General Counsel, Intellectual Property, and Assistant Secretary at Eastman Chemical Company. He has prior experience as Assistant Patent Counsel at United Technologies Corporation and Patent Examiner at the United States Patent and Trademark Office. He has served as President of both the Tennessee and Connecticut Intellectual Property Associations and is currently a member of the Board of Governors of the Tennessee Intellectual Property Law Association.

Kelly H. Hale is the Intellectual Property Manager for the Rockwell International Semiconductor Systems Division. His background includes several years of semiconductor device development work at various companies, including American Micro Systems, Inc., and RCA (now Harris Semiconductor). He graduated from Idaho State University and received his law degree from the University of Denver.

Brian P. Hall, Ph.D., is an international values consultant to education, government, and industry throughout the world. He specializes in the development of tools and methods for values measurement that enable leaders of international organizations to improve the alignment and agility of those institutions. Currently, he is Chairman of the Board and Chief Executive Officer of Values Technology.

Martin L. W. Hall, Ph.D., is a management consultant and frequent lecturer. His research focuses in issues of systems thinking and human values as they relate to organizational intervention and transformation. Dr. Hall is a Principal in Values Technology of Santa Cruz, California. Past experience includes working in the software industry in various management and consulting roles with a focus on quality issues.

Suzanne S. Harrison, MBA, has worked for over ten years in the emerging field of intellectual capital management (ICM). Prior to her current assignment, she was with Coopers & Lybrand's Financial Advisory Services as a financial consultant, specializing in intellectual property issues. She has also worked for Hewlett-Packard as a financial analyst. She has conducted economic and financial analyses in support of intellectual property litigation and has advised clients on maximizing value from their patent portfolios. Ms. Harrison is the recipient of the Licensing Executives Society North America Fellowship.

Pamela Jajko, BA, MS, is Manager of the Library Information Center (LInC) and the Corporate Record Systems Department at Roche Bioscience.

Sam Khoury, Ph.D., is the Senior Intangible Asset Appraiser of The Dow Chemical Company. He specializes in the valuation of patented technology, trade secrets, and valuation of over 200 patents and trade secrets that range in value from $0 to $50 million. He is the Chairman of the Valuation and Taxation committee at Licensing Executives Society (LES).

Kari Laento, LLM, is Corporate Vice President for Telecom Finland Corporation. Formerly, she was with the Neste Group, where she served as part of the Group Marketing Company and Special Products and Gas Division. Ms. Laento is President of the Finnish Basketball Federation and is a member of the Board of the Olympic Committee.

Willy Manfroy is Director, Corporate Development, at Eastman Chemical Company in Kingsport, Tennessee. Previously, he was Manager in the Mergers, Acquisitions, and Licensing Department of The Dow Chemical Company. Mr. Manfroy is the current President of the Licensing Executives' Society USA/Canada, an international professional organization devoted to technology transfer and licensing.

Lorraine S. Morrison, MA, has worked at Avery Dennison for the past 11 years and is currently Manager, Intellectual Property for the Corporate Research Center. In addition to her role in valuing the intangible assets of Avery Dennison, she works to integrate the knowledge learned with strategic planning.

James P. O'Shaughnessy, JD, is Vice President and Chief Intellectual Property Counsel, Rockwell International Corporation. Before assuming that position, Mr. O'Shaughnessy was a Senior Partner at Foley & Lardner, where he was a leader in the growth of the firm's intellectual property practice. He is founder of Innovatech Co., a company devoted to the development of innovation strategies. Mr. O'Shaughnessy is a frequent lecturer and an author on a wide range of intellectual property topics.

Gordon P. Petrash is the Global Director of Intellectual Asset and Capital Management for The Dow Chemical Company, one of the world's largest chemical companies. Mr. Petrash has been a speaker at numerous conferences on the subject of Intellectual Asset

Management and its implementation. He has authored and contributed to a number of articles related to the work his company has done in this area.

Eugenie Prime, MA, MS, has been Manager of Corporate Libraries at Hewlett-Packard Company since 1987. Before that, she headed a large hospital library while simultaneously serving as President of CINAHL Corporation, publishers and database producers of the Nursing and Allied Health Index.

Kevin G. Rivette, JD, is cofounder and President of SmartPatents, Inc., where he is responsible for the strategic vision and direction of the company. He has served with several high-tech and investment-related companies. As a patent attorney, Mr. Rivette has represented several high-tech clients, including Apple Computers and Seeq Technology.

Trent E. Walker, Ph.D., is a Professor at the University of California at Berkeley. He has written for various journals in the areas of mathematics and engineering, and specializes in operator algebras and H control.

Paul B. Westberg, MBA, is Senior Financial Analyst at Genentech, Inc. He has pioneered several financial and strategic planning initiatives involved with managing the uncertainties and value of innovations in the development pipeline. He has conducted financial and economic valuations of knowledge companies as well as of developing technologies. He has also advised companies on the application of ICM frameworks and techniques for the resolution of client problems.

Contents

Part II Intellectual Property Management

Part III Intellectual Asset Management

Foreword

The worldwide emerging focus on intellectual capital is part of a search for more intelligent approaches to managing the corporate enterprise. The attention being given to intellectual capital has grown from a ripple to a groundswell as ever new insights demonstrate that intellectual capital is one of the major forces driving corporate performance and earnings. Not only current performance, but of even greater strategic importance, we now know that it is the firm's intellectual capital that defines its future.

In its broader context, intellectual capital is comprised of human capital and structural capital. Its subelements include organizational capital, customer capital, supplier capital, and more. These terms are not new. What is new is the energy and commitment of organizations trying out the concepts surrounding intellectual capital to leverage ideas into value. Terms like *intellectual asset management, intellectual property management,* and *knowledge management* are frequently being interchanged as firms describe their new management focus. The cross-company confusion created by this emerging taxonomy does not prevent the advancement of the discussion of intellectual capital management or any of the other focused discussions regarding these terms. Though each of these terms is unique, they all concern the intangibles of an organization and how to better leverage and manage them for value.

Intellectual capital is about the creation of value out of human talent, transforming it through the resources provided by the firm's structure, and multiplying it on a global scale by the value extraction recipes contained in this book. In many corporations, there are a lot of hidden values, imbedded in both the human and structural capital of the firm. Corporations recognizing the importance of this hidden value have been working to understand how to release its potential through systematized value extraction processes. Dow, Skandia, and the member companies of the ICM Gathering have been exploring and experimenting with systematized value extraction and the creation of new ways of profiting from this elusive "hidden value."

A number of books on the topic have been written and more are on their way. The books written to date focus almost exclusively on knowledge management or how to create new knowledge or new value. This book, different from its predecessors, focuses on how to *profit* from the firm's knowledge. The value extraction perspective discussed in detail in these pages is being shared by Gathering companies in other ways as well. For example, companies interested in emulating successful

ICM practices are actively benchmarking with each other, and organizations such as the Licensing Executives Society (LES) are devoting more time and effort to learning about ICM and sharing their knowledge broadly. Leading organizations know that the pursuit of best practices is important and have made this an active part of their intellectual capital management process. The member organizations of the ICM Gathering are examples of this.

There is a community of interest surrounding ICM. The community is global and is comprised of IC practitioners who exchange and refine their learning both about value extraction and value creation.

This book presents a number of different perspectives, experiences, and practices from companies in the ICM community. It also highlights a range of perspectives on how to extract and leverage the hidden value of our enterprises for current and future benefit. It is not a book filled with simple answers or silver bullets. It is a book of experiences and learning about how to create the future of your firm through harnessing the power of the firm's IC. It is about profiting from intellectual capital.

Gordon Petrash
Midland, Michigan

Leif Edvinsson
Stockholm, Sweden

Preface

My interest in the field of intellectual capital management began in 1988 when I read an article by David Teece, a colleague and Mitsubishi Professor at the Haas School of Business, UC Berkeley. The article, "*Profiting from Technological Innovation: Implications for Integration, Collaboration, Licensing and Public Policy,*" included a diagram of the steps necessary for commercializing a technology. Although I had been working in the Silicon Valley for more than 20 years, I had never seen the steps defined before. Typically, in the Valley, the people who commercialize technology do so using a set of "secret rituals" or "black arts" that are carefully guarded at the same time that their results are ballyhooed. David's revelation of the steps, if accurate, offered amazing possibilities. Companies as a whole (rather than individuals or consultants) could begin to understand how to commercialize a technology, develop ways to do it better, teach employees how to do it, create whole new capabilities, and commercialize neglected technologies.

For the next four years I worked closely with Professor Paul Alder at Stanford, David Teece, and a range of other industry and academic experts to develop a simpler, more direct explanation of the commercialization process than David's. I began to make presentations to technology companies, defense contractors (swords into plowshares, thought I), and anyone else who would sit still long enough to hear the message about how to generate more profits from their existing portfolios.

In 1992 Tom Stewart of *Fortune* magazine wrote the first "brainpower" article. He mentioned a number of people working in the general field of knowledge creation and brainpower. Although my interests focused on value extraction, different from Tom's brainpower interest, we nevertheless seemed to be involved in the same general area, now being called *intellectual capital management.* I called him and gave him a précis of my work and my interest, which he politely typed into his computer (I could hear the clacking of the keyboard keys during our conversation).

Tom was becoming the person who connected people with related interests in the new field called *intellectual capital management.* One day I received a phone call from someone with a decidedly Swedish accent who announced himself as the Vice President for Intellectual Capital at Skandia, a Swedish finance house. Tom Stewart, he told me, had given him my name. The caller, Leif Edvinsson, subsequently visited me in Berkeley, where I introduced him to David Teece and another Berkeley faculty member, Baruch Lev, a professor of accounting with an interest in valuing and measuring intangibles.

During that visit, Leif and I began a relationship that was to endure. In one conversation we talked about bringing together companies that were actively managing their intellectual capital and looking at the management of intangibles through the eyes of companies that were actually profiting from them. Unfortunately, neither of us had the time or the energy to follow through at that time.

In 1993 I gave a talk on commercializing innovation, this time at the annual meeting of the Licensing Executives Society (LES) held that year in San Francisco. In a 20-minute presentation I did my enthusiastic best to demonstrate to the audience how technologies can be commercialized and also how theory and practice have revealed methods for making more profits than firms typically do. As usual, people were interested but couldn't quite see how to apply it at their companies.

Afterward, a man from the audience approached me and announced, "You were using my slides!" Recovering quickly, I asked who he was and why he thought the slides were his. "Oh," he said affably, "not actually my slides, but I do give almost the same talk. I'm Gordon Petrash with Dow Chemical. I manage Dow's intellectual assets, and I frequently give talks just like the one you just gave." Gordon and I went off to the cafeteria to talk some more about this over coffee. During the next year, Gordon invited me to consult at Dow and to share my now evolving views on profiting from intellectual assets with a spectrum of potentially interested Dow people.

The following year, at the next meeting of the LES, in Hawaii, Gordon and I were having coffee on the veranda overlooking a spectacular scene of mountain, sea, and pool. "Wouldn't it be fun to bring together all of the companies in the world who actively manage their intellectual capital?" said I. Gordon immediately responded that it would be very interesting and wondered what we could all learn from each other. All of a sudden this sounded like "déjà vu all over again". . . . I suggested that Leif Edvinsson might be interested as well. Gordon's enthusiasm for the idea was just the push I needed to agree to be the point person.

Gordon, Leif, and I pooled our knowledge of the companies who were actively managing their intellectual assets and invited them to meet. In Berkeley in January 1995, we gathered this group of practitioners together to share what they knew. The participating companies included Dow, Du Pont, Hewlett-Packard, Hughes Space and Communications, Hoffman LaRoche, Skandia, and The Law & Economics Consulting Group (my then business affiliation).

The meeting participants set as their purpose to define the term *intellectual capital* and to determine how it is managed, at least for those companies attending the meeting. At the end of an opening round of show-and-tell, it was clear that each company saw intellectual capital differently and managed its resources in this area differently as well. At the end of the day we were all perplexed and troubled; no common pattern seemed to be emerging. The next morning we met again and, using some group-discussion techniques as well as lots of blackboard drawings, slowly came to realize that we were, in fact, all talking about the same thing but that, while using the same terms, we were all defining them differently. We proceeded to develop a common set of definitions and descriptions.

Having agreed to meet for one and a half days, by noon on the second day the excitement level in the room was almost electric; no one wanted the meeting to end. We agreed to meet again, and four months later we reconvened to continue the conversation. We have continued to meet every four months since. The group formally calls itself "The ICM (Intellectual Capital Managers) Gathering." The members of the Gathering agree a priori on the "hot topics" to be featured at each forthcoming meeting, speakers are invited, and hotels are booked.

Meetings usually begin slowly, with show-and-tell around the table concerning the agreed topic. On the first day, participants jot down issues and potential topics for the next morning's discussions. At the beginning of the second day, a long list of potential discussion topics is quickly winnowed down to the two or three "hottest." The discussions that follow take on a life and an energy of their own. In the room are people who are among the most knowledgeable in the world about the practice of managing intellectual capital. They share a collective knowledge that is probably unequaled. When this collective knowledge is focused on topics of mutual interest and importance, the result represents the very best thinking possible.

The interest and energy generated by being in the company of others who were interested in extracting value from intellectual capital led me (with several others) to form The ICM Group, a consulting company focused on developing innovative methods, procedures, and techniques for companies to use to extract the most profits possible from their intellectual capital. The number of companies interested in learning more about this new field of management continues to grow. Their interest is in learning how to make more profits from their existing intellectual capital, and how to use their intellectual capital as a basis for creating the profits, both now and in the future.

By virtue of their early commitment and head start, Gathering companies are perhaps five years ahead of others in their thinking on technology commercialization. This book contains many of the lessons these companies have learned, from themselves and from one another. These are not proprietary or secret. The Gathering companies realize it is in their self-interest to have more companies learning and sharing how to manage and profit from intellectual capital. They and I invite you to read this book and to use as much from it as possible. In so doing, you become a part of this process of creating a world where ideas can have more value and where they can make greater contributions to society.

The idea for this book first came from Marla Bobowick, the John Wiley & Sons editor on a book I had done with Russell Parr on extracting value through licensing. Marla and I had been talking about my view of the emerging importance of intellectual capital and the then slow but persistent increase in interest in how to profit from it. Marla encouraged me to write a book on the topic, while I expressed my reluctance to committing the time to such an undertaking. She then suggested that the companies in The Gathering might write some of the chapters; after all, weren't they too a source of knowledge as well as participants in the learning that comes from Gathering meetings? I broached the idea with some trepidation. This book is evidence of the response from the companies in the Gathering.

This book is about extracting value from intellectual capital. It is a book about how to change our view of a company to see the hidden value and to take advantage of it. It contains information on methods, approaches, and techniques for extracting value already in use by the companies in The Gathering. Everything in this book is tested, tried, and true.

This book is different from the several others recently published on intellectual capital. The author and contributors are not professional writers; consequently, the book is undoubtedly less well-written than others. Written for practitioners, this book describes the basic concepts and theory as well as the actual experiences and practices used by a range of companies, all of whom are successfully extracting value from their intellectual capital. Every contributor to this book shares a set of beliefs about intellectual capital and its management: that what we have learned from each other has benefited us, our companies, and many others; that what we have learned and what we are doing with that learning contributes to society at large by creating more profits, more products and services, and more economic value for society. Finally, we believe that the more companies there are practicing the principles we have learned, the more we ourselves can learn, thereby benefiting ourselves, our companies, and society.

As you read this book, we hope you will sense our passion and perhaps even develop one of your own.

Acknowledgments

A book is a snapshot that freezes into a moment of time the thinking processes that span years and sometimes decades. During the course of those years of thinking, learning, and experiencing, we are exposed to and nourished by many people. This book, like any other, is the product of all of those interactions with friends, colleagues, coworkers, and clients.

Early in my consulting career, at SRI International, I was working (and learning) with technology companies on increasing the profits they made from technology. While there, I met and was deeply influenced by Paul Skov, from whom I learned the power of decision analysis in examining business issues, and how to structure analyses in ways that business schools don't teach. From J. Patrick Henry, another colleague who had a major impact on my intellectual development, I learned to think strategically. Pat taught me how instincts and intuition (along with a touch of Irish insight) provide dimension and perspective that enriches and breathes life into business facts, calculations, and data.

I was intrigued and stimulated by David Teece's original article on extracting value from innovation. Discussing the steps to commercialization from that article with David, as well as with Paul Adler, then of Stanford University, led to a greater understanding of the sources of innovative value as well as of the ways to convert value into cash.

I have been supported and encouraged by friends and colleagues Blaine Nye of Stanford Consulting Group, Syed Shariq of NASA, and Chelton Tanger of Coopers & Lybrand. Clients-turned-colleagues have also added a significant dimension of insight and learning that have increased my knowledge and understanding. At Dow Chemical, Sharon Oriel, Carl Lucas, and Sam Khoury have been the source of many open and honest dialogues and debates that led to greater levels of understanding; Kelly Hale at Rockwell, who taught me more about the semiconductor industry than I taught him about ICM; Cheri Porter at Eastman Chemical, who kept asking me "how" and "why" until I could adequately describe; Roger Hailstone of Du Pont and Dan McGavock of IPC, who forced me to think through and define the differences between managing intellectual property, intellectual assets, and intellectual capital; Thierry Sueur of Air Liquide, whose gentlemanly manner and soft-spoken style belie his intelligence, insight, and intuitive grasp of the practical possibilities for often incomplete ICM concepts.

I have been intrigued and challenged by a range of intellectually interesting if not provocative people—some of whom I know as friends, some I have only met, and some I know only through their writings—now friends as well as colleagues Gordon Petrash and Leif Edvinsson, Joe Daniele of Xerox, Stephen Fox of Hewlett-Packard, Willy Manfroy and Harry Gwinnell of Eastman Chemical, Jim O'Shaughnessey of Rockwell, Hubert Saint-Onge of The Mutual Group of Canada, and Brian Hall of the Values Institute; Tom Stewart of *Fortune* magazine, Steven Wallman of the U.S. Securities and Exchange Commission, Baruch Lev of the NYU Stern School's Center for Research on Intangibles.

On the production end, Janet Mowry has been wonderful at editing the rough draft chapters into well-expressed English; my assistant Lizabetta Young has worked us carefully through a labyrinth of chapters, drafts, contributors, and format requirements. Martha Cooley at Wiley whose unflagging support, encouragement, and helpful suggestions made this easier than it should have been.

Finally, and most important, I would like to acknowledge my business partner, colleague, friend, and daughter, Suzanne (Sullivan) Harrison, who carried the business load more times than I can recount, who provided me with time, inspiration, and intellectual space, and who made this book possible.

Part I

Definitions, Concepts, and Context

1

Introduction to Intellectual Capital Management

Patrick H. Sullivan

ICM Group, LLC

Intellectual capital is a topic of increasing interest to firms that derive their profits from innovation and knowledge. In many cases, these "knowledge firms" find that the marketplace values them at a price far higher than their balance sheets warrant. What is the true value of a company like Microsoft? It is more than the tangible assets: The company's value is in its intangible intellectual assets as well as in its ability to convert those assets into revenues. The market premium for Microsoft and other knowledge companies is in their intellectual capital as well as in the firms' abilities to systematically leverage it. But, surprisingly, few managers in knowledge firms can define intellectual capital—what it is, where it resides in their firms, and how they manage it to produce the profits for their shareholders.

This book differs from those already published on intellectual capital management (ICM) in several ways. First, this is the only one to present "inside information" from several companies that have succeeded in extracting profits from their intellectual capital. Second, this is a how-to book that contains best practices from some of the most managerially sophisticated companies in the world. Third, whereas other books on intellectual capital focus on knowledge management, learning communities, information technology, and the human side of the management equation, this one focuses on "value extraction." It discusses the experiences of pioneering companies that have been actively managing their intellectual capital for some years. The companies contributing to this book span the range of U.S. and international industry: Xerox, Dow, Hewlett-Packard, Eastman Chemical, and Rockwell International.

In April 1996, the Securities and Exchange Commission (SEC) convened a meeting to discuss what it saw as an emerging problem. Increasingly, a new kind of company has been finding its way onto U.S. securities exchanges. This new kind of company has intellectual capital (intangibles) as its major asset. Unlike tangible assets such as money, buildings, and equipment, intellectual capital is not visible; it is neither measured nor reported. Of concern to the SEC is that many of these companies are trading at prices far in excess of the value of their tangible assets. This gap between market value and the value of tangible assets is associated with the value the marketplace puts on the firm's intellectual capital as well as its ability to leverage that value in its marketplace. No information is reported to investors about this intellectual capital—not its amount, how it is created, or how it is used to generate profits. The major reason for this lack of reporting is that intellectual capital is not directly managed or measured. Most firms do not know how to describe or define their intellectual capital, much less how to manage or report it.

The interest in intellectual capital was sparked by Tom Stewart's series of articles in *Fortune* magazine on the topic. Stewart focused his articles (as well as his recent book, *Intellectual Capital, the New Wealth of Organizations*) on how firms *create value* through their "brainpower" (intellectual capital). Indeed, virtually all of what has been written on the subject to date focuses on the strategic issue of how to better create knowledge and intellectual capital for the firm to achieve its strategic objectives. This literature deals with the knowledge creation and information sharing aspects of ICM. But what about the other side of the equation? How can firms develop financial benefits and routinely extract ever more value from their intellectual capital? Extracting value from intellectual capital is the focus of this book

Companies that make their profits by converting knowledge into value are called *knowledge companies.* As a practical matter, those companies whose profits come predominantly from commercializing innovations are at the core of the knowledge company definition. Companies such as Microsoft, 3M, and Netscape are examples of firms whose knowledge or intellectual capital is the firm's major asset. They are clear-cut examples of knowledge firms. Other firms, whose profits come largely from commercializing their innovations but, where the commercialization requires large and expensive business assets (such as manufacturing facilities and distribution networks), are also considered here to be knowledge firms as far as the management of their intellectual capital is concerned.

What is intellectual capital? Is intellectual capital, as one company has defined it, "what walks out the door at the end of the business day"? Is it the people? A firm's know-how? Intellectual capital, as defined by the companies represented in this book, is the sum of a firm's ideas, inventions, technologies, general knowledge, computer programs, designs, data skills, processes, creativity, and publications. *Intellectual capital may be thought of simply as knowledge that can be converted into profits.*

There are other definitions of intellectual capital. For example, Hubert Saint-Onge, Vice President for People, Knowledge and Strategies for Canada's Mutual Group, a pioneer in the field of knowledge creation, prefers the term *knowledge capital* to intellectual capital: He defines *knowledge capital* as the sum of human capital (the capabilities of the individuals required to provide solutions to customers); *customer capital* (the depth, width, attachment, and profitability of the franchise); and *structural capital* (the organizational capabilities of the organization to meet market requirements). Leif Edvinsson of Skandia, another pioneer, defines it as "the sum of the firm's human and structural capital." Tom Stewart of *Fortune* magazine has defined intellectual capital as "the intangible assets of skill, knowledge, and information."

In contrast, the ICM Gathering (all of whose members have value extraction as their primary focus), at its first meeting, developed a definition of intellectual capital that has served them well ever since: *Intellectual capital is knowledge that can be converted into profits.* For these companies, intellectual capital comprises two major elements: human capital and intellectual assets.

- *Human capital* consists of a company's individual employees, each of whom has skills, abilities, knowledge, and know-how. To take advantage of any of these, the employee (an individual "unit" of human capital) must be physically positioned wherever that skill, ability, or bit of knowledge is to be used. Within each employee resides the tacit (uncodified) knowledge the firm seeks to utilize.
- *Intellectual assets* are created whenever the human capital commits to media any bit of knowledge, know-how, or learning. Once "written," the knowledge is codified and defined. At this point, the firm can move the intellectual asset, rather than the individual, to wherever it is needed. Examples of intellectual assets include plans, procedures, memos, sketches, drawings, blueprints, and computer programs, to name but a few. Any items in this list that are legally protected are called *intellectual property.* Intellectual property includes patents, copyrights, trademarks, and trade secrets.

Exhibit 1.1 depicts the intellectual capital of the firm. Imagine that the large shaded box represents the firm's intellectual capital. Inside the box are its two

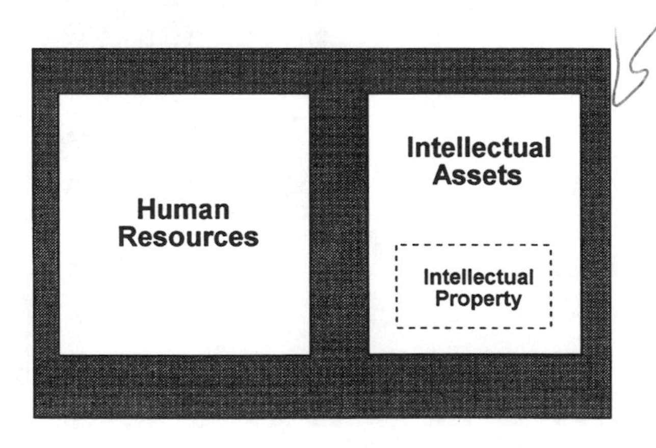

Exhibit 1.1 A Model of Intellectual Capital

major elements: human capital and intellectual assets. The portion of the firm's intellectual assets that are legally protected are called *intellectual property.*

Note that the firm does not own the human capital. Employees are not owned by the firm. They may quit, be fired, take leaves of absence, or in many other ways sever their working relationships with the firm. But the firm does own its intellectual assets: These were created by the human capital in the firm's employ and are now the property of the company. With this in mind, it is in the firm's best interest to encourage employees to codify their knowledge thereby creating more intellectual assets and more opportunities to leverage it into profits.

But intellectual capital by itself is not sufficient for a knowledge firm to succeed. The intellectual capital must be supplemented by the firm's infrastructure or structural capital:

> *Structural capital* is the "hard" assets of the firm. These include all of the items found on the balance sheet: financial assets, buildings, machinery, and the infrastructure of the firm. The structural capital also includes the complementary business assets that are often necessary to convert an innovative idea into a salable product or service. (Complementary business assets include such necessary business elements as manufacturing facilities, distribution capabilities, and sales outlets. These are discussed in more detail later.)

Adding structural capital to intellectual capital provides a much more accurate picture of what constitutes a knowledge company. Exhibit 1.2 shows a more complete view of the model of a knowledge firm.

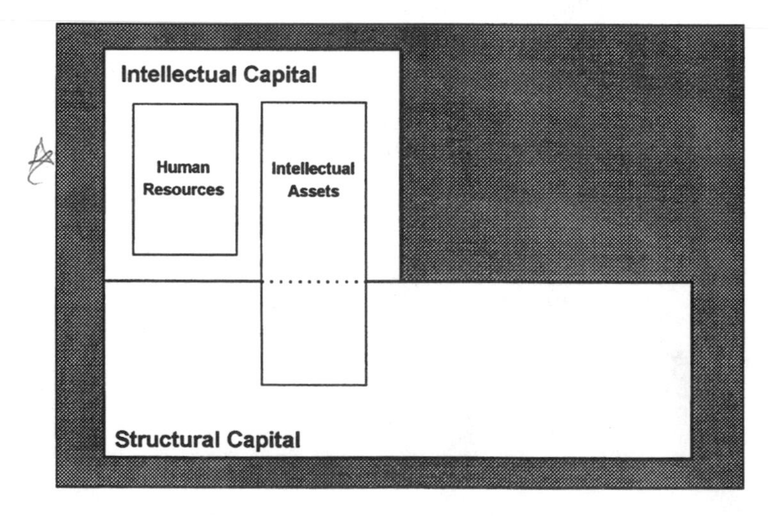

Exhibit 1.2 Model of a Knowledge Company

WHAT COMPANIES ARE DOING

Companies that operate according to the model presented in Exhibit 1.2 may focus their intellectual capital management activity on different portions of the model. For example, two major chemical companies see the major focus of their IC work in the intellectual asset portion of the model; their unprotected intellectual assets are the most likely source of new or innovative products. Hence, their focus is on identifying and managing their intellectual assets. Other firms, such as tightly managed computer and product companies, have innovation management systems in place that allow them to focus their IC activities on selecting only the "best" technologies to be patented and commercialized. This puts the focus of their IC activity at the frontier between intellectual assets and intellectual properties.

Companies desiring to create a large portfolio of ideas need to encourage their human capital to codify knowledge and know-how; from this knowledge they can select the most promising ideas for commercialization in the marketplace. Such firms operate at the interface between human capital and intellectual assets. Still other firms are involved in all of the foregoing and place themselves at the juxtaposition of human capital, intellectual assets, and intellectual property. Exhibit 1.3 illustrates where a number of the Gathering companies see the focus of their intellectual capital management activity.

THE IMPORTANCE OF CONTEXT AND VALUES

To manage and extract value from its intellectual capital, a company must understand the context in which it operates and be able to define its own values. Context

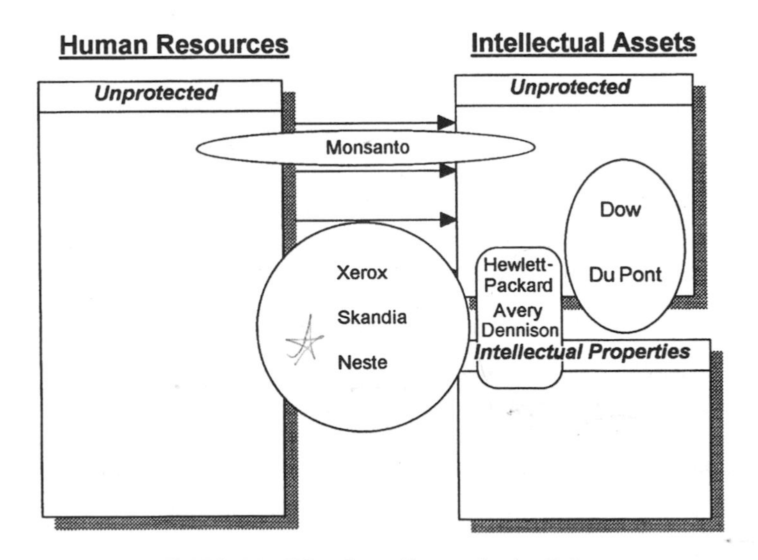

Exhibit 1.3 What Some Companies Are Doing

may be considered to be external to the firm; values are internal. Context includes the characteristics of the business environment within which the firm operates. For example, some firms (e.g., software, fashion clothing, consumer electronics) operate within short product life cycles, sometimes measured in months. Others, such as chemical companies, banks, and many retail companies operate on product life cycles measured in years. Some firms operate in regulated environments, but most do not. Some firms operate in rapidly changing market environments and others in stable markets. The combination of such external factors constitutes the business context within which a firm operates. A firm must have a full understanding of this external context to evaluate and fully utilize its intellectual capital.

In addition to the external context, firms have values or shared beliefs that guide the day-to-day decisions and actions of employees. Some firms, usually those that operate in stable environments, prize order, hierarchy, standardized thinking, guidelines, and the minimization of risk. Other firms, typically those that operate in rapidly changing environments, value risk-taking, grasping opportunities, and thinking "outside the box."

Understanding a firm's values makes it possible to identify what is important to the firm. Values also represent a double check on reality for a firm. For example, suppose the managers of a firm that values order, low risk, and hierarchy redefined its strategic vision to state that it aspired to become a fast-moving, entrepreneurial growth company. What would be its chances of achieving such a vision with employees whose values were standardized thinking, guidelines, and minimization of risk?

Values and context underlie all intellectual capital management activity. They form the backdrop and baseline against which all company intangibles are described, defined, measured, valued, and managed. A full understanding of a firm's values and the effects they can have on its activity is critical to understanding the potential success of any current or future activity.

THE TWO-PARADIGM COMPLEXITY

One of the complexities that makes the management of intellectual capital more difficult to understand is the existence of two entirely different paradigms in play, covering some of the same territory and using terms that are common to both and yet are defined differently in each. The two paradigms are the social and the economic.

Knowledge Creation and the Social Paradigm

The social paradigm holds that knowledge is both an outcome of human social evolution and part of the process. It looks at the evolution of human beings from instinctive animals to reasoning and rational ones. That evolution was made possible through the slow development and awareness of a cumulative heritage of knowledge and values built up over generations and accessible to all. The term *civilization* refers to the refinement of customs and their link to the progress of humanity. Culture became an objective set of perceptions, patterns, rules, and values. Activities or beliefs that earlier were considered *natural* came to be described as *cultural.* Culture was described by Crespi, a researcher in the field of knowledge, as having five dimensions:

- A subjective dimension accounting for the human side of culture; it includes learned behavior as well as a way of life.
- An objective dimension that captures the content of the culture; this includes the body of knowledge owned by a group.
- A cognitive dimension that defines individual and group identities.
- A prescriptive dimension that includes the normative regulation of behavior and standard orientations to recurring problems.
- A traditional dimension that allows for the transmission of experiences through a collective memory.

The sociologist would say that knowledge is never the product of a neutral description of an external observation. It always takes off from a particular point of view. Since culture is an agreed social reality that makes sense of the complexity of life, culture forms the basis for the development of knowledge. Changing (increasing) the knowledge of individuals or groups is fundamentally a cultural activity. A culture provides the environment in which knowledge creation occurs; and the values of any individuals or groups involved in learning set the direction as well as the measuring stick for what will be considered knowledge that adds value or meaning to the group.

Knowledge creation is an activity associated with social processes, structures, and norms. It involves human capital directly. The humans involved in learning may be assisted by machines or supporting systems, but knowledge creation is essentially a human and social activity where the value of particular knowledge is determined by the culture and values of the group.

Value and the Economic Paradigm

To the economist, "value" is a measure of the utility that ownership of an item brings to its owner. Utility is often viewed as a stream of benefits, stretching into the future, that an owner foresees as the "rent" he or she receives from owning the item. Utility may be measured in a number of ways. To the visual artist, utility may be the pleasure his or her work gives to the viewer. To the designer, utility may be the functionality of a design. To the accountant, utility may be measured in the accuracy of historical expenditure data. To the economist, however, utility is most often measured in dollar terms.

Economists typically view a future stream of benefits in dollar terms and can discount and sum these amounts to determine the current dollar equivalent of a future stream of income. This discounting and summing calculation is the determination of the net present value of a future stream of benefits. This is most often the economist's measure of value.

Looked at through economic eyes, the knowledge firm would be expected to create knowledge for future commercialization and extract current profits from existing knowledge. Hence, we have come to describe the knowledge firm's two basic IC functions as *value creation* and *value extraction.*

- *Value creation* is primarily an activity that involves the firm's human capital. It is the set of activities that create new knowledge through learning or knowledge acquisition. It also includes those activities associated with systematizing or institutionalizing the firm's processes for knowledge creation.
- *Value extraction* involves harvesting the level and degree of value required to achieve the strategic vision and long-term objectives of the firm.

All the firms represented in this book, as well as all of the contributors to it, operate within the economic paradigm. Although the social paradigm is a factor in value creation, the economic paradigm best meets the needs of value extraction.

Using the value extraction perspective, firms may be categorized as practicing one of three types of management:

1. *Intellectual Property Management.* Firms with significant legally protected intellectual assets (called *intellectual property*) focus on generating more intellectual properties as well as on leveraging them in the marketplace. First these firms develop a portfolio of defined intellectual properties, then they devise the broadest number of avenues for commercializing the properties in the portfolio. Intellectual property managers are typically tactically oriented, dealing with the near term and seeking profits sooner rather than later.
2. *Intellectual Asset Management.* Firms that seek to significantly increase the flow of innovations that can be considered for patenting and for commercialization focus their energies on the broader set of intellectual assets, the unprotected as well as the protected. Their management systems and processes are more complex because they deal with many more kinds of commercializable assets than just legally protected ones. Most often firms that operate with IAM are large and very sophisticated, with access to the vast internal resources needed to identify, evaluate, and leverage the intellectual assets. International asset managers operate both tactically and strategically, with near- to midterm profits from the company's intellectual assets in mind, as well as longer-term strategic positioning.
3. *Intellectual Capital Management.* A few firms operate according to the strategic opportunities offered by the IC view of their firm. For example, the intellectual capital of the knowledge firm, its driving force, can be displayed externally in a manner that describes and defines the company's ability to harness its "hidden value" as a powerful tool for leveraging itself into the future. Further, the IC perspective is insightful in determining the degree to which the intellectual capital of the firm is balanced and aligned with the firm's vision. Experience shows that most knowledge firms have significant imbalances between the actual deployment of their intellectual capital and the deployment that would move them more rapidly toward their vision.

Recently we identified a relationship between the fundamental business nature of the knowledge company and its need for one or more of the three systems for managing intellectual capital described here. This analysis divided companies managing their intellectual capital into two sets: (1) product and process companies and (2) service companies.

- *Product companies* are those whose primary value-added activity is the production of a product. Their focus is on product technologies, typically on product features as a way of differentiating themselves in the marketplace.
- *Process companies* are those that use a process to handle physical materials, such as refineries, manufacturers, and distributors. For all such companies, the primary business goal is to reduce processing costs and increase the quality as well as the volume of output.
- *Service companies* (*continuous service*) are companies such as the telephone and utility companies that expend resources to create a network for the distribution of services; they utilize their intellectual capital to create and market an ever-broader set of services to customers, which they deliver through the network. The focus of most of their intellectual capital is on developing and marketing new services. They have little need or use for portfolios of patents or other protected assets (although these kinds of companies often have a large number of brands or trademarks).
- *Service companies* (*discrete service*) offer services one-at-a-time, and a sale to a customer means only a limited number of units of service rather than a continuous provision of service. Companies in this set typically provide professional services, such as law and accounting firms, consulting firms, and others that commercialize their well-trained human capital.

As Exhibit 1.4 shows, these companies use their intellectual capital differently, use different intellectual capital management systems, and have different degrees of interest in the tactical and strategic uses of their intellectual capital. Not all aspects of the intellectual capital management perspective are appropriate for all knowledge firms. Each company must assess for itself the nature of the benefits realizable through managing the firm's intellectual capital, and which type of intellectual capital management to consider.

DIFFERING NEEDS FOR VALUE EXTRACTION

For each of the different kinds of knowledge companies identified above, there is a different need for value extraction from their intellectual capital. These needs differ in a tactical versus strategic sense, as well as in a human capital versus intellectual assets sense.

	Product Companies		Service Companies	
	Process Emphasis	Product Emphasis	Continuous Service Provided	Discrete Services Provided
Examples	Refinery Company Oil & Gas Pipeline	Automobile Companies Computer Companies	Electric & Gas Utilities Telephone Companies Banks Insurance Companies	Law Firms Consulting Firms
Intellectual Property	Large Amount	Large Amount	Small Amount	Very Small Amount
Intellectual Assets	Large Amount Technical, Admin., Managerial	Large Amount Technical, Admin., Managerial	Small Amount of Technical, Large Amount of Managerial & Administrative	Small Amount of Technical, Large Amount of Managerial & Administrative
Human Capital	Yes	Yes	Yes	Yes
ICM Focus	Tactical & Strategic	Tactical & Strategic	Strategic	Strategic
Management Systems Needed	IPM, IAM, ICM	IPM, IAM, ICM	ICM	ICM

Exhibit 1.4 ICM Preferences by Company Type

Tactical Value Extraction

Tactical value extraction, usually thought of as involving the technology company subset of knowledge companies, requires the close coordination of a range of intellectual capital activities that revolve around the technology or technologies to be commercialized. These activities are conducted at the level of intellectual property management (IPM) or intellectual asset management (IAM).

IPM—Intellectual property management, discussed in more detail in Part II, concerns the activities, decision processes, work processes, and databases used for commercializing individual *patented technologies or innovations.*

IAM—Intellectual asset management, discussed in greater detail in Part III, considers the broader set of intellectual assets that include both legally protected and nonprotected intellectual assets. It, too, concerns the activities, decision process, work processes, and databases used for commercializing and *obtaining additional extracted value from the firm's intellectual assets and innovations.*

Strategic Value Extraction

Strategic value extraction by knowledge companies is typically concerned more with the firm's future or its long-term value extraction needs. Firms involved with strategic value extraction activity are usually concerned with aligning their intellectual capital with the firm's long-term interests or concerns. The strategic value extraction activities usually concern: using the intellectual capital of the firm as a basis or building block on which to define the vision; aligning intellectual capital resources with the vision and strategy to enable their achievement quickly and efficiently; reporting externally to the financial markets on the firm's strategic uses of intellectual capital and the implications of these uses on the firm's long-term ability to create value for shareholders.

As Exhibit 1.4 has shown, not all knowledge companies have the same interests in intellectual capital or needs for value extraction. It follows from this that there should be a range of ICM directions, purposes, and methods. In later chapters, there are discussions of IP-, IA-, and IC-focused management models, the capabilities required, techniques available, and examples of companies successfully implementing the concepts in the management model.

OVERVIEW OF THE BOOK

One should not expect, nor will one find, any company exactly copying and implementing any of the models outlined in this book. Indeed, every company is unique, each has its own wish to tailor concepts and ideas to make them its own. Nevertheless, as the concepts, methods, and models contained in this book arose from companies themselves, they are already well-tested, and their use has been verified as successful. They are not simply theoretical sets of interesting but untested ideas. The concepts and models found between these covers are all tested, proven, and already implemented in one or more companies.

This book is about value extraction and the three levels of intellectual capital management. The intellectual capital management portions of this book relate to all knowledge companies, whether they be technology based or service based. We have learned that all knowledge companies have an interest in extracting value from their intellectual capital. At the intellectual capital level of management, value extraction involves two kinds of activity: alignment of resources to produce an efficiency of operation, and strategic positioning to produce improved visibility in the marketplace.

For technology-based knowledge companies, value extraction from intellectual capital focuses almost exclusively on their intellectual assets and intellectual properties. The work of the author and contributors to this book has largely been with technology companies. For this reason, a considerable amount of focus is on value extraction from intellectual assets and intellectual properties.

Part I Definitions, Concepts, and Context

Chapter 1 Introduction to Intellectual Capital Management

Chapter 2 Basic Definitions and Concepts

Patrick Sullivan provides the basic language, terms, and definitions to be used throughout this book. This chapter includes a discussion of the value extraction models for intellectual capital and for knowledge companies. It describes some of the basic concepts underlying vision, strategy, value, and valuation.

Chapter 3 Advanced Definitions and Concepts

Patrick Sullivan discusses principles underlying value creation and value extraction, including concepts and general strategies as well as the approaches used by specific companies. He identifies the sources of value for knowledge companies and discusses the mechanisms used to convert value into cash. Finally, he reviews the decision to commercialize, in which companies determine the number and kind of mechanisms they will use to develop cash from their innovations.

Chapter 4 Values and Their Importance to ICM

This chapter discusses the importance of values to intellectual capital management. In it, Brian Hall reviews the effects values have on company operations and uses actual examples to demonstrate how important a knowledge of values can be to executives of the firm. He discusses the impact values have on the firm's ability to determine what is and is not valuable. Finally, he discusses techniques that he has developed to use values knowledge to leverage corporate activity, such as intellectual capital management, toward profit improvement.

Chapter 5 In Search of a Paradigm

The existence of a range of models for intellectual capital and the confusion of common terms with different meanings complicates the search for a common language and framework for discussing intellectual capital. In this chapter, Paul Westburg and Patrick Sullivan review the current slate of intellectual capital models and identify their purpose, usefulness, and contributions to the confusion. They further suggest some characteristics that an overarching paradigm might contain.

Chapter 6 The Confusion of Capitals: Surveying the Cluttered and Confused Landscape of Intellectual "Capitals" and Terminology "Capital"

Martin Hall picks up the theme begun in Chapter 5 and reviews the plethora of definitions for commonly used IC terms, such as human capital, customer capital, structural capital, and others. He also provides a road map to link the different definitions into the set used in this book.

Chapter 7 Irreconcilable Differences? Managing the Knowledge Creation Interfaces

Peter Grindley and Patrick Sullivan discuss the two different philosophical bases for the two major perspectives on intellectual capital. They include is a review of the effect of these two different philosophies on discussions of intellectual capital and suggestions for improving communications between the two communities.

Part II Intellectual Property Management

Chapter 8 Extracting Value from Intellectual Property

Patrick Sullivan sets the stage in this chapter for the structure of the remainder of the book, showing how, for most firms, value extraction begins with intellectual properties. For firms without intellectual property, he discusses tactics, a fundamental concept of importance to all firms in managing their intellectual capital. He includes reviews of the importance of a well-articulated strategic vision and business objectives; the value of identifying the firm's intellectual properties and how they are expected to be used; how to select the "winners" from the portfolio; and how to develop systems for routinely managing all of the foregoing activities.

Chapter 9 The IP Portfolio as a Competitive Tool
The portfolio of protected intellectual assets contains a wealth of insights, often invisible to the firm, useful for developing more profits from existing portfolio contents as well as the identification of new areas of innovation that could provide increased technology or market leverage for the firm. In this chapter, Suzanne Harrison and Kevin Rivette discuss several new analytical methods for identifying ways to increase the current and future income potential of a patent portfolio.

Chapter 10 Creating a Portfolio Database
Here the reader learns how companies may create a portfolio database that suits their management needs. Kelly Hale discusses the general principles underlying the creation of a patent database as well as some of the practical considerations. Specifically, he discusses the experience of Rockwell International in creating and using its patent databases.

Chapter 11 Intellectual Property Management: From Theory to Practice
How do firms create strong portfolios that are effective tools in business negotiations and for protecting individual technologies? Stephen Fox tells how Hewlett-Packard has created one of the most powerful patent portfolios in the business world.

Chapter 12 Intellectual Capital Development at a Spin-off Company
Willy Manfroy and Harry Gwinnell discuss the processes used by Eastman Chemical to identify and evaluate the commercial potential of a range of nonstrategic technologies contained in its portfolio. They include an overview of the process, showing how it complements the firm's strategic thrust. Further, they discuss the firm's programs for technology management and value extraction and show how this special effort complements and supports both of the foregoing.

Part III Intellectual Assets Management

Chapter 13 Extracting Value from Intellectual Assets
Patrick Sullivan discusses intellectual assets in detail; describes the relationship between intellectual assets, human capital, and structural capital; and discusses how intellectual asserts are valued from both a qualitative and quantitative perspective. He also provides the basis of understanding on which Chapter 14, "The Intellectual Asset Manager," builds.

Chapter 14 The Intellectual Asset Manager

Joseph Daniele describes the totality of what is involved in managing intellectual assets: functions, information, processes, and information sources. Because the role of intellectual asset management (IAM) is evolving, he includes in this chapter the most practical and advanced thinking of a dozen companies that actively practice IAM. He defines the functions and roles for managers and describes the decision-making process and the supporting work processes and databases.

Chapter 15 Intellectual Asset Management at Dow Chemical

Much has been said about Dow Chemical and the system it developed for managing its intellectual assets. In this chapter, Dow's Director for Intellectual Asset Management, Gordon Petrash, discusses why Dow decided to develop this in-house capability and how he made it happen. This is a revealing discussion of what was done, and a frank appraisal of lessons learned.

Chapter 16 Intellectual Asset Management at Avery Dennison

Paul Germeraad, Avery Dennison's Director of Research, and Lori Morrison, Avery's Manager, Intellectual Property, discuss the sophisticated system Avery has installed to manage and extract value from its intellectual assets. This is an excellent example of an IAM that is aligned with the firm's business vision and long-term objectives.

Chapter 17 Intellectual Asset Management at Neste

Neste was formerly the national oil and chemical company of Finland. Since privatization, the company has conducted a thorough audit of its intellectual assets as part of developing and installing an in-house capability for their management. Neste's Director of Intellectual Capital discusses what the company did, how it was accomplished and how Neste has made this a part of its normal management decision processes.

Chapter 18 Making It Happen

How can companies create an in-house capability for managing their intellectual capital? Patrick Sullivan lays out a step-by-step approach, building on the information in the preceding chapters and the learning of all of the companies discussed. Using the information in this chapter, firms can improve, start up, or modify their own capability for extracting value from innovation.

Part IV Intellectual Capital Management

Chapter 19 Measuring and Monitoring Intellectual Capital

Beginning with an overview of current reporting systems and their capabilities, Suzanne Harrison and Trent Walker discuss the current needs for measuring intellectual capital, both internal and external. They identify the key stakeholders in measurement and the focus of interest for each, and they discuss an evolving measurement tool that companies currently use to measure their intellectual capital.

Chapter 20 Managing Intellectual Capital at Skandia
Leif Edvinsson discusses ICM activities at Skandia. He reviews the Skandia ICM evolution and the major steps the company took in its IC development. Edvinsson further discusses in detail the leadership phases of IC development followed by Skandia.

Chapter 21 The Role of Intellectual Capital in Valuing Knowledge Companies
When determining how much to pay to acquire a knowledge company, how does the potential purchaser make the calculation? Is the frame of reference an accounting or financial one? Or is it an intellectual capital one? Too often, companies being acquired are valued based on old-fashioned or no-longer-applicable methods. In this chapter, James O'Shaughnessy and Patrick Sullivan discuss some new ideas about how to value knowledge companies for acquisition or merger.

Chapter 22 Reporting on Intellectual Capital
Patrick Sullivan reveals up-to-date methods used by companies to report on the use of their intellectual capital and discusses both internal and external reports. He reviews what companies can do to determine their current context and to report that to their internal constituencies. He also discusses some of the issues that impede companies from accurately measuring the most meaningful elements of intellectual capital. Finally, he discusses some of the measurable items that may be considered, and why, and reviews the available measurements and discusses how and why they should be considered for incorporation into a firm's intellectual capital management monitoring system.

Chapter 23 Understanding and Managing Knowledge Assets for Competitive Advantage in Innovation and Product Development
Joseph Daniele, Xerox's Director of Intellectual Assets, has been called one of the country's most innovative thinkers in the area of intellectual asset management. In this chapter, he reveals some of his thinking about knowledge management. Sometimes controversial but always innovative, Joe Daniele's thoughts represent the thinking in many of the most innovative companies managing the creation of knowledge.

Chapter 24 Maintaining the Stock of Intellectual Capital
Discussions about how to capture the knowledge a firm generates in ways that allow other members of the firm to access and utilize it is the core of this chapter. Here, librarians Pam Jaejko and Eugenie Prime, the people most knowledgeable about the cataloging and retrieval of information, make a case for the use of the library resource as the mainstay for cataloguing and obtaining routine access to new knowledge within a firm. Their arguments are persuasive and suggest a new and continuing role for the corporate library within a firm.

Chapter 25 The Future of Intellectual Capital Management
The field of intellectual capital management is new and rapidly evolving. The lessons learned by practitioners are shaping the practices and procedures used by

others. What is the future for this new and challenging approach to profit extraction? How can we expect it to evolve? What are some of the leading indicators and trends? How can companies position themselves ahead of these trends so as to be more competitive in the future? In this chapter, Patrick Sullivan offers his own ideas about the field of innovation management.

Appendix Valuing Intellectual Properties

The Dow Chemical Company's Dr. Sam Khoury has developed and implemented an interactive method for valuing Dow's technology. This method, called the Technology Factor, is detailed in a Dow publication on valuation which defines the range of valuation methods available for use within the company. Dr. Khoury, Dow's expert on valuation, has agreed to include this paper here as an example of how the valuation of intangibles may be approached systematically.

2

Basic Definitions and Concepts

Patrick H. Sullivan

ICM Group, LLC

Discussing intellectual capital management can be a frustrating experience. Conversations that begin with apparent understanding can soon become confused and unclear. When this occurs, it is almost always because those involved in the conversation lack common definitions for frequently used terms—in other words, they do not share a language with which they can communicate. The reason for the lack of commonly understood definitions appears to be twofold. First, managers of intellectual capital use different models or perspectives, each of which describes intellectual capital differently. For example, there are both knowledge-based and economic-based views of intellectual capital (IC). Depending on which view or model you use, the commonly used terms have different meanings. This chapter defines the perspective or the intellectual capital model, the terms, and the definitions that are used throughout this book.

But terms and definitions are not the only source of confusion in discussions of intellectual capital, particularly when the discussion concerns the management of IC and is held between managers in two different companies. Each organization has its own worldview. Within that worldview, each organization is faced with a different set of external and internal realities. The worldview combined with the internal and external realities form the context within which each firm defines, manages, and values its intellectual capital. When two firms with different contexts discuss how best to manage intellectual capital, it is to be expected that they will find communication and agreement difficult. This chapter discusses some of the principal elements of context and how they affect a firm's management of its intellectual capital.

INTELLECTUAL CAPITAL MANAGEMENT

Intellectual capital management is an evolving field of management. Its roots are in the mid-1980s, developed in seminal publications by UC Berkeley professor

David Teece, on the extraction of value from innovation,[1] and by the Swedish consultant Karl Eric Sveiby, on managing knowledge.[2] Since then, the motivation as well as the new ideas and innovations in the field have been developed almost entirely by the companies actively managing their IC. Through the experiences of these companies, the field of ICM has evolved into two distinct areas of focus: *value creation* and *value extraction.*

Value creation concerns the generation of new knowledge *and* its conversion into innovations with commercial value. In the area of value creation, the management focus is on people, the human capital. Value creation activities include training; education; knowledge; innovation; building organizational structures; developing customer, organizational, and individual relationships; and managing values and culture.

Value extraction focuses largely on the paper (the codified knowledge) created by an organization's human capital. Value extraction focuses on valuation, decision processes, databases, screening and culling, conversion mechanisms, and asset management systems and capabilities.

This book is written for people interested in value extraction. All of the models, methods, processes, and perspectives discussed herein are concerned with optimizing the value the firm extracts from its intellectual capital.

INTELLECTUAL CAPITAL

The new term used to describe companies that focus on intellectual capital is *knowledge companies.* Knowledge companies use their knowledge (intellectual capital) as a major source of competitive advantage. They use their specific product or market knowledge to differentiate themselves from their competitors. Indeed, knowledge companies are leveraging newly defined kinds of capital: human, structural, and intellectual.

In this discussion we focus primarily on intellectual capital because it is viewed by knowledge companies as their source of competitive advantage. What exactly is intellectual capital?

Although there are many descriptions of what constitutes intellectual capital (see Exhibit 2.1), virtually everyone agrees intellectual capital includes a range of kinds of knowledge, lore, ideas, and innovations. We also know that industrial knowledge may be divided into two kinds: tacit and codified (see Exhibit 2.2). Tacit knowledge resides within an individual, often as a skill, an ability, or know-how. It can be demonstrated or taught to others. Examples of tacit knowledge and abilities are artistic skills such as pottery, sculpture, and painting. Although in modern times these skills have become codified, in earlier days such knowledge was passed from teacher to student, and from master to apprentice.

Codified knowledge is knowledge that has been committed to some form of communication medium. It might be a handwritten document, a computer program, a blueprint, or a cartoon.

In knowledge companies, intellectual capital comprises both tacit and codified knowledge. From the perspective of someone wanting to extract value from it, a

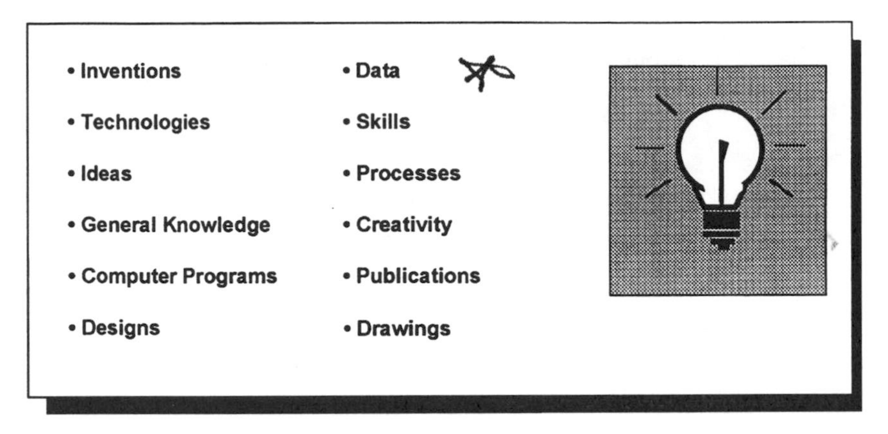

Exhibit 2.1 What Constitutes Intellectual Capital

working definition of intellectual capital is "knowledge that can be converted into profit." Exhibit 2.3 shows that there are two major components of intellectual capital: human capital and intellectual assets.

The distinction between human capital and intellectual assets is of particular importance to owners of knowledge companies. Unlike human capital (people), which is not interchangeable and cannot be owned by shareholders, intellectual assets are and can be. For this reason, it is clearly to the advantage of the knowledge firm to transform the innovations produced by its human capital into intellectual assets to which the firm can assert rights of ownership. One major task of IC managers is to transform human capital assets into intellectual assets.

Industrial Knowledge

	Tacit	Codified
Definition	Knowledge which is difficult to articulate & may be embedded in ways of doing things	Knowledge which is written down in some medium
Ownership	Ownership resides with the holder of the know-how; difficult to copy and/or transfer	Technology easier to protect using the mechanism of the law; yet also easier to transfer
Examples	Experience Lore Group skills	Blueprints Code Formulae Computer Programs

Exhibit 2.2 Types of Industrial Knowledge

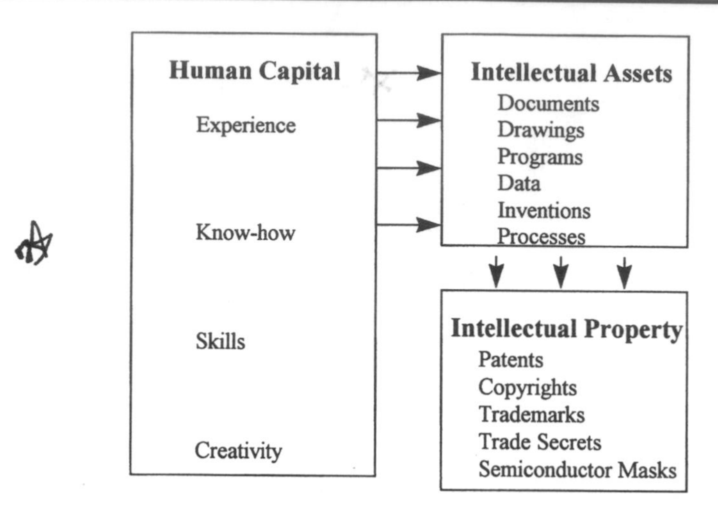

Exhibit 2.3 The Intellectual Capital of the Firm

Human Capital

The *human capital* of the firm may be defined as the capabilities of employees, contractors, suppliers, and other company-related people to solve customer problems. The firmwide human capital resource is the know-how and institutional memory about topics of importance to the company. The human capital includes the collective experience, skills, and general know-how of all of the firm's people. It is a resource because it can generate value for the company, yet it would be difficult for the company to deliver this value without the employees themselves. For example, a law firm might count its staff of lawyers as its income-producing or commercializable human capital. The lawyers appear in court and advise clients on legal matters. It is difficult to imagine how a law firm could provide such legal services to its clients without the carrier of the skills, the lawyer.

Other kinds of companies use their human capital very differently in creating value. A software company may use its programmers to create a new software program. The program, once codified, becomes an intellectual asset that is then reproduced, manufactured, and sold to customers. In this case, the human capital does not create value for the customer directly, as the lawyer does; he or she does it indirectly, by creating an intellectual asset that can be manufactured and sold.

Creating intellectual assets is not easy. It requires managing the firm's human capital in ways that give people incentives and encourage them to codify their knowledge. But it is often difficult for managers to know which employee has specific knowledge and how quickly it can be accessed. When companies are small, it is easy for everyone to know what information is relevant to a situation and how to gain access to the knowledge possessed by the human capital. As companies grow and become more complex, and the size of the human capital pool increases, such information is less widely shared and becomes more compartmentalized. In an ideal world, the corporation would evolve to possess some form of *collective intelligence,* a term coined by George Por, founder of Community

Intelligence Labs, in which all members of the organization had access to all of the firm's relevant knowledge instantly available at all times. With increasing size it becomes ever more important for knowledge firms to motivate their human capital resources to codify their knowledge and know-how, thereby creating intellectual assets.

Intellectual Assets

Intellectual assets, the second component of IC, are the codified, tangible, or physical descriptions of specific knowledge to which the company can assert ownership rights. Any piece of knowledge that becomes defined, usually by being written down or entered into a computer, qualifies as an intellectual asset and can be protected. Intellectual assets are the source of innovations that the firm commercializes.

Intellectual assets that receive legal protection are *intellectual property.* Intellectual property law, the body of law that deals with the protection of intellectual assets, recognizes five forms of intellectual property that are entitled to legal protection in the United States: patents, copyrights, trade secrets, trademarks, and semiconductor masks. For each protected asset, the nature and amount of protection available varies, as does the degree to which that protection applies to an innovation.

Intellectual assets, by definition, may be legally protected, although often the firm has not yet decided to do so. Indeed, regardless of whether formal legal protection is sought, intellectual assets are usually protected by the trade secret provisions of the law. A firm may choose not to legally protect all of its intellectual assets. Nevertheless, both intellectual assets and intellectual properties are the most usual elements of intellectual capital to be commercialized.

Structural Capital

Intellectual capital by itself is of little value. Picture, for a moment, a group of skilled people, huddled together on a hillside, thinking great business thoughts and scribbling them onto scraps of paper. The ideas may be good, but without the supporting resources of a firm, the people have no ability to do anything with their ideas. They have no production staff or manufacturing facility; there is no telephone to call potential customers; there is no distribution system to ferry products from warehouse to retailer. In short, the intellectual capital lacks the firm's supporting resources, called *structural capital.*

Structural capital is the support or infrastructure that firms provide to their human capital. It includes both direct and indirect support, and for each there are both physical and intangible elements. Direct support, which touches the human capital directly, includes physical elements such as computers, desks, and telephones, and intangible elements such as information systems, computer software, work procedures, marketing plans, and company know-how. Indirect support, which does not touch the human capital directly, includes such physical elements as buildings, lights, electricity, and plumbing, and such intangible elements as strategic plans, payroll systems, costing structures, and supplier relationships.

Indeed, structural capital provides the environment that encourages the human capital to create and leverage its knowledge. The structural capital is the part of the firm that remains in place when the human capital goes home.

Complementary Business Assets. Complementary business assets are one element of the firm's structural capital that deserves special mention. These are the business assets of the firm that are used to create value in the commercialization process. Typically, for knowledge companies, the business assets of the firm complement the innovations developed by the human capital. These complementary business assets frequently include manufacturing facilities, distribution networks, customer lists and relationships, supplier networks, service forces, complementary technologies, trademarks, and organization capabilities. Complementary assets may be thought of as the string of assets through which the innovations must be processed to reach the customer. No matter how exciting an intellectual asset itself may be, it will have little commercial value unless paired with the appropriate complementary assets.

There are two kinds of complementary assets. The first are business assets that are widely available—*generic complementary business assets.* They can be bought or contracted for on the open market and may be used in commercializing a wide range of technology applications. The second kind, which offer more leverage, are called *specific complementary assets.* Suppose an inventor devised a unique product with a large market appeal. If this product could be made using manufacturing equipment that is readily available in the marketplace, then its manufacture would involve the use of generic assets. If, on the other hand, the product required some manufacturing process or technique that was unique to the technology or the product's design, so that generic manufacturing equipment was not capable of producing it, then that specific manufacturing capability would be a *specific* complementary asset. A specific complementary business asset can be used strategically: It can be used as a barrier to competition; it can be licensed out as a source of income; it can be sold; it can be used to attract joint venture partners. Most important, it can be used to protect a technology from competitors when legal protection is either not desired or not available.

Specific complementary assets, then, are a source of value in addition to the value created by the innovation. The use of a business asset in the commercialization process adds value to the innovation on its way to the marketplace. It is this additional value that the owner of the complementary asset can capture and retain. The value realized by the manufacturing process can be captured as profit by the owner of the manufacturing system; the value of distribution can be captured as profit by the owner of the distribution system, and so on. Where the business assets are unique to the innovation, their owners can charge a greater premium for the value they add to the innovation. Thus, complementary business assets are also a source of hidden value; in fact, they provide a greater value to the firm than their book value as tangible assets.

Specific complementary business assets are usually created in conjunction with the commercialization of a specific application of an intellectual asset. They are therefore unique, and they are often themselves protectable. In effect, controlling the specific complementary assets is equivalent to controlling the underlying intellectual asset and its ultimate commercial value. This has the advantage of protecting a technology without having to reveal the technology itself. Patenting does not provide this advantage.

VALUE: SOURCES AND CONVERSIONS

For a knowledge company whose profits come primarily from the commercialization of its ideas and innovations, there are only two fundamental sources of value: the innovations themselves and the complementary business assets of the firm that are applied to the commercialization of its innovations. Further, there are only six ways that firms can convert innovations into profits: direct sale, out-licensing, joint venture to obtain and use needed complementary business assets, strategic alliance to obtain and exploit markets, integration, and donation (tax write-off).

For sophisticated knowledge companies, the route to maximizing profit extraction for any innovation is to maximize the number of combinations of unique complementary business assets and conversion mechanisms (see Exhibit 2.4).

The Commercialization Decision

Any firm that intends to commercialize an innovation should undertake an analysis of its profit extraction potential. The decision to commercialize should be made only after a firm asks itself a series of questions, the answers to which determine the mechanism to be used to convert the technology to cash as well as the degree of risk involved in successfully completing the cash conversion (see Exhibit 2.5).

Sources of Value	Conversion Mechanisms

• Innovations
• Complementary Business Assets
    • Purchasing
    • Manufacturing
    • Distribution
    • Sales
	• Sale
	• Out-license
	• Joint Venture
	• Strategic Alliance
	• Integrate with Current Business
	• Create New Business
	• Donate

Exhibit 2.4 Sources of Value and Conversion Mechanisms

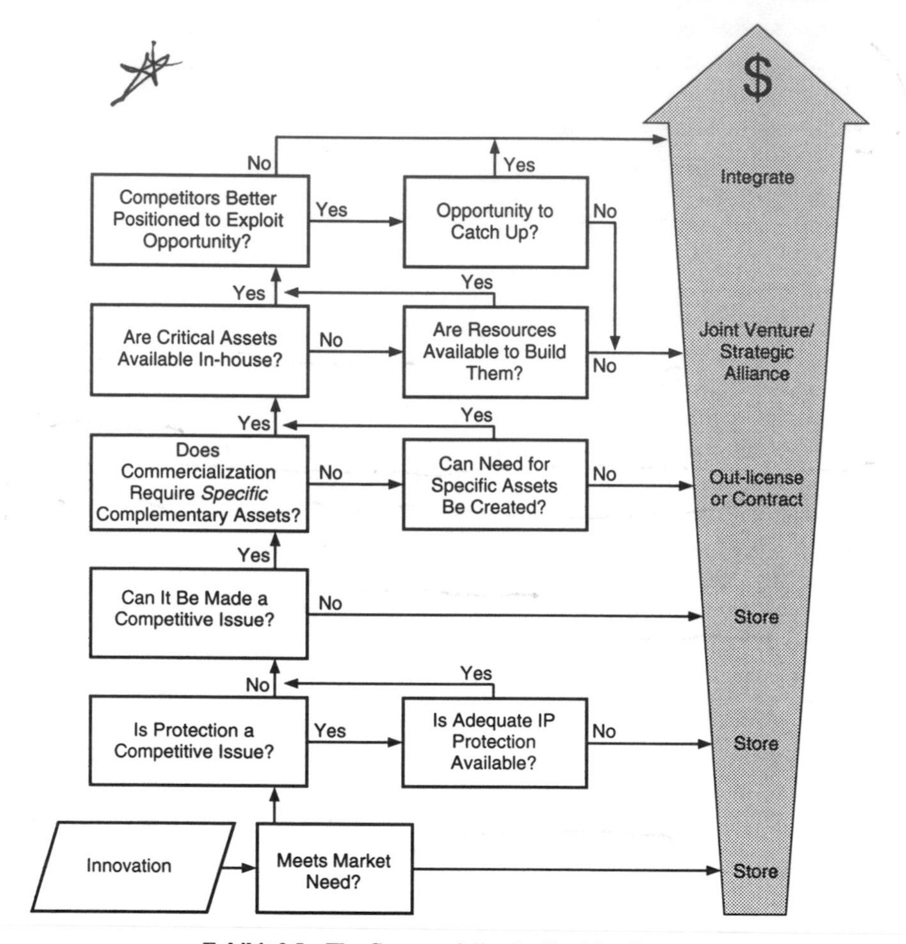

Exhibit 2.5 The Commercialization Decision Process

The first question to be asked is, does the innovation meet a market need? If the answer is no, then the innovation has no immediate commercial value and should be "stored" until some other innovation is created which, when matched with the first, will produce something that does meet a market need. But if the innovation does meet a current market need, then the second question can be asked.

The second question concerns legal protection and whether it is a competitive issue. For some innovations as well as for some industries, legal protection is not required for an innovation to be commercializable. Perhaps the most famous example is Coca-Cola. The formula for Coke syrup is a tightly held secret within the firm. To patent it legally, it would have to be revealed. Rather than do so, the firm maintains it as one of the best-kept secrets in the world. In most industries, however, legal protection for an innovation is necessary before the innovating firm will decide to invest its funds in commercialization. If protection is an issue, the related question involves the degree to which adequate protection is available. The adequacy of protection depends on many things, usually a mixture of legal, technological, and business considerations. Where the degree of protection is not considered adequate, the innovation is "stored," awaiting an adequately protected partner innovation.

The third question concerns the innovation's commercialization and whether it requires specific complementary assets. Where commercialization does not require specific complementary assets, the firm must ask whether the innovation could be redesigned or reconfigured to require specific complementary assets. The reason for this is simple. Where specific complementary assets are required, the firm has the opportunity to obtain profits not only from the innovation, but from the unique complementary asset as well. Indeed, an innovation that requires more than one unique complementary asset has more value to the firm that owns those specific assets.

If the innovation under review does not require specific complementary assets for its commercialization, then the firm has a limited number of ways of profiting from the innovation. For this reason, it is often best to out-license the innovation to some firm that owns the generic assets required for commercialization. On completion of the out-licensing transaction, the firm should sequester the licensing income, look inside the firm for another innovation that requires specific complementary assets, and invest the licensing income in bringing that innovation to market.

If specific complementary assets are required, the next question concerns these assets and whether they are available in-house. If they are not, does the firm have the resources available to build, buy, or acquire these resources? If specific assets are required and the commercializing firm cannot obtain access to them directly, then the most profitable course of action is to find a firm that owns such assets and obtain access to them through a joint venture.

In the parlance of intellectual capital, a firm may consider three types of business alliance: (1) a contract, used to obtain access to generic business assets; (2) a joint venture, used to obtain access to specific business assets; or (3) a strategic alliance, used to obtain access to markets.

If access to specific assets can be arranged, the final question concerns the commercializing firm and whether it is adequately positioned in the marketplace. The market-competitive position of the firm is considered adequate if it has access to the market for the product. If other firms have better access, can the commercializing firm catch up? If the answer to these questions is no, then the commercializing firm should form a strategic alliance with the firm that does have access to the markets.

If, however, the commercializing firm has adequate access to the markets, then it should "integrate" the innovation, the protection, and the complementary assets, and manufacture and bring the innovation to market itself. It should be noted that the further the firm can progress in the commercialization decision before settling on a conversion mechanism, the greater the available profits. (It is also true, of course, that the greater the profit potential, the greater the risk.)

In summary, the commercialization decision involves asking five sequential questions, the answers to which determine the optimum cash-conversion mechanism for an innovation. The decision process relies on a knowledge of several underlying concepts: complementary business assets, conversion mechanisms, and the sources of value from innovation.

THE IMPORTANCE OF CONTEXT

Value, a concept addressed throughout this book, is discussed from the perspective of the economist. Economists view value as the sum of a stream of benefits (or income) stretching into the future, summed, and discounted to a net present value (NPV) dollar exhibit. Yet value has meaning for many others besides economists. Consider a painting of some fishing boats in a tropical harbor. To an interior decorator, the painting might have value if its colors complement the color scheme of the room. To an artist, the painting's value might be related to its creator, the technique used to paint it, or its perspective on the subjects. To an art dealer, its value might lie in the price it can command, and to the owner its value might be sentimental, because it was painted by Aunt Maisie on her trip to Tahiti. In all of these situations, the value depends on who determines it. In other words, the value depends on the values of the valuer.

If there can be so many views of value for a tangible object like a painting, then what must be the case with an intangible? Its value, too, depends on who determines its value and in what context. For example, a plastic bottle filled with water, located at the bottom of a swimming pool in rainy England might have little value; indeed, it might be seen as a nuisance to the pool owner who wants it out of the pool. That same container of water in the middle of the Sahara could have enormous value.

The relative value placed on innovative ideas is largely dependent on the firm's view of itself and on the reality of the marketplace. Put another way, each firm exists within a context that shapes the firm's view of what is or is not of value.

Context may be defined as the firm's internal and external realities. Internal realities concern direction, resources, and constraints. They define the firm's strengths and weaknesses as well as its capabilities for competing in its external world. The external realities concern opportunities and threats and focus on the fundamental forces affecting the long-term viability of the industry as well as the immediate opportunities available to the firm.

Internal Dimensions of Context—Questions asked to determine the internal context center on direction, resources, and constraints. What business is the firm really in? How does the firm define its business? What are the firm's strengths and weaknesses? What are the "levers" to pull for growth? What strategies are available? What strategies has the firm selected? Why? What is the firm's current performance against goal? Is this performance acceptable?

External Dimensions of Context—Questions asked to determine the external context center on identifying the fundamental forces affecting the industry as well as the immediate opportunities available in the firm's marketplace. What are the major environmental forces affecting success in this business (e.g., economic, governmental, technological, sociological, political)? What is the firm's market? How is it changing (getting larger, declining, etc.)? Who are the firm's competitors? What are their strengths and weaknesses? What are the best market strategies?

Companies that manage their intellectual capital successfully realize that two fundamental elements of the context are particularly useful to know: *values* and *vision* (see Exhibit 2.6). In that regard, two short mantras are useful in determining the context for valuing something:

1. Values ⇒ Value ⇒ Valuation
2. Vision ⇒ Strategy ⇒ Value

In the first mantra, the underlying idea is that the values of a firm are major determinants of what it holds to be of value. Once the firm's values are known, it becomes possible to know how a firm should value an item. The second mantra is based on similar but different reasoning—if a firm has a vision of what it wants to become, then it will be able to know whether an item (of intellectual capital) will help move it toward that vision. If an item would be helpful, then it has value for the firm. If it has no usefulness in moving the firm toward its vision or objectives, then it has little value. Combining the two mantras suggests that understanding the company's vision as well as its values may be basic to understanding the value of intellectual capital to a firm.

The following two sections expand on the meaning of vision and values, how they are used, and why a firm's vision and values are basic to understanding how it values its intellectual capital.

VISION

A firm's vision describes the firm as it wishes to be in the future. The vision often provides the standard against which a new innovation is measured: Will the innovation help the firm achieve its long-term vision? Can the firm capitalize on or somehow use the innovation to improve internal operations, how it is viewed by the marketplace, or the list of innovations to commercialize? Will it lead to

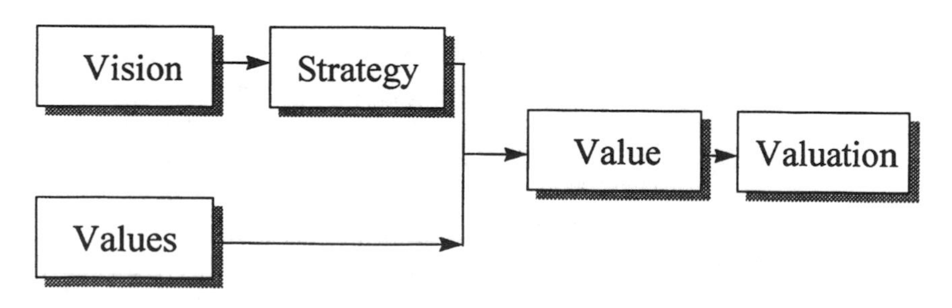

Exhibit 2.6 Vision, Values, and Value Relationship

increased sales? Will it improve internal efficiency? Will it improve the firm's ability to develop new innovations? Are these things important to the firm? If so, the idea has value. If not, then the idea has little value.

The importance of a well-conceived and well-articulated vision of the future is perhaps the most important piece of intellectual capital a firm can develop. Once known and widely acknowledged, such a view of the future allows employees at all levels of the firm to know whether pursuing an idea or an activity makes sense. It helps people know which path to take.

Lewis Carroll explained it best with tongue-in-cheek in *Alice in Wonderland:*

Said Alice to the Cheshire Cat:
"Would you tell me, please,
which way I ought to go from here?"

"That depends a good deal on where
you want to get to," said the Cat.

"I don't much care where—," said Alice.

"Then it doesn't matter which way you go."
Said the Cat.

Strategic Thinking

Experience has shown that firms with a desire to shape their own futures can successfully do so. The essence of being able to determine the corporation's future is the effective use of strategic choice. In the context of strategy development, choice means that a firm can identify a set of significantly different yet equally desirable futures for itself. These futures represent the choices available to the firm. With these potential choices in mind, the firm can decide which future to bring into being. This process of developing control of the future through choice rests on two fundamental beliefs: (1) The future of a firm can be known in advance, and (2) a firm can take actions that will bring that desired future into being.

The process of thinking into the future (developing plans and strategies) is a well-known one, and there is general agreement that it flows along a spectrum of planning activity much as outlined in Exhibit 2.7. This spectrum divides strategy development into two distinct segments: *strategic thinking* and *strategic planning.*

Strategic Thinking: Strategic thinking is a component of the strategy development spectrum and may result, eventually, in a strategic plan. For organizations beginning the strategic thinking process, the starting point is usually the development of a broad mission statement, which outlines why the firm exists. This is followed by a description of what the firm wishes to be in the future (the vision). Next comes a definition of the steps, both giant steps (objectives) and near-term or one-year steps (goals), for achieving the vision. Only at this point does a strategy, or the decisions about how to achieve the vision, objectives, and goals, emerge. These steps are col-

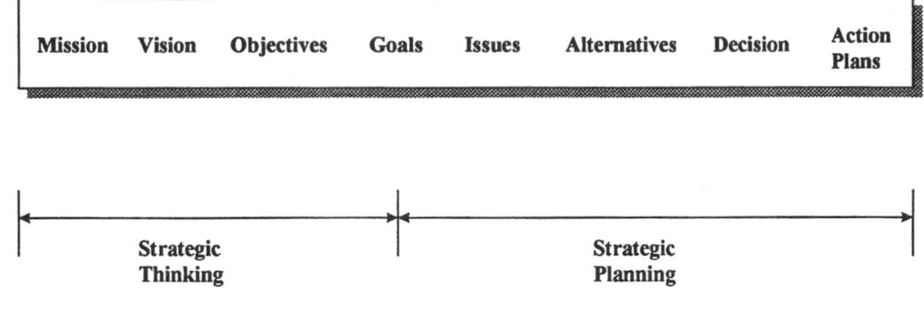

Exhibit 2.7 The Strategy Development Spectrum

lectively the contents of the strategic-thinking end of the strategy-development spectrum. They are followed by strategic planning.

To think strategically requires developing a mindset that focuses on the long-range view of the company, its constituencies as well as its micro- and macroenvironments, to describe what it can become in the future. Strategic thinking involves:

- Describing the company as it exists. Describing the desired form of the company in the future.
- Identifying the growth steps necessary to get from here to there.
- Developing a schedule for taking each step.

Strategic Planning: To plan strategically requires identifying the major obstacles to achieving the firm's targets and milestones, and developing action plans to reach them within the available resources of time, money, manpower, and facilities.

How Visions Are Defined

A strategic vision is *a set of operationally meaningful statements describing the organization as it wishes to be in the future.* It is more specific than a mission statement, which sets forth objectives in broad business terms. It differs from a strategic plan in that the latter describes specific steps leading to the achievement of long-term goals. The strategic vision focuses on operational activities that will make the organization into what it wishes to become, leaving the matter of "how" to later planning or to individual initiative. The vision selected must be feasible as well as compatible with the organization's mission and its values.

Another way to understand strategic vision is to focus on the reasons for creating one. Here are some observations about what a well-conceived and broadly accepted strategic vision can do for an organization:

1. The vision provides strategic meaning for the organization. Vision permits the organization to focus its energies—for if everything is important, nothing is important. Vision differentiates foreground from background. Because the foreground acquires meaning only in relation to the background, an important part of vision development is to say what is excluded from the vision.

2. The vision provides a common definition of subjective social reality for the organization's members. It defines a vocabulary and a framework for discussing alternative plans, actions, and potential outcomes. It symbolizes an infrastructure of values, culture, and context that helps individual actors relate to one another and to the more abstract organization of which they are a part.
3. The vision provides a reference point for managing the organization's *beforemath.* It pulls people toward the desired future, reducing the need for formal directives.
4. The vision is most important when there are dimensions of the proposed change that are quite large; the change involves organizational values, culture, or structure; and the time to adjust is long. It provides a continuing focal point as people and conditions change during the implementation of the strategic plan.

A final word on visioning. Many organizations believe they have a vision for the future, but few have visions that are strategically helpful. To be helpful, a vision must state what the company wishes to become in operational terms, not how it intends to get there. And it is very important that visions describe the future state in a way that allows progress toward it to be measured. (Otherwise, the use of terms such as *best,* or *preferred,* or *number one* are meaningless.) With a well-articulated vision for the future and a secure grasp on where the company is now, any firm is in a position to make the strategic decision that will help it achieve the vision.

VALUES

The values of the firm represent the consensus beliefs of its members. The sum of these views, the collective values of the firm, determine the worldview held by the employees. Values drive the day-to-day decision making of employees. If the values of the employees differ from those of the executive management, the employees will be unlikely to effectively implement the firm's strategic plan.

In Chapter 4, Dr. Brian Hall discusses values as ideals that shape and give significance to our lives. They are reflected in the priorities we choose, the decisions we make, and the actions we take. Values are ideals that individuals select and use as the basis for many decisions in day-to-day life. As decision prioritizers, values are reflected in behavior. As ideals, they provide meaning for people's lives. Values are also measurable. Using a list of 125 values that are important to individuals, teams, and organizations, and that are inherent or referred to in an organization's documents, Hall provides a common language or yardstick for discussing values and the issues they influence.

VALUE

Value is a concept that has many meanings, each of which may apply in a narrow or unique set of circumstances. For example, the value of a piece of rental property may be assessed somewhat differently by a seller, a potential buyer, an insurance company, a tax assessor, the executor of an estate containing the property, a government entity considering taking possession by "eminent domain," and a potential mortgage lender. The value of an item depends primarily on the needs of the person or organization that will be using it. Defining and measuring the value of intellectual capital is a topic that is discussed extensively throughout this book, beginning with the sections that follow.

In the business context, value measurements are used for decision making. The value of an intangible or a piece of intellectual capital is often the basis for deciding whether to invest further in developing the intangible, to continue holding it, or to sell it. This kind of value measurement may be called *economic;* that is, it is a measure of the utility the intangible brings to the firm.

In measuring economic value to the firm, it is necessary to have a reference point, something that can be used as the basis for measurement. In the case of ongoing enterprises, such as knowledge companies, a particularly useful reference point is the firm's vision of itself in the future. This vision (as well as the firm's strategy for achieving it) may be used as the basis for measuring the utility or value of intangibles such as intellectual capital. If an intellectual asset such as an idea, a patent, or a process can assist the company in implementing its strategy or achieving its vision, then it has value to the firm. The amount of value depends on the degree to which the intellectual asset enables the strategy or vision.

THE IC FRAMEWORK

The concepts and definitions discussed so far form the major elements of an IC framework, or a way of defining and looking at a company that differs from traditional views. Intellectual capital (and its major subcomponents of people and paper) and structural capital are the fundamental elements of the IC framework in a knowledge company. The economist's concepts of complementary business assets and sources of value help a firm to chart a path toward maximizing the value of the firm's intellectual capital. The commercialization decision process, which demonstrates the relationships among protection, complementary assets, and the conversion mechanism alternatives, allows a firm to project the flow from tacit knowledge, to codified knowledge, to protected knowledge, to complementary assets, to conversion to profits.

The IC framework, as described so far, provides a different perspective for managers interested in developing profits from a firm's innovations. But it leaves unanswered questions about how the firm goes about accomplishing what the framework suggests. The "how" of IC management is covered in later chapters of this book, which address the management of intellectual capital, intellectual assets, and intellectual properties. The "how" questions require answers in terms of systems, decision processes, work processes, and databases. They also require knowledge about how intellectual capital elements are defined, described, and measured. Further, they require more information about how the elements of intellectual capital relate to the firm's bottom line. Whereas this chapter has dealt almost exclusively with the concepts underlying intellectual capital and its management, the remainder of the book is devoted to how intellectual capital is defined, measured, managed, and monitored as well as to how to demonstrate its relationship to the firm's bottom line.

NOTES

1 David J. Teece, "Profiting from Technological Innovation: Implications for Integration, Collaboration, Licensing and Public Policy," *Research Policy 15* (April 1986): 285–305.

2 Karl Erik Sveiby and Anders Risling, *Kunskapsföretaget* (The Know-How Company) (Malmö: Liber, 1986).

3

Advanced Definitions and Concepts

Patrick H. Sullivan

ICM Group, LLC

We have already defined *intellectual capital* as "knowledge that can be converted into profits." We have also shown that intellectual capital includes the company's tacit and explicit knowledge, its know-how and uncodified knowledge, as well as its written plans, procedures, patents, and customer lists. This chapter discusses basic concepts about value: What it is, how the concepts of value and intellectual capital relate, and how companies can convert their intellectual capital into profits.

Value extraction from intellectual capital, unlike value extraction from intellectual assets or intellectual properties, is fundamentally a strategic activity. Firms that actively extract value from their intellectual capital do so in two ways. First, they internally align their intellectual capital with the firm's vision and strategy to ensure that their intellectual capital, as well as structural capital, is focused on achieving the right goal. Second, they report to the external world on the firm's intellectual capital—both the amount of it and the company's ability to leverage it in the marketplace.

STRATEGIC ALIGNMENT OF INTELLECTUAL CAPITAL

The alignment of the firm's intellectual capital with its vision and strategy is a powerful idea. Indeed, the idea of alignment underlies virtually all management theories, concepts, fads, and fashions. The power of the concept of alignment is its suggestion that companies can focus their resources and activities on a set of objectives for the purpose of achieving them faster or without unnecessary effort.

Intellectual capital management, as has been stated elsewhere in this book many times, is an integral part of creating the future of the firm. Although its intellectual property component is used (and is useful) in generating current profits, its major utility is in making the future happen. Alignment of the firm's intellectual capital and strategy requires the presence of a well-articulated and well-understood vision. As Exhibit 3.1 shows, the concept of alignment is a simple one.

A company with a well-defined vision of the future and a well-conceived and executed strategy can define the role its intellectual capital should play in helping it to achieve the vision through the strategy. The roles for intellectual capital tend to fall into one of two areas: value creation or value extraction. Companies that have asked and answered the question about the role of IC can then audit their current actual use of intellectual capital. The degree to which the current use is inconsistent with the desired is the degree of misalignment.

Alignment of intellectual resources with a benchmark such as the vision requires the ability to define and measure the existing intellectual capital. Chapter 19 describes methods and measurement schemes available. The critical issues for strategic alignment of intellectual capital are: Does the firm have a clear, well-conceived, and well-articulated vision of the company it wants to become in the future, and does it have the ability to define and measure the current use of its intellectual capital assets?

Firms that wish to alter the external view of the company, particularly where the external view does not include an appreciation of the knowledge content of the firm's activities, are increasingly considering reporting publicly on their intellectual capital. At this writing, only one firm has done so, reporting distinctly positive information. Skandia AFS, a Swedish finance and insurance company, published an intellectual capital supplement to its 1994 annual financial report. Shortly thereafter, the price of Skandia's stock rose by some 40 percent.

In the United States there has been a sharp increase in the interest in external reports of intellectual capital. In 1996 the Securities and Exchange Commission sponsored a symposium to discuss the needs and concerns surrounding such reporting. As a direct outcome of that meeting, New York University founded the

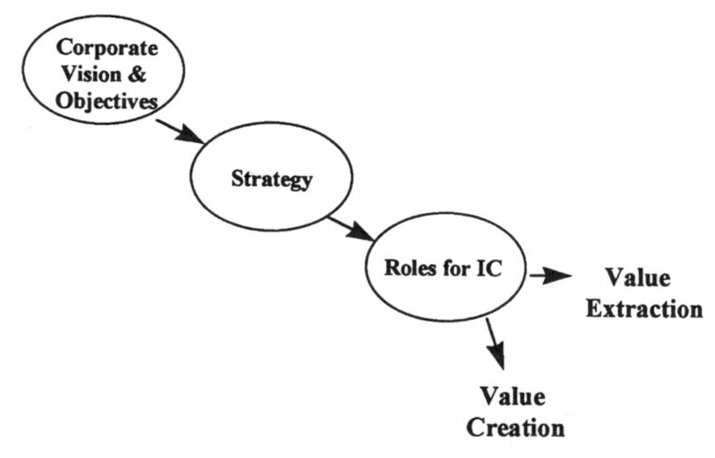

Exhibit 3.1 Strategic Alignment of Intellectual Capital

Center for Research in Measurement of Intangible Assets headed by Professor Baruch Lev, a professor of accounting. In 1997 think tanks and other organizations nationwide held numerous unofficial meetings and discussions about intellectual capital measurement and reporting issues.

The issues underlying external reporting of intellectual capital involve measurement. Of particular interest to the SEC is valuing intellectual capital according to some consistent and agreed-upon measurements, and having the trust of people outside the company that the measurements are accurate and relevant to their needs.

But measurement issues extend beyond questions of value. Which measures of intellectual capital are best depend on the context of a firm's own circumstances and management needs. It is not productive to discuss the measurement of intangibles such as intellectual capital without first understanding the context within which the company manages its intellectual capital. Lacking context, it is impossible to assess whether any measure of IC has meaning for the firm.

DEFINING, DESCRIBING, AND MEASURING INTELLECTUAL CAPITAL

Generally, three different groups have an interest in describing and measuring intellectual capital. One group is knowledge companies themselves, whose employees must manage these intangibles. As yet, they have inadequate methods for measuring either the stocks of intellectual capital at their firms or, more important, the changes in those stocks that result from management efforts. The company managers need operating measurements of intellectual capital, leading toward what amounts to an intellectual asset operating statement.

Another group concerned with the definition and measurement of intellectual capital is the financial community. An increasing number of knowledge firms (those whose major assets are intellectual and not tangible) are valued highly in the stock market on the basis of the market's perception of each firm's intellectual capital. But, lacking any systematic or common ways of measuring intellectual capital or its value, it is difficult for the members of this group to determine whether the investing public is well served by its perceptions of value. The financial interest group wants to see intangible assets capitalized in a standard and reliable way: on an intangible balance sheet, where the intellectual assets are measured in dollar terms and the valuation methods are credible.

A third group consists of macroeconomists whose interest is knowing whether firms' existing use of intellectual capital resources is economically sound for the country. Their need is for companies to provide data on their intellectual capital that will allow them to conduct analyses of those companies at the national accounts level.

These interest groups have very different reasons for wanting to measure intellectual capital; and their different reasons, while not incompatible with one another, are not likely to focus on measuring exactly the same things.

Defining Intellectual Capital

Both people and paper are sources of "knowledge that can be converted into profits" (see Exhibit 3.2). From the perspective of value extraction, the work activities of the human capital, as well as the knowledge creation activities the human capital engages in, are of long-term interest. But the managers responsible for value extraction are most concerned with how to realize the full value of both the people and the paper assets.

Measuring and Valuing Intellectual Capital

There are two types of measurement that a firm may use to determine the value of its intellectual capital: (1) a measurement of the effectiveness of managerial decision making; and (2) a measurement of the amount of intellectual capital the firm has amassed. This chapter deals with measures concerning both the effectiveness of managerial decision making and the value of the corporation.

Market Value and the Knowledge Company

As the stock prices of knowledge companies have risen, the financial community has shown more and more interest in them. The market value of a knowledge company as determined by the stock exchanges is calculated by multiplying the stock price by the number of shares of stock outstanding. This simple calculation provides the market's value of the company. Where the market value is greater than the value of the firm's total tangible assets, then the value in excess of this amount may be said to be the premium the market places on two aspects of the firm's intellectual capital: its perception of the amount of intellectual capital held by the firm, as well as its perception of the firm's ability to leverage this intellectual capital in the business marketplace.

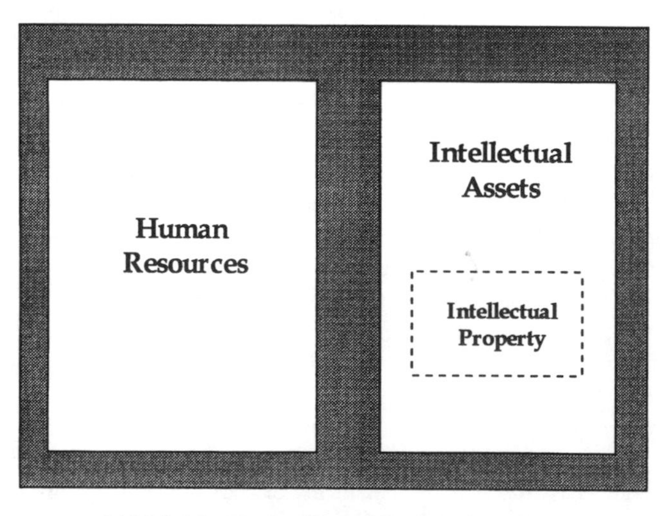

Exhibit 3.2 The Intellectual Capital of the Firm

Exhibit 3.3 shows the value the stock market places on several different knowledge companies (or companies that profit from commercializing their innovations). As can be seen, the market does not assign a premium for intellectual capital to all knowledge companies. Indeed, three of the four firms are trading (in 1997) at less than the value of their tangible structural capital. Why is this?

Simply stated, the reasons for the lack of premium are that the financial markets place little value on either the knowledge firm's stock of intellectual capital and/or its ability to leverage it in the marketplace. One way of rectifying this may be to develop methods for reporting on the amount and leveragability of the firm's intellectual assets. Because information about the value of the firm's stock of intellectual assets is of such interest to the financial marketplace, efforts are under way on several fronts to create methods for accurately and effectively pricing the firm's stock of intellectual capital. Interestingly, although measures of the asset value of intellectual capital are important to the financial community, they hold little or no meaning or interest for the operating management of these firms, whose interest is in measuring the future income streams that their intellectual capital will generate.

CREATING AN INTERNAL CAPABILITY TO MANAGE INTELLECTUAL CAPITAL

The two different kinds of knowledge companies, technology companies and service companies, share an interest in managing their intellectual capital. In both cases, the management of IC is a strategic activity that requires the alignment of intellectual capital with the company's vision and strategy, as well as the external positioning of the firm.

Strategic value extraction by knowledge companies is typically focused more on the firm's future than on its immediate needs. The firm's strategic vision and positioning are usually based on the current or intended intellectual capital capabilities of the firm. Strategic alignment usually involves focusing the firm's

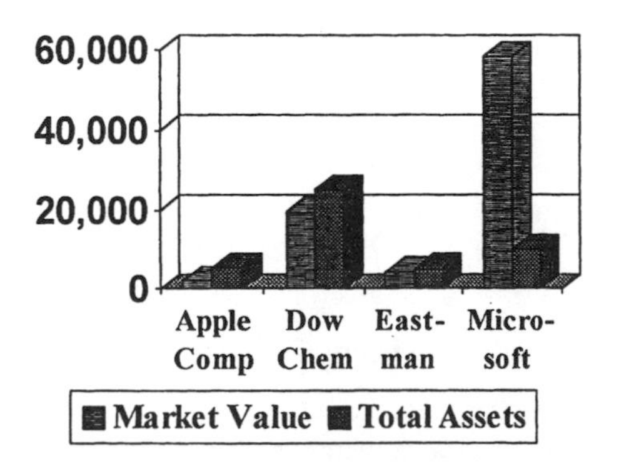

Exhibit 3.3 Example Market Premiums

intellectual capital resources on the activities that will enable the strategy and move the firm toward its vision. Both strategic positioning and strategic alignment involve managing the firm's intellectual and structural resources to enable the rapid and efficient achievement of the vision, and reporting externally to the financial markets on the firm's strategic uses of intellectual capital and the implications of these uses on the firm's long-term ability to create value for shareholders.

A Framework for Managing Intellectual Capital

For many years knowledge companies were not differentiable from other kinds of businesses. They used the same standard business model as other firms; they managed and reported on their physical assets in the same ways; and they used the same protocols for financial reporting and internal accounting. That standard business "model" is useful largely because it is well understood and widely accepted. But that business model emerged when most companies were largely concerned about physical and financial assets. Intellectual assets had not yet become a factor to contend with in business.

With the rise in importance of intellectual capital and the management of intangibles, and with the emergence of knowledge companies, the intellectual capital framework has emerged as a model for companies to consider. Looking at a knowledge company through the intellectual capital framework is like tilting the company 30 degrees on one of its axes and 15 degrees on another. The view that this new perspective provides is different from the standard business model and also complementary. It provides knowledge companies with yet one more tool for managing their resources to produce larger profits.

At this stage in its evolution, the IC framework consists of several elements:

- The company vision for its future, and its business strategy for achieving the vision
- A definition of the role intellectual capital is to play in enabling the vision and the strategy
- A definition of the roles of value creation and value extraction
- Value extraction mechanisms
- Systems for routinely administering, managing, and directing the firm's intellectual capital:
    - Management and information systems
    - Decision processes
    - Work processes
    - Databases

Measuring and Monitoring Intellectual Capital Activities

The value of a firm's product to its customers is referred to as the *value added*. In addition to the *business* terms with which this value added is normally expressed, knowledge firms have the additional perspective to be gained from determining its *intellectual capital* value added. This bit of additional perspective also allows these firms to determine what it is that drives the intellectual capital–created value. These activities, once identified, are the *key drivers of value* and are the activities most important for knowledge firms to monitor, measure, and report.

Identifying the firm's value added is often done using the value chain tools described by Michael E. Porter in his book *Competitive Advantage.* Porter contends that a systematic way of analyzing a firm's sources of competitive advantage is to examine how the activities it performs interact to create value. A Porterian analysis would require firms to identify their primary value-added activities and the support activities that also may add value for customers. Exhibit 3.4 shows the kind of structure suggested by Porter as the basis for defining and pinpointing the sources of competitive advantage or value added for the firm. The axes of the matrix show key firm activities and the phases of each activity.

Defining the firm's activities and then highlighting those that create competitive advantage or added value is a standard business exercise. But to convert that into an intellectual capital framework, you need to translate the highlighted activities into IC terms. To accomplish this in at least a coarse way, the framework displayed in Exhibit 3.5 divides the firm's activities into two: major *IC activities* on the one hand versus phase-of-business activity on the other.

Using the IC matrix allows the firm to determine which of its IC activities are key drivers of value or competitive advantage. A comparison of this finding with the allocation of intellectual resources should be an easy method of determining the relationship between resource allocation, key IC driver activities, and value added or competitive advantage for the firm.

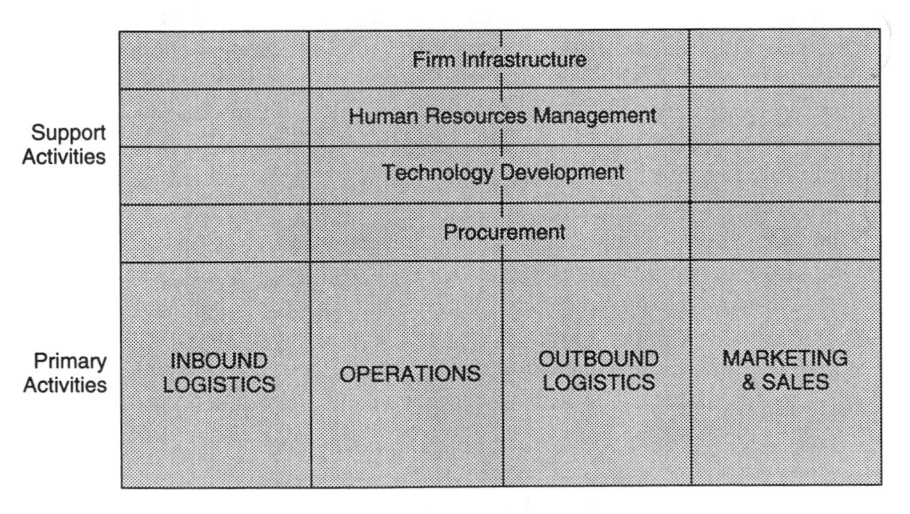

Exhibit 3.4 Traditional Business Value Matrix

	Value Creation				Value Extraction			
	Skills Acq	Envir Imp	Knowledge Creation	Systemization	Gen & Maint	Eval	Extract	Alignment & Systemization
Support Activities				Firm Infrastructure				
			Human Resources Management					
			Technology Development					
				Procurement				
Primary Activities								

Exhibit 3.5 Intellectual Capital Value Matrix

SUMMARY

Extracting value from intellectual capital is a complex activity. A firm's understanding of its values and vision, as determined by its context, is crucial to value extraction. Defining, describing, and measuring intellectual capital requires a descriptive model of IC, as well as an understanding of the sources of value in knowledge companies and the mechanisms available for converting value to cash. Market value, operational value, current and future value, quantitative and qualitative value, and, finally, economic value in money terms are the various types of value that must be understood.

For technology-focused knowledge companies, value extraction relies heavily on the creation and use of management systems involving patent and technology databases, and decision processes focused on technology, business, and legal strategies. For service companies, value extraction is largely strategic, with heavy emphasis on visioning, alignment, and reporting to the external world.

This chapter has outlined the concepts that underlie the extraction of value from the three types of intellectual capital. The remaining chapters discuss the details.

4

Culture and Values Management: Context for the Development and Measurement of Intellectual Capital

Brian P. Hall

Values Technology

The largest intangible in any organization is its people and their collective intelligence. That is to say, intellectual capital is largely driven by and derived from the human side of the enterprise. In Chapter 6, Martin Hall defines intellectual capital as follows:

> The most prevalent concept is to describe intellectual capital (also known as intangible assets) in terms of being constructed from the other "capitals" of organizational design. These capitals are, for the most part, qualifiable elements that can be determined to aid in, or contribute to, organizational success.

But it is financial capital (the "bottom line") measurement and maintenance that preoccupies most senior managers. What is the connection between these two? Measurement. Measurement is key to management of any type of asset (financial or otherwise). After all, measurement is a way of making sense out of what the organization is doing, whether it is a measurement of monthly profit and loss or of time to market. Measurement is an aspect of deriving meaning from something, making sense out of what is going on.

If we are to measure intellectual capital—the intangible dimension that contributes to organizational success—the measurement of people's creativity, their ability to coöperate, and even their sensitivity to the customer and the marketplace, is essential. Recent discoveries have made this possible through the measurement of values. Values are the glue that holds all human relationships together and the foundation that underpins human motivation and creativity. The management of values is so important because, in any company, it is the human relationships that produce its intellectual capital.

The proposition of this chapter is that, if we are to measure intellectual capital—the intangible dimension that contributes to organizational success—the measurement of the people dimension is essential: their creativity, their ability to cooperate, and even their sensitivity to the customer and the marketplace.

The paradigm in Exhibit 4.1, described by Hubert Saint-Onge of The Mutual Group insurance company in Canada, looks at the intangible assets of an organization through three essential dimensions of what he terms *intellectual* (or *knowledge*) *capital:*

What Saint-Onge discovered after five years as Director of the Leadership Center of the Canadian Imperial Bank of Commerce (CIBC) in Toronto is that the business success of a corporate culture is the consequence of the harmony and right balance between human, structural, and customer capital. Human capital, he notes, goes home every night, so it is capital that is on loan to the organization. It is the people, their goodwill, their motivation and creativity that keep the organization alive. The structural capital is all that stuff from computer software to policies, procedures, and business practices (hidden and declared) that allows the human capital to be its best. "Therefore," says Saint-Onge, "if the structural and human capital are not minimally aligned, it is the customer who loses. Customer capital are the clients or customers that pay us for what we do and produce—they are our lifeline to the future."

Saint-Onge's point is that the agility of a company, its capacity to be adaptable in the marketplace and a winner in a global environment, is the congruence or alignment between the three capitals. At a very basic level, it is the human relationships in any company that result in knowledge capital. What we are talking about is the culture of the organization. What allows any organization to work and perform efficiently, is its culture.

In *Built to Last,* James Collins and Jerry Poras put the issue of cultural alignment as follows:

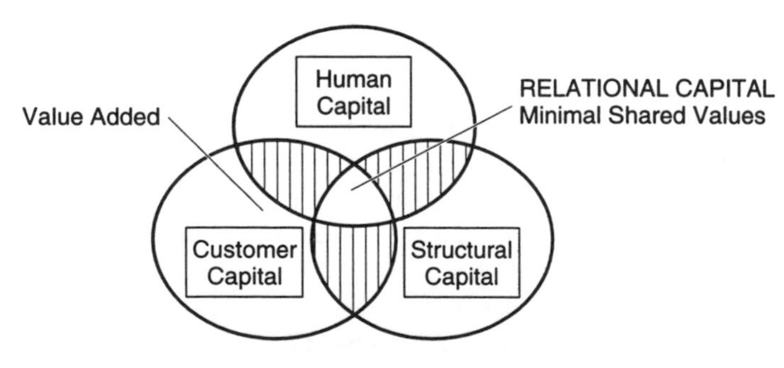

Exhibit 4.1 The Three Capitals

> If you look around at your company right now, you can probably put your finger on at least a dozen items misaligned with its core ideology or that impede progress—"inappropriate" practices that have somehow crept through the woodwork. Does your incentive system reward behaviors inconsistent with your core values? Does the organization's structures get in the way of progress? Do goals and strategies drive the company away from its basic purpose? Do corporate policies inhibit change and improvement?

Poras and Collins have shown the business world by their studies of the most successful organizations over the last 70 years that cultural alignment is based on core values, and that it is this that has made the best organizations successful. In Saint-Onge's terms, it is the core values of an organization that that can bring about minimal congruence between human, structural, and customer capitals. To get a handle on this, we need to explore what we mean by values.

WHAT ARE VALUES?

Answering this question leads to the concept of the "values string," which is the continuum from human values to economic value. In the last decade these concepts have been separated as if they were different and distinct entities. In fact, they are integrally connected. Most often when we see the word *value* or *values* it is related to money or price. For example, we are invited into a grocery store to purchase their apples or eggs because they will give us better value for our money than another store. We are asked to value or place a priority on buying from this store because it will cost us less or we will get more for our money than we would somewhere else. The added value is better fruit for less money. How do we know? The idea, that we have been taught since Adam Smith, is that we can measure value in financial terms. The key is how we make our priority choices based on the financial measure. In Exhibit 4.2, we are looking at the right-hand side only:

What we now call *values* were historically thought of as qualities of human excellence that were underpinned by habits and skills. Aristotle described about half a dozen of them 2,500 years ago. In our research, we found that Aristotle's 6 values can be transformed into 125 values that are the foundation of all our behaviors. These 125 values might be considered a "universal" set. The following definition makes values understandable in our modern reality: *Values are inner ideals that give significance to our lives through the priorities we choose to live by.* Ideals are wider than qualities. Self-preservation is an ideal if you are homeless, for example. As we grow, family or education may become ideals, and so forth.

Exhibit 4.2 is a pictorial representation of the spectrum of "value(s) in human society. When we go to the left-hand side of Exhibit 4.2, we see human or personal values. The concept is that values are consciously chosen priorities reflected in human behavior. In addition, they are what give meaning to people, what drives and motivates them. Values are never in isolation; they form clusters or attitudes and underpin all our behaviors. This component, which has appeared mysteriously for so long, is now identifiable and measurable.

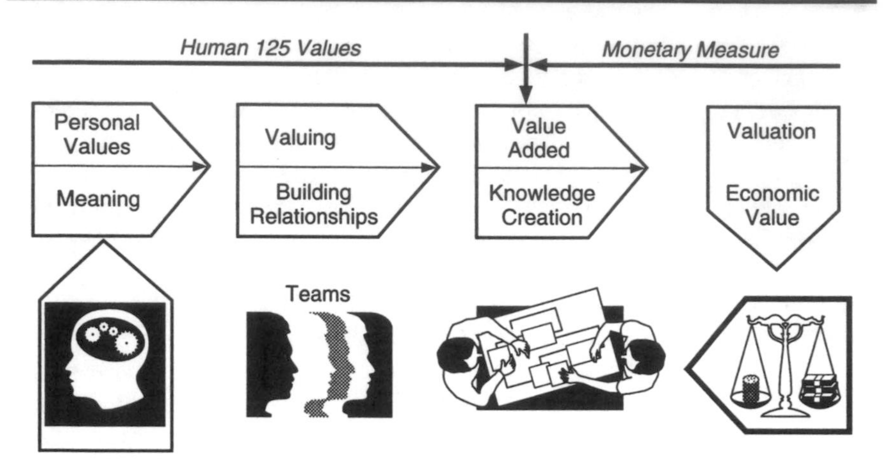

Exhibit 4.2 The Values String

The left side of Exhibit 4.2 begins with the values or priorities that each person chooses. Each of us lives on about 20 of the 125 values priorities. Economic values are simply about 10 percent of the universal set. What the values point out is that they underpin all our relationships. Therefore, the right values mix in a team, particularly in a high-performance team, is going to produce added value. For example, an efficient team might bring a product to market in double the time of one that is full of conflicted relationships due to a lack of values alignment. At a team level, valuing occurs that can create "added value" for the organization. This then gives "added value" that has an economic consequence necessary to perpetuate the organization's life.

The point is that human values and economic value and capability are all connected—a part of a cultural whole. At the personal level, valuing is a matter of choosing priorities that give one value priority or meaning at a day-to-day level. In relationships, common values can lead to team priority and action that gives added value to the company that converts them into economic consequences. Of course, all these things work together—a team works in harmony and consciously makes choices that have a positive effect on the bottom line by, for example, increasing the speed with which a product comes to market.

VALUES AND BEHAVIOR

Three to four values (in different priority orders) will explain any known extant human behavior (see Exhibit 4.3). This was really the basis of the validity studies that stood behind the measurement tools we developed in the mid-1980s. There is, therefore, a direct relationship between the values priorities we live by and our behavior. For example, take four simple values—play, work, family, and education—and prioritize them as follows:

Exhibit 4.3 Three Different Values Priorities

Priority One	Priority Two	Priority Three
1. Play	1. Work	1. Education
2. Family	2. Education	2. Work
3. Education	3. Family	3. Play
4. Work	4. Play	4. Family

The same four values in different orders of priority will change our behavior considerably. In column one, work and study are far less important than leisure and being with family. Column three would be the opposite and might be the behavior of a person who pursues the truth, working long with little time for leisure and family. Perhaps the person in column two works all the time without regard for personal health and relaxation.

VALUES AS A MEASURE OF CULTURAL READINESS

Once it was determined that 125 values underpin human behavior, it was recognized that they correlated with normative models of human, group, and leadership development (see Exhibit 4.4). This work was done at the University of Santa Clara in the early eighties and became the foundation for developing the measurement instruments that will be explained later in this chapter.

Of the 125 possible values, each of us lives with about 20. On a day-to-day basis, we operate on about a third of these, on what we call *focus values*—they guide our decisions and motivate us. The focus area consists of two stages (the gray area) that shift depending on the life or organizational circumstances. A well-developed organization might focus on the values in stages 5 and 6 as illustrated in Exhibit 4.4, or an organization going through severe downsizing might be in stages 2 and 3. Another third of our values make up our foundation—like security and economics—as illustrated by the first three stages on the values map. Another third exist in us as things that are constantly pulling us into the future—these are our vision values.

The values map (Exhibit 4.4) illustrates that values form patterns that reflect human development. What we found is that the collective values of all the employees of an organization, or business units, or specific teams, reflect and go through the same stages of development. In other words, the collective values of all the employees are a measure of the developmental stage of the corporate culture. We also found that by measuring the values development of various groups in the organization, we could see the degree of conflict and alignment. This turns out to be an important connect to intellectual capital measurement.

It turns out that if you want a group to do knowledge leveraging and extraction, examining patents, and increasing knowledge distribution throughout the organization, as described in much of the work of Pat Sullivan and Gorden Petrash in

Values & Culture Development

	Stage 2	Stage 3	Stage 4	Stage 5	Stage 6	Stage 7	
Goals Self-interest Self-preservation Wonder/Awe/Fate	Security Physical Delight	Family/Belonging Fantasy/Play Self-worth	Belief/Philosophy Competence/ Confidence Play/Recreation Work/Labor	Equality/Liberation Integration/Wholeness Self-actualization Service/Vocation	Art/Beauty Being Self New Order Human Dignity Knowledge/Insight Presence Faith/Risk/Vision	Intimacy/Solitude Truth/Wisdom	Ecology Global Harmony Word
Means Food/Warmth Function/Physical Safety/Survival	Affection/Physical Economics/Profit Property/Control Sensory Pleasure Territory/Security Wonder/Curiosity	Being Liked Care/Nurture Control/Discipline Courtesy/Hospitality Dexterity/Coordination Endurance/Patience Equilibrium Friendship/ Belonging Prestige/Image Rights/Respect Social Affirmation Support Peer Tradition Obedience/Duty	Achievement/ Success Administration/ Control Communication/ Competition Reason Design/Pattern/ Order Duty/Obligation Economics/Success Education/Certification Efficiency/Planning Hierarchy/Order Honor Law/Rule Loyalty/Fidelity Management Membership/ Institution Ownership Patriotism/Esteem Productivity Responsibility Rule/Accountability Workmanship/Art Technology/Science Unity/Uniformity	Adaptability/Flexibility Authority/Honesty Congruence Decision/Initiation Empathy Equity/Rights Quality/Evaluation Expressiveness/Joy Generosity/ Compassion Health/Healing Independence Law/Guide Limitation/Acceptance Mutual Obedience Relaxation Search/Meaning/Hope Self-assertion Sharing/Listening/ Trust	Accountability/Ethics Collaboration Community/Supportive Complimentarity Stewardship Creativity Detachment/Solitude Discernment Education/Knowledge Growth/Expansion Intimacy Justice/Social Order Leisure Limitation/Celebration Mission/Objectives Mutual Accountability Pioneerism/Innovation Research Simplicity/Play Unity/Diversity Ritual/Communication Contemplation	Community/ Personalist Interdependence Prophet/Vision Synergy Minessence	Convivial Technology Human Rights Global Justice Macroeconomics
←	**Foundation**	→		← **The Focus**	→	← **Vision**	→

					STE
Autocratic	Familial	Layered	Facilitating	Collaborative	Self-Organizing Dynamic

this book, this works very well if the group is functioning at stages 3 and 4. However, if the issue is knowledge creation, the skill and capabilities reflected in stages 3 and 4 would not be adequate. Knowledge creation—the development of entirely new ideas or the leveraging of an idea in one industry into another with an entirely different field of operation—requires the group to be operating minimally at stages 5 and 6 or higher. That is to say, if the individual's values in a group are not aligned at the right stages, knowledge leveraging or creation is impossible. To go deeper into this idea, let us look at how human values are measured.

VALUES MEASUREMENT: THE TOOLS

One very important asset that has been gained from the scientific and industrial periods of history is the importance of measurement. Modern accounting is a clear example of this. First, we must be clear that any measurement system is limited within its purpose and that it is a way for us to increase our understanding of a given circumstance. For example, accounting can tell us a lot about our financial affairs, about how we have been coping financially up until yesterday. But it is very poor at telling us what we might do in the future. Values measurement, on the other hand, does tell us something about the possible futures of an organization and its capacity to move into a future successfully. Values measurement has a two-fold purpose:

1. To inform us about gaps and discrepancies, or states of nonalignment, in the organization.
2. To make human relational and decision-making information that is tacit, explicit. Values measurement moves values from what we feel we know intuitively to what can be confirmed and known explicitly by a group as a shared consensus experience. Once values are explicit, then we are more in control of where we are going, which in turn can be monitored and measured. It is a critical methodology for empowerment of any management.

Three basic types of measurement instrument were developed in the 1980s:

Document Analysis. This is a computer-driven values thesaurus program that scans the words in a document for the 125 values and 6,000 synonyms. It scans for words, their synonyms, sentence structure, word combinations, and, finally, paragraph structure. As a final check, a human interface check is conducted. The computer output then gives the values priorities of the overall document or any part of a document that is required. It also prints out a values map showing the values priorities by stage and where the focus, future, and foundation values are.

Individual Profile Analysis. This is a program that requires an individual to fill out a 125-question questionnaire. The values output is similar to that of document analysis, and it is used for the same purposes.

Group Audit Analysis. A questionnaire is completed by a group. For example, a recent audit of a global organization polled 8,000 employees

> in four regions of the world to determine how values priorities in different cultures affect the management and decision-making styles of leadership in the regions. The data were used as the basis for improving cultural alignment worldwide, while at the same time respecting the differences in the local cultures. The idea was to create minimal misalignment to promote creative decision making.

The measurement system is a comprehensive way of looking at the culture of an entire organization through a values perspective. The purpose of such an assessment is for strategic planning, increasing organizational alignment, and managing declared values.

In Saint-Onge's language, this gives us an opportunity to measure intellectual capital by measuring the alignment between human, structural, and customer capital:

1. Customer capital is measured by using document analysis scans of advertising, customer focus groups, and special interviews.
2. Human capital is measured through individual executive coaching using the 125-values questionnaire and a 63-question questionnaire to measure the values of the employee population by groups.
3. Structural capital is measured in a number of ways:
   - Policy, communication, and business practice analysis using document analysis
   - Audit analysis in global organizations to measure the degree of alignment between cultural business units
   - Audit analysis to see degree of alignment between business units, leadership, and management

Tom Carter, formerly of the Executive Leadership Development Program for Alcoa International, made the following observation:

> The training of personnel in skills and capability, generally related to the management sciences, were never effective until the values ceiling of the organization were made explicit at a higher level. That is to say, they found that the values that any group held in common around their vision for the future determined their skill and performance ceiling. It is not enough for management to know what knowledge it wishes to impart to personnel, it must also know what values it ought to hold explicitly in common.

THE EFFECTS OF RESEARCH AND MEASUREMENT

In the last 25 years, we have worked with hundreds of organizations in all fields of endeavor. However, in the last ten years, we have had the privilege of conducting audits and using transformation processes based on values measurement in 20 or so global organizations. The following illustrates some of the discoveries we made that will inform us more about intellectual capital measurement.

- Each column showing the eight stages of values development (see Exhibit 4.4), lists "goal" values at the top; these are long-term objectives. At the bottom of each column are the short-term objectives or "means" values that contain over 5,000 skills coded to the values.
- Each stage reflects the worldview of a person and his or her leadership style. That is to say, when you know the values focus of a person, you know his or her worldview and the context through which he or she will make decisions and view the culture of the organization.
- In the modern institutional climate, the demands of the global reality at stages 6 through 8 are causing organizations to move from a traditional management and task-efficiency orientation at stages 3 and 4 to a partnering and collaborative way of doing things at stages 5 and 6.
- *The consequence of this shift* is that most organizations are bridging stages 3 and 4 and moving directly to stages 4 and 5, which is an often chaotic transition stage of development. It is a move from the first half of the diagram to the second half. The transition is characterized by some or all the following:
    - Lack of clarity or uncertainty about one's identity or values, particularly in global organizations
    - Awareness of gaps or discrepancies in the organizations, experienced as lack of collaboration, radical independence rather than interdependence
    - Unclear decision making in a uniform direction due to growing conflicts between old and new ways of doing things
    - Decline in loyalty to the institution
    - Lack of customer focus
- Values emphasis at a particular stage results in a particular leadership style. For example, a person with dominant values at stages 2 and 3 is going to be parental or benevolent in his or her leadership style, which would be very commanding and controlling. Not only is the leadership style going to reflect these values, but the administrative structure that such a person put in place would reflect the same values, encouraging dependency and obedience to the leaders value system. Personal values expression would not be tolerated. On the other hand, a person whose values dominated in stage 6 is going to set up an administration that encourages self-initiation and collaboration at all levels of the organization. *The point is, if the leadership style differs from the group experience, conflict will occur.*
- Any person or group to be healthy must have the appropriate balance of values in the foundation, focus, and future or vision sectors.
- An individual or a group will have values in most of the stages on the values map: in the foundation, focus, and future areas. However, a group will make its decisions and view leadership and personal authority through the focus stages of the group. Two factors are of special significance:

When there is a gap of more than one full "stage" between two individuals, the understanding of a person at the earlier stage may be as little as 20 percent of the communication from the person at the later stage. For example, a leader speaking about collaboration at stage 6 will mean self-initiating partnering with other persons to accomplish a given task. The stage 6 person would assume no need for further discussion. If he or she were speaking to a person at stage 3, that person would be confused and want more clarity and permission to speak to others, as well as guidance on what to say and what decisions to make. The stage 3 person is viewing the world through dependency orientation, expecting to be told what to do and would not comprehend what it means to be independently self-initiating.

When there is a gap of more than a full "stage" between members of a group or administrative team, the team will automatically function at the lowest common denominator. However, if the values of the group are measured and made explicit, and the group itself chooses its values, then the group could function at the highest level.

VALUES TRACKING AND ETHICAL INTEGRITY

We have discussed values patterns and what they mean, values gaps and an organization's need for alignment. But we have not addressed what particular values and what priorities are needed to give an institution ethical integrity. What we have found in this regard is that most leadership, once it is clear about its own values, has very little difficulty seeing what values are essential for the modern corporation to succeed, treating its employees fairly and humanely, and contributing to the wider society. But *what is not understood is that such values cannot be adopted and deployed unless the appropriate antecedent values and tracks are in place.* What does this mean?

Let us take the example of knowledge management. Let us assume that we are interested in both knowledge leveraging and knowledge creation in the organization. We also understand that knowledge and the concept of learning are connected. We stated earlier that for knowledge creation to occur, the organization must be operating at stage 6, at least in its strategic intent. Then the question is what minimal goal values and means (one of each) would we need for this to occur at stage 6?

- Example values would be knowledge/insight as the goal—after all, we are looking at knowledge management. The means could be research or perhaps pioneerism/innovation, or collaboration.

The point is that the values are not activated unless there is a goals and means value at each of the preceding stages, for example:

- Stage 5: Self-actualization (professional development) and sharing/listening/trust to distribute the knowledge
- Stage 4. Competence/confidence (capability) and efficiency/planning or management
- Stage 3: Self-worth and perhaps peer support or control/order/discipline

In our experience, the most often repeated reason that values fail to be deployed throughout an organization is that the antecedent values are not in place. For example, the values of knowledge/insight and collaboration might be critical for an organization wanting to improve collaborative processes in knowledge management. However, these values cannot be activated unless the values in the prior stages are in place. That is, there would have to be additional values in stages 5, 4, 3, 2, and 1 that are also explicitly known. It is the track that fully informs us about the values priorities and overall behavior and skills needed to deploy or manage the values in the organization.

Many corporations today think of values as a set of five or six "governing principles" that govern the success of their businesses. Sometimes these are called *corporate values.* These are at the heart of what they feel their businesses are about. Typically, these corporate values or principles cover such topics as "team excellence," "quality," "customers first," "stewardship," or "innovation." These are really corporate virtues. They are usually thought of as an expression of the corporate culture in that they are unique to a given industry and company. They are what make it unique and excellent. But what is the relationship of these "corporate values" or "governing principles" to the 125 values we have been discussing? *They are, in fact, the values tracks.*

For example, knowledge management as a track might contain all the values and their antecedents we have listed above. This is important because values are what underpin the corporate value or principle and make it unique and different. Without the values, the principle is empty and without content, and impossible to deploy throughout the organization. Principles are an excellent device for focus and communications, but they need to be related to the underpinning basic values for values management to occur. This is because each of the values has a behavioral description and a list of skills (5,000) that lie behind the values. But what is more central to our discussion is that values underpin relationships.

The management of values at an organizational level requires a lot more than assessment and identification of values by the leadership. *Having values as beliefs is one thing, but getting personnel in our institutions to agree to them and to try to live them through their behavior is quite another.*

MANAGEMENT OF THE ORGANIZATIONAL CULTURE

Values are the realignment dimension of culture. Management of values has to do with management of the corporate culture. It is precisely the culture of an organization that reinforces in a positive or negative manner beliefs it declares are essential to its mission. The following case example illustrates how corporate alignment takes place using a values metric. The principle here is to use values measurement to help:

- Align human, structural, and customer capital
- Upgrade the development level of the organization to make knowledge leveraging and creation possible
- Develop organizational principles through values tracks that support the desired mission of the organization

IDENTIFICATION AND DEPLOYMENT OF VALUES: CORPORATE EXAMPLE

This case is about three client populations (divisions) over a five-year period. The company was a government telecommunication agency that was privatized and became a publically traded stock company. Each division had experienced downsizing. Naturally, every institution has to enter into this process with its own strategic plan; however, there are clear lessons to be learned from this process, which can always be repeated.

Context

- Some 8,000 employees with serious fears of downsizing due to recent changes in the marketplace and growing international interests
- New CEO
- Acquisition of a new company with an additional 3,000 employees

What they ended up with were divisions that thought they were entirely different. One was dedicated to engineering and research, another to administration and legal affairs, one was mobile telecommunications, another was advertising, etc. The top 35 leaders in the head office were very mistrustful of each other, and to make it worse, they had a new president, appointed by the Board, who was from another country. To make things even more complicated, they had decided to acquire another company that would increase their employee population by a third, greatly expanding their services into a new geographic and international arena.

Cultural Assessment First Six Months

- The organization had a principles and philosophy statement, which they referred to as the "company values." A *document analysis* was done on this document, on the previous three years' annual reports, and on a speech from the new president on his view of the future of the company.
- Because of mistrust in the leadership, the 35 executives went through values mentoring to get a better sense of their values, using the individual values profiles to help achieve this.

- These 35 individual profiles were then entered into the audit software program resulting in a group executive profile showing the values and stages they held in common.
- A group audit was done on 33 percent of the personnel using 17 open-ended questions that were document-scanned, and later expanded to the organization they were anticipating acquiring: It was a merger analysis of 4,000 personnel and included the additional 17 open-ended questions.

Review of Results and a One-Day Consensus Meeting

The data and results were shared with the executive team. The results were as follows:

- Document analysis showed an absence of stage 3 and 5 values. These stages emphasize interpersonal relations. Other evidence supported the initial conclusion that the company had insufficient customer and employee sensitivity and a lack of internal collaboration between departments and divisions. A lack of sharing of critical knowledge was also a problem, so that in some instances divisions were competing with each other.
- Employee audits showed the same "bridge" interpersonal values absent. They also showed that half the group feared losing their jobs through downsizing. At the same time, they saw the need for the company to move to a partnering culture reflected in values stages 5 and 6 on the values map. What was additionally interesting is that employees had the same priority values in stages 5 and 6 as the executives had after the coaching process.
- Executive group analysis was congruent with the employee results.
- The results of the merger analysis were that the organization they were to acquire had very similar values to their own, giving the board the courage to complete the merger.
- The consequence was that the executives agreed to come to a one-day values seminar.

One-Day Consensus Seminar

The 50 executives (15 from the newly merged organization) came together and within one day agreed on a consensus of 32 values with all the appropriate antecedents for their organization. This was broken down into five principles or corporate values, each tracked with the appropriate values:

- Excellence in community service
- Teaming and partnering
- The most innovative in the industry
- Relationships for the future
- The learning organization

An overall vision document was developed that included a complete definition of each principle based on the standard definitions of the values that stood behind each principle. The process was efficient and straightforward because of all the measurement that had been done beforehand. The process was actually completed in two hours, and the rest of the time was spent on looking at blocks to their vision. The concluding issue was: How are we going to get the other 10,000 employees committed to the new vision?

Commitment and Deployment

Traditionally, the stumbling block to values deployment has been employee commitment. After completing this process with over 15 organizations, we have learned that the keys are as follows:

1. Measurement and monitoring
2. The concept that employees will commit to the corporate values as long as they recognize those values in themselves
3. Educational Process. A team of two executives met with 50 employees for two-hour sessions. All employees had this experience within a six-week period. Before the sessions, employees filled out a personal values questionnaire, with 33 percent already completing questionnaires in the audit process.

Based on this simple process, the executives got near total commitment from management and all employees. For the following two years they used the agreed-on values to look at:

- Policies, rules, and business practices to remove any impediment from the vision
- Hiring practices to ensure new personnel would share the values and have the appropriate education and skills
- Communications to ensure they conformed with their new vision
- The structure of the organization to reduce layers of management that prevented high-quality direct service to their customers
- Values and behavior of all management leadership using a special values-based 360 degree instrument based on their chosen values to coach leadership in living the values of the organization on a day-to-day basis

To complete the process, an organization must first integrate the values behind the principles into the mission statement and business strategy of the company through the business units by region. When we measured the values of the organization two years later, the system had moved a full stage of development toward its desired values. Performance evaluations were replaced by growth evaluations, and leadership values were monitored through a confidential measurement and coaching process. In this particular case, the customer base expanded considerably, and stock value rose by 20 percent. (While it may not be attributable directly to the values work, there have been public statements by the president suggesting that it contributed greatly.)

CONCLUSIONS

To quote Martin Hall, referring to intellectual capital as made up of customer, structural, and human capital: "These capitals are, for the most part, qualifiable elements that can be determined to aid in, or contribute to, organizational success." At the beginning of this chapter, I posited the question: What is the relationship between the profitability of a company and the ability of its employees to form partnerships? The other way we put it was: What is the relationship between values alignment and economic value?

What my associates and I are demonstrating and proposing is that intellectual capital measurement must include both financial and values alignment measurement to give a more wholistic picture.

What I have tried to illustrate is that the people and culture dimensions of the corporation are not only indispensable dimensions of intellectual capital, but that they contribute directly to the bottom line. In this sense we expect that, in the future, values measurement as the metric for human, customer, and structural capital, together with the standard financial measures, will give the stockholder a much better measure of the total value of the company.

Exhibit 4.5 illustrates where the future is.

The context is cultural alignment, where the values of the employees are aligned with the values of the culture. The effort is to make sure the employees' values and the policies and practices for the company are supportive of each other. The basic assumption is that the work of any company is knowledge management; it is the company's knowledge that gives rise to products and services that the public will want to buy. Therefore, looking at Exhibit 4.5, knowledge creation is an essential part of any company's practices, whether it's a manufacturing company developing new chemicals or electronic products, or a financial services company bringing new insurance services to the public. Over time, as patents and copyrights are developed particularly for historical companies, they are going to

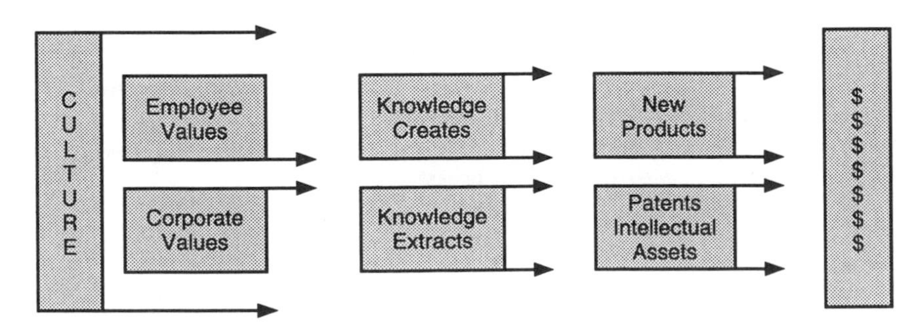

Exhibit 4.5 Values Alignment

become a means to leverage the bottom line. An important question for any company will be when to leverage knowledge creation and knowledge extraction, but both are necessary. However, knowledge creation is a more difficult issue, since you are dealing with completely new products and services, compared to knowledge extraction, which is dealing with a known entity.

However, what we still have not demonstrated is a direct measurement relationship between intellectual capital measures, the direct relationship between knowledge extraction, knowledge creation, and the bottom line using values-based metrics, and the financial outcome. People like Leif Edvinsson of Skandia would have us believe it is not necessary—just tell the story and the stocks will go up. This is not perhaps smoke and mirrors, but I think it is too far from the reality we need to address. A better approach is to understand that values and value are, in fact, intricately connected. Values are what support the culture to make knowledge creation and extraction possible. Value is simply the direct financial consequence of both of these streams.

The answer, I believe, is in the center of Exhibit 4.2 and has to do with rate of change of a system.

BIBLIOGRAPHY

Albizuri, Itziar, et al. (1993). *Los Valores en la Ley Organica de Ordenacion General del Sistema Educativo: Un Analisis Documentos a Traves de la Metodologia de Hall-Tonna.* Bilbao, Spain: I.C.E., Universida De Deusto.

Argyris, C. (1990). *Overcoming Organizational Defenses.* Boston: Allyn and Bacon.

Aristotle. *The Nicomachean Ethics.* Bk. 2, *The Works of Aristotle.* Vol. 2, *The Great Books of the Western World.* New York: Encyclopaedia Britannica, Inc., 1952.

Capra, Fritjof (1996). *The Web of Life: A New Scientific Understanding of Living Things.* New York: Jossey Bass/Anchor Books.

Collins, James, and Jerry Porras (1994). *Built to Last: Successful Habits of Visionary Companies.* New York: Harper Business.

Covey, Stephen R. (1990). *The Seven Habits of Highly Effective People.* New York: Simon and Schuster.

DePree, Max (1992). *Leadership Jazz.* New York: Dell.

Hall, Brian P. (1986). *The Genesis Effect.* New York: Paulist Press.

——— (1994). *Values Shift: Understanding Human and Organizational Development.* Rockport, M.D.: Twin Lights Publishers.

Hall-Tonna Inventory of Values 3.0 (1993). Santa Cruz, C.A.: Values Technology.

Schein, Edgar R. (1992). *Organizational Culture and Leadership.* San Francisco: Jossey Bass.

Toffler, Alvin (1990). *Power Shift.* New York: Bantam Books.

Tonna, Benjamin (1982). *Gospel for the Cities: A Socio-Theology of Urban Ministry.* Translated by William E. Jerman, Ah. Maryknoll, N.Y.: Orbis Books.

5

In Search of a Paradigm

Paul B. Westberg

Genentech, Inc.

Patrick H. Sullivan

ICM Group, LLC

INTRODUCTION

> There is no appropriate scale available with which to weigh the merits of alternative paradigms: they are incommensurable.
>
> *Thomas Kuhn*

A reading of the popular business literature reveals much about the current state of mind in the business community: Titles such as *Inside the Tornado, Crossing the Chasm,* and *Guerrilla Marketing* evoke images of the unpredictable and sometimes precarious nature of business today. In fact, few would dispute that the almost incomprehensible pace of technological advancement and globalization (among other factors) is driving firms to rapidly become more nimble and responsive. On one hand, senior managers have been battered by wave after wave of new techniques for achieving greater and more consistent efficiency and operational effectiveness. On the other hand, there has been an increase in the availability of tutorials on managing turbulence (e.g., in chaos theory and complex adaptive systems), each attempting to draw parallels to the new business climate. Despite the insightful perspectives, few have provided concrete guidance on how to translate their observations into a sustainable increase in financial returns. Ironically, today's senior managers and executives seek greater insight to win the profitability wars and to exceed the optimistic earnings expectations of red-hot equity markets.

The preceding chapters of this book have presented a rationale and framework for a new way of looking at and managing knowledge companies. Several definitions, concepts, and models related to the management of intellectual capital have been put forth with a critical focus on extracting value from a firm's knowledge assets. Does IC represent a new paradigm for companies whose profits come from ideas? How would we know? What is a paradigm? Why should we care? This chapter is dedicated to discussing whether IC represents a new paradigm for business, and, if so, why business should find this significant.

THE CONCEPT OF A PARADIGM

Thomas Kuhn's *The Structure of Scientific Revolutions* first appeared more than 35 years ago, in 1962. In this profoundly influential work (not only for scientists, but for sociologists, economists, and others as well), the word *paradigm* appeared so frequently that he is often credited with popularizing the term. According to Dr. Kuhn, paradigms are "universally recognized scientific achievements that for a time provide model problems and solutions to a community of practitioners." Furthermore, a paradigm is characterized by two critical phenomena: (1) It is sufficiently unprecedented so as to attract an enduring group of practitioners, and (2) it is sufficiently open-ended so as to leave a variety of problems still unresolved. In other words, this body of thought must seem better than any of its competitors, although it does not have to explain all circumstances with which it will be tested.

Management Paradigms

If we are to benefit from a meaningful translation of Kuhn's definitions and framework for change, though, we must begin by understanding the business (and social) context for which we seek parallels. While comparisons to the Industrial Revolution have become almost trite, it is not invalid to compare the current changes to that earlier revolution.

The earliest view of economic enterprise arose out of agrarian society, whose farmers realized that they could trade produce for other family necessities. The agrarian business model was rooted in the land, developed by manual labor, and funded by the seeds of a small portion of the previous year's harvest. It grew out of a society organized around families, tribes, small towns, and local marketplaces. The agrarian model changed over time, driven by the development of newer technologies—the iron-tipped plow, irrigation, hybrid plants, and so on. Land and labor were always the fundamental sources of value.

The agrarian model and its social structure were replaced by the industrial model, which emerged from the Industrial Revolution of the mid-nineteenth century. The Industrial Revolution changed all aspects of economics, society, and lifestyles. It eliminated local craftspeople and replaced hand tools with large-scale industrial machinery powered by water or steam. The Industrial Revolution transformed society from an agricultural to a technology-based economy. Financial capital and access to cheap sources of labor and raw materials were the fundamental keys to value.

During its early stages, the industrial model was characterized by a one-sided focus on finance and economics. Great injustices for the human capital were the norm rather than the exception. The latter stages of the industrial model saw the rise of humanism in the workplace, where concerns for and the tending of the firm's human capital became more the norm. Thus, the late industrial model included a social model in its management toolkit for dealing with human capital. Indeed, it is often argued that the firm is now a social as well as an economic enterprise.

The knowledge firm, by virtue of its reliance on the innovations produced by its human capital, specifically focuses its managerial attention on knowledge creation and the development of new and better innovations for commercialization. Therefore, managing knowledge firms in today's environment requires use of both the economic and the social models.

Until recently, the coexistence of these two very different managerial perspectives on the firm has been characterized as a relatively symbiotic relationship. The economic perspective encouraged a sustained, focused academic study of the firm's physical and financial resources. This effort produced a range of new management tools such as portfolio management, risk analysis, capital investment decision making, learning curves in manufacturing processes, and the value chain. Meanwhile, the social perspective has allowed for a better understanding of the interactions among the individual, the team, the culture, and the working environment. This increased understanding of social phenomena within a firm has yielded great advancements in the areas of organizational behavior, corporate culture and structure, and employee incentives and compensation, among others. However, the industrial economy itself is being replaced by an information economy, driven by stunning advancements in telecommunications and information transfer. The question now arises whether these two perspectives can be extended to this era of information and knowledge, or a new paradigm is necessary.

Emergence of a New Paradigm

Despite the abundant and often erroneous references to paradigm change, the magnitude of the change is rarely discussed. For the business community, a change in paradigm usually signifies the largest change possible, equivalent in nature to the mathematician's concept of infinity. Unfortunately, the current usage is inadequate because it fails to recognize and distinguish the type of change. Only after the type of change is known, however, can we hypothesize meaningfully about the place intellectual capital will ultimately occupy in the new business lexicon. A brief discussion of Kuhn's approach to this issue is especially instructive.

Kuhn put forth an extensive framework for scientific revolutions in his treatise. Critical to this framework is the fundamental role of a paradigm and the means by which changes in it occur. Initially, acceptance of a particular paradigm is predicated on the belief that it will successfully address the practitioner's problems. Construction of more elaborate tools, development of an esoteric vocabulary and skills, and a refinement of concepts all follow. This professionalization leads at once to a severe restriction of the practitioner's vision as well as to additional clarity within the allowable area of focus. Measurement techniques are continually enhanced to aid the need for further precision. It is here, under the backdrop of expectation, that anomalies, or deviations from the norm, are discovered.

A shift in paradigm will occur if an anomaly is assimilated after detailed study, and the resulting components of the paradigm will account for a wider range of phenomena or more precise measurement. However, if the anomaly persists and penetrates the confidence of the practitioners, then a crisis ensues. This crisis has several defining characteristics, which are discussed later in this chapter, and is resolved only by the emergence of a completely new paradigm. It is this dichotomous role of anomalies that gives rise to Kuhn's theory that science is not a cumulative acquisition of knowledge but, instead, composed of intellectually peaceful interludes terminated by violent revolutions.

A BUSINESS ANOMALY

What happens to the symbiotic relationship between the economic and social paradigms when the successful interplay between social factors, resulting in knowledge creation and innovation, becomes the dominant asset of a company, outstripping the importance of the physical and financial resources of a company? A knowledge firm emerges—a new type of company using knowledge as its source of differentiation and competitive advantage, and effectively leveraging newly defined kinds of capital. Moreover, an anomaly to the current paradigms now exists. No longer can the old conceptual models apply. Perhaps more important, the measurement tools previously developed are no longer adequate for describing a knowledge company.

The knowledge company emerged effortlessly, as if created out of whole cloth. Its evolution seems so natural that it is difficult to pinpoint its source or its roots. However, it is possible to begin to trace the development of the belief that innovation (and, hence, knowledge) is fast becoming the firm's major source of value. Acknowledgment of this phenomenon is illustrated by Exhibit 5.1.

Besides demonstrating the increasing frequency and specificity of contribution to ICM, Exhibit 5.1 also provides insight into the amazing diversity of contributors and their influence on each other. The names on the timeline in Exhibit 5.1 are briefly explained below.

- **David Teece**—Teece's long-term interest in licensing led to his 1986 article, "Profiting from Technological Innovation," which was instrumental in demonstrating the economist's view of technology commercialization and contained several ideas that were key to a management capability for extracting value from innovation. This article (and subsequent work) identified sources of value in technological innovation, the mechanisms for converting value to profits, and the steps necessary for commercializing innovation.
- **Brian Hall**—For more than 25 years, Hall has studied human values. In collaboration with Benjamin Tonna, he has developed a hierarchy of human values as well as several instruments for measuring and describing the value sets of individuals and corporations. On his retirement from the University of Santa Clara, Hall founded a company, Values Technology,

Exhibit 5.1 Timeline of IC-Related Events

1986	Sveiby publishes "The Know-How Company" on managing intangible assets
April 1986	Teece publishes "Profiting from Technological Innovation"
1988	Sveiby publishes "The New Annual Report"
1989	Sveiby publishes "The Invisible Balance Sheet"
Summer 1989	Sullivan begins research into "commercializing innovation"
Fall 1990	Term "intellectual capital" coined in Stewart's presence
Jan. 1991	Stewart publishes first "Brainpower" article in *Fortune*
Spring 1991	Sullivan and Stewart meet by telecon. . . . discuss value extraction
Sep. 1991	Skandia organizes first corporate IC function, names Edvinsson VP
Spring 1992	Stewart publishes "Brainpower" article in *Fortune*
Summer 1992	Stewart meets Edvinsson
Fall 1992	Sullivan meets Edvinsson
1993	Hudson publishes *Intellectual Capital*
Spring 1993	Edvinsson visits Sullivan at Berkeley
Fall 1993	Sullivan meets Petrash
Jan. 1994	Stewart interviews Sullivan for forthcoming "measurement of IC" article
July 1994	First meeting of Mill Valley Group
Oct. 1994	Stewart authors "Intellectual Capital" cover article in *Fortune*
Nov. 1994	Sullivan, Petrash, Edvinsson decide to host Gathering of IC managers
Jan. 1995	First meeting of ICM Gathering
Jan. 1995	Second meeting Mill Valley Group
May 1995	First Skandia public report on IC
1996	Brooking publishes *Intellectual Capital*
April 1996	SEC symposium on measuring intellectual/intangible assets
Sept. 1996	Sullivan and Parr book *Licensing Strategies* published
Oct. 1996	Lev founds Intangibles Research Project at New York University
Mar. 1997	Edvinsson and Malone book *Intellectual Capital* published
April 1997	Tom Stewart book *Intellectual Capital* published
1997	Sveiby book *The New Organizational Wealth* published

and now works with firms to identify their values, to analyze how those values aid or impede the firms in achieving their business goals, and to change the values, if necessary, to make them more supportive of the firms' business goals.

- **Karl Erik Sveiby**—Sveiby was an early conceptual thinker about knowledge, its relationship to current financial statements, and its management in Sweden. One of his first clients was Skandia AFS, which incorporated his thinking into their own early thinking on the development of intellectual capital.
- **Hubert Saint-Onge**—The father of the concept of "customer capital," Hubert Saint-Onge is considered one of the most creative thinkers in the field of learning and knowledge management. Saint-Onge, responsible for developing learning programs for the Canadian Imperial Bank of Commerce (CIBC), was interested in how to translate learning into both human and structural capital (note: Saint-Onge's definition of structural capital is largely the equivalent of our definition of intellectual assets). He began by exploring the ratio between the firm's human and structural capital and the firm's financial capital. Saint-Onge realized that for the firm

to be commercially successful in the long term, the first two capitals inevitably must focus on customer-related interests. In so doing, the firm creates a stock of capital around its customers, which he dubbed *customer capital.* The Saint-Onge model shows that the confluence between human, structural, and customer capital is the area where long-term profits are created.

- **Patrick Sullivan**—The focus of Sullivan's work has been the extraction of value from IC. As one of the founders of the ICM Gathering, Sullivan has encouraged companies and individuals involved with value extraction to share information and to jointly develop decision processes, methods, and systems that produce practical results. This book is one of the outcomes of that approach. As a founder of the ICM Gathering, he has been closely associated with the ICM model of a knowledge firm, which was formulated at the first Gathering meeting using much of his thinking as its basis.
- **Thomas Stewart**—Stewart began his association with intellectual capital when, as a feature writer for *Fortune* magazine, he wrote a brief article in 1991 about new ideas in business. This led to a longer story, which became *Brainpower,* published in 1992. Stewart's interest in knowledge management led him to write a second *Fortune* cover story, "*Intellectual Capital,*" which appeared in 1994. Stewart has become one of the most visible spokesmen for the field of intellectual capital management and continues to write articles that focus on the brainpower and knowledge management themes he has done so much to popularize. Now a member of the board of editors of *Fortune* magazine, Stewart published *Intellectual Capital, The New Wealth of Organizations* in 1997.
- **Gordon Petrash**—Originally trained as an architect, Petrash joined Dow in 1986 as a development manager for construction materials. After successes in both construction materials management and in managing Dow's Styrofoam films business, he was asked to create an intellectual asset management function to identify and bring to commercialization any innovations or ideas that might have been overlooked by the corporation. Petrash developed an intellectual asset vision and implementation model, including approaches and tools to enable the company to maximize the value of its existing portfolio of intellectual assets. The success of this work led Dow to expand his responsibilities. Petrash is now the Director of Intellectual Capital/Knowledge Management focusing on creating a learning culture and management focus to enable better utilization of the company's human and organizational capabilities. Gordon Petrash is one of the founders of the ICM Gathering.
- **Leif Edvinsson**—As Corporate Director of Intellectual Capital at Skandia AFS, a Swedish insurance company, Edvinsson is responsible for creating ways to describe hidden value and develop an intellectual capital management model for the firm. With a career in banking and an MBA from the University of California, Edvinsson's work at Skandia has involved identifying, capturing, cultivating, and capitalizing on the firm's

intellectual capital. As one of the best-known spokesmen for intellectual capital management, Edvinsson pioneered the concept of reporting on intellectual capital. Skandia has now issued some six IC supplements to its annual financial reports, outlining the ways in which this "hidden value" is used for the benefit of customers and shareholders. Edvinsson coauthored *Intellectual Capital: Realizing Your Company's True Value by Finding Its Hidden Brainpower* with Michael Malone in 1997. He is also one of the founders of the ICM Gathering.

- **Baruch Lev**—Currently a professor of accounting and finance at the Stern School of Management at New York University, Lev first began his research into valuing intangibles in the early 1990s when he was at Berkeley and a colleague of David Teece's at the business school there. Lev moved to NYU where, in September of 1996 he founded and now runs The Intangibles Research Project. Lev's work focuses on quantifying the value of intangibles and correlating those values with financial measures observable in the capital markets. Lev's project has current liaisons and working relationships with the OECD, the International Accounting Standards Committee, the Center for European Policy Studies, the National Research Council (National Academy of Sciences), and the ICM Gathering. There are currently 15 research projects and two Ph.D. dissertations conducted under the auspices of the Intangibles Research Project.

In fact, our war chest of critical observations regarding knowledge companies is much fuller than the timeline or the current literature suggests. There now exists a spectrum of knowledge firms that can be distinguished on a variety of axes. One particularly important axis is the product versus service orientation of a firm. Firms with knowledge embedded in products (Hewlett-Packard, for example) may be afforded legal protection for their innovations, whereas a firm whose knowledge is manifested in the provision of services (such as Price Waterhouse) has a relatively low level of legal protection available. A logical extension to this observation is that the level of protection (and methods for leveraging this protection) are common to particular industries.

Beyond these observations (and those discussed in the remainder of this book), there are two very different approaches taken to defining and managing the intellectual capital of a knowledge firm. Not so surprising, these approaches mirror the economic and social trajectories of the industrial era. One approach is based on the premise that by increasing the knowledge resident in the firm, you can increase its ability to generate profits over the long term. This belief leads to a view of intellectual capital that is focused almost entirely on human capital—in particular, on the firm's employees concerned with knowledge creation, learning, communicating, and sharing. According to this approach, intellectual capital management itself is based on a set of disciplines grounded in the academic study of education, philosophy, religion, and sociology.

A second approach to intellectual capital management comes from people who view intellectual capital as an economic asset of the firm that can be treated using economic and financial methods. Their premise is that the firm's intellectual capital is a valuable asset to be maintained over time and from which profits can be extracted. Managers of IC in this framework are concerned with economic and financial value, systems approaches, and business strategy. Intellectual capital management is based on academic concepts rooted in economics and finance theory, according to this approach.

The point to appreciate is that the study of the anomalous knowledge firm has reached a level of critical momentum. The initial stages of discovery and recognition are now a part of business history, and we have collectively progressed to a stage of focused assessment and deduction of conceptual models that is already yielding valuable information and insight for senior managers. What are these conceptual models? How were they developed?

MODELS OF KNOWLEDGE FIRMS

Models allow us to abstract from the infinite levels of detail and facts without material loss of meaning. Yet, somewhat counterintuitively, additional understanding and insight are gained from the resulting simplification. What qualifies as a model for intellectual capital? The topic of intellectual capital has roots in many diverse fields—psychology, sociology, information systems, operations research, finance, and strategy, among them—and each possesses a multiplicity of models and an accompanying bevy of definitions important to the understanding of intellectual capital. Reviewing and summarizing all of the elements that contribute to the understanding of intellectual capital would be a futile effort with little value in the end. Therefore, we limit this discussion to explicit models of intellectual capital (with one exception) in the hope of promoting an improved understanding of knowledge creation and an elucidation of the mechanisms by which value is extracted.

To date, at least four models have been used to conceptualize intellectual capital:

- ICM/Model (Sullivan)
- Skandia Navigator (Edvinsson)
- Hubert Saint-Onge Model
- Hall-Tonna Values Map

We have gone to great lengths to ensure that the following representations are as current as possible. Nevertheless, many of these models have been years in the making, and it is only realistic to recognize that they continue to be modified and enhanced. We believe that much of what follows will not change materially, however, and that our observations and conclusions will remain valid.

It will be important to develop an understanding of the similarities and differences between each of these models. First, however, we must spend a moment addressing the confluence of terminology that occurs as we try to summarize the IC models. Each of these models relies on its own set of unique definitions and concepts to support its framework, hypotheses, and conclusions. The problems associated with this confluence of terminology do not emanate from different terms being used to describe the same phenomenon. In fact, it is exactly the opposite. Several of these models actually use the same terminology yet define the terms differently. What could be a greater misfortune for understanding and communication of this field of study? A few of the terms which suffer this misfortune are:

Intellectual capital
Human capital
Customer capital
Structural capital
Economic capital
Organizational capital
Process capital
Intellectual assets
Innovation & renewal
Knowledge & know-how
Values

Fortunately, this black cloud of potential miscommunication has a silver lining. After an extensive comparison of the models and their respective terminology, it is our hypothesis that there is actually very little significant variation in most of the definitions posited. If true, we are witness to a much more remarkable phenomenon than we might recognize at first glance. Several pioneers across various countries, industries, and professions seem to have arrived at the same essential building blocks of intellectual capital. In this light, rather than provide a comparative analysis of each model's definitions, it would seem infinitely more valuable to adopt a representative definition for each of the key terms so that we can focus on the genesis, contribution, and implications of each model.

Key Definitions Related to IC

Because the extensive vocabulary associated with the topic of intellectual capital is growing exponentially, we have selected a short list of the most critical terms necessary to understanding the four models. Each of the following definitions benefits from many sources. We are indebted to the many people who have proposed, commented on, and collaborated on each. Our goal, though, remains simple and utilitarian: to capture the essence of each term for use in deriving other important insights.

Human Capital. Human capital consists of the firm's know-how and institutional memory about topics important to its business. It includes the collective experiences, skills, and general know-how of the firm. At the individual level, it may be defined as the capabilities of employees, contractors, suppliers, and other related people to solve customer problems. Human capital is largely, if not totally, tacit in nature and is not owned by the firm.

Intellectual Assets. Intellectual assets are the codified, tangible, or physical descriptions of specific knowledge to which the firm can assert ownership. Examples include plans, procedures, memos, sketches, drawings, blueprints, and computer programs, among others. Intellectual assets that receive legal protection become intellectual property. There are five generally recognized forms of intellectual property: patents, copyrights, trademarks, trade secrets, and semiconductor masks.

Structural Capital. Structural capital consists of the supporting resources and infrastructure of a firm. It includes all of the assets found in the financial statements of a firm, such as cash and equivalents, property, buildings, and equipment. Note that substantial information technology infrastructure is often included in these assets, although you must be sure not to confuse certain elements of information technology with process capital (see the following). Structural capital also includes the complementary business assets of a firm (i.e., assets that are necessary for a firm to process an innovation, such as a manufacturing facility or sales force).

Customer Capital. Customer capital is the historical, demographic, and psychographic information related to past, current, and potential customers of a firm. In addition, it includes the relationships that a firm has with its internal and external customers. Relationships within the value chain (i.e., with distributors and vendors) are a critical part of customer capital. Such concepts as brand equity, image, and community visibility are also included in customer capital.

Process Capital. Process capital consists of the methods a firm uses to conduct its business. These include the indoctrination of new employees, training, and all other forms of knowledge transfer. Process capital also includes the deployment of technologies for the transfer of information within and outside of the firm. Because of its similarity to and overlap with elements of human and structural capital, several IC models include process capital within these other types of capital.

ICM Model (Sullivan)

This and earlier chapters of this book have referred to the ICM model for intellectual capital. Exhibit 5.2 is a complete graphic depiction of this model.

Notice that the ICM model relies on the concepts of human capital, intellectual assets, and structural capital, which have previously been defined. In addition, this model incorporates complementary business assets. The inclusion of complementary assets is grounded in Sullivan's work with David Teece, whose seminal work led to a greater understanding of the links between innovation, markets, value, and profit. In addition, the relationship between intellectual property (IP) and intellectual assets was greatly influenced by Sullivan's work with technology clients interested in extracting greater value from their IP portfolios. Therefore, this model emphasizes the systemic relationships within the firm and addresses intellectual capital from a value extraction viewpoint.

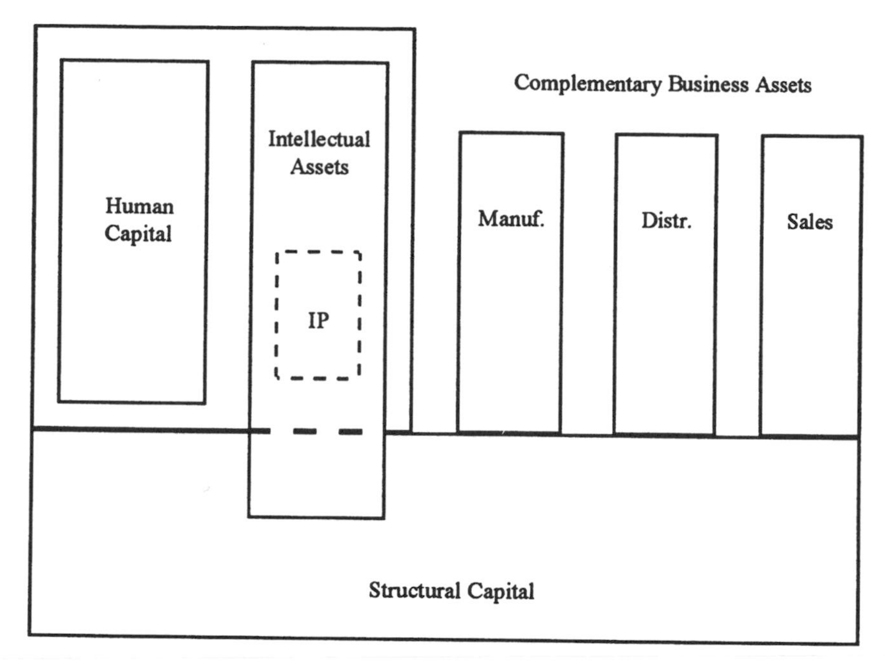

Exhibit 5.2 ICM Model of Intellectual Capital

The Skandia Navigator (Edvinsson)

Perhaps the best publicized of all the models, the Skandia Navigator is the pioneering work of Leif Edvinsson at Skandia AFS (see Exhibit 5.3).

Development of this model benefited from a supportive chief executive and from Edvinsson's extensive collaboration with most of the leading thinkers on this, and related, topics over a period of several years. Notice that the Navigator does not explicitly use any of the terms already discussed. Implicitly, though, the Navigator incorporates human capital, customer capital, and structural capital. The Navigator also adds the concept of renewal & development, which are the activities necessary for capturing opportunities that will define the company's future. The traditional financial statements, annual reports, and the like, are termed *financial focus* and are the final component of the model. The addition of these two terms allows for the inclusion of the concept of time: The financial focus relates to past results and extends into the future with renewal & development. The Navigator is a milestone result of Skandia's efforts to adapt to the deregulation of the mature financial sector and to a new environment of increased competition and innovation. The Navigator can be seen as a model that addresses intellectual capital from a value creation standpoint and greatly benefits management explanation (both internally and externally).

Karl Erik Sveiby was an early influence on the Navigator, despite conducting his early work in a completely different industry (printing). His early work, published in Sweden, focused largely on intangible assets and their three key compo-

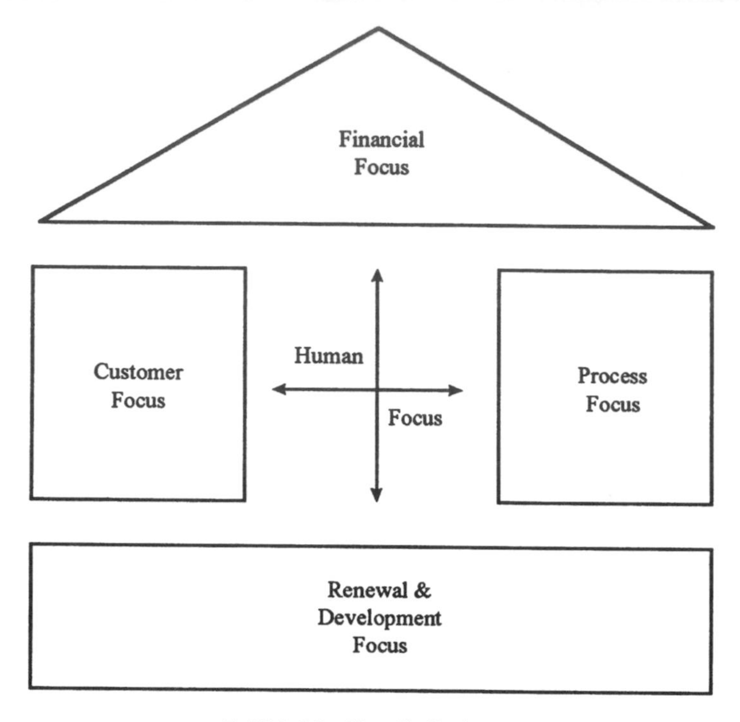

Exhibit 5.3 Skandia Navigator

nents: employee competence, internal structure, and external structure. Besides his continued efforts to delineate human and structural capital and the processes that transfer knowledge within a firm, it was, perhaps, Sveiby's early discussions with Skandia that were of the most import.

Hubert Saint-Onge Model

Another key influence on Skandia's Navigator was Hubert Saint-Onge. Much of Saint-Onge's groundbreaking developmental work was done while he was vice president of learning organization and leadership development at the Canadian Imperial Bank of Commerce (CIBC). Saint-Onge sees the firm's intellectual capital as including three elements:

Human capital. The capabilities of the individuals required to provide solutions to customers

Customer capital. The depth (penetration), width (coverage), attachment (loyalty), and profitability of customers

Structural capital. The capabilities of the organization to meet market needs (see Exhibit 5.4).

The focus of the Saint-Onge model is on the firm's tacit knowledge and how to renew and manage it most effectively. His model is fundamentally based on the

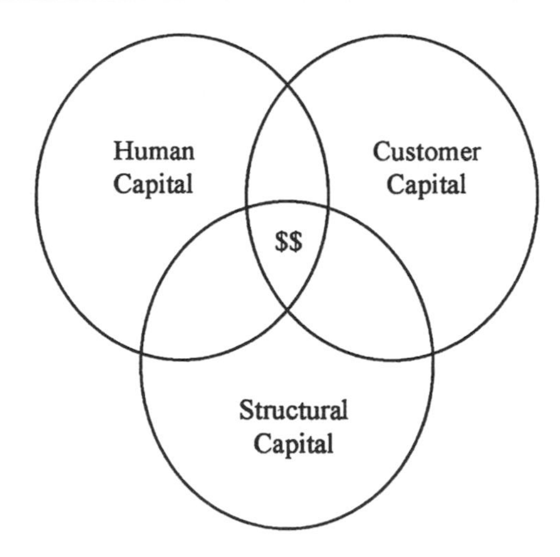

Exhibit 5.4 Hubert Saint-Onge Model of Intellectual Capital

belief that by understanding tacit knowledge, the firm can find ways to build a dynamic internal cohesiveness that will enhance its future performance.

The Values Map

While not strictly a model for intellectual capital, the Values Map developed by Hall and Tonna nonetheless is vital to the understanding of intellectual capital (see Exhibit 5.5).

In short, a human-centric viewpoint of intellectual capital shows that values are the critical underpinning for many of the concepts and definitions in these other models. An understanding of values gives fundamental meaning to concepts such as human and customer capital. Values also play a critical role in defining the interaction and relationships between the different kinds of capital. The importance of alignment becomes obvious through this lens.

Several observations regarding the four models just discussed are now possible. To reiterate, the usually slight differences in definitions are largely immaterial in our opinion. In fact, when we make allowances for differing perspectives and the intended use of each model, much of the ambiguity among definitions disappears. For example, if your mission is to increase the rate of innovation, then the main concern is to define the leverage opportunities that will most dramatically influence this process. This would undoubtedly include a detailed examination of human capital. But your view, and thus definition, of structural capital would likely focus on such things as information technology, which facilitates interaction among individuals, teams, and so forth. These efforts would naturally differ from those undertaken by a firm that possesses a large portfolio of intellectual property and is focused on converting this asset into increased profits via the firm's structural capital (e.g., its manufacturing facility).

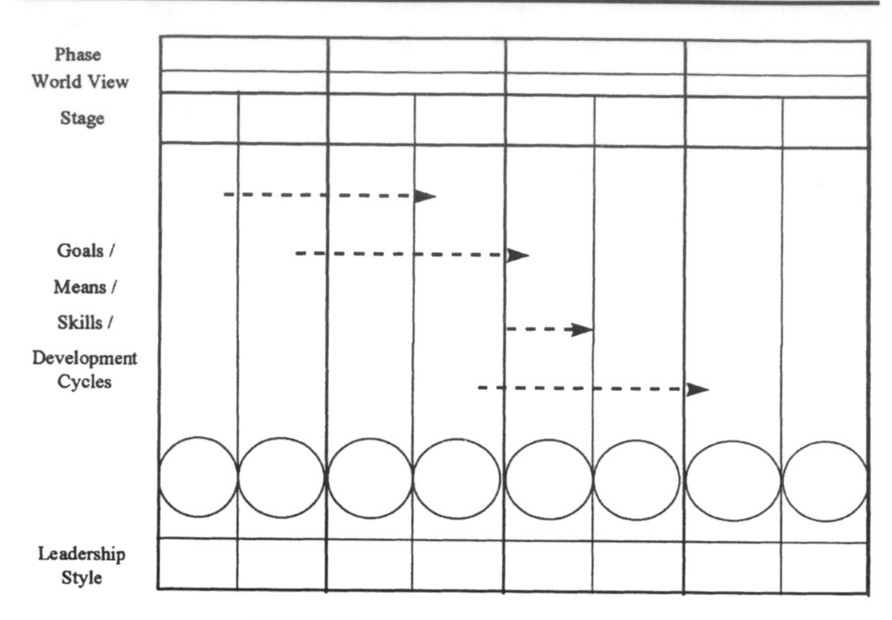

Exhibit 5.5 The Hall/Tonna Values Map

PERSPECTIVES ON INTELLECTUAL CAPITAL

Perspective is perhaps the single most influential factor in the development of intellectual capital and its models.

Value Creation

We have already alluded to the first major perspective several times: *value creation.* This perspective recognizes the human contribution to innovation and the creation and transfer of knowledge. It is largely held by companies such as law firms, consulting firms, and financial service firms, which do not rely on legal protection of their intellectual assets, as a computer hardware or software company might. Within the value creation perspective, though, several distinct agendas are apparent. Much of the recent efforts at Skandia have involved educating the capital markets on the topic of ICM and, now, reporting to them in a supplement to the firm's annual report. Hubert Saint-Onge and Charles Armstrong (of S.A. Armstrong, Inc.) have made great strides to further elucidate the concept, role, and relationships of customer capital, especially for their respective firms. Due to the focus on human and customer capital, these companies have been most involved with Hall in the area of values and alignment.

Value Extraction

We have also previously alluded to the second major perspective: *value extraction.* This perspective is different from value creation in that it places a premium on the concept that innovation and the creation of knowledge are necessary but not sufficient. The mechanisms for converting IC to corporate and shareholder profit are paramount. Of course, this perspective tends to be that of technology and manufacturing companies, whose intellectual assets are often embedded in their physical products and, consequently, qualify for greater legal protection. Several initiatives with different roots have led to the adoption of this common perspective, but with differing emphases. For instance, both Dow Chemical and Eastman Chemical have largely focused their corporate resources on extracting more from their existing portfolios of intellectual assets. In a similar effort, Xerox has focused on the systematic review and classification of innovations and techniques for extraction. Meanwhile, Avery Dennison has chosen to focus on managing the future and developing a vision that will benefit it most effectively later. Finally, the ICM Gathering and Pat Sullivan have done a tremendous amount of work on the topic of measurement.

One valid interpretation of the current state is that there is a gap between the value creation view of intellectual capital and the value extraction view (see Exhibit 5.6). Both views are valid, and both function effectively for the narrow purposes for which they are intended. Neither view is complete, however; and, unfortunately, there are not sufficient activities underway to move the two efforts from a parallel development toward one unified coaxial approach.

Logically, this quandary results in one of two outcomes: a synergistic reconciliation whereupon the resulting paradigm incorporates all facets of the old and new perspectives, or a destructive schism that leads the business community to crisis. Indeed, it is this qualification of our journey which we are attempting to describe and predict.

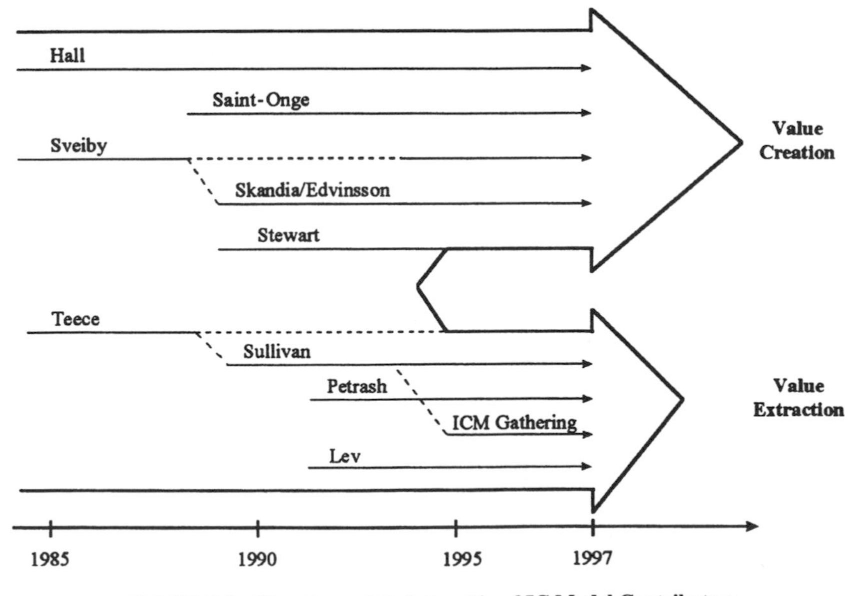

Exhibit 5.6 Timeline and Relationship of IC Model Contributors

PARADIGM SHIFT OR REPLACEMENT REVISITED

The growth in the number and importance of knowledge-based companies in the global economy has had an unsettling effect on the business community that is too profound to ignore. Too frequently, the current models do not work for the equity analyst on Wall Street who attempts to assess the market value (and, hence, the price) of a knowledge company. The SEC and FASB are mobilizing to ensure that these knowledge companies are continuing to properly account and report to regulators and shareholders. Senior managers and executives of knowledge firms are desperately implementing stop-gap measures to ensure that their institutional knowledge becomes codified and is partially secured against recruiters, who would use nearly any means necessary to lure away key personnel.

But are we really in a state of crisis? Unfortunately, the evidence to date is decidedly mixed. According to several indicators adopted from Kuhn, the scales are beginning to tip toward a crisis.

1. There has been a continued failure of the rules that operate under the economic paradigm and that are well documented in Edvinsson and Malone's book *Intellectual Capital: Realizing Your Company's True Value by Finding Its Hidden Brainpower.* Consequently, the social paradigm has become largely self-referential, posing many curious problems of its own.
2. The fundamentally different approach required by knowledge-based firms has been isolated, and studies have been designed to refine it. Witness the SEC hearings in the summer of 1996 to launch its efforts to account for intellectual capital and the recent efforts of Baruch Lev at the request of the SEC for a multiyear study of intangibles and accounting policy.
3. The management of intellectual capital has been partially anticipated: Over the past ten years, futurists have emphasized the growing importance of intangibles and human capital.
4. Several general environmental conditions make the management of intellectual capital a likely candidate for a new management model. The combination of several years of downsizing, rightsizing, and outsourcing coupled with the rise in individual empowerment in society and the workplace suggests that a new management philosophy with a focus and respect for the individuality of employees is ripe for adoption.
5. There has been a proliferation of new conceptualizations, and derivations thereof, offered to the business community.

SUMMARY AND CONCLUSIONS

The emergence of the knowledge firm has christened the dawn of a new era. Still in its infancy, this new era is fraught with uncertainty and many conflicting observations and viewpoints. There is no more profound a difference than the divergence of the value creation and value extraction perspectives of intellectual capital's pioneers. Without question, the business community does not currently have a common, integrated perspective that meets the diverse needs of its constituents. The schism between these groups must be resolved and a unified perspective agreed on. Quite likely, the focal point of many discussions will be the critical issue of measurement, where relativistic and standardized philosophies will be pitted against one another and possibly crossbred. It is the astute manager or practitioner who will not be distracted but will persevere to a higher ground where value from innovation and knowledge is both created and extracted within a partnership that is more powerful than the sum of its parts.

BIBLIOGRAPHY

Brooking, A. (1996). *Intellectual Capital: Core Asset for the Third Millenium Enterprise.* Thomson Business Press.

Chalmers, Alan, and Jonathan Tidmus (1996). *Practical Parallel Processing, An Introduction to Problem Solving in Parallel.* London: International Thomson Computer Press.

Edvinsson, Leif, and Michael Malone (1997). *Intellectual Capital: Realizing Your Company's True Value by Finding Its Hidden Brainpower.* New York: Harper Business.

Hall, Brian P. (1995). *Values Shift, A Guide to Personal and Organizational Transformation.* Rockport, M.D.: Twin Lights Publishers.

Hudson, W. J. (1993). *Intellectual Capital: How to Build It, Enhance It, Use It.* New York: John Wiley & Sons, Inc.

Kuhn, Thomas S. (1962). *The Structure of Scientific Revolutions.* Chicago: University of Chicago Press.

Levinsson, Jay Conrad (1993). *Guerrilla Marketing.* New York: Houghton Mifflin Co.

Moore, Jeoffrey A. (1991). *Crossing the Chasm.* New York: Harper Business.

——— (1995). *Inside the Tornado.* New York: Harper Business.

Porter, Michael E. (1996). "What Is Strategy?" *Harvard Business Review.* (November–December).

Stewart, Thomas A. (1997). *Intellectual Capital: The New Wealth of Organizations.* New York: Doubleday/Currency.

Sveiby, Karl Erik (1997). *The New Organizational Wealth: Managing and Measuring Knowledge-Based Assets.* San Francisco: Berrett-Koehler Publishers.

Teece, David J. (1986). "Profiting from Technological Innovation." *Research Policy* (April).

6

The Confusion of the Capitals: Surveying the Cluttered Landscape of Intellectual "Capitals" and Terminology

Martin L.W. Hall, Ph.D.

Values Technology

Different definitions of or about intellectual capital (IC) are being concocted about as fast as the field is developing, which is to say, very fast. Tom Stewart defines intellectual capital as the "intellectual material—knowledge, information, intellectual property, experience—that can be put to use to create wealth."[1] This definition is probably as good as any. But good definitions are only meaningful within the context of models. The most prevalent concept is to describe intellectual capital (also known as *intangible assets*) as being constructed from the other "capitals" of organizational design. These capitals are, for the most part, qualifiable elements that can be determined to aid in, or contribute to, organizational success. These capitals are the pillars that describe the overarching concept of intellectual capital. From this, people extract value, either in better understanding or in economic gain. The idea of IC is to have conceptual structures from which formerly intangible elements in an organization can be understood and discussed.

This short chapter hopes to enlighten and educate those who wish to better understand the rocky landscape that is the burgeoning field of intellectual capital (IC). Even if it does not define the best model, it should give you the ammunition to decide and understand what works and, hopefully, begin to apply it.

There appear to be two primary reasons why people use the models: One is to help understand and discuss how an organization might develop intellectual capital; and the other (which is the focus of this book) is to understand IC so that value may be extracted and used by the organization.

THE IC LANDSCAPE

Intellectual capital (IC) so far has utilized at least five models, and in many ways they are more alike than they care to admit, and there are many more descriptions and definitions within each model. The common models include: the Skandia model made popular by Leif Edvinsson, Intangible Assets (Karl Erik Sveiby), the Saint-Onge and Armstrong models, the ICM Extraction Model (Pat Sullivan), and the Hall-Tonna Values Map model (though this is not strictly an IC model). These models will be discussed elsewhere in the book. It is important to note, however, that the models usually follow one of two primary focuses: understanding or extraction. *Understanding* focuses on trying to understand the issues of intellectual capital in an organization with the hopes of increasing or developing intellectual capital. *Extraction* focuses on extracting value for the organization by looking at the extant intellectual capital.

Many of the IC models seem to use some form of trinity to help explain their intellectual capital and intellectual asset models. Three pillars or three circles are commonly used to describe the subcomponents of IC. These subcomponents are usually also referred to as "capitals," so, for example, human capital refers to the human side of the enterprise, etc. The concept of describing everything in terms of "capitals" is an obvious reference to the banking and other financial roots of the intellectual capital discussion.

The aforementioned capitals are conceptual structures used to discuss the intangible elements of organizations. Unfortunately, there is not a lot of consensus in terms of strict definitions except at the highest levels. But that said, there is a fair amount of similarity in what everyone is saying with their own definitions. The various capitals are seen as interacting with each other to define IC.

The following is a list (absent the models) of the various "capitals" that clutter the landscape:

- Human
- Customer
- Stakeholder
- Cultural
- Relationship
- Spiritual
- Organizational
- Structural
- Process
- Economic

Let's take a look at the specific definitions to see what they tell us about the various elements of IC. (Note: Not all of these are featured in the most popular models but are often used when discussing intellectual capital.)

DEFINITIONS OF THE CAPITALS

Human Capital. This is the way in which many of the current thinkers in IC choose to define the human side of the enterprise. Usually they are focusing on the knowledge and know-how captured by looking at individuals or groups within an organization. This is quite often understood as the area in which many companies need to spend more time developing their IC. Companies that develop human capital well are thought of as doing well in managing people and knowledge-intensive activities. Values are seen as key components to understanding Human Capital.

Customer Capital. This is where some of the IC models describe the customers and customer relationships that affect the perceptions and the valuation of a company. In other words, this is often where the *image* or *reputation* of the company is kept. This is often where issues of marketing and image are dealt with in intellectual capital management.

Stakeholder Capital. This is essentially the same as customer capital with the exception that the definition is broadened to include other stakeholders in the organization—such as customers, vendors, suppliers, and stockholders. Employees are often considered stakeholders, but more from a perspective of how their perceptions of the company are understood and managed. This is particularly important in hire-and-retain issues. Stakeholder capital is distinctly different from human capital.

Cultural Capital. As values are seen as a key to understanding and managing IC, cultural capital is seen as one way for the values to be understood in a cultural context within an organization. Specifically, it is the internal organizational environment that includes communication issues with individuals and groups, values and vision.

Relationship Capital. Values are relational and, consequently, so are people. Since IC is a collection of "capitals" interacting with each other, relationship capital is seen as the value or potential value of different capitals in interaction with each other. It might be, for example, the interaction between human capital and structural capital. Relationship capital is essentially the by-product of the interaction of these two capitals (see Exhibit 6.1).

Spiritual Capital. This is one of the least defined of the capitals. It does not specifically show up in many of the models and is usually reserved for defining elements that we do not know how to otherwise identify with one of the other elements. The concept here is the discussion of the essence of a high-performing, high-level communicating culture. The idea is to capture the essence or positive spirit of the organization and "harness" this essence in developing IC. Since it is less defined, it is very unclear how this might have practical ramifications on the extraction side of IC except possibly in the relationship it has to high-quality communication between individuals and the relationship of that to IC.

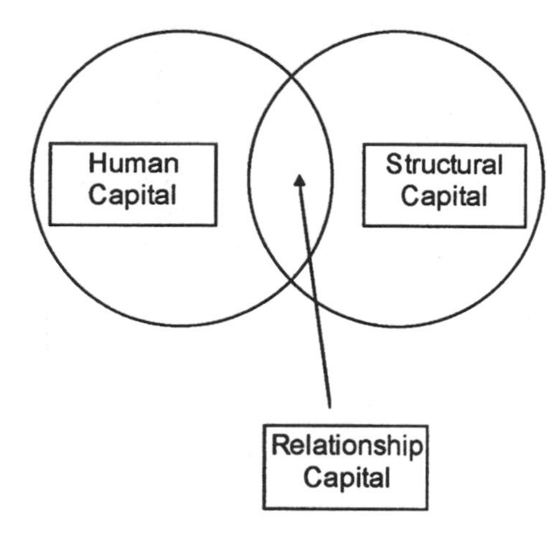

Exhibit 6.1 Relationship Capital

Organizational Capital. Organizational capital gets at the relationship between how an organization and its people are organized to best take advantage of environmental (market) conditions. To some this is simply structural capital (see Exhibit 6.2), to others this is the relationship of human and structural capital. Since organizations are made up of both individuals and the structures and processes within which they work and operate, the definition that seems to work is that of a combination of human and structural capital. Organizational capital is the managing of this relationship. It is important to watch the organizational capital because this is where the organizational agility is developed (see Exhibit 6.2).

Structural Capital. Structural capital essentially comprises the hard assets and structures that make up an organization. Often this is seen as the tangible side of

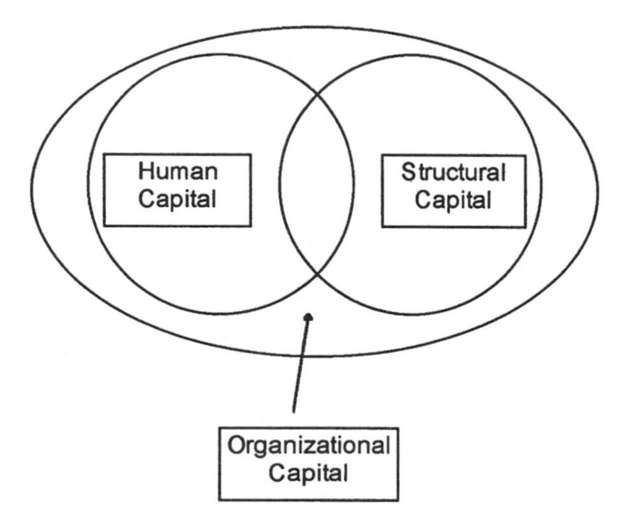

Exhibit 6.2 Organizational Capital

the organization because this is where the assets, buildings, machines, and other tangible examples of organizations are kept.

Process Capital. This is the process elements of the organization. It includes the training and other processes in the organization (purchasing, hiring, decision making, etc.) that control the flow of information. Anything organizational that is not strictly structural would be process capital. This is where organizational barriers to communication can occur. In some models, this is subsumed into the human capital because it mainly deals with human process. In others, it is subsumed into the structural or organizational capital. The reason for spelling it out on its own is that it does not necessarily fit into either category as currently defined.

Economic Capital. This is really what is classically thought of as financial capital. These are the elements that are usually seen on the balance sheet or year-end report. In intellectual capital terms, this is what extraction is trying to optimize. Economic capital is the intersection of organization (human and structural capital) with the needs of the customers or stakeholders to generate value (see Exhibit 6.3).

If we were to try and put these all together, you would see that it becomes confused very quickly because there has been no real effort to reconcile the models (see Exhibit 6.4).

PUTTING THE CAPITALS IN PERSPECTIVE

Elsewhere in this book, we are going to be discussing the different models. The individual capitals themselves may be more obvious or understood through that lens. But it is important to note that there is currently no comprehensive model of the IC landscape. Consequently, you have models with similar but different definitions.

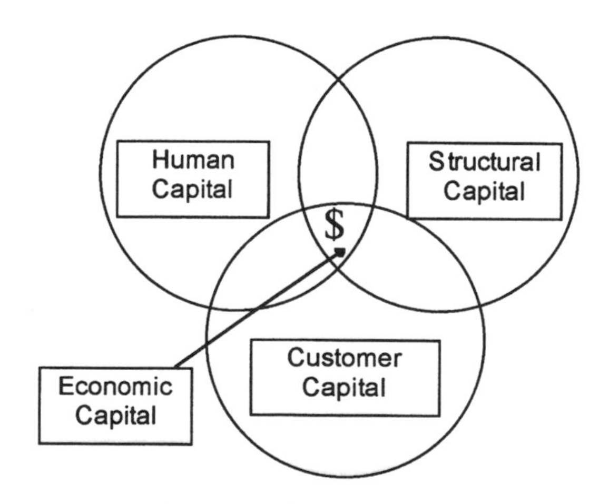

Exhibit 6.3 Economic Capital

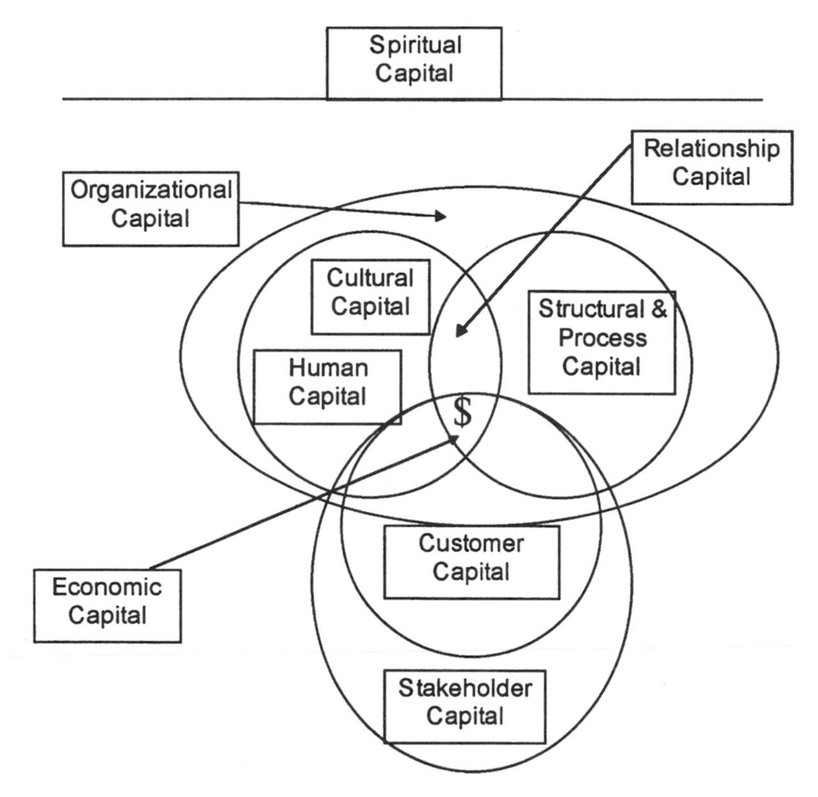

Exhibit 6.4 Cluttered Landscape

One way to look at the IC puzzle is to think of it as a box (see Exhibit 6.5), where the box is intellectual capital but you can look into or at the box from different perspectives to get what you need.

You may look at one model as more of a diagnostic tool for understanding intellectual capital; you may use another model to extract value from your organization's IC activities. What this makes apparent very quickly is that there is no common model. If there is no common model, it can be difficult to reconcile the activities of two different IC activities using the same definitions, etc. A model for extraction may not be complete enough for a discussion of IC development and vice versa. While I will not attempt to solve this issue here, I would like to add a perspective to the debate that might, with clearer definition of the elements, allow the development of a newer more comprehensive model.

SYSTEMS AND VALUES: CONCEPTS FOR INTEGRATION NOT DISINTEGRATION

It may not be well understood, but these descriptions of capitals come out of mixed similarities, almost out of a sense of not wanting to be defined too closely.

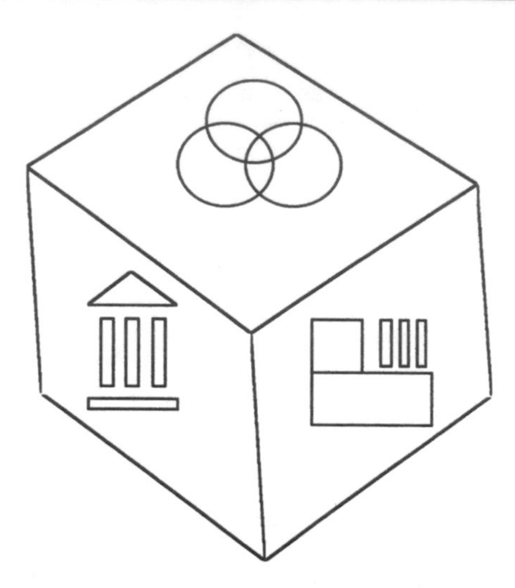

Exhibit 6.5 Box Diagram—The Different Perspectives of IC

But if we step back, it is clear that there are a few key underpinning concepts. The issue could probably be best described in two planes that act synergistically to encompass all activities of organizations, systems, and values. Or more specifically, systems thinking and human values activities. The first one, and the one that drives much of the behavior involved in intellectual capital, is human values. In the earlier list of capitals, values directly influence the following types of capital: relationship, spiritual, cultural, and human, and secondarily affect organizational, stakeholder, and customer. As you can see, values are hard to get away from because human beings are doing and defining these activities.

Systems thinking is about understanding the "big picture" and organizational issues such as boundaries, structures, and processes. All activities that involve the resources of an organization are systemic, as are all the things needed to organize people, resources, and activities. Systems thinking and methodologies govern the manipulation of the other models. In other words, the way in which the elements of the capitals interact with each other is governed by such systems concepts as structures and process that govern all systemic (big picture) models.

Values are about understanding organizations as systems made up of humans. Systems is about understanding all this systemically. When looking at any human-centric system, there is an inevitable yin-yang that occurs of systems and values. It is the managing of the tension between these that grows and cultivates IC (see Exhibit 6.6).

The systems and values context is only being used here to give a sense of order to the different capitals. When they are all presented out of context, it is much more difficult to see similarities. With this context you can see quickly where to place the emphasis and can also understand quickly the nature of the tools that might be used to measure the activities in a given area. If it is on the human value's side, you know that it will likely be a human-oriented tool such as a customer satisfaction survey, values inventory, or something that looks at buying patterns of

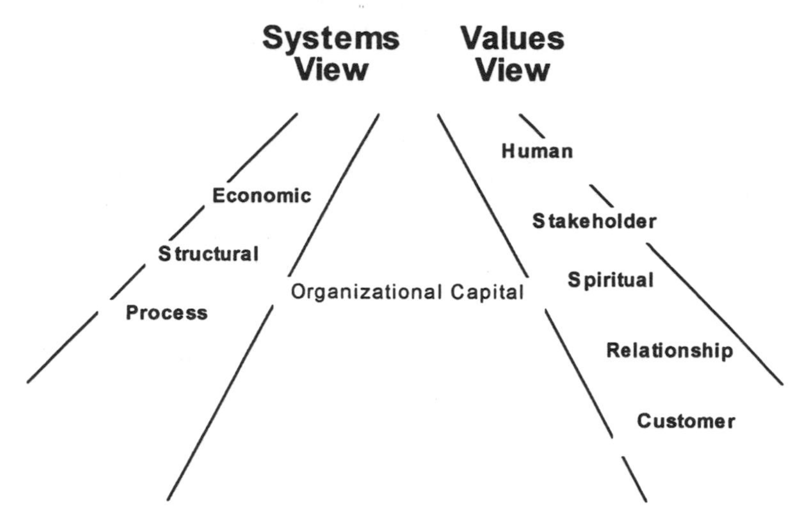

Exhibit 6.6 Systems and Values as a Context for Understanding Intellectual Capital Activities

the organization's products. On the system's side, issues will likely concern organizational wealth, assets, or the policies and guidelines that instruct the organization in its business. Organizational capital straddles the two sides, and tools here might be hybrids such as corporate culture surveys.

FUTURE MODELS

Future models will need to take into account the essence of the capitals previously defined and the dual-planed understanding of the systems and values issues that influence organizations. While this article may raise more questions than it answers, the intent is to focus the development of intellectual capital in a direction where there is a greater drive toward holism rather than toward the plethora of diverging models that currently exists and is growing steadily. Better definitions and solid context will aid this in happening. Systems and values are what drives this. Systems gives it definition and boundaries, values gives it meaning. Intellectual capital is about taking information, knowledge, behaviors, and experiences and applying them to the development understanding about our organizations and extracting values for all this hard work.

NOTES

1 Thomas A. Stewart, *Intellectual Capital: The New Wealth of Organizations.* (New York: Doubleday/ Currency, 1997).

7

Irreconcilable Differences? Managing the Knowledge Creation Interfaces

Peter C. Grindley

Law & Economics Group, Inc.

Patrick H. Sullivan

ICM Group, LLC

INTRODUCTION

Approaches to Management

When considering the management of intellectual capital, it soon becomes apparent that there are two very different approaches to how this should be done. This reflects differences that go deeper than the intellectual capital debate. One of the continuing challenges in business strategy and management in general has been to reconcile two equally valid views of what composes strategy and management. On one hand, we have the competitive strategy tradition, which looks at the economics of markets and products, costs and prices, accounting value, investment, and strategies for positioning the firm for competition. In the extreme this is a "bottom line" approach to business strategy, which focuses on the value chain and assumes the organization and people will be in place when they are needed. Representative approaches in the "rational" approach to strategy include Ansoff (1965, 1969); Chandler (1962, 1990); Boston Consulting Group (1968); Ackoff (1970); Andrews (1980); Porter (1980, 1985); and Kay (1993).

On the other hand, we have the organizational management tradition, which focuses more on organizational structures, procedures and controls, and human relations. It includes "soft" aspects, such as individual motivation, coordination and communication, creativity, and learning. This tradition studies organizational process and individual behavior but does not directly address product and market strategies. The implication is that strategy is facilitated by organizational process and may emerge out of it, but is not the main realm of the organizational specialist. The organizational approach grew partly out of a reaction against the certainties of rational strategy. Some representative approaches are Simon (1976); Minzberg (1977); Pettigrew (1977, 1979); Quinn, et al. (1988); O'Reilly (1989); and Senge (1990).

The two approaches described here are simplifications of the complexity of business management and are meant as no more than a characterization of two salient aspects of the same problem—managing the firm for success. Clearly, successful management combines product and organization. A product strategy is of no use without the organizational management to put it into effect. A smoothly functioning organization will not survive long if it does not have the right products at the right prices to pay the bills. Many of the most influential management theorists combine aspects of both markets and organizational management, although these tend to focus on generic market strategies and management structures rather than organizational process. Examples include Drucker (1977); Peters and Waterman (1982); Teece (1986); Peters (1987); Hammer and Champy (1992); and Prahalad and Hamel (1992).

The object of management is to focus effort in ways that make money. This requires the integration of organization and market strategy. Yet this integration is difficult. A first step is to acknowledge and reconcile two different approaches. Management strives to bring the two into alignment. Indeed, it may be that a main focus of management is bringing both aspects together in a functioning whole. Individual goals may not match those of the firm as a whole. A grand strategic vision for the marketplace may not be feasible with the existing organization and capability.

The task is not made easier by the fact that students of the different aspects tend to talk and think in different terms. They may be focused on their specialisms, and each side "cannot understand where the other is coming from." Progress in strategic management is slower the further apart the two approaches remain. We need to acknowledge the differences more fully before we can make further progress on reconciling economic and organizational management.

Application to Knowledge Management

Problems of finding a common language are most pressing in knowledge-based industries and the management of innovation. Finding this language is a primary task for advancing our understanding of intellectual capital management (ICM).

The importance of aligning strategic and organizational management, as defined here, changes from industry to industry, and from firm to firm. In some industries, perhaps financial services, the emphasis on markets may be so intense that, although organization and interpersonal behavior are important, the core competences for success are unlikely to be organizational. They are more likely to be analytical, and individual rewards are linked closely to economic performance. In manufacturing, by comparison, the balance may be different. Product success is still key, but to achieve that requires a more complex blend of strategic and organizational management, and the coordination of resources in a timely fashion to meet changing market needs.

The contrast is illustrated most clearly in high-technology industries, where knowledge and innovation management are central. Especially, although not solely, in these industries, knowledge has become critical to business success. The challenge is that this is an area in which the differences between economic strategy and organizational management are most apparent.

Complementary or Irreconcilable?

The economic and organizational approaches may be so different that they should be left to develop independently, and the business strategist may draw on whichever is most pertinent to the project on hand. Or should we try to understand how they are related, to find and clearly identify the common ground and the differences? If we can do so, will this enable us to manage this very important area more effectively?

An area in which these two approaches come together is in knowledge creation. This is the point at which the views are most likely to be reconciled. It is important that we should do so. The interface between creation and commercialization is central to success in progressive markets.

This chapter focuses on knowledge creation as common ground that brings organization and economic strategies together. From one view, knowledge creation is an underlying goal of organization; from the other, it is a basis for performance. It links forward to valuation of the firm's knowledge stock, as it does to its ability to manage intellectual capital for economic success. It links back to learning processes and individual fulfillment, to corporate cohesiveness and culture, and personal intercommunication. The task for intellectual capital management is, then, to foster the creation and extraction of value from this firm knowledge.

DEFINING THE PROBLEM

Why Knowledge-Based Organizations?

Business is developing more quickly than ever; ideas travel around the world in seconds, and there are fewer boundaries to finding and applying knowledge than ever. In an increasingly global economy, innovation and technology are vitally important in maintaining competitiveness. This puts a premium on knowledge-based competences, applied to rapidly changing needs and continually being renewed. Skills requirements are rising across industries, putting more stress on learning and on retaining knowledge within the firm.

The degree of emphasis on knowledge is relatively recent, as product life cycles have shortened and pressures for technical and managerial sophistication have risen. Traditional means of competing through state-of-the-art manufacturing and superior marketing have been short-circuited by widespread national and international availability of equivalent capabilities. As firms have scrambled to revamp their operations and product development processes, they have needed to put more emphasis on all aspects of knowledge management.

What Are the Differences?

There are two basic approaches to economic and organizational management of innovation and intellectual capital.

- **Innovation as business strategy.** This focuses on managing intellectual assets (IA), including the commercialization of innovation, the use of technology for competitive advantage, and the identification, protection, and commercialization of intellectual property (IP). This often stresses the importance of understanding market needs in helping direct R&D, but treats the management of creative innovative processes as a "black box."
- **Management as learning and knowledge creation.** This focuses on the organization and management of creative organizations, making them more effective and flexible. Often this does not focus on the business consequences of innovation except by implication. Strategies emerge from political processes within the firm.

There are also different interests within each camp. The "rational" approach to intellectual asset management includes at least two major differences in viewpoints that have become apparent recently, depending on whether the aim is to evaluate the worth of the asset base of the firm, or to use knowledge management to improve firm earnings.

- The "asset value" strand seeks to put a value on knowledge as an intangible asset of the firm, to obtain a clearer idea of how much the firm is worth. Firms in knowledge-intensive industries, such as computer software or biotech, routinely sell for large multiples of their book value. The hope is that assessing the value of intangibles such as accumulated R&D may help give a more accurate sense of value. The audience for this information is essentially outside the company, in the financial markets, and among regulators or policy makers. The idea of knowledge measures to supplement annual financial reports has become a lively research topic; interested parties include the SEC, financial community, accounting profession, and policy makers. For the current state of play, see recent work by Baruch Lev and a chapter in this book. For a critical view see *Forbes ASAP*, April 7, 1997.
- The "knowledge management" strand is more concerned with the dynamics of developing and using knowledge more effectively in the business activities of the firm. This should eventually affect firm performance and, hence, the value of the firm's stock, but the main objective is to provide tools and indicators for use within the firm to help manage innovation and increase earnings. The audience are the knowledge practitioners within the firm. This strand is more likely to use whatever indicators seem to work as knowledge measures, rather than formal R&D evaluation rules that can be standardized across firms. This is closer to the definition of intellectual capital management as a dynamic process, discussed later in this chapter and elsewhere in this book.

Within the organizational knowledge management approach, there are as many or more different viewpoints. An important distinction is between organizational theories that consider the effectiveness of organizational structures and procedures in achieving the objectives placed on them, and those that stress the means by which strategy "emerges" from process. What is most important, learning or control?

- The "traditional" organizational approach considers structures and procedures, such as divisional or M-form organization, which make the corporation more effective. This is part of the principal-agent problem of inducing individuals to operate in ways which, while in their own best interest, are also in the interest of the company as a whole.
- The "emergence" approach starts from the proposition that what makes an effective organization depends on its environment or context. For example, a bureaucratic organization may be a perfectly efficient response to a set of needs that call for routinization and repetition, whereas more free-form processes may be more appropriate where needs call for creativity and rapid responses. Representative approaches include Burns and Stalker (1961); Woodward (1965); Cyert and March (1963); and the Minzberg, Quinn, and Senge references previously given.

Why the Interfaces?

The object of knowledge management is to focus learning to improve market performance. To do this we need to reconcile the different approaches. There have been many attempts to bring the different aspects of knowledge management together. Success has been achieved when apparently following either approach. But the greatest success may be when the two are melded. Examples related most specifically to innovation include work on complementary assets in commercializing innovation (Teece, 1986); on identifying the firm's core managerial and technical competences as bases for sustainable competitive advantage (Hamel and Prahalad, 1990; Teece et al., 1994); managing the R&D, manufacturing, and marketing interfaces (Riggs, 1983; Imai et al., 1985; Reich 1989); and the evolutionary approach to technological development (Nelson and Winter, 1982). Some approaches to innovation management are discussed further in the Addendum to this chapter.

At the least complex in reconciling two views, we are talking about the interface between them. Firms that can handle this by keeping innovation close to market knowledge, by improving communications between functions, and by developing personnel through different types of positions, succeed. Other firms that succeed may still be handling the interfaces effectively but in ways that are not apparent—possibly via individuals who bridge the approaches, or through informal mechanisms that operate as interfaces.

At a deeper level we are talking about embedding the "interface" throughout the organization, so that it is not clear where one approach starts and the other stops. The interface is "holistic."

APPROACHES TO ICM

Embedding IC Management in Strategic Thinking

The problem of reconciling human organizational management with economic market strategy, however these are defined, is not new. It is generally well understood, if not expressed as it has been here. The problem, then, is not simply one of management. We may be aware of the difficulties, but merely exhorting us to change will not work. Attitudes may first need to change at a fundamental level. Organizational management and strategic management may already be combined in direct and indirect ways. Several aspects of interface management are already in place in innovative companies, where it is vital to bring products from research into commercialization quickly.

Interfaces may also have found ways to overcome the people problem. The same individual may behave in one way in one context and another way in a different context. For example, an R&D manager may need to be flexible and intellectually curious in the lab, but objective regarding hard-line cost effectiveness when acting in a research project steering committee. Different groups within the same firm may have different cultures, depending on the purpose of the group. Acting in an interface group may involve different behavior than in a functional area, and the cultures may be independent of the personalities in each group (see Brian Hall's discussion of value systems in Chapter 4).

But such integrated management can only go so far without deeper understanding and attitudes to back it up. Ideas, ways of thinking, have to be developed, which bring the two aspects closer together. Upper management may need to be convinced of the problem before they will devote resources to solving it; individuals may need broader understanding before they can implement the interfaces effectively. In all, this is a new problem, and much depends on getting it right.

Groundwork—Defining the Approaches

Intellectual Asset Management

Intellectual asset management, the "rational" part of knowledge management, is the process of creating and extracting value from knowledge. This is the core relationship between human resources, intellectual assets, and intellectual property in ICM, as shown in Exhibit 7.1. Intellectual asset management consists of phases, as described in more detail elsewhere in this book:

- **Value creation.** There are several stages to this, but a main step is "fixing" knowledge in codified form, so that it becomes part of the firm's base.
- **Value extraction.** There are also several stages to this. The main step is to use intellectual property to obtain value by increased earnings, either by the protection this gives to products or from value via licensing, joint ventures, or similar means.

The general direction of this process is that intellectual assets move from human resources, to intellectual assets, to intellectual property as they become

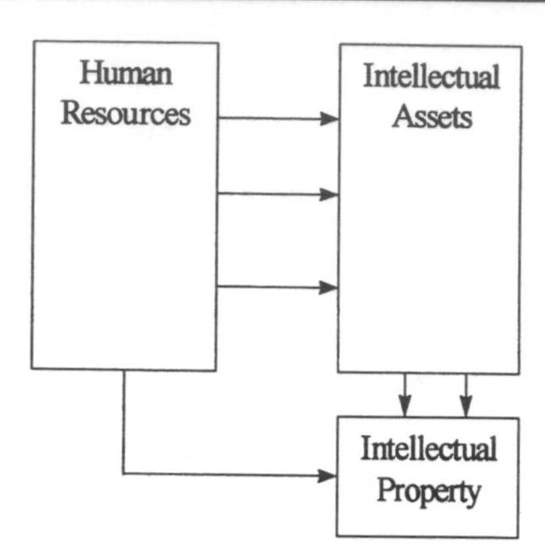

Exhibit 7.1 Basics of Intellectual Asset Management

more specific and identified. Some knowledge will become codified assets. A smaller percentage will become legally protected intellectual property. Other knowledge may be so diffuse that it remains as human resources in individuals' heads, hopefully still used to make better products and increase earnings.

The process may be seen as stages in a value chain, running from basic know-how structure, to specific knowledge creation, to product/process innovation, to codification of intellectual assets and intellectual property, and finally to earnings generation. This is included in Exhibit 7.2.

Organizational Management

The "process" approach involves organizational management, creative development, and learning. Strategies may be directed or may evolve. This focuses on process, the "how" rather than the "what." It relies on broad motivation, or visionaries, or direction from upper management to keep the process moving in productive directions. We have distinguished two aspects of this process.

- **Direction and structure.** This is the basic managerial structure and procedures to control the organization and keep it focused on the firm's objectives. This stresses routines, hierarchy, formal relationships, and certainty.
- **Emergence and interaction.** This is the aspects focused on creativity and interaction. This stresses emergence, flexibility, informal relationships, and innovation. It allows individual creativity and breadth of ideas to flourish.

Knowledge creation is most likely to be affected by the efficacy of the emergence process. Emergence creates value, though indirectly. It builds competencies directed toward markets, that is, as a basis for market strategies.

The organizational process may also be seen as stages in a "knowledge value chain," or a "tree of knowledge." Knowledge creation is a building process. It begins with basic sociology—the external and internal sociological environment

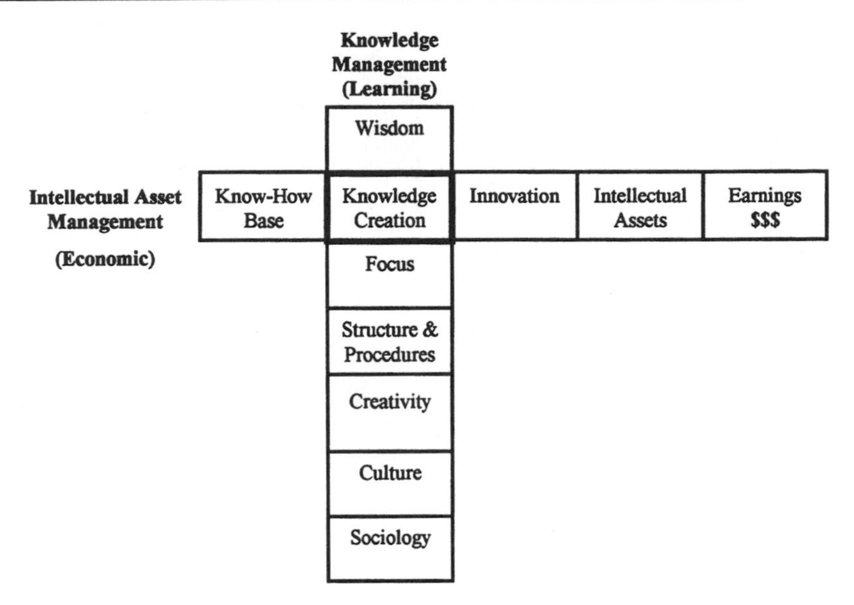

Exhibit 7.2 Intersection of Knowledge and Intellectual Asset Management

of the firm. This is the foundation for the firm's underlying culture, including the values and beliefs of those in the firm, how people behave, and the values of the firm as a whole. An important aspect of culture is creativity, an urge to create something new, which might be a new product, a new operational process, or a new organizational form. Culture and creativity in turn are embedded in the formal and informal structures, procedures, and routines of the organization. These determine behavior in the firm—what activity is rewarded, who is hired, how people interact, how skills developed, how the organization is changed? Some structures foster greater creativity, some less. This focuses creativity on particular knowledge areas, which in turn leads to specific knowledge creation. Over time this is abstracted as higher wisdom. These steps in developing knowledge are also included in Exhibit 7.2.

Intellectual Capital Management

ICM recognizes both intellectual assets management and organizational management. The most clearly defined aspects of ICM are the intellectual assets management elements, identifying and exploiting intellectual assets and intellectual property, as shown in Exhibit 7.1. However, it also recognizes that much of the strategic capability of the firm, what make it effective and innovative, relies on the human and organizational capabilities within the firm. Thus, both the valuation and management of intellectual capital must allow for the organizational capital as well as the intellectual capital itself.

What we mean by ICM as a whole is shown in Exhibit 7.3. The overall process of ICM goes beyond the human capital aspects of extracting intellectual asset value, to include the organizational processes and human capabilities of the firm. A complete picture of ICM should also include the complementary business

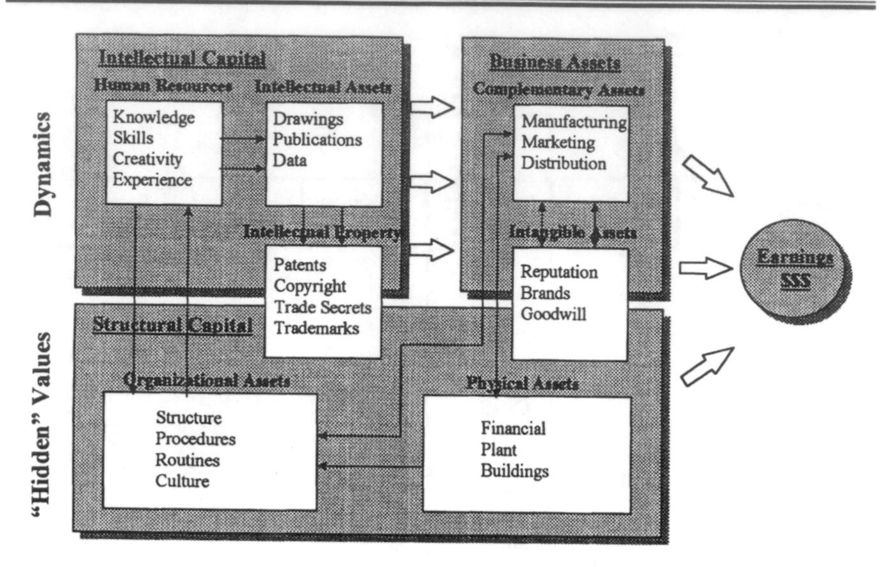

Exhibit 7.3 Intellectual Capital Management—Composite View

assets needed to commercialize innovation (and provide information on market needs) and the relevant physical assets.

There are several different models of ICM. Each contains similar features to the model described here. For discussions see Chapter 5.

Knowledge creation is not yet modeled closely. Although ICM encompasses aspects of organizational management, these are conceptually less developed in the model than the economic processes for extracting value. For example, the dichotomy is apparent in different interests within the ICM Gathering of intellectual capital professionals. The ICM Gathering consists mainly of members involved directly in identifying and licensing intellectual assets and intellectual property. The relationship between this and knowledge management, such as context dependence of value and the requirements of knowledge creation processes, are gradually being investigated in the model. It is also apparent that different members place different stress on the importance of organizational inputs.

Intersecting Knowledge Processes

The intersection of the asset management and the knowledge management value chains is shown in Exhibit 7.2. This shows knowledge creation as the common ground where organization develops something specific that potentially has commercial value, and intellectual assets management has something from which to extract value.

This understanding of the two processes and the intersection in knowledge creation should help make it clearer how to manage intellectual assets. Management may focus on the intersection or, more precisely, the interfaces between knowledge and intellectual assets management processes. The idea of the knowledge creation interface also adds meaning and urgency to the less-defined "soft" processes of ICM, to facilitate ideas creation and exchange. ICM may refer to the "flowering of broader understanding," or the importance of informal "conversations that matter." These are often interface ideas.

HOW THE DISTINCTION AFFECTS ICM

Stocks and Flows of Knowledge

Valuing the stock of knowledge is important in some contexts, less so in others. The different objectives within intellectual assets management noted above, of external valuation versus internal management, are stock/flow distinctions. If the aim is to evaluate a firm's innovative value from the outside, then the value of the stock of knowledge is important. Yet the capability to create and use knowledge may be invisible to the outside observer; the capability is too involved in the organization for simple measures to mean much to the outside. What can be seen is the ability to perform.

If the main objective is to use and create knowledge to make more successful products, then the process of management may be more important to the outside than the presentation of the stock of knowledge capability. To be effective, management of knowledge must reach down into the organization, into the creative processes as well as the exploitive functions.

Learning and Functioning in Knowledge Creation

There are further distinctions in the knowledge creation area. If the firm has to "grow to survive," then organizational learning is important. If the firm's main need is to operate smoothly and efficiently in a relatively stable environment, then a bureaucratic organizational model is more appropriate and the cultural interests are more in cohesion than creative tension.

An important point is that organizational characteristics are defined partly by the structures, procedures, and routines of the organization and partly by the people and relationships. In some organizations, individual capabilities as leaders or innovators may be more important. In others, the relationships between individuals are more important, and individuals are most effective as part of a team, with a team culture that spans individuals.

These relational organizations have a continuity over time that goes beyond individual members; it takes time to integrate new members into the organization. A result is that such organizations may be difficult to change, barring large-scale personnel changes. However, a more positive consequence is that these organizations are difficult to replicate and may be an important source of competitive advantage. If embedded in the firm structure, the dynamic capabilities of a creative organization can provide a lasting resource.

Context and the Balance of Creating and Extracting Value

It is also clear that the relative importance of different aspects of ICM, and how these are managed, depends strongly on the context or environment of the organization. Context includes the nature of the market and competition, the speed of change, rate of decline or growth, regulatory environment, education, availability of skilled workers, and many others.

It also depends on the *status quo,* where the organization is starting from. Organizations are difficult to change, as previously noted, and any analysis of where a firm wants to take ICM must consider the context of the organization itself. This applies not just to top management, whose support is of course vital, but also to efforts to bring the whole of the organization to an understanding of the overall aims of ICM.

In some contexts, it is important to create knowledge, in others to exploit it. This affects the balance and which aspects of the interfaces are most active.

IMPLICATIONS FOR MANAGEMENT

Make Interfaces More Effective

It is beyond the scope or intent of this chapter to make detailed suggestions for managing the interaction between two approaches. The object has been to point out the differences in approach between knowledge creation management and intellectual asset management within ICM. There are some implications, however, which illustrate how these differences are to take effect by indicating how they might be may be modified.

Having said that, there are some general issues that are relevant to going forward in our understanding of ICM and techniques that are implied. The most immediate implication of this dichotomy is the importance of making the management interfaces more effective. This may involve more complete communication between different functions, brought in at earlier stages of the development process. It may involve specifically designed reporting relationships between functions, with responsibility for the success of a project from start to finish, not just through the development stage or the marketing stage.

This idea of overlapping development stages with wide communication across functional barriers is generally well understood in product development management, such as described in Imai et al., (1965) and elsewhere. The aim is simply to avoid the situation where a product is developed in engineering then "thrown over the wall" to manufacturing to make it and to marketing to sell it.

Expand the Interfaces

Managing the existing interfaces, however, to an extent misses the point. The two approaches are so ingrained that more effective management at the existing points of intersection is not going to achieve much, even though it may help. The changes, the broadening, must go deeper.

One way to achieve this is to expand the scope of the interface, to bring more knowledge creation into knowledge exploitation, and vice versa. The points of interface may be increased "laterally." This is shown in Exhibit 7.4. Different organizational processes contributing to the same set of knowledge creation

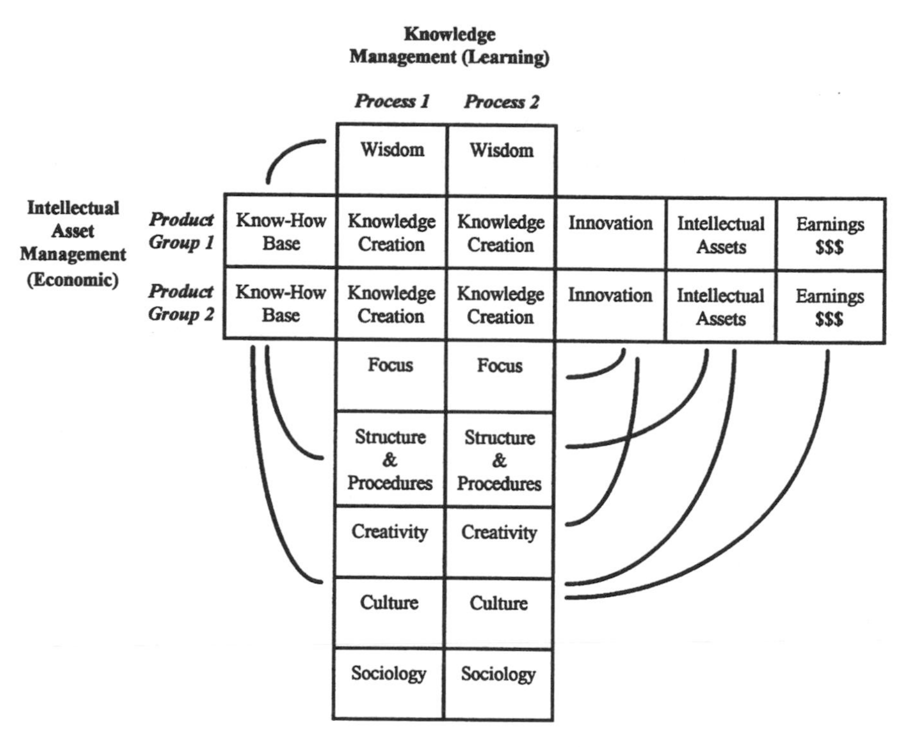

Exhibit 7.4 Broadening and Bypassing the Knowledge Interfaces

should be brought into the same interface pool. Similarly, if the same knowledge is to be used in different product families, these too should be brought into the same mechanism for sharing knowledge within the interface.

Bypass the Interfaces

To go further, the interaction between creation and exploitation may become broader yet by including ways to bypass the interface altogether. Provided the circumstances permit it, there may be opportunities to allow and provide feedback information directly from commercialization of the intellectual assets to research functions, without being filtered out on the long route back through the organization.

This is also shown in Exhibit 7.4. Direct communication and interaction links may occur between knowledge creation and value extraction at a more basic level than through the formal interfaces. What this might mean in practice is that knowledge creators are exposed to practices in the commercialization of knowledge, in ways they can relate to in their work and make their work more effective. Knowledge extractors may obtain a deeper understanding of the creation processes and adapt their own structures and procedures to make them more supportive of development. This may be aimed at specific products or broad competences.

CONCLUSION

The aim of this chapter has been to point out some differences in approach to ICM between the traditions of knowledge creation management and intellectual asset management. Before we can manage the knowledge organization effectively, we must be aware that different rules are being followed in different parts of the organization.

Only after we have a more complete picture of the organization, its structures and routines throughout the functions, and have an understanding of what is involved in reconciling the two approaches, can we expect to find more effective means of managing the whole. Given the widespread trend toward knowledge-based competition, this is of vital importance. There is much to be done.

ADDENDUM: INNOVATION STRATEGIES

Competence Strategies

Extracting value from knowledge, or exploiting innovation, is more than placing a new innovation on the market. Successful commercialization depends on the effective management of complementary assets, and utilization of core competencies and other firm-specific capabilities (Teece, 1986; Hamel and Prahalad, 1990; Prahalad and Hamel, 1990; Teece et al., 1994). These strategies stress the importance of developing the firm's resources and may be seen as a step further into the organization of the firm than more specifically market-oriented approaches based on market positioning and competitive strategies (Porter, 1985; Tirole, 1988). They stress organizational integration and are related to those stressing the importance of tripartite investment in manufacturing, marketing, and management in the integrated corporation (Chandler, 1990).

Yet another strand of innovation literature advocates "chaos" management, perhaps as an antidote to too much integration and lack of innovation (Quinn, 1985; Peters, 1987). Debate over the long-term performance of entrepreneurial versus integrated firms contrasts the possibility of "chronic entrepreneurialism" with that of clogged lines of innovation (Gilder, 1988; Ferguson, 1988; Florida and Kenney, 1990; Saxenian, 1990; Rappaport and Halevi, 1991).

Innovation and Organization

A feature of innovation is that it requires both creativity and commercial control. This makes organizational, or cultural, aspects such as motivation, identification with team goals and attitudes to change, very important.

Innovation is an expression of creativity and needs freedom to operate. It calls for effective communication of knowledge within the firm and a capacity for learning. At the same time, as a commercial activity the objective is competitive advantage. This implies some form of strategic direction and control. The combination of creativity and control requires a synthesis of economic strategy and organizational process. Firm culture is identified closely with the firm's institutions. It is likely to be interrelated with organizational structure and incentives. It is also likely to persist over time, implying that it depends as much on the organization as on the individuals who make up the organization.

Yet notice that this also implies that culture, as well as other aspects of the organization, are under the firm's control and may be drawn into strategy. Above all, it depends on the relationships between individuals and the organization.

An environment where knowledge accumulation (if not exploitation) is encouraged may build on a skills base, which implies long-term employment, trust relationships between employee and management, and open communications. There may be a strong effort to instil identification with corporate goals of high quality, customer regard, and integrity. Individual rewards may be taken over a long period as increased responsibility and job satisfaction. These relations embody the culture at the corporate level.

They are coupled with more specific control and direction at the product group level. Frequent close communication keeps the group fully informed and able to evaluate performance and coordinate strategy. In this way contracts combine specific and relational aspects, the mix depending on the management level and the particular organizational objectives. Specific control may be strongest in divisions where there is greatest need to coordinate strategy and to integrate complementary assets in marketing, manufacturing, development, and service. Other product divisions, which are more "individualistic" and depend on products developed on an engineer-to-engineer basis, may be more flexibly managed.

Organizational learning has another strategic importance. The relational network makes the organization hard to reproduce and hard for individuals to appropriate the capabilities of the network. This makes imitation harder and gives competitive advantage.

Elements of Innovation Management

The next step is to identify key features of the innovative and adaptive organization that is able to develop and retain competitive advantage. The aim is an organization that can develop streams of new products or repeatedly introduce new process technology to give the firm lasting advantage in the marketplace. Three basic elements may be identified, stressing the management of the knowledge base of the firm (Grindley, 1991, 1993).

Functional Integration

Cross-functional integration between areas such as research and development, design, manufacturing, and marketing ensures that products fill user needs, can be manufactured at low cost, and that these and other complementary assets are available on time (Teece, 1986). It involves communication, knowledge sharing, and substantial understanding within the firm and, to some extent, outside it. It requires openness and trust within the firm, as well as some form of controlled information sharing outside. This may arise from job rotation and cross training as well as from routines for involving different areas in the innovation process. It requires attention to the interfaces between innovation functions and the rest of the firm (Burns and Stalker, 1961; Reich, 1989).

Learning and Capability Building

Core capabilities and learning include business skills and organizational integration as well as technical knowledge. Capabilities are built up over relatively long periods and need constant replenishment. This implies an orientation toward encouraging learning. As much of this is firm-specific "know-how," it depends on long-term commitment as well as identification with firm objectives. This requires continuity of employment for trained and knowledgeable personnel, to keep the "know-how" and "know-why" inside the organization. Skills are difficult to acquire "off the shelf" or change quickly (Riggs, 1983; Imai et al., 1985).

Strategic Direction

Integration and learning may occur, but we still need strategic direction to guide the capabilities into commercially rewarding areas. Strategy provides the overall guidance toward long-term goals. It may be seen as a shaping function, which selects and forms capabilities into basic competencies which are applied over a series of products. However, strategy also evolves as technological and market opportunities arise. It is a combination of forward planning and responsiveness to ideas inside and outside the firm. It should combine broad direction with flexibility, top-down leadership with bottom-up ideas. Ultimately, the motivation for innovation is from competition, though the link may be long term and indirect (Prahalad and Hamel, 1990; Teece et al., 1994).

BIBLIOGRAPHY

Ackoff, R. L. (1970). *A Concept of Corporate Planning.* New York: John Wiley & Sons, Inc.

Andrews, K. R. (1980). *The Concept of Corporate Strategy.* Chicago: Irwin.

Ansoff, H. I. (1965). "The Firm of the Future," *Harvard Business Review* 43:5 (Sept.–Oct.), 162–78.

Ansoff, H. I. (ed.) (1969). *Corporate Strategy.* New York: McGraw-Hill.

Boston Consulting Group (1968). "Perspectives on Experience," *Boston Consulting Group,* Boston, M.A.

Burns, T. and G. M. Stalker (1961). *The Management of Innovation.* London: Tavistock.

Chandler, A. D. (1962). *Strategy and Structure.* Cambridge, M.A.: MIT Press.

Chandler, A. (1990). *Scale and Scope: The Dynamics of Industrial Capitalism.* Cambridge, M.A.: Belknap.

Cyert, R. and J. March (1963). *A Behavioral Theory of the Firm.* New York: Prentice-Hall.

Drucker, P. (1977). *People and Performance: The Best of Peter Drucker on Management.* London: Heinemann.

Edvinsson, L. and P. Sullivan (1996). "Developing a Model for Managing Intellectual Capital," *European Management Journal* 14:4 (August, 356–363).

*Florida, R. and M. Kenney, (1990). "Why Silicon Valley and Route 128 Can't Save Us," *California Management Review,* (Fall): 66–88.

Grindley, P. (1991). "Turning Technology into Competitive Advantage," *Business Strategy Review* 2:1, 35–48.

Grindley, P. (1993). "Managing Technology: Organizing for Competitive Advantage," In *New Technology and the Firm: Innovation and Competition,* edited by G. M. P. Swann. London: Routledge, 36–53.

Hamel, G. and C. K. Prahalad (1990). "Strategic Intent," *The McKinsey Quarterly* (Spring): 36–59.

Hammer, M. and J. Champy (1994). *Reengineering the Corporation.* N.p.: Harperbusiness.

Imai, K., I. Nonaka and H. Takeuchi (1985). "Managing the New Product Development Process: How Japanese Companies Learn and Unlearn." In *The Uneasy Alliance* edited by K. Clark, R. Hayes, and C. Lorenz. Boston: Harvard Business School Press.

Kay, J. (1993). *Foundations of Corporate Success.* Oxford: Oxford University Press.

Minzberg, H. (1979). *The Structuring of Organizations: A Synthesis of the Research.* New York: Prentice-Hall.

Nelson, R. and S. Winter (1982). *An Evolutionary Theory of Economic Change.* Cambridge M.A.: Harvard University Press.

O'Reilly, C. (1989). "Corporations, Culture, and Commitment: Motivation and Social Control in Organizations," *California Management Review* 31:4, 9–25.

Peters, T. J. (1987). *Thriving on Chaos.* London: Macmillan.

Peters, T. J. and R. H. Waterman (1982). *In Search of Excellence.* New York: Harper and Row.

Pettigrew, A. M. (1977). "Strategy Formulation as a Political Process," *International Studies of Management and Organization* 7:2, 78–87.

Pettigrew, A. M. (1979). "On Studying Organizational Cultures," *Administrative Science Quarterly* 24:4, 570–581.

Porter, M. E. (1980). *Competitive Advantage: Creating and Sustaining Superior Performance.* New York: The Free Press.

Porter, M. E. (1985). *Competitive Strategy: Techniques for Analyzing Industries and Competitors.* New York: The Free Press.

Prahalad, C. K. and G. Hamel (1990). "The Core Competence of the Organization," *Harvard Business Review* (May–June): 79–91.

Prahalad, C. K. and G. Hamel (1994). *Competing for the Future.* Boston: Harvard Business School Press.

Quinn, J. B. (1985). "Managing Innovation: Controlled Chaos," *Harvard Business Review* (May–June): 73–84.

Quinn, J. B., H. Minzberg, and R. M. James (1988). *The Strategy Process.* New York: Prentice-Hall.

*Rappaport, A. and S. Halevi (1991). "The Computerless Computer Company," *Harvard Business Review* (July–August): 69–80.

Reich, R. (1989). "The Quiet Path to Technological Preeminence," *Scientific American* (October): 19–25.

Riggs, H. (1983). *Managing High-Technology Companies.* New York: Van Nostrand.

*Saxenian, A. (1990). "Regional Networks and the Resurgence of Silicon Valley," *California Management Review* (Fall): 89–112.

Senge, P. (1990). *The Fifth Discipline: The Learning Corporation.* New York: Basic Books.

Simon, H. (1976). *Administrative Behavior, 3rd ed.* New York: Macmillan

Stewart, T. (1997). *Intellectual Capital: The New Wealth of Organizations.* New York: Doubleday.

Teece, D. (1986). "Profiting from Technological Innovation," *Research Policy* 15, 285–305.

Teece, D., G. Pisano, and A. Shuen (1994). "Firm Capabilities, Resources and the Concept of Strategy." CCC working paper 90:8 (rev.). UC Berkeley: Center for Research in Management.

*Tirole, J. (1988). *Theory of Industrial Organization.* Cambridge, MA: MIT Press.

Woodward, J. (1965). *Industrial Organization: Theory and Practice.* Oxford: Oxford University Press.

---

* Addendum only/unused

Part II

Intellectual Property Management

8

Extracting Value from Intellectual Property

Patrick H. Sullivan

ICM Group, LLC

Intellectual assets that receive legal protection are called *intellectual property.* Intellectual property law, the body of law dealing with the protection of intellectual assets, recognizes five forms of legal protection in the United States: patents, copyrights, trademarks, trade secrets, and semiconductor masks. For each form of protection, the nature and amount of protection available, as well as the degree to which that protection applies to an innovation, may vary.

For technology companies, a well-constructed system for managing intellectual properties is fundamental to being able to extract full value from the properties *and* to being able to create IA and IC management systems to successfully extract value from all three tiers of the firm's intellectual capital. In this sense, technology companies have an advantage over service firms, or firms not holding a portfolio of intellectual properties. Technology firms can develop the decision processes, databases, and work processes required to successfully extract value from their intellectual properties. In so doing, these firms create the culture, structure, and decision-making capability for systematically extracting value from their intangibles. With the building block of an IP management capability in place, it is easy for firms to expand it to encompass their intellectual assets and, finally, their human capital. Lacking the foundation of an IP management system, nontechnology firms typically do not extract the degree of value from all of their intellectual capital they otherwise would be capable of.

There is a time or *current versus future* dimension associated with the tiers of intellectual capital. Intellectual properties may be thought of as the source of *current* value for the firm. Much of what is currently in the portfolio is the basis for protecting current products in the marketplace or for current joint ventures and strategic alliances. Intellectual properties represent current value where the value extraction activities are rife with tactical considerations. Intellectual assets, the next tier of intellectual capital, are the assets with less current definition, and often more promise for the future. Extracting value from these assets usually involves thinking into the future, and discussing positioning and strategies for value extraction rather than near-term tactics. For this reason, intellectual assets are usually considered as assets that bridge the transition from the present to the future (also from the tactical to the strategic) value extraction. The intellectual capital tier, to complete the thought, operates almost entirely at the strategic level of decision making and future value extraction, but uses the same fundamental decision processes as those found in the most fundamental and well-constructed systems for extracting value from intellectual property.

For many firms, extracting new or extra value from their intellectual properties means a shift in focus away from a *portfolio-as-protection-only* view to a *portfolio-as-corporate-business-asset* view. This shift in perspective opens up more alternative ways to use the portfolio for the firm's benefit and thereby allows firms to create more value extraction opportunities. For example, a manufacturing firm making the shift in perspective might find it has opened up new opportunities for out-licensing it never considered before; it might find new strategic alliance opportunities; it might find new joint venture opportunities. But, to *maximize* value extraction from the portfolio, firms must go a step further. Value maximization involves the creation of a full range of value extraction mechanisms and their *simultaneous use* with individual technologies. The manufacturing company in our example might find itself simultaneously manufacturing and distributing a technology application in the North American market, licensing it to manufacturers in the South American market, doing a joint venture with Asian manufacturers or distributors, and entering a strategic alliance with one or more European companies, *all involving the same technology innovation, and all at the same time!*

There are at least two widely held and different philosophical views of the function of IP management, and these philosophies fundamentally shape the context within which portfolio use is viewed. One view is that the portfolio's highest and best use is to protect the firm's innovations from competitive attack (this is the portfolio-as-protection view). Other uses of the portfolio, proponents argue, might direct energies away from the firm's main business—commercializing innovation. The contrasting view (the portfolio-as-business-asset view) is that the portfolio is a great source of corporate value for firms willing to exploit it. Companies holding this latter view believe that the portfolio has the potential to significantly enhance the value of the firm.

Portfolio as Protection. Companies holding the aforementioned first (largely defensive) view oppose the idea that the IP portfolio should be used for any strategic purpose other than protecting the firm's innovations. They believe that the portfolio's use should be restricted to achieving the four primary objectives for patenting. Their overarching goal is to exclude others from using their patented innovations. These companies are often decentralized and structured around strategic business units (SBUs). Their profits are created in the near term through the sales of the products and services of the SBUs. For the most part, the business units in these firms "own" the innovations: They decide what is to be patented and how those patents will be used. For these companies, patenting is primarily a legal and a local business issue and is often managed or coordinated by the SBUs and the firm's office of general counsel.

Portfolio as Corporate Asset. Companies taking a more aggressive view use their portfolios to create superior value. These companies believe that extracting value from their protected innovations is not limited to bringing a better mousetrap to the market. For example, a company may decide to license its mousetrap technology to others for manufacturing and distribution because it does not have the required capabilities itself. Similarly, it may enter into a joint venture with another company, set up a strategic alliance with a partner that can give it access to markets it might otherwise be unable to reach, or simply sell a technology in which it no longer has a strategic interest. Such companies take a broad view of their patent portfolios. They seek to extract value from the portfolio by treating it as a collective corporate asset rather than as a collection of individual patents.

It requires more than a shift in perspective for firms to *maximize* their value extraction. It requires a shift in context. It requires the firm to realize that it is no longer in the technology-application manufacturing business. It is in the business of commercializing technology. Companies able to shift their context or, in other words, their self-view, are companies with the strategic perspective necessary to fully extract value from all of their intellectual assets. This chapter is written for companies capable of shifting their context about commercializing their intellectual properties. It discusses methods and systems for effectively linking intellectual property with business strategy, as well as methods for extracting the most value from the intellectual properties themselves.

HISTORICAL PERSPECTIVE

For firms holding patents, the most usual form of protection that companies actively manage, some significant changes have taken place since the late 1980s. Before that time, the judicial environment was decidedly antipatent. The U.S. Supreme Court was generally antimonopoly and antipatent during the so called Black/Douglas era (1946–1965). The chances of a patent being held valid, infringed, and enforceable in litigation were only about one in three. Moreover, the U.S. Department of Justice (DOJ) subscribed to the view that patents were bad monopolies that stifled competition in the marketplace by preventing companies from copying each other's products. Companies using their patent and technology prowess aggressively sometimes found themselves the subject of a governmentally enforced consent decree requiring low or zero patent royalty payments to competitors.

This state of affairs made an about-face in the early 1980s. The report of the President's Commission on Industrial Competitiveness identified intellectual property as one of four critical areas for achieving and maintaining competitiveness in American industry. A new court of appeals for the federal circuit was created to unify legal precedent in patent cases, previously fragmented among the 11 circuit courts of appeal. Antitrust restrictions were relaxed; the National Cooperative Research Act (1984) became law and permitted competitors to do joint research more freely.

Subsequent to 1982 and the creation of the new court of appeals, the number of significant domestic and international intellectual property cases heard, as well as the dollar amounts of settlements, make it clear that intellectual property has become an asset of significant value. The market value of patents has increased dramatically; their value in business negotiations has gone up significantly; and their importance as a major source of value for knowledge firms has increased greatly.

Because of the increased value of intellectual property in general and patents in particular, knowledge companies must ask themselves whether they are using these valuable assets to their best advantage for the firm. How are these assets being managed? How are they being exploited to improve the firm's position in the marketplace? How are they being used to improve the firm's position versus its competitors?

EXTRACTING VALUE FROM INTELLECTUAL PROPERTIES

This chapter is about intellectual property management and the creation of a basic building-block management capability on which the other tiers of intellectual capital may be based. Extracting value from intellectual property is accomplished most effectively when the value extraction activities meet two criteria. First, they must be aimed at improving the firm's competitive position as defined in the corporate business strategy. Second, they must become part of a systematized set of decision processes supported with information-producing activities and databases that collectively allow the firm to manage its IP assets.

Knowledge firms usually think of value extraction in terms of converting an innovation into cash or profits. Indeed, any activity that increases income or reduces expenses (or both) while requiring few resources to do so, may be considered an attractive value extraction alternative. Extracting value from intellectual properties, because of its strong current time frame and tactical focus, is usually thought of as a near- to midterm profitability opportunity. But what are some of these profit-generating activities?

Short-Term Value Extraction

Corporations that want to extract value from, or improve the "profitability of," their portfolios immediately have at least two courses of action available to them: (1) Reduce portfolio expense by reducing the amount of patent maintenance "taxes," and (2) increase portfolio income by improving the royalty income stream from out-licenses.

- **Reducing Portfolio Expense.** Much of the expense of maintaining a patent portfolio comes in the form of patent maintenance fees or taxes.

The Dow Chemical Company, for example, estimates that by 1996 it had created $40 million in savings, forecast in maintenance taxes over a ten-year period.

It is not unusual for a firm to find that approximately 5 percent of the patents in its portfolio are no longer useful and could be eliminated. Thus, just by reviewing their portfolios, many firms could realize an immediate savings of about 5 percent per year in maintenance fees.

- **Increasing Portfolio Income.** Many companies are not realizing the full value of the income that can be drawn from the business asset that is the portfolio. Dow Chemical, to use them again as an example, was generating $25 million in licensing income from their portfolio in 1994, without a focused effort on licensing. The corporation determined that it would more systematically "milk" the portfolio for licensable technologies. They set a target of $125 million in annual licensing fees to be achieved by the year 2000. They actually reached and surpassed this goal by 1997.

  As another example of how portfolio income may be increased, consider the existing stream of royalty income. In general, companies that have out-licensed their technologies receive far less in royalty payments than they expected, based on the terms contained in the firm's licensing agreements. That this is so should not be surprising. Licensees under cash management pressure create reasons why they need not make their royalty payments immediately. For example, some licensees say they are holding the royalty payments in an accrual account until the licensor asks for it; others say that they are having cash flow problems and decided to defer payment (without notifying the licensor). Still others make payments, but of a lesser amount than called for. In the latter case, the mere announcement of a licensor's intent to audit royalty payments often produces an unsolicited check for back payment of royalties owed. Firms that audit their royalty income usually find that the amount of income received as a result of the audit far outweighs its cost.

Midterm Value Extraction

Whereas the short term is viewed as the forthcoming year, the midterm is defined here as meaning a two- to four-year period. During this midterm period, value extraction activities focus on:

Increased Portfolio Quality

This is accomplished by developing a series of "screens" for filtering out any potential patent not bringing specific value to the company's portfolio. Each patent in the portfolio should be included for specific reasons, where the reasons relate to specific elements of the firm's business tactics or strategy.

Increased Use of the Portfolio in Business Negotiations

As the portfolio improves in quality, it will probably contain fewer total patents but relatively more usable ones. With increasing quality, the portfolio brings more strength to the company's bargaining position in cross-licensing discussions, in discussions with potential litigants, and in a whole range of negotiating situations.

Expanded Licensing, Joint Venturing, Strategic Alliance Activities
With an enhanced portfolio, there are new opportunities for out-licensing, joint venturing, and the creative and market exploration of strategic alliances.

THE ROLES OF INTELLECTUAL PROPERTY IN CORPORATE BUSINESS STRATEGY

Companies create intellectual property portfolios for one major corporate purpose: near-term competitive advantage. For technology-based companies, this translates into three objectives: protection for innovations, design freedom, and litigation avoidance. For companies capable of shifting to a portfolio-as-corporate-asset view, the list of objectives is further modified to include the creation of a basis for establishing alliances and joint ventures. Technology-based businesses create portfolios of technology that are fundamentally a collection of innovative ideas for whose use the company wishes to be granted a legal monopoly. In most cases the individual patents, trademarks, and other protected assets are intended to generate near-term income. They do so by providing limited protection to a mark, a product, or process innovation to allow its commercialization without fear of imitation. As companies grow and produce improved and new innovations, they often build a significant portfolio of patents and other intellectual properties.

IP STRATEGY AND COMPANY STRATEGY

Whether a company's IP strategy is, or should be, offensive or defensive in nature depends in large measure on the company's business strategy and the role intellectual property is expected to play in that strategy. Returning to fundamentals, the company has a vision of the company it wishes to become in the future. The vision, a set of operationally meaningful statements describing the organization it wishes to become, establishes a long-term goal to focus employee day-to-day activity (see Exhibit 8.1). For knowledge companies, the firm's strategy—the set of decisions about the strategic issues affecting progress toward the vision—includes mention of the role the firm's intellectual capital is expected to contribute.

The roles of intellectual capital are typically specified for both the value creation and the value extraction sets of activities. This chapter focuses on the value extraction set of activities, in particular on those relating to the firm's intellectual property and its management.

Need for an IP Strategy. For firms that expect that the role of intellectual property in the corporate strategy will be significant or for firms with a significant

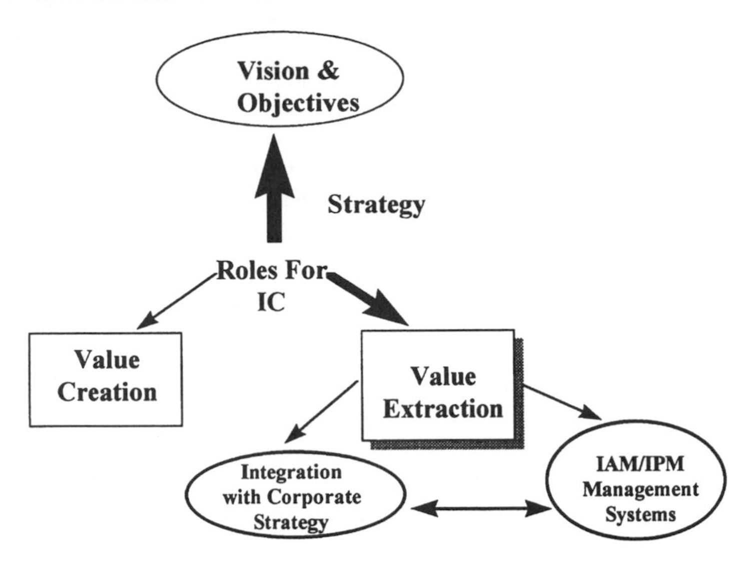

Exhibit 8.1 Relationships among Vision, Strategy, and Intellectual Capital

number of intellectual properties, an IP strategy can guide employee decision making on issues and outcomes that will move the firm toward its strategic vision. IP strategies are particularly helpful when they outline the strategic objectives of the firm and its related IP activity, as well as the expected use to which the firm's IP is to be put.

Breadth of IP Strategy. Strategic objectives as well as strategic use may vary considerably depending on the business strategy of the firm.

Broadly focused business strategy. Technologies are developed and patented in anticipation of some future use. The portfolio is created with an expectation that it can contribute to the creation of some future market demand. The corollary of this is that often a technology is patented to stake out an early claim to future design freedom. Companies with a broadly focused business strategy tend to be strategically opportunistic.

Narrowly focused business strategy. Technologies tend to be the results of targeted R&D and are often developed to meet a known or narrowly defined current (or potential) market demand. The time horizon for commercialization typically is short. Companies in this group tend to cull their portfolios routinely to ensure that the portfolio's contents continue to be tightly arranged around the focused business strategy.

In most firms the patent portfolio is an outgrowth of the firm's business strategy and merits the attention from senior managers that you would expect for a valued corporate asset. In firms such as these, there is usually a well-articulated set of definitions of the firm's strategic objectives for its intellectual properties, as well as the use to which those properties are expected to be put.

Strategic Objectives and Intent. All companies with patent portfolios create them with an expectation of how they will be used in the near term and in future technology-based opportunities:

1. *Protection from competition.* The holder of a patent is granted a fundamental monopoly right that prohibits others from commercializing the patented technology without express permission from the patent holder.
2. *Complementary protection.* Some patents are developed with no view toward direct commercialization. They provide complementary protection for a similar innovation but are created using different materials or processes. Complementary groups of patents formed around a key patent afford it a higher degree of protection and guard against thicket formation by competitors.
3. *Design freedom and litigation avoidance.* A portfolio often contains patents on future technologies, created to ensure that the firm has a prior claim to a specific area of technology. It signals that the firm is seriously in business in this area and can be expected to defend its intellectual property position forcefully. These prior claims are made to ensure the ability to commercialize new technologies over an extended period of time without threat of infringement.
4. *Basis for alliances.* An alliance is any business relationship formed with another party to meet a critical business need. Such needs include market access, product line expansion, technology transfer, and manufacturing competency. As customer demands become more complex, so do the technologies and services required to create solutions that will sell in the marketplace. Since no single company is likely to have expertise in the ever-widening span of technology, putting together a winning market solution often requires putting together a partnership or an alliance.

A large and strong portfolio and the means to continue generating large numbers of quality innovations is a measure of the technological and commercial strength of a technology-based firm. This can be a major advantage when seeking alliance partners who themselves are looking for a company with strengths to complement their own.

Strategic Use. While strategic intent focuses on what the firm wants to happen in the future, strategic use focuses on portfolio activity in the present. Strategic use may be thought of in terms of business opportunities, either those currently being pursued or those to be pursued in the near future. Portfolios are structured mainly for offensive and defensive strategic uses, but often are put to other uses such as establishing strong negotiating positions and enhancing the technological stature of the firm.

1. *Offensive use of the portfolio.* Offensive use includes both direct commercialization and tactical blocking. Direct commercialization can be achieved by clustering groups of patents together in estates around

planned or future products, around the core competencies of the firm, or both. These estates are aimed at producing a proprietary position in specific product areas. Offensive estates can also be clusters of improvements formed in a picket fence or thicket around the foundation patents of a competitor or a potential licensor. Offensive use usually involves excluding competitors from using the technology or business application for the life of the patent. Through careful use of licensing to excluded competitors, a firm may use the portfolio offensively to gain partial access to markets not otherwise within its reach. Similarly, a firm might develop alliances to gain access to needed technologies or markets.

2. *Defensive use of the portfolio.* Defensive uses of the portfolio tend to require a broad array of patents covering future uses of technology, processes, and materials that broadly cover as-yet-undefined products. In addition to ensuring exclusive use of a technology, defensive use of the portfolio usually means ensuring design freedom for the future. Successful defensive use also avoids litigation resulting from cross-licensing and other related strategic moves.
3. *Negotiation.* For the most part, the portfolios of firms interested in using them in negotiations have developed in one of two ways. A portfolio may contain a set of patents focused around a specific technology or business area. Firms negotiating a cross-licensing agreement or a business arrangement can be aided by the mere existence of a highly focused portfolio with strengths in the area of interest of both firms in the negotiation. Alternatively, the creation of a large brood portfolio including both existing and potential technologies can itself be intimidating to a negotiating firm.
4. *Enhancing the technological image of the firm.* A large and strong portfolio and the means and will to continue generating large numbers of quality patents is a measure and indication of the technological and commercial stature of the firm. This is a factor in seeking joint venture partners, and in the silent effect a strong portfolio (and the ability to continuously regenerate it) has on potentially infringing competitors.

The development of an IP strategy for the firm, in addition to focusing its scope on activities associated with the firm's intellectual property, must also be focused on supporting the long-term business strategy which itself is supporting the achievement of the strategic vision. The logic behind the development of a firm's IP strategy includes *a priori* review of the firm's vision and corporate strategy and the identification of the roles intellectual capital and its subset, intellectual property, may play. The roles available for intellectual property may then be codified into a set of activities and practices which themselves are the foundation of the firm's IP strategy.

The Intellectual Property Management System

Strategy implementation inevitably involves many parts of the organization. In the case of the IP management function of a knowledge firm, many activities are ongoing in the day-to-day activity concerned with maintaining the portfolio. Some of these involve improving the flow of potential patents into the patenting decision process; others relate to the cost management of the portfolio, others to the processes of valuing patents, still others to determining the optimum set of conversion mechanisms for extracting value from a patent the firm has decided to commercialize. With this bustle of activity, mass confusion is a distinct possibility unless the firm creates a systematic way of conducting all of these activities, each in its own time frame, and each coordinated with the others. Such a capability is often thought of as a system. Systems have the capability of being describable, their flows and processes made explicit, their relationships to one another made visible, and the requirements for each relatable to the company's business strategy.

The management of a complex series of activities such as those described for managing the firm's intellectual property, requires a system and a systematic approach. Anything less leads to chaos, misunderstanding, and wasted effort.

Components of an (IPM) Intellectual Property Management System

Managing intellectual property involves a series of activities and functions, each necessary to provide the basic information on which business decisions may be made, decisions about specific pieces of intellectual property that activate the link between individual patents in the portfolio and the company's business strategy.

How should the firm's intellectual property manager conceive and direct this series of activities and functions? The answer lies in understanding not only what the functions of IP management are but also what capabilities a firm must develop to make the functions happen (see Exhibit 8.2). A complete generic IP management system has five areas of responsibility:

1. Generation of Candidate Intellectual Properties. This includes all activities associated with identification of candidate innovations, analysis, categorization, and the decision to patent. The elements of the generation portion of an IPM system include:

a. *Overseeing the innovation process.* IPM includes a monitoring of the firm's innovation management activity: stages of innovation, decision processes, and status of development for key innovations. Firms with strong IPM have usually institutionalized the innovation process, defining and describing the serial stages of research, innovation, development, and product creation. The management of innovation for these firms includes evaluating the progress of innovations toward commercialization, reevaluating the strategic importance of each innovation in conjunction with the business plan, determining the amount of investment required for commercialization, and deciding to continue or cancel the innovation's development process.

b. *Generating new patents.* Because the decision to patent a technology has so many implications for the firm, it is one of the fundamental deci-

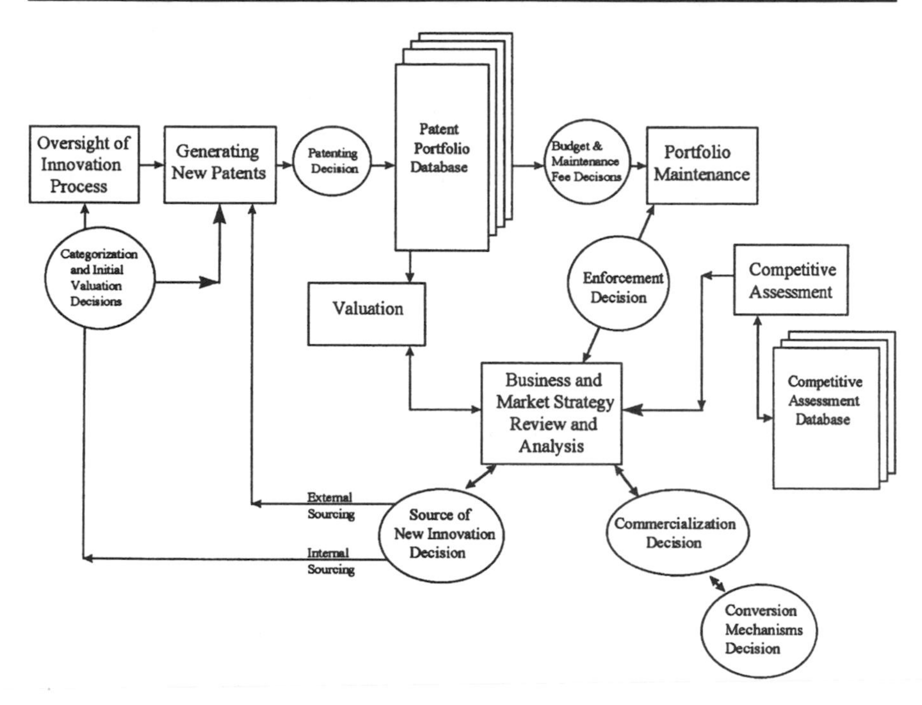

Exhibit 8.2 An IP Management System Showing Functions, Decision Processes, and Databases

sions a technology-based knowledge company can make. It determines the basis from which product and process applications are developed and subsequently sold. This decision more than any other determines the future course of the company. It can affect the quality (utility) of the patent portfolio; it can affect the future fee costs of the portfolio; it can affect the business strategy in those cases where a business is based on one or more technologies; it can affect the company's legal or protection strategy. For all of these reasons, the selection of innovations to become part of the patent portfolio is carefully considered in companies that are particularly successful in managing their patent portfolio.

The generation of patentable innovations must be preceded by identifying the technology areas in which new or more patents are desired, providing the incentives necessary for generating an amount of patent requests sufficient to meet the company's needs, and creating screening criteria and decision processes for deciding which of the patent requests to pursue and which to drop.

Each potentially patentable innovation should be analyzed twice, first from a technical perspective and subsequently from a business perspective. The technical analysis is conducted to determine the technical merits from the firm's perspective: Is the technology consistent with the firms's technical strengths? Does it add to the firm's technical position? Is it a technology the firm will wish to pursue in the future? Would staking out a technological interest in a new area be of benefit to the firm in the future?

Business-oriented analysis of a potential patent might include concerns about the market acceptance of applications developed from the technology. Would the products or processes that evolve from applications of the technology be in the firm's current or planned areas of business? Would products or processes resulting from the technology require new investment? If so, how much? What level of income would these products generate? When could that income stream begin?

There are other business-oriented questions that may be asked. What are the intended business uses for the patent (e.g., direct commercialization, protecting some other business asset, use as an anticompetitive weapon)? What would be the ability of the patent to exclude others (e.g., excellent, nominal, poor)? How easy would it be to detect infringement of the patent (that is, would infringement be visibly detectable, or would the technology be used inside another apparatus, making infringement neither visible nor easy to detect)?

c. *Patent categorization decision process.* Many of the selection criteria may also be used to qualitatively value the patent once it is issued and placed in the company's patent portfolio. The *value grid,* described later in this chapter, is a useful method for categorizing patents.

2. Portfolio Management. Most companies maintain a patent in its portfolio throughout the life of the patent and pay the patent maintenance fees required to maintain the patent in force. Successful patent managers, however, routinely review their budgets for maintenance fee payments and cull their portfolio of properties that once offereed value to the firm but no longer do so. The portfolio is routinely screened for patents no longer of value to the firm, and payment of maintenance fees on these is discontinued. Companies that actively managed and maintain their portfolios report dramatic reduction in portfolio maintenance fee costs.

a. *Budget and maintenance fee decisions.* The costs associated with maintaining patents can be high. Many companies, because of the design of their accounting system, do not even know the actual costs. Nevertheless, the cost of obtaining and maintaining patents is considerable and should represent a firm's conscious decision to invest in the creation and generation of technology products that themselves create future income.

To make rational decisions about the costs, companies should budget funds for this purpose and assign a portfolio manager to ensure that this and other portfolio goals are met. The portfolio manager may present management with tradeoffs related to managing the portfolio. For example, it may make sense to discontinue the maintenance on some less-useful patents in the portfolio to make funds available for new technologies with more potential for contributing to the firm's capabilities in the marketplace.

b. *Patent enforcement decisions.* When infringement of a company's patented technology has been detected, the firm must decide how to enforce its rights. The relevant considerations include the company's context, its competitive position, the effect enforcement could have on customers' perceptions of the firm, the strength of an enforcement action, the nature and kind of resolution to be sought through an enforcement action, the probability of success, and more. Enforcement decisions are often significant enough that they are made at the firm's strategic level.

3. IP Valuation. Knowledge firms are routinely faced with a need to value their technologies, patented or not, and inevitably a portfolio manager is asked to value one or more patents in the portfolio. A significant new function that technology-based knowledge firms are adding to their management system capability is the ability to produce valuations of their technology.

4. Competitive Assessment. This function involves the development, assimilation, and promulgation of information on two kinds of competition: business and technology.

5. Strategic Decision Making. The analysis of an individual or group of intellectual properties to determine whether and how to commercialize them for the benefit of the firm is the strategic decision-making function within IPM. Using the firm's business strategy as the guide, managers evaluate properties for their commercial use. The two decisions that may be reached are (1) the decision to commercialize, or (2) the decision to "store" the technology until some other technology becomes available that will make the technology under analysis more appropriate to commercialize.

a. *Commercialization decisions.* In a sophisticated IPM company, the commercialization decision is largely anticlimactic. In such companies, innovations under development have been continuously tracked and evaluated. Increasingly detailed analyses have determined the market need, the degree of market acceptance, the complementary assets required for commercialization, access to those assets, and the most appropriate conversion mechanisms.
b. *Defining the need for more technology.* A firm uses the results of the business and marketing strategy analysis along with the competitive assessment information to determine whether its competitive position could be improved through the addition of a specific technology to its portfolio. If it determines that a patented commercializable technology is unsuitable for commercialization, often one of the following has been realized:
   - The expected market for applications of the technology has not materialized or is not adequate to support further investment. The firm should seek other or related technological innovations which, when

paired with the one under examination, could demonstrate acceptable levels of market acceptance.

- The innovation cannot be adequately protected legally. The firm should seek to pair this technology with other technologies that have greater ability to qualify for legal protection to proceed with commercialization.

In either case, the firm seeks other technologies to match with the technology under review. Outside the company there may be a licensable technology residing with companies that can be merged with or acquired, or people who have the requisite skills or knowledge to create the technology directly and who are currently working at other companies and might be hired away. Alternatively, the firm may have the ability to create the new technology itself. In either case, the sourcing decision is one that, like the enforcement decision, sometimes requires strategic decision making.

ALTERNATIVE METHODS OF PROTECTION (EXTRALEGAL)

Legal protection is only one of several ways to give the firm a monopolylike position and, thereby, capture value from the innovation. In extracting value, strategy and positioning are usually more important than protection. Patents are crucial in some industries, such as chemicals and, more recently, electronics. In other industries, such as semiconductors, speed in getting the product to market is the most important factor in maximizing sales revenue. The difference by industry allows us to divide the world into two regimes, according to the strength of the legal protection available to the innovating firm. An industry with good intellectual property protection operates under one regime, and an industry or technological area with poor intellectual property protection (i.e., where imitation is easy) operates under another. The discussion in this chapter so far has concerned firms in the first regime, where good intellectual property protection is available.

For firms without good intellectual property protection, other, nonlegal methods for developing a near-monopoly position may exist, but they must have the required complementary business assets.

As explained in Chapter 2, specific complementary assets are unique to a product or technology and can be used strategically to isolate a technology from competitors and extract more value. For example, manufacturing facilities capable of handling rapid growth while maintaining high quality constitute an extremely valuable complementary asset. Thus, Compaq Computer was able to grow rapidly in the MS-DOS personal computer (PC) market in the 1980s at the expense of technological pioneer IBM, largely because IBM lacked the critical manufacturing assets to meet the PC demand it had created. Because Compaq quickly recognized and took advantage of complementary capability necessary for success in the PC market, it was rewarded with rapid market penetration.

Thus, where firms can limit their rivals' access to complementary assets, they can significantly slow down the rate of competition. Imitators desiring to enter the marketplace must not only replicate the technology of the product; they must also develop the complementary assets required to commercialize the technology. When AT&T tried to enter the PC business in 1984, it lacked the marketing assets (sales force and distribution systems) necessary to support PC products. The lack of these assets and the time AT&T spent trying to acquire them may explain why four years and $2.5 billion later, AT&T had still not become a viable competitor to Compaq and IBM in the PC marketplace.

Because specific complementary assets are usually created in conjunction with the commercialization of one specific application of an innovation and are, therefore, unique, they are often themselves able to be protected. In effect, controlling the specific complementary assets is equivalent to controlling the underlying intellectual capital.

Thus, ownership of specific complementary business assets may often provide reasonable or adequate de facto protection when legal protection is not available. A corollary is that, if the complementary asset is critical and unattainable, a firm that can find an unconventional way of eliminating it can also be advantaged. For example, when Canon was exploring the introduction of a new line of copiers in the U.S. market, it learned that it lacked an adequate distribution network to service them. In a creative use of technology, Canon redesigned the machines' toner cartridge, making its replacement the equivalent of a service call, and eliminated the need for a service network.

SUMMARY

Companies engaged with technology have the advantage of two forms of intangible assets not available to companies not engaged with technology. For technology-based companies, there are intellectual assets as well as intellectual properties that are available as assets from which value can be extracted. This chapter has discussed the key concepts associated with value extraction from the perspective of intellectual property management.

For firms wishing to maximize the value extracted from their portfolio of intellectual properties, there are several key elements which must be in place. First, a clearly defined and well-articulated vision of the company as it wishes to become, as well as a strategy for achieving the vision, are fundamental building blocks for the maximization of value extraction from IP. In addition, a knowledge of the firm's actual and desired values is desirable to ensure their consistency with the values and strategy. Second, it is important for the firm to develop a clear portfolio strategy, one that identifies the defensive and offensive elements of portfolio use. Companies with intellectual properties may create a portfolio of IP assets that may be used either as a defensive asset (portfolio-as-protection) or an offensive asset (portfolio-as-corporate-asset). Third, firms must clearly identify the role(s) intellectual property is to play in the strategy and then create a plan for moving IPM toward its strategic capability.

An intellectual property management *system* is also a required element of successful IPM. Such a system must contain the key elements described in this chapter and must also explicitly include identification of key decisions. For each of the key areas of decision, the decision processes must be defined, including who is involved, what information is needed by the decision makers, what work processes are necessary to provide this information, what databases are needed to store the information, and how the decisions are made in each decision process to be implemented.

Intellectual property management is a key set of concepts, methods, and processes specifically designed for aligning the intellectual properties of the firm with its business strategies and objectives. It represents one of the fundamental approaches to maximizing the extraction of value from a firm's intellectual capital.

9

The IP Portfolio as a Competitive Tool

Suzanne Harrison

ICM Group, LLC

Kevin Rivette

SmartPatents, Inc.

In the war for global economic dominance, the fiercest battles today are over intellectual property. Where nations once fought for control of trade routes and raw materials, they now fight for exclusive rights to ideas, innovations, and inventions.

Fred Warshofsky, The Patent Wars: The Battle to Own the World's Technology, *1994.*

At its simplest, the patent portfolio is a collection of innovative ideas waiting to be exploited. The key issue is how best to convert those ideas to profit. Most companies understand that their patent portfolios have value that can be realized through technology commercialization. As has been highlighted earlier in this book, commercialization is but one of several "conversion" mechanisms for extracting value from the portfolio. The appropriate tools for converting knowledge to profit can be used to generate both near-term or longer-term returns. In the near term, the emphasis should be on immediately increasing revenue while reducing the cost of maintaining the portfolio. In the longer term, the emphasis should be on managing the firm's intellectual capital by providing an organized framework for decision making. Answering the following questions will help executives begin to assemble information that will be useful in managing the patent portfolio.

- What opportunities are available to increase income from the current patents in the portfolio?
- How can the costs of creating and maintaining the portfolio be reduced?

- How can the firm obtain greater protection for the key patents in the portfolio?
- Which IP assets are linked to core and noncore technologies?
- How can the firm evaluate the effectiveness of the current patent management strategy?
- Based on the present patent position, what R&D activities or acquisition strategy would help to fill any "patent gaps" in the portfolio?
- What business assets are critical for company and/or business unit success?
- What is the relationship between investing in internal development and the acquisition of technology? Can the risks and rewards be quantified?
- What are the signs that a competitor is encroaching on the firm's intellectual property assets?
- What is the best way to identify and evaluate acquisition targets based on their patent portfolios and market positions?
- How can the firm routinely predict future market opportunities?

This chapter discusses some of the patent portfolio tools developed and utilized by the ICM Group LLC and SmartPatents that managers can use to help their firms systematically extract the maximum value from their IP assets.

PATENT-RELATED REVENUES ARE INCREASING RAPIDLY

Corporations cannot ignore their patents when making business decisions. In 1980, U.S. patent-related revenues were only $3 billion. In 1997 this number is projected to reach a staggering $100 billion (see Exhibit 9.1).

The rate at which corporations are filing patents is rising rapidly. Corporate managers not only realize the strategic value of patents, but are also rapidly realizing that the life cycles for products, technologies, and processes are not the same. Products can rapidly become obsolete, but technologies and processes can be redeployed to new uses (either within the firm or through out-licensing) and thus continue to generate revenue in a myriad of ways long after their initial use.

INCREASING SHAREHOLDER VALUE THROUGH INTELLECTUAL PROPERTY

Patents are the most tangible and enforceable form of intellectual property. In addition to being legal documents, patents contain information that can enable a company to develop and protect a business strategy that cannot be replicated easily by competitors. Most executives intuitively understand the value of their patent assets. However, they do not have the requisite systems and tools in place to enable them to quantify the value of their patent portfolio, map the competitive landscape, and develop strategies to protect market positions.

Computer software is a must for proper portfolio analysis. A software system must be capable of not only handling textual information, but also displaying

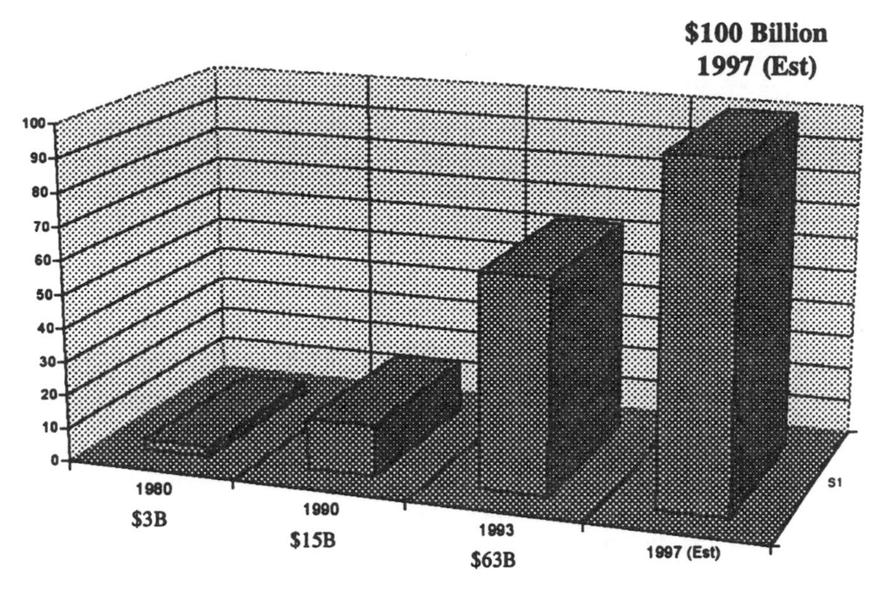

Exhibit 9.1 Gradual Increase in U.S. Patent-Related Revenues
Source: Fred Warshofsky, *The Patent Wars: The Battle to Own the World's Technology,* 1994.

sophisticated graphs. Until recently, only large companies have been able to computerize their patent portfolios, because they have designed custom software applications. Now, however, there is a standardized software system that allows the systematic integration of text and graphical information in a relational database. The SmartPatent Business Decision System is analytical software designed to revolutionize business decision making by integrating patent data with other corporate data, including financial and product data. This integration produces a wealth of patent information that can become a potent corporate weapon. It is crucial to have at the core of your toolkit a robust computerized search engine to effectively utilize all of the data embedded in patents.

Getting Started: The Portfolio Audit

To begin tapping the value of the patent portfolio, a firm must understand the components of its portfolio. A patent portfolio audit should be conducted for the purposes of:

- Documenting the contents of the portfolio
- Identifying leverage opportunities that can improve the firm's strategic and tactical business position and quickly increase the bottom line

Documenting the Portfolio's Contents

The first step is to develop a profile of the firm's patent portfolio and display the profile in different dimensions. The portfolio profile can be displayed in three complementary ways:

1. Using U.S. patent baseline data, the first step is to develop a listing of all of a firm's patents by U.S. Patent Class code. This listing allows the creation of charts that describe the technology profile of the firm's portfolio. Exhibit 9.2 shows the distribution of patents for a sample portfolio.
2. Using the baseline data, the firm can then aggregate and summarize the portfolio by technical group, a different and more specific categorization that begins to show how the portfolio is distributed by technologies and by subtechnologies, a more disaggregated categorization that further reveals underlying distributions of a firm's technologies.
3. Last, the ICM Group LLC has devised a proprietary methodology for translating U.S. Patent Class codes into 4-digit SIC codes within which each patent is most likely to be commercialized.

Creating a Classification Scheme

Once the patent portfolio has been profiled, a more detailed classification scheme is needed to help identify opportunities for enhancing revenue and reducing patent maintenance costs. We generally recommend classifying the portfolio by groupings: core or noncore technologies or patents, SBU, division, or product. For illustrative purposes, we will use core and noncore patents.

Mapping Patents to Products

Following are several examples of reports that show how patent data can be integrated with product data to reveal which patents directly or indirectly protect technology embodied in key products, which patents are likely to protect the trajectory along which technology is evolving, and which patents are still key to revenue-generating products. From this mapping, executives can determine which patents will contribute to the success of the company. Executives can also decide which

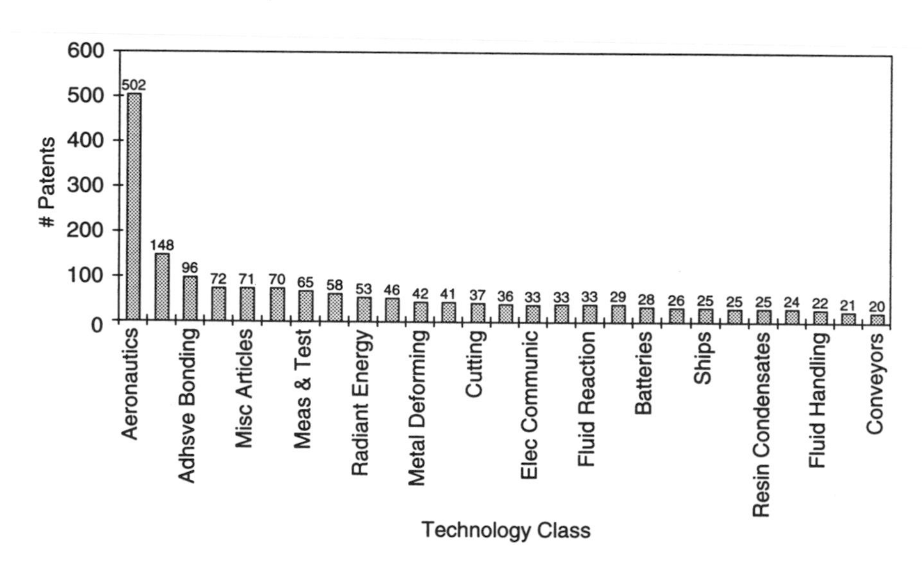

Exhibit 9.2 Frequency Distribution of Patents

patents they no longer want to pay licensing or renewal fees for, thus achieving cost savings.

The first step is to evaluate the firm's patent portfolio in relation to its key products. The firm must assemble a multifunctional implementation team to drive the effort, because it requires input from the corporate patent counsel, research and development, product management, and other divisions. The end result will be a patent-centric, integrated, organized knowledge base that is far more valuable than individual data sources for making strategic decisions.

Cluster and Bracket Analysis: What Are Competitors Doing? Cluster and bracket analysis—the clustering around the core technology of key technology patents required for the final product—allows businesses to ascertain that they have protected a core technology. Businesses can routinely protect their core patents from competitors by obtaining patents for the supporting technologies required to extend the area of invention. If key products and technologies are not protected when patents expire, any competitor can enter the market and affect the firm's margins. Cluster and bracket analysis can also reveal mixed results in which further research, thought, and analysis can lead to the development of effective business licensing strategies (see Exhibit 9.3).

Case 1: A company is protecting its core technology by protecting related technologies. This method of extending protection is called *clustering.*

Case 2: A competitor has protected technologies needed by the firm to extend a core technology, thus effectively "bracketing" or preventing the

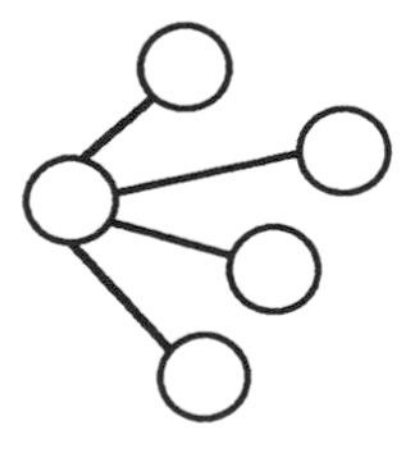

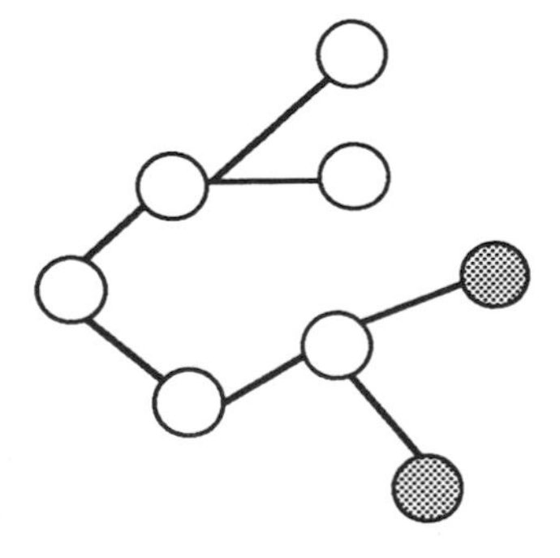

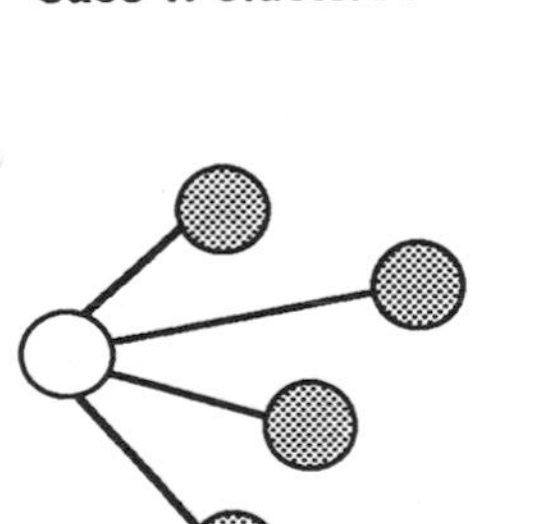

Exhibit 9.3 Cluster and Bracket Analysis

company from extending their product. The gray represents the competitor's protected technologies surrounding a company's core technology.

Case 3: A company has its core technology partially protected and partially blocked by competitors. It can explore options such as a new product strategy, a merger or acquisition, or a licensing opportunity.

Patent Aging Analysis. Patent aging analysis shows the number of years left on a company's patents. A patent is a time-limited right to exclusive use granted by the government in exchange for disclosing the technology. When a patent expires, it becomes a part of the public domain. Knowing how much life any given patent has left provides extra insight for marketing and R&D strategies as well for licensing negotiations.

Inventor Employment Analysis. Inventor employment analysis reveals which inventors are still with the company and which divisions they work in. This information is crucial for developing inventor retention programs and for determining whether inventors of key product technologies who have left the company are working for a competitor or a potential partner.

Patent Counts by Inventor. By integrating patent data with other corporate data such as human resource information, this analysis details how many and which patents each inventor has. The linking of inventors to specific patents makes it easy to determine which inventors are working on core products. If top inventors are assigned to noncore products, companies can reassign them as appropriate to keep talent in the company.

Depending on a firm's interests, the portfolio profile information can be augmented by other company-specific data to make possible several other useful analyses.

Determining Leverage Opportunities

Identifying Candidates for Out-Licensing. Often one technology has a variety of potential applications. Patents that are not strategic to a firm's current or potential businesses may be licensed into new business areas or to different markets within a given business area. Using the USPC/SIC database, technology managers can identify potential licensees for whom the patent is likely to provide significant value. These licensees presumably have the highest willingness to pay for the license.

Minimizing Patent Maintenance Fees. Also using information on current and potential business areas, an analysis of the data will reveal a number of patents that are candidates for cessation of patent maintenance fees. Minimizing patent maintenance fees can save a client, on average, 10 percent of the overall portfolio cost.

Integrating Portfolio Strategy with Corporate and Business Unit Strategies

Ranking Patent Importance. The frequency with which a firm's patents are cited or otherwise referred to is an indicator of the relative importance competitors place on its patents. Companies that own complementary patents are often potential joint-venture partners, acquisition candidates, or competitors. Such information is very useful when negotiating cross-licensing agreements because it allows a firm to determine and value the patents potential licensees are most interested in.

Identifying Potential New Business Areas. A company's analysis of its patent portfolio can help it identify business areas it is not presently in but in which it might have technical advantage. Consider company X, which was looking to expand into several new markets/businesses in which it believed it dominated technically. After combining the SIC codes for its existing and new businesses with its patent portfolio (also sorted by SIC code) and potential business opportunities, it was able to determine that it would have difficulty competing in market E because it had no patent position; at the same time, it identified a different new business opportunity in market J that was being ignored (see Exhibit 9.4).

Identifying Hidden Competitors. The same analysis, conducted in reverse, allows a firm to explore patent data by SIC code as well as by technology area and to identify companies that also hold patent positions in a business area of interest. This allows the firm to know who its existing and potential competitors are and to determine a rough technology trajectory for each.

Determining Technology Trajectory. The database can also permit time-sensitive analysis. An analysis of competitor portfolios over time highlights their pace of technology development as well as their developmental directions. Such a database can also warn a firm when a competitor seems to be altering its technology trajectory, thus alerting the firm to potential future competitive threats.

Identifying Potential Joint-Venture Partners or Acquisition Targets. A similar analysis would allow the identification of companies whose technology position

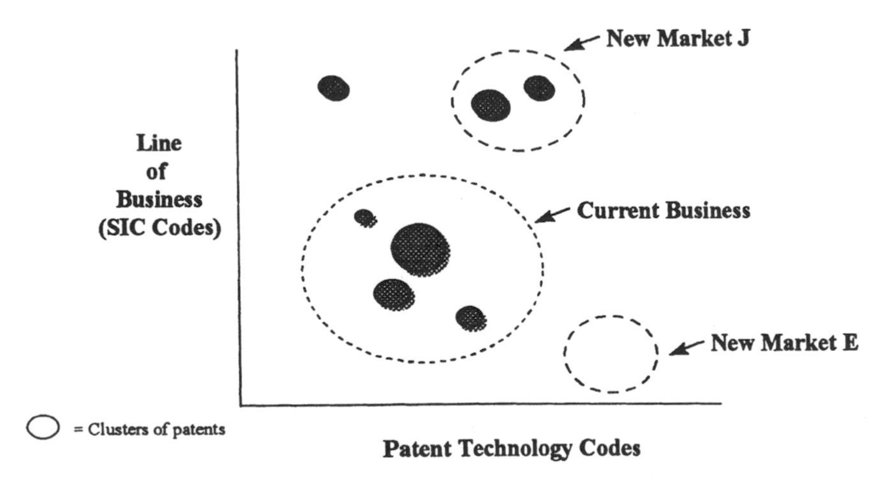

Exhibit 9.4 New Business Opportunity Identification

is complementary and therefore might be a potential partner in an R&D joint venture. Similarly, the analysis could be used to identify potential acquisitions as a means of obtaining access to a key or costly to develop technology.

While the USPC/SIC code database allows a firm the ability to view its patent portfolio (and its competitors') in a variety of different scenarios, it does not adequately address "patent gaps" or determine the strength of a particular patent. To acquire this information we suggest a patent tree analysis.

The Patent Tree

A patent tree is a tool to aid in guiding management activities in technology commercialization and R&D management. The tree arranges a large amount of disorganized and often disjointed information in a manner that allows the firm to obtain new information and insight.

The patent tree approach, pioneered by Dow Chemical, is used to bring focus to and to optimize protection for near-term existing or planned businesses in which technology is an important element of the income-producing capability of the business. In this approach a business opportunity is identified, and the vertical chain of activities required by the opportunity is outlined. The vertical chain is typically divided into common sense segments (determined by the business). The major activities of each segment are identified (raw materials, processing, products, processes). Further delineation of subordinate categories of interest underneath each of the activities is identified. Additionally, the firm's patents are laid out and prioritized according to the breadth and strength of claims. On paper, the resulting structure looks something like a tree (see Exhibit 9.5).

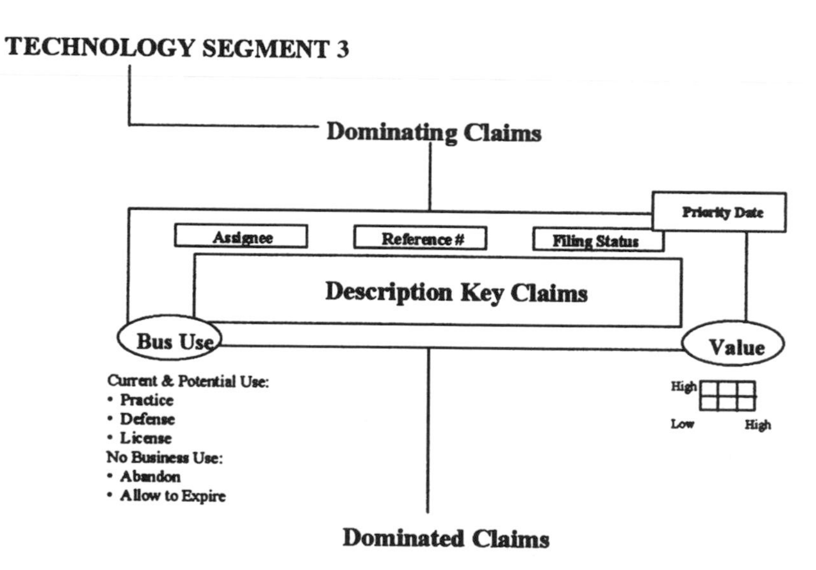

Exhibit 9.5 Assessing a Firm's Overall Patent Protection

Similarly, patents owned by other firms are identified, structured in their appropriate relationship to the company's patents, and then also placed on the tree. At the end of the process, it is possible to assess the company's overall patent protection for the business opportunity, including areas of strength and weakness. Further, a company can identify areas of business or technological activity in which another company holds a dominant position and new activity in that area would risk infringement.

Additional applications of the patent tree in technology-based companies include:

Strategy Alignment. Often, particularly in large companies, differences emerge between the company's overall strategic direction and the firm's subordinate strategies or plans. Executives would like to believe that the contents of their patent portfolios are consistent with the company's technologies, direction, overall strategy, and R&D plan. Experience shows, however, that this is rarely the case. Patents are often in the background of strategy and tactics, although in technology-based companies they should be in a lead position. This happens when the company's technology and R&D strategies and the overall strategic plan are misaligned. The patent tree is a useful device for showing the optimal alignment of the technical and business elements of the corporation's strategies.

R&D Direction. Patent trees can help a company identify technologies that would be desirable inclusions in the portfolio. A portfolio that contains a range of complementary patents creates design freedom for the future as well as opportunities for immediate commercialization in new business areas. The patent tree also creates the ability to identify "patent gaps" or needed technologies.

Cost Savings. Patent trees allow companies to learn where they have more patent protection than necessary within a business area. A subsequent review of selected patents will determine whether the company can terminate maintenance payments and still retain effective coverage.

New Income. Patent trees also allow companies to identify potential new vertical licensing opportunities for their existing technologies. These examples make clear the value of patents in increasing shareholder value, protecting business strategies, and making tactical decisions. But the real value of undertaking a patent tree analysis lies in understanding all the options available to a company and making decisions that further the strategic direction of the company, based on a greater understanding of the competitive landscape.

CONCLUSION

A fundamental source of profits for knowledge-based companies is the patent portfolio of the firm. The patent portfolio, the most tangible of the intangible assets, is the first step to extracting the firm's "hidden value." This chapter has outlined various tools to enable both near-term and longer-term revenue generation available to firms quickly and easily. It is imperative that the firm ensure a sufficient number of focused innovations are developed to fuel the business as it strives to achieve the firm's strategic objectives. Additionally, it should view the patent portfolio as a valuable business asset in this quest.

10

Creating the Portfolio Database

Kelly Hale

Rockwell International

INTRODUCTION

Individual intellectual assets can have vastly different value, depending on a host of factors. Understanding, identifying, and managing the many factors that define the value of each asset is critical to any activity that seeks to exploit the value. For most companies, the easiest and most logical place to start this task is with intellectual property, because most companies already have a collection of patents or copyrighted works and they feel they have some understanding of the collection's value.

While a large body of information is available regarding the valuation and use of intellectual property, management strategies for the important factors are not well known. This chapter presents some highlights from our attempt to collect the necessary information to effectively develop, manage, and exploit patent assets.

WHY DEVELOP A PORTFOLIO DATABASE?

Many, if not most, technology-based companies in America secure a collection of patents during the normal course of business. Typically, the patents originate according to no particular strategy—rather, they are the products of certain individuals within these companies who feel compelled to produce them. With no strategy for patent procurement, it is not surprising that the same companies have no real strategy for managing them. Additionally, the nature of the business of most high-technology companies renders patent procurement and exploitation relatively unimportant in their business plans. Whether they know it or not, managers of high-technology businesses are, and have always been, responsible for collecting and exploiting the business's intellectual property. Inventors seldom have an understanding of the strategic direction of their companies, and they are, therefore, incapable of determining the relative value of their inventions. Patent attorneys are likewise not privy to the strategic direction of the company and lack training in valuing the inventions they secure protection for. Only the business managers are sufficiently aware of all the critical factors that define the strategic value of patented technology. Additionally, they are ultimately responsible for the impact intellectual property will have on their companies' profitability.

Where a business begins based on some new idea or technology, it is readily apparent that the probability of success for that new business (assuming the idea or technology is useful) is directly related to the business's ability to control who will practice the subject technology. Intellectual property, usually in the form of patents, is the primary instrument of that control. For these companies, patents are valuable and coveted. Once the same company gains success, particularly as a manufacturer of technology, the focus changes, with more effort being given to managing the tactical aspects of the everyday business. Securing and exploiting intellectual property is not even on the radar screen of these managers, and, given their lack of familiarity with patent law and patent valuation, they prefer to avoid dealing with it altogether. Managers blessed with insight, however, know that they must get a handle on intellectual property procurement and exploitation or risk being bested by the businesses that do. This is where Rockwell International (as well as a good number of other companies) found itself some years ago.

BACKGROUND

Well known for its involvement in the space program and various high-tech military programs, Rockwell International was the primary contractor for the space shuttle and the B-1 bomber, among other things. But, as of December 6, 1996, Rockwell International can no longer be considered a government contractor, having sold the last of its aerospace and government contractor businesses to Boeing. With the divestiture of its automotive business in 1997, Rockwell will have completed the shift to commercial electronics.

While Rockwell was able to effectively transform itself in a relatively short period of time to a commercial business (no small task), the collection of assets representing the intellectual part of Rockwell still reflects the business as it was. Until recently, no attempt has been made to understand the collective value of these assets, since doing so would have added little value to Rockwell's business. Licensing has rarely been an issue, and even if it were, the assets included in any such activity were well known and understood prior to the licensing attempt, because the particular assets were procured for expressly the licensing purpose. As with most aerospace and government contracting firms, intellectual assets (more particularly patents) have been used primarily for defensive purposes at Rockwell, when they have been used at all.

As startling as it might seem, the environment described above is not uncommon among aerospace and defense contractors. If one examines the policy, it is easy to understand. Suppose a defense contractor, as part of a U.S. government contract, invents new technology that promises to revolutionize a particular aspect of its business. Even if a patent is applied for (and one usually is), there is no right of exclusion against other defense contractors, since the government grants them a royalty-free license to use the patented technology by or on behalf of the government.[1] Government contractors learn to seek the best technology available, regardless of who might own it, even in their nongovernment businesses. For these participants the patent system is not a source of inspiration for new innovation as it was designed to be but, rather, has devolved into a safe haven for copiers. This artificial system leads to strange practices on the part of technology borrowers, such as not learning about competitors to avoid treble patent damages. This impacts the perceived and actual value of patents in the portfolio—rendering them a less useful investment and, therefore, less interesting to manage.

That was then; this is now. Rockwell, like all commercial businesses, must exploit *all* of its assets to be competitive, or risk finding itself on the wrong side of an uneven playing field. Rockwell has been redefined as a commercial electronics supplier and, thus, must adhere to a new set of rules. Rules that require the characterization, acquisition, and exploitation of intellectual assets. Additionally, there has been a shift in the attitude of the Department of Justice, the U.S. federal court system, and the federal government generally since the early 1980s toward higher damage awards and more frequent injunctions for patent infringement.[2] Patent holders are increasingly willing to extract licensing income from putative infringers and sue those who are unwilling to pay.

With the environment just described, it is only too apparent that "business as usual" is not acceptable. Technology companies clearly need patents, but almost as important, they need access to those patents. Without an understanding of the attributes of the patents a company owns, there is no access; the patents are not available to aid a company in achieving its strategic goals and objectives. In short, management of patent assets is imperative. Informed databases are necessary tools of portfolio management.

In 1994 the management of Rockwell Semiconductor Systems (formerly Rockwell Telecommunications), realizing that the nature of Rockwell's business was changing and that the value of patents was increasing generally, determined to understand the value of these assets and to go about protecting them. It is important to note that it was not the patent department that embarked on this journey. Every patent department has a database of patents, but the database is usually lifeless, unable to predict or quantify the value of the assets within. The motivation for a useful database (and this is important) comes from those who would benefit from it most—within the business itself. If a program such as this emanates from the patent department, it will be seen as an activity designed to benefit them and will, therefore, receive little support from the strategic and technical personnel, whose input is fundamental.

Rockwell Semiconductor Systems sought to secure a team capable of taking on this task without the burden of conflicting responsibilities. From the outset our goal was to develop an understanding of the process in place and the assets already existing, then to increase the number and average value of the assets.

When this project began in mid-1994, there were very few easily accessible examples of programs like that which we were looking for. In fact, only recently had the function of "intellectual property management" been known anywhere as it is understood in this context. Timely resources, such as the now well-known *Fortune* article[3] describing a new group of professionals purporting to be managing intellectual assets, gave us a structure with which to begin.

As part of our management task, we realized the need to develop a database of the patents and disclosed inventions. This chapter deals with what this database should (or could) look like, using anecdotal information where available. Keep in mind that there is an inseparable link between the database of assets and the process by which those assets are created. We will try to point out, wherever possible, the implications the invention disclosure and procurement processes have on the form and substance of the database.

BUILDING THE DATABASE

Perhaps the most difficult aspect of developing a database is determining where to start. Database designers will be faced with a particularly difficult decision immediately: "Should I start with the databases that we already have, or would it be more efficient to start with a clean slate?" The need to show results quickly will make for an almost irresistible temptation to develop the database attributes "on the fly," using whatever platforms are currently available. Unfortunately, however, early decisions can and will constrain the eventual usefulness of the database.

Begin with the "Ideal Database"

One way to avoid "analysis paralysis" and still provide a useful tool is to begin the development project by focusing on the end uses for the database. This tends to drive the end product toward a format that is both more useful and more easily understood. At this point, we found it useful to engage in brainstorming sessions with potential users to consider the likely applications, both present and future, for our database. Here is partial list of our observations:

1. The database should readily identify patents that have value but that are not being used by the corporation (i.e., good licensing candidates).
2. The database should allow its administrators to easily identify nonperforming assets so that they can be sold or abandoned.
3. The database should be designed such that it can dynamically reflect and accommodate the strategic direction of the company.
4. The database should provide access to the costs associated with maintaining the portfolio and individual assets.
5. The database should provide the users with the ability to easily group patents comprising similar technologies.
6. Within a technology area, patents should be easily grouped and identified as being fundamental versus iterative in nature.

7. Where a particular asset is iterative in nature, it should be easily grouped with patents that are fundamental within the same technology group.
8. The database should have a mechanism to allow its users to group patents that might be applied to a particular product or class of products.
9. The database should identify competitors and potential competitors for each patent.[4]
10. The database should be designed so that it is easily (if not automatically) appended with new information from a variety of sources.
11. The database must be designed with hierarchical access control, so that only those with a "need to know" have access to sensitive information.
12. Each patent should identify alternatives to itself and the associated costs (advantages versus disadvantages) of each.
13. The database should be a constantly updated (interactive) source of information on individual assets.
14. Procuring the information required for the database must add little or no extra burden to inventors or to their management.

Who Are the Intended Users of the Database?

Once the uses for the database are defined, it is important to focus on the users. While the database is intended primarily for those tasked with managing the properties (whether that function is discrete or shared between groups), others within the organization will find the information useful and necessary. Here are some examples:

1. *Strategic business planners* will want to know whether the business entity has sufficient pertinent intellectual property to defend itself against incumbents in new businesses the company is considering.
2. *Staff intellectual property attorneys* will want to identify patents that might be useful to ward off litigation challenges from competitors.
3. *Business managers* will need to know which patents might be useful to attract potential joint ventures and other cooperative business arrangements.
4. *Engineering* will want to be able to find the company-owned patents useful for new designs, both to leverage engineering efforts and to avoid encroaching on the patents of others.
5. *Intellectual property managers* will want to use the database to identify technology areas in which the company is active, but which have not been (or are not being) adequately protected.
6. *Licensing personnel* will want to know which patents would be good candidates for licensing programs.
7. *IP managers and staff IP attorneys* will want to be automatically informed of any actions required to protect the patents in the database.
8. *IP managers* will want to be able to use the database to create metrics for patent activity and portfolio value for business managers.

What Is Doable?

Armed with knowledge of what an ideal database might contain and who the users might be, the next task is to determine what can be achieved given the constraints of a normal business, that is, which tools add the most value to the business for the effort. Every business is constrained by opportunity costs. Obviously, the trick is to provide the maximum level of functionality in the database while making the minimum investment. We determined to consider the attributes (or tools) we had at our disposal or which we could easily get our hands on before proceeding. One of the more enlightened decisions (in retrospect) was the use of consultants at an early stage in database development. Although consultants can be expensive, the right consultant can save a great deal of time and, in the long run, save money while producing better results.

Intellectual Property Management Flowchart

We used a variety of tools during the development of our database, and one of the more useful tools was a flowchart describing our intellectual property management process. The flowchart (Exhibit 10.1) was designed to identify the sources and decision spaces for our patent management project. We found that we could use it as a template for our database to ensure identification of the important fields. We will define these fields further later in this chapter.

U.S. Patent and Trademark Office Classifications

We found that U.S. Patent and Trademark Office (PTO) technology classes and subclasses are useful as a starting point when categorizing patents into technologies. While the PTO classification is not always reliable, often there is enough accuracy to do cursory evaluation of the portfolio. Additionally, software to convert the PTO classification numbers into well-defined technology terms is available.[5] We also found that our effort to convert existing commercial patent databases to use as a platform for our interactive database was well worth the effort.

Business Strategies as a Source for Intellectual Property Management Data

The business strategy is the primary source for patent management information. As a source, the business strategy supplies the criteria to evaluate and disposition new and existing assets. For each asset in our possession, we must know how we expect it to be represented in both our products and our competitors' products, and how strategically important those products are to the business. Additionally, the value of the patents in the database is dynamic, so we need a mechanism to update the strategic information associated with each asset. How is business strategy codified in the individual assets in our collection? There are obvious methods to link each asset to business strategy, including identifying the product in which it is found and identifying how long the invention will likely be found in similar products. Patent databases normally include this sort of information. But such data quickly becomes obsolete, often even *before* issuance of the underlying patent. More important, this information is lost once the product's link to the company's

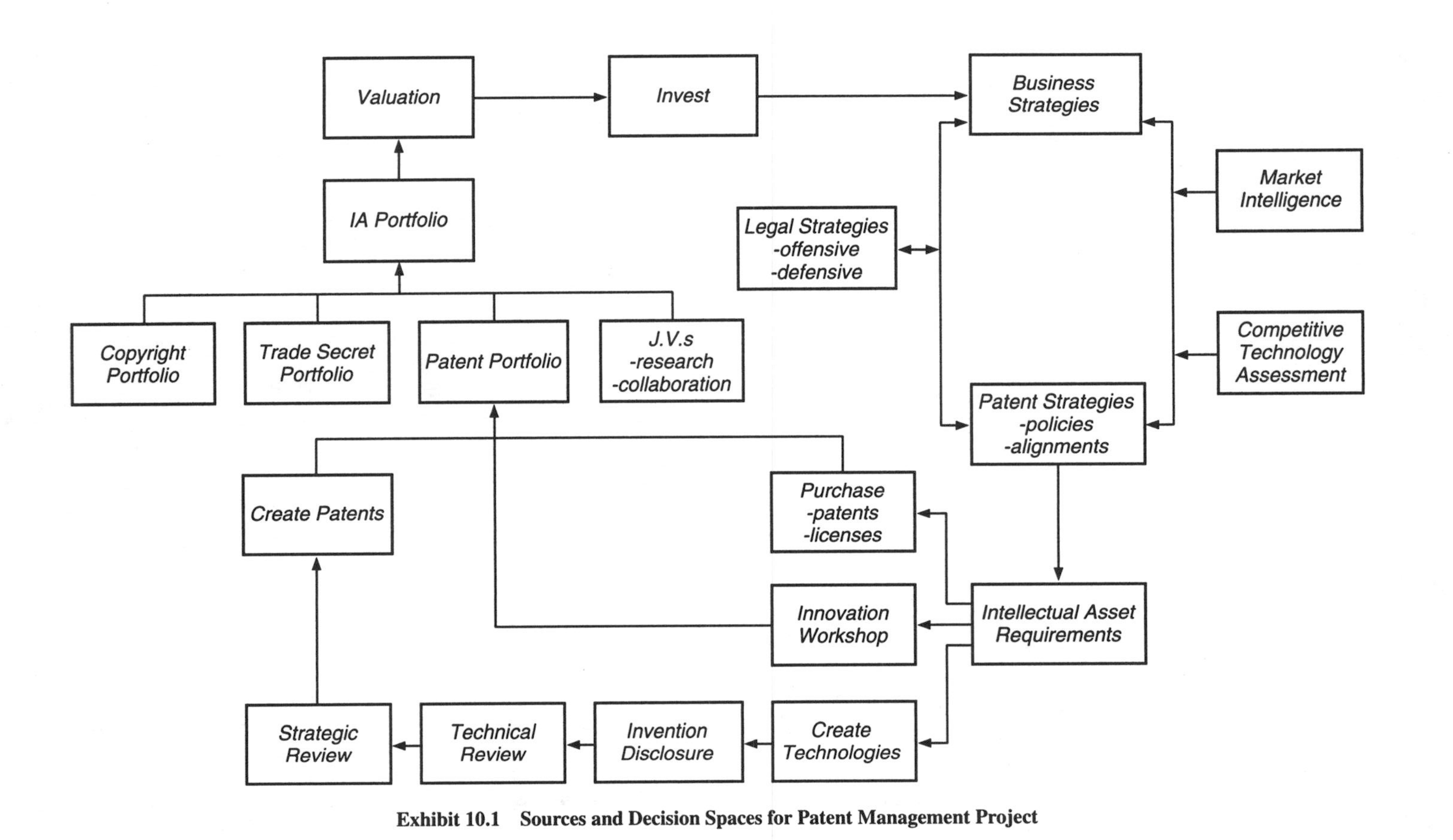

Exhibit 10.1 Sources and Decision Spaces for Patent Management Project

strategic future is severed. Once the product dies, the patent's link to the strategy dies with it.

Business strategists usually identify the migration of products into later versions and establish a link between a company's core competencies and the products they intend to produce. From here one can identify the technology that the business believes is responsible for the company's success in the marketplace. Patents in the database that comprise strategic property should be readily identifiable, and they should be classified based on their relationship to specific strategic objectives.

We have found that inventors can tell us quite easily what the alternatives are to a given technology; they can also explain the key future technologies or events which, if they were to come to fruition, would render the present invention and its alternatives obsolete. While information acquired in this manner is not always absolutely correct,[6] it can offer much insight when reviewed later—even after the product utilizing the patented technology is long gone. As strategies evolve, this information may be used to find candidates for licensing and/or sale.

The Business Purpose Field

In addition to assets revolving around core competencies, well-run businesses attempt to identify technology areas that are being investigated by their current and future competitors. Where the business is focusing on such "market strategic technology"[7] challenges and securing market strategic patents, the database should identify with the particular market strategic goal behind each such asset in the portfolio. While identifying known competitors using similar technology is often impractical, one useful approach is to identify the "business purpose" envisioned for the patent. Obvious business purposes include reference to potential licensing candidates or protection against particular types of competitors. Where a patent covers technology that potentially will be included in an industry standard, the business purpose "field" should make reference to the standard. Identifying the standard by name allows nearly automatic correlation to subsequent standards and to new products that might use the technology.

If a patent is part of a larger group of patents designed to create an obstacle in the aggregate for copiers, the business purpose for each patent should be the same, allowing for easy grouping of the related patents. Subsequent licensing activities or cost-cutting measures can then treat these patents as a group.

The business purpose field should, once again, be easy to update so that it will reflect the current asset value of the portfolio. In our experience, the business purpose field is more useful when the inputs come from a known set of possibilities. We use a lookup table, adding new terms only when the existing candidates fail to adequately describe the purpose. Exhibit 10.2 is one input view from the database which illustrates how lookup tables may be used. For nearly every field, the input derives from a pull-down menu (▣) of choices.[8] Even the inventors' names (collected on a different form) are pulled down from a common address book, saving the inventor time and ensuring that the data is consistent throughout the database. This practice forces our organization to be more disciplined with our entries into the database. One can recognize that the database is far more useful when the metrics used to assess value are closely associated with the input fields. This is the goal of our pull-down fields. While this practice requires much more effort in the beginning, it forces us to understand new technologies and products as they evolve. Wherever possible, we try to use lookup tables in place of ad hoc entries.

Market Intelligence and Competitive Technology in the Database

Market intelligence and competitive technology assessment are implied in market strategic technology activities. Both are fundamental to any well-designed busi-

Rock. Case No.: [REF] **Division:** [REF] **Bus. Area:** [REF] **Status:** [REF]	**Inventors:** [REF]	**Ser. No.:** [REF] **Pat. No.:** [REF] **Filed:** [REF] **Issued:** [REF]

Title: [REF] **Current Rockwell Technical Rank:** [REF] **Current Rockwell Strategic Rank:** [REF]

Technology:	**U.S. Class:** [REF]
Product:	**Int. Class:** [REF]

Abstract: [REF]

U.S. Maintenance Actions

Received	Filed	Status	Last Action	Action Due	Due Date	Last Date
[REF]	[REF]	[CALC]	[REF]	[CALC]	[CALC]	[CALC]

Foreign Maintenance Actions

Exhibit 10.2 Model Lookup Table

Foreign Filing	Foreign Filed	Foreign Status	Foreign Last Action	Foreign Action Due	Due Date	Last Date
Germany	[REF]	[CALC]	[CALC]	[CALC]	[CALC]	[CALC]
Japan	[REF]	[CALC]	[CALC]	[CALC]	[CALC]	[CALC]
U.K.	[REF]	[CALC]	[CALC]	[CALC]	[CALC]	[CALC]
France	[REF]	[CALC]	[CALC]	[CALC]	[CALC]	[CALC]
		[CALC]	[CALC]	[CALC]	[CALC]	[CALC]

Enforceability:	**Excludability:**	**Previous Action:** [CALC]
Business Use:	**Commercial Pot.:**	**Action Due:** [CALC]

Cost to Maintain as a Foreign Patent until Expiration: [CALC]	**End Date:** [CALC]
Cost to Maintain as a U.S. Patent until Expiration: [CALC]	**End Date:** [CALC]

Sunk costs to File and Maintain Patent to Date: [CALC]

Problem Solved: [REF]

Obsoleting Technology or Event(s):

Primary Technology:

Sub-Technology:

Product: **1.** **2.** **3.**

Entered: Bruce Cox @ 07/15/96 07:46 AM

Modified: Bruce Cox @ 07/15/96 07:49 AM

Revision History:

Revised: No Edit Date

Exhibit 10.2 ***(Continued)***

ness strategy and, likewise, to intellectual asset management. If the business strategy relies on particular market intelligence, this information should be part of the database. By including this information, the database not only becomes useful for evaluation of candidates for patenting, but it may be used later to identify patents with licensing value as the market evolves.

Business Strategy as a Destination

We stated above that a corporation's business strategy is a primary source of information for the patent management database. The database can also provide highly relevant and useful information for managers formulating business strategies. Some consultants have opined that, eventually, companies will consider their collection of intellectual assets before the business considers overall strategy. While no company appears to be there yet, the database must anticipate the increasing role of patent assets in development of business strategies.

Where correctly designed and implemented, the database can be a ready source of information for business managers to determine where the protected assets in their company reside and where they do *not* reside. With this information, these managers are able to more accurately assess the risks and benefits associated with their decisions.

Invention Disclosure

As previously stated, the process by which inventions are disclosed to the company is closely linked to the quality of the portfolio. Efforts to recreate the patent database will not be successful without visiting the invention disclosure process itself. Not only is the invention disclosure a ready source of relevant information, but a poorly crafted disclosure process discourages inventors from making the effort at all. The key factor with disclosure of inventions is the comfort level the inventors feel with the system. Developing a more easily used disclosure form not only pays off with more useful information—you also get more disclosures! The ready availability of electronic mail, the Internet (in our case "intranet"), and so-called "groupware" applications such as Lotus Notes™ provide plenty of options for disclosure process renovation. One should resist forcing inventors to learn a new system, because usually they will not tell you if the process hinders them—they will simply not use it. There is no substitute for an easy-to-use electronic disclosure filing system combined with zealous proselytizing as to the benefits of its use.

Technical and Strategic Review of Inventions

Patents are not cheap. Filing one patent in the United States and Europe will easily exceed $80K[9], even without including maintenance costs, which easily double the filing costs if the patent is maintained to term. And this estimate does not consider time invested by the inventor during preparation and prosecution. But, *failing* to file a patent can be far more costly, for obvious reasons. Even so, most companies review and file patents on an ad hoc basis, without recording the rationale (in some retrievable format) before a file or discard decision is made. By formalizing the review process and linking it to the patent in the database, this information is available later. Details that are usually forgotten are useful later to assess the value of the patent as well as for feedback for the review process itself.

Exhibit 10.3 is one example of how the review process might address pertinent issues.

Exhibit 10.3 Review Process

Completed by Peer Group

1. Docket number ____________Title____________
2. Detectability—How hard would it be to detect the invention in a competitor's product? How would we detect it?
3. Is the invention or will the invention be used in our products? If yes, go to *a, b, c*
   a Which products?
   b How can we use the benefits of the invention as a marketing tool? Is there a cost to using it?
   c How long will the invention be useful to us or our competitors?
4. Will competitors be interested in or need this technology?
5. Is the invention related to any standards activities (official or unofficial)?
6. Summarize why the invention should or should not be patented:
7. Technical merit (1–3 ranking):____________
   1= A significant advance which allows for very few feasible technological alternatives with the same benefits.
   2= A moderate advance which allows for few feasible technological alternatives with the same benefits.
   3= An advance in technology which allows for few feasible technological alternatives with the same benefits.
   NA = Many feasible technological alternatives exist with the same benefits.

Completed by Invention Review Committee

8. Strategic value (*A–C* ranking):____________
   A= key strategic area
   B= strategic area
   C= area of product interest

Those present at review:
Date:____________Appraiser:

SUMMARY

The better intellectual property is understood, the more effectively it may be exploited. Due to the unique nature of these assets, traditional methods of cataloguing, evaluating, and valuing are not adequate. By focusing on the company's strategic plan, a database can be created whereby these assets can be managed to be useful tools for business management.

NOTES

1 See 15 USC Sec. 3710 and 48 CFR 27.302.

2 Patrick Sullivan and S. Fox, "Establishing an Out-Licensing Activity," in *Technology Licensing: Corporate Strategies for Maximizing Value,* eds. R. Parr and P. Sullivan (New York: John Wiley & Sons, Inc., 1996).

3 Thomas A. Stewart, "Your Company's Most Valuable Asset: Intellectual Capital," *Fortune* (October 3, 1994).

4 Modern markets are obviously too complex to be defined in terms of competitors only. See J. P. O'Shaughnessy, "Strategy for the Times: Intellectual Property Can Drive Corporate Profitability," in

Technology Licensing. O'Shaughnessy uses terms such as "substitutor" and "complimentor" to describe the complicated competition model found in today's markets.

5 Contact Brian Silverman from ICMG.

6 Inventors, as a rule, tend to see the world in terms of their inventions. Where a product fails for reasons related to technology, it usually, but not always, comes as a surprise to technologists. Inventors are often aware, however, of the alternatives to *their* technologies and can usually point out the drawbacks of alternatives with relative ease.

7 See O'Shaughnessy, "Strategy for the Times," Note 4.

8 "[REF]" indicates that this field is supplied from a referring form; "[CALC]" indicates that this field is derived from other inputs.

9 A. Lawrence, "Patents for Profit," in Computer Business Review Online (vol. 3, no. 8) [cited August 1995].

11

Intellectual Property Management: From Theory to Practice

Stephen P. Fox

Hewlett-Packard Company

THE NEW CONTEXT

Intellectual capital has become a trendy term in the '90s. Although the popularity of the term is only a few years old, there are already numerous books and seminars on this topic. Law firms, accounting firms, consulting firms, universities, and professional groups are all involved. We have moved from a society based on nuts-and-bolts manufacturing to one based much more on human brainpower and other intangibles, and it seems that everyone has an opinion on this subject.

What follows includes a description of how the precepts of intellectual capital management are actually practiced in a large multinational organization such as Hewlett-Packard Company, but first a little background is in order. Suppose that company stock is selling at $60/share and there are a billion shares outstanding. The market value of the company would then be $60 billion. At the same time, however, suppose that the book value of the company, including things like land, buildings, machinery, inventory, and cash, is on the order of $15 billion. What accounts for the $45 billion difference between market value and book value? One answer: *intellectual capital.*

A number of institutions are looking at ways to quantify intellectual capital, including the Securities and Exchange Commission. The challenge is to figure out how to put values on intangible assets in financial statements. Ultimately, this may turn out to be a good idea, but it is not likely to happen anytime soon because it would interfere with years of accounting tradition. Currently, there are no standards and only fuzzy measures for valuing intangibles; hence, there would be fertile ground for shareholder lawsuits if any financial reporting were attempted.

Meanwhile, taking more of a liberal arts approach, intellectual capital has been defined as "knowledge that can be converted into profit."[1] There are two broad categories: *human capital* and *intellectual assets.*

To grasp the notion of human capital, let me relate an anecdote. During an annual Hewlett-Packard service awards lunch, the audience was asked how much someone would pay for the company if it were put up for sale. Dollar amounts were called out from the audience: $20 billion, $50 billion, $90 billion. The question was changed a little and asked again: How much would the company sell for if none of its employees were included in the deal? There was a brief silence, followed by a general consensus that the company would not be worth very much at all. The point had been made. A very large part of company value is inherent in the people who work for it and the knowledge they possess. They are the human capital component of intellectual capital.

Human capital represents the know-how and institutional memory about matters of importance to the company, matters such as the creation of innovations. Also included are things described by terms such as *intra-organizational capabilities, dynamic networking,* and the *cross-correlation of knowledge.* All of these forms of human capital are of considerable value, but they are difficult to capture, quantify, and measure. They don't fit well into the accounting world because accountants report what they can easily see, an approach that sometimes misses the mark.

Another component of intellectual capital is called *intellectual assets.* These are slightly more tangible and may be defined as the quantified, physical descriptions of specific knowledge to which the company can assert ownership. Generally speaking, such knowledge relates to three categories: (1) commercializable products, processes, and services; (2) customer relationships, agreements, and history; and (3) structure-related things like plans, guidelines, and procedures. From a functional standpoint, they relate to a wide variety of "complementary business assets," such as supply side logistics, research and development projects, patents, manufacturing techniques, advertising programs, and distribution channels.

Lastly, we come to the subcategory of intellectual assets that is more familiar, namely *intellectual property.* These are assets protected by specific bodies of laws directed, for example, to patents, trademarks, copyrights, and trade secrets. Some of these have been called our "constitutionally enshrined golden eggs," particularly when used to create product differentiation in an increasingly competitive world where commoditization is becoming dominant. The traditional wealth in land, natural resources, and industrial/agricultural capital has given way to new wealth in intelligence, information, and knowledge. Just as food and manufactured goods can be packaged and sold, there are ways to package knowledge for commercial benefit, using the intellectual property laws. Considering the vast scope of this topic, the focus of this chapter is on the kinds of intellectual property protectable by patents.

A STARTING POINT: FOCUS ON PROCESS

Most assessments of intellectual property (IP) start with an IP audit. Usually this entails a broad-scope examination of corporate operations using various checklists and templates to identify what is being done in protecting inventions, trademarks, copyrightable materials, and trade secrets. Auditors will superimpose recommended practices onto corporate activities to look for holes and find out where there are inadequate measures for protection. Oftentimes this is achieved using a scatter-shot approach. The recommendations for improving IP protection may be good ones and, in fact, once put in place may serve corporate purposes quite well for a while. However, it is important to recognize that for optimum effectiveness, IP protection schemes need to last for years, not just a few months after implementation. The key is to develop adequate *processes:* (1) that are easily identifiable and simple enough to be remembered; and (2) that have clearly designated long-term owners to assure perpetuation.

In IP protection process design, it is helpful to view industrial activity from several different vantage points. A few are discussed below:

1. There are two classes of companies operating on different paradigms. One type of company is small enough and simple enough in structure that employees can still enjoy frequent direct contact through all management levels. Projects tend to be more focused and more rapidly implemented. There are fewer products and an invention on one of them is likely to be readily identifiable and easily visible throughout the organization. A patent on such an invention is likely to be viewed as very important. The other type of company is larger, and activities are diffused over a broader range of market interest. More patents are obtained on more products. While a single invention covering a product may be just as important as for smaller companies, the inventions and the patents on them are often viewed more collectively.
2. Innovation can occur several different ways. Innovation may begin as part of a linear process, sometimes starting with a major scientific breakthrough. It then moves from idea to design, then development, then production, then finally to market. The assumption is that with a major scientific breakthrough, everything else takes care of itself. The breakthroughs are relatively easy to identify and protect with patents. More often, however, in the current competitive environment, there is no clear scientific breakthrough; and the focus of innovation is more on making incremental improvements. The innovation process is less linear and considerably more interactive, where the ball passes back and forth among the various players both inside and outside of the company. Within this environment, inventions are more of a challenge to identify, yet patents on the incremental advances are important to competitiveness.
3. Inventions are often made at the same time by several people right after the logical foundations for them fall into place. Sometimes there are

> simultaneous discoveries made by two or more people working completely independently of one another, where each is ignorant of the other's work. Such simultaneous discoveries happen because they depend on the development of enabling technology before they can be completed. One interesting example of simultaneous discoveries resulting from the appearance of an enabling technology is first-time human heart transplants independently achieved by Barnard, Shumway, and Kantrawitz all during a short six-week period from 1967 to 1968. The enabling technology was the development of the heart/lung machine that made the surgery possible. Other examples of simultaneous and independent discoveries include the airplane (the Wright Brothers and Dumont in 1903), the telephone (Bell and Gray in 1876), the telegraph (five inventors, including Morse, about 1837), and the telescope (Jansen, Lippershev, and Metius in 1608).[2]

We are in an age when innovation is proceeding more rapidly than ever and where the effective use of information is vital in developing processes to capture and protect innovative ideas. At Hewlett-Packard, for example, over one-half of the order dollars in any given year are derived from new products introduced in just the last two years. In this environment, the cycle from product research to maturity is quite short, and the challenge is to design IP protection processes that can keep up with the fast pace.

Today, all intellectual property is more important than ever. The power of patents in particular has been expanded over the last 15 years. Companies are devoting more time to futuristic positioning to preempt competition and to ensure the right to compete. The single most important aspect of succeeding in this fast-paced environment is the creation of durable and effective *processes* that capture new innovations and adequately protect them.

THE ROLE OF R&D AND IP ACTIVITY IN A COMPETITIVE ECONOMIC MODEL

Research and development (R&D) plays an important role in the overall economic model of a successful business. To create effective IP protection processes, the underlying assumptions on which a going business is based should be specifically identified. First, there is the assumption that a business has the freedom to compete in the marketplace; second, that the research and development activity will lead to something commercially feasible; third, that there is or will be significant results from the R&D, such as a breakthrough or creation of a dominant design; and, fourth, that the company has control of the complementary assets that surround the R&D activity. As noted earlier, complementary assets include patents, manufacturing capability, advertising effectiveness, and product distribution channels. If any of these factors are missing, there will likely be impediments to integrating the results of R&D into a successful business strategy.

The typical activities in product life cycle management are shown in Exhibit 11.1.

Exhibit 11.1 Activities in Product Life Cycle

Phase	IP Activity
• Set Requirements/Plan	Conduct IP right-to-use searches
• Study/Define	Conduct IP right-to-use assessments
• Specify/Design	Gather invention disclosures; hold invention review meetings; file patent applications; obtain necessary IP licenses
• Develop/Test	Perfect other IP rights (e.g., software copyrights)
• Ramp-up	
• Enhance/Support	Assess enhancements for IP protection

Some steps in the cycle are more intensive than others with respect to R&D and the protection of intellectual property. For example, in the early phases, the emphasis is on assuring freedom to compete in the marketplace by conducting IP right-to-use searches of the patent art and, then, conducting assessments of the patents found as a result of the searches to assure that there are no impediments to introducing products on the market. The most labor-intensive patent activity occurs during the third phase (Specify/Design), which comprises two principal activities, namely: (1) identifying inventions made with respect to any given product under development and filing patent applications on those inventions; and (2) obtaining any patent licenses from other parties that may be necessary to assure that the product can be marketed without interference with the rights of others.

INVENTOR INCENTIVES AS PART OF THE PROCESS

Sometimes it is a challenge to inspire inventors working on a project to disclose their inventions to the legal department. They may have the feeling that their contributions are obvious and, hence, not of value from a patent standpoint, or that their contributions are not good enough to rise to the level of patentability. There once was a well-known television commentator who would close a weekly hour-long TV magazine program with a five-minute monologue, and one time he focused on the issue of inventions. His hypothesis was that all of the "good" inventions had already been invented, for example, the telephone, the airplane, and the light bulb, and the only ones left were the "bad" inventions, which inventors kept on inventing. Examples he gave included tongue-in-cheek things like refrigerator wrap that is hard to get out of the box and that sticks to itself when finally extracted. In this same category, he put spot removers that just spread the spot around and don't really remove it, and organizer cabinets with little drawers that don't do a thing for organization if you're not already an organized person.

It is important to dispel the notion that there is nothing good left to invent and encourage inventors to give themselves the benefit of the doubt when assessing whether they have invented something. Inventions are not always readily apparent to those involved in the day-to-day rigors of product research. Usually, there is no lightning bolt, "flash of genius," or brightly burning light bulb to signal a new idea. Inventor encouragement should be kept in mind when designing effective IP protection processes.

The timely capture of inventions from researchers is very important. Technologists are busier than ever keeping up with rapid advancement of technology and at the same time meeting their personal productivity requirements. Work pressures often result in low prioritization of time for writing invention disclosures and submitting them to the legal department. Under the law, there is usually a short window of opportunity to file a patent application after an invention is made, and thereafter, the right to a patent may be lost forever. Lack of timely action may compromise a company's position and create long-term adverse impacts. Cooperation and motivation of the inventors is needed to ensure that the inventions are disclosed in a timely manner and that patents can be obtained on them.

Traditionally, inventors have been expected to write invention disclosures during the course of research, and this activity has been considered part of the job. Some companies still rely on this understanding to capture and protect inventions. However, many companies recognize that more may be needed to motivate the timely submission of invention disclosures, particularly if the drafting of a disclosure is going to be done on an inventor's personal time because the pressures of project deadlines leave little time during the course of a normal day. A common solution is to create an inventor-incentive program, which rewards inventors with cash payments. Such programs serve to increase the number of invention disclosures and assure their timely submission. In addition, these programs can be used to encourage disclosures in certain specifically identified technology areas where more patents are needed in the portfolio.

The inventor-incentive program developed by Hewlett-Packard Company includes the following elements:

1. Adoption on a business-by-business basis: A program is usually approved for one year at a time, with renewals as appropriate. This provides the business with an opportunity to measure results annually and make modifications as needed.
2. Awards paid to inventors: There is a small cash award on submitting an invention disclosure; a larger cash award when a patent application is filed on the invention; and a personalized plaque when the patent is granted.
3. Recognition: This is strongly encouraged in public fora, peer groups, annual banquets, etc.
4. Administration: The financial aspects are handled by the business R&D function, while eligible inventor identification and the patent plaques are handled by the legal department.

There are two features of the HP program that may differ somewhat from programs adopted by other companies. The one-year term with a sunset provision, coupled with renewals as appropriate, provides greater program flexibility. Also, in the U.S. cash payments to the inventors are made only on submission of the invention disclosure and on filing the patent application, whereas on the later patent grant, the award is a personalized plaque. The front-end emphasis on cash incentives serves to motivate the inventor at the critical time when the contours of the invention are being shaped before the application is filed. Overall, this type of program has achieved considerable success in increasing the number of invention disclosures submitted and permitting more selectivity of important inventions for protection by patents.

INVENTION AND PATENT REVIEW COMMITTEES

The review of invention disclosures and consideration of other matters involving obtaining and using patents is an activity that should involve business managers, R&D management, and intellectual property attorneys in joint efforts. It is important that all participants have a broad-scope understanding of the objectives in obtaining patents. These are preferably communicated widely within the company in a variety of ways. At Hewlett-Packard Company, it is generally understood that patents are obtained for the following reasons:

1. To protect the company's ideas and innovations from being copied
2. To obtain design freedom, such as through patent license agreements with other companies
3. To preclude others from patenting inventions first developed within the company
4. To generate an optimal return on the company's R&D expenditures.

It is helpful for inventors throughout the company to have an understanding of some of the criteria used in determining whether an invention is likely to be patentable, before an invention disclosure is submitted for review. From the inventor's standpoint, there are exemplary questions that he or she can ask before drafting an invention disclosure. If the answer to any of them is yes, the invention is a candidate for patentability review. A list widely disseminated within the company is as follows:

1. Have I developed a new product, feature, or process that seems unique?
2. Did my work produce results greater than expected?
3. Have I used a known technology, circuit, or process in an unusual way?
4. Is my development a new step in a rapidly changing technology?
5. Is my development in an area where different technologies are converging?
6. Did I make an improvement to an existing technology, product, or process?
7. When I discussed my work with my coworkers, did they express surprise at the results achieved or the approach used?
8. Did my work result in something being better/faster/cheaper?

At Hewlett-Packard, invention review and the consideration of other patent matters takes place as part of a patent coordination process that involves R&D management and the legal department working together, with additional input from business general managers. The focus is on maintaining a strong link between patenting activities and the company's business strategies. In fact, the entire process is frequently referred to throughout the company as "Strategic Patenting." The process itself centers on patent coordinator meetings held periodically, preferably each quarter, for each business entity that is engaged in R&D. There are a least three people at a typical patent coordinator meeting: an IP attorney responsible for the particular business, a legal department manager with oversight responsibility, and an engineering manager who is appointed to his or her role by the entity general manager to represent the R&D function and technology management aspects of the process. Although the meetings generally occur according to a schedule, they may take place on an ad hoc basis if special attention is needed with respect to any particular invention disclosure, such as when an invention may involve an eminent critical date for publication or product introduction.

An overview of the patent coordination process is shown in Exhibit 11.2. There are six steps, some of which represent subprocesses in the overall process, as will be described shortly in more detail:

At the patent coordinator meetings, the following issues are considered:

1. Whether to seek patent protection in the United States or elsewhere and, if so, what priority should be assigned to the filing of patent applications

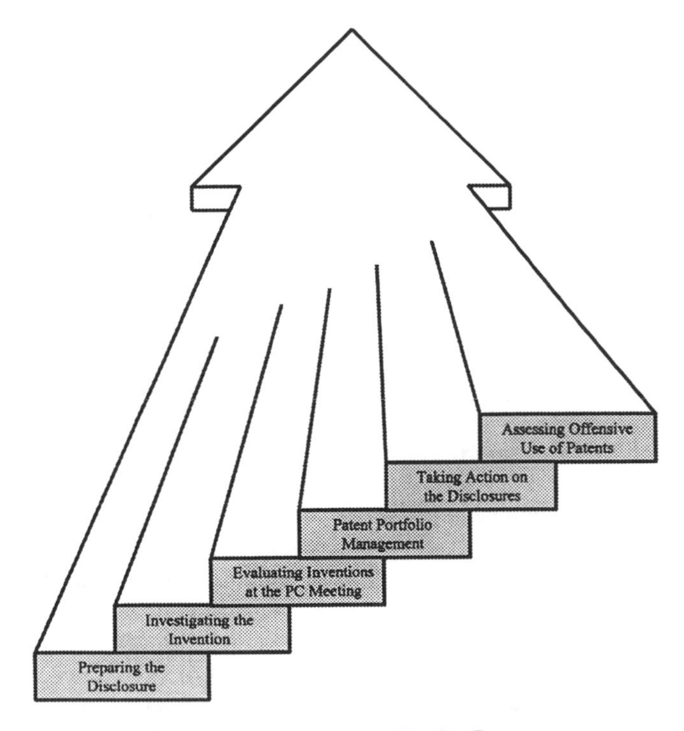

Exhibit 11.2 Patent Coordination Process

2. Whether to suspend further consideration of some inventions until additional information can be developed or until further experimental activity is completed
3. Whether there are opportunities for identifying and patenting futuristic developments
4. Whether to pay the government maintenance fees required to keep previously filed patent applications and issued patents in force in various countries throughout the world
5. Whether to maintain certain concepts as trade secrets or, instead, to publish them, if patent protection is not to be pursued
6. Whether new R&D projects may require patent right-to-use or clearance searches, to identify any patents owned by other parties that may cover proposed products or processes
7. Whether to consider using patents offensively against competitors

The invention evaluation activity at the meeting is diagrammed in Exhibit 11.3. Note that the meeting includes input from a number of sources. Exhibit 11.3 focuses on the processing of invention disclosures and omits some of the other activities that occur in the meeting as previously listed. Each invention disclosure is reviewed in light of established evaluation guidelines and checklists, as well as technology priorities that are provided by the business general manager on a survey form, as described shortly in more detail. Patent application filing recommendations are made both by the engineering managers responsible for the technology and by the IP attorneys responsible for procuring patent protection. Engineering management is usually represented by the designated patent coordinator for the particular entity; however, there may be participation by multiple engineering managers, depending on the technologies involved. For each invention under review, a decision is made whether to file a patent application, keep the invention as a trade secret, or publish the invention disclosure to establish it as prior art with respect to potentially similar work being conducted by others. As shown by the decision tree, for those invention disclosures on which patent applications will be filed, a filing priority is set, for example, to file immediately or to file within a reasonable time.

Occasionally, invention disclosures are put on hold and reevaluated at a subsequent patent coordinator meeting after additional information becomes available about the feasibility or patentability of the invention. Invention disclosures which do not fall within the decision tree, shown in Exhibit 11.3, are generally inactivated.

In assessing an invention disclosure, key considerations are technical and commercial merit, the projected life of the technology, the strategic importance to the overall patent portfolio, patent cross-license activities, the comparative value of maintaining the invention as a trade secret, and the prospects of detecting infringement by another company. All of these factors are reflected in the evaluation guidelines and checklists which explore in detail how the invention will be *used,* how the invention will *benefit* the company, and how the company will benefit from a *patent* on the invention.

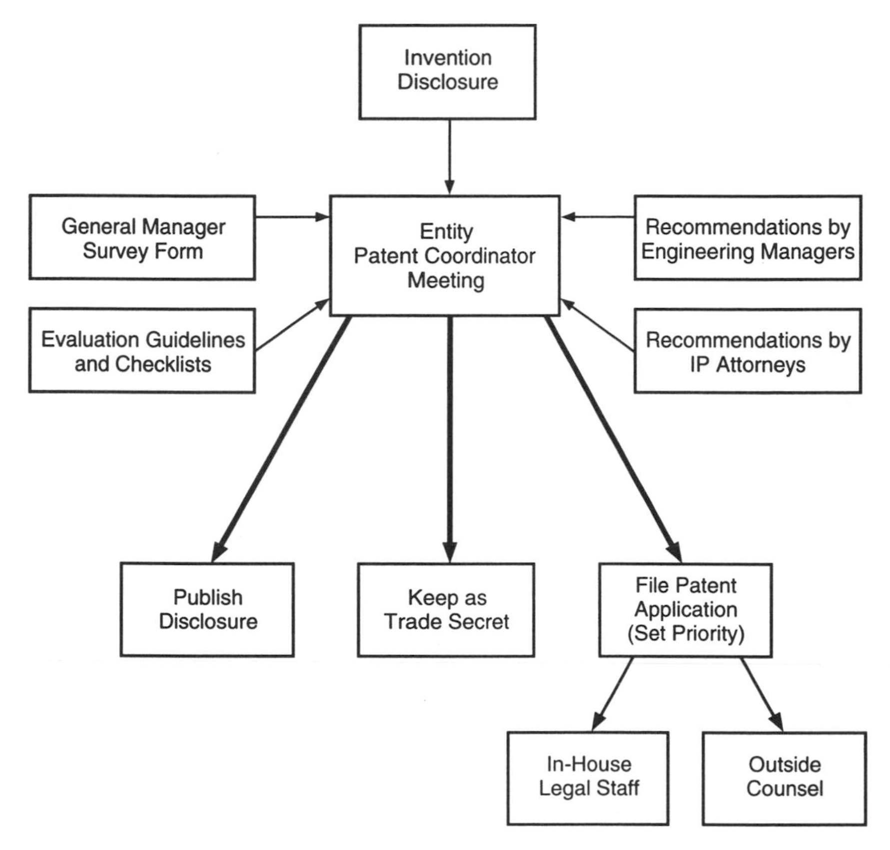

Exhibit 11.3 Invention Review Process

Exhibit 11.3 also shows the general manager survey form as one of the inputs to the patent coordinator meeting. The survey form helps to maintain the focus on invention selection and patenting of inventions that have high strategic value for the company. The survey form is sent to general managers who are responsible for the different company businesses, along with a request that the manager complete the form to provide his or her perspective for the patenting process. The form serves as an additional guideline to optimize invention selection during the patent coordinator meeting. An exemplary version of the form is shown below in Exhibit 11.4.

To help build a strong patent portfolio, the survey form has two parts: the top part directed to strategic technologies/products for the next five years, and the bottom part directed to new technologies and futuristic patenting opportunities that may preempt competitors or fill technology gaps. The preemption aspect is time sensitive and the survey answers help participants in the patent coordinator meeting to take prompt action in identifying inventions to be patented, so as to reduce exposure of the company to patents that might be obtained by others and used against the company.

With regard to the top part of the survey form, strategic technologies/products are listed in the first column and then prioritized using a weighting scheme called

Exhibit 11.4 Patenting Survey Form

STRATEGIC TECHNOLOGIES/ PRODUCTS	$100 TEST	NON-U.S. PROTECTION
List the technologies or products that have the highest strategic importance over the next five years. 1 2 3 4 5	Allocate $100 to pay for patenting activity among all listed.	Name non-U.S. countries where patents should be obtained.

NEW TECHNOLOGIES AND FUTURISTIC PATENTING OPPORTUNITIES	RATING
(e.g., to preempt competitors or to fill technology gaps) 1 2 3	Rate potential importance as "high," "likely," or "unknown."

the "$100 test," as shown in the second column. In addition, the third column provides an opportunity for identification of significant countries outside the United States where patent protection is deemed desirable. Additional considerations for filing patent applications outside the United States are contained in the evaluation guidelines and checklists, which comprise one of the inputs to the patent coordinator meeting. Note that the survey form and the discussion herein are directed to inventions that originate in the United States. For business entities and R&D activities in other countries, the survey form and the guidelines/checklists are modified appropriately for inventions and patents that originate in those countries.

Effective patent coordination calls for considerable interaction among the participants at the coordination meeting. In Exhibit 11.3, this is represented by the boxes that refer to recommendations from the engineering managers and the IP attorneys. At HP, the patent coordinator meetings are replicated many times a year in order to adequately serve the needs of the company's numerous R&D facilities.

USE OF OUTSIDE COUNSEL

Once it has been determined that a patent application will be filed on an invention, the next step is to decide whether the application will be drafted by the in-house legal staff or by outside counsel, as shown by the decision tree in Exhibit 11.3. Generally, the use of an in-house attorney for this purpose is preferable because the attorney possesses unique knowledge of the company's technology, products, and business strategies. However, case volume and in-house attorney workload often dictate that a percentage of the patent applications be prepared by outside counsel. Use of outside counsel should be carefully weighed against the disadvantages that may arise from diminished internal control of a case or the business client's activity. If outside counsel is used, there still should be an in-house attorney primarily responsible for the patent application to ensure that services are properly provided.

The selection and use of outside counsel is itself a subprocess of overall patent coordination. A list of approved outside counsel is maintained by the legal department, and names are added to or removed from the list based on quality of work product, responsiveness, and cost effectiveness. Only outside counsel on the approved list are eligible for drafting patent applications. To ensure uniformity among outside counsel in both administrative and substantive matters, each outside counsel is provided with a set of standardized procedures, including patent forms and an engagement letter agreement setting forth mutual understandings with respect to how the patent application will be prepared. Accompanying these materials, for each case, is a request for quote form that addresses estimated fees for completing the application. It has been found that these outside counsel procedures are not only necessary but quite effective as the volume of patent applications sent outside increases in a decentralized environment where R&D and patent procurement take place in many different locations.

BROAD-BASED PATENT PORTFOLIO MANAGEMENT

As reflected in the survey form previously described, there is a broad, more futuristic aspect of the patent coordination process, which goes beyond the primary focus on evaluating invention disclosures that result from current research and development efforts. At Hewlett-Packard Company, this approach is called *patent portfolio management.* It is part of the overall process and is somewhat collateral to the more traditional invention review and selection activities. Patent portfolio management (PPM) is a form of intellectual property asset management. Fundamentally, it differs from the invention review process in having more drivers in addition to the invention disclosure. Also, process participants include more technology futurists in the company businesses. The goal of PPM is not only to pursue patents for inventions actually used in products, but also to patent commercially viable alternatives and conceivable future variations of the technology relating to any given product line. Patent portfolio management entails analyzing technologies and patents of competitors and inventing and patenting to both fill identified technology gaps and to secure exclusive rights to technologies that may become important in the future. Patents have long lives, and there are potentially significant advantages to looking ahead and perceiving technology trends and market needs and then obtaining key patents in these areas.

Opportunities for PPM are periodically considered at patent coordination meetings. The patent coordinator and entity IP attorney determine when a PPM team may be needed for a particular technology or product line. A PPM team will typically acquire a broad-scope perspective to understand the role that technology plays in a particular business and to understand whether company patents protect the key technologies. Next, there are efforts to identify significant competitors, learn their technology strategies, and monitor their patent output. Also, the team will work to identify technology holes that need to be plugged to improve competitiveness and to direct resources to these areas for R&D and/or for patent procurement. Sometimes, this activity leads to synergistic technology alliances with other companies or to obtaining technology licenses from other parties. In summary, PPM initiatives include the following activities:

1. Predicting the future, i.e., looking outward and forward at technology trends and evaluating likely future courses of action in identified business areas
2. Searching for key developments that will be needed to permit inventing and patenting early, before others do, or publishing to prevent patents by others
3. Identifying critical patents of others so that they can be designed around, invalidated, or licensed in a timely manner

SUSTAINING, DISCONTINUOUS, AND DISRUPTIVE TECHNOLOGIES

Patent portfolio management process techniques have considerable potential when viewed in the context of how new technologies and products are developed, particularly in a fast-moving, high-technology industry. A common view is that product improvements proceed incrementally, driven largely by customer needs and market demand. Companies that already have an established position in a given product area tend to be the most effective at creating these incremental improvements, because there is high motivation to devote both human and financial resources to sustain an existing customer base. Ultimately, however, evolutionary development may be interrupted by new creativity, discontinuous change, and disruptive technologies.

Numerous case histories have been described by those who have studied these phenomena.[3] In the typewriter industry, discontinuities occurred when development progressed from manual to electric typewriters, then to dedicated word processors and, finally, to personal computers. In the lighting industry, oil lamps went to gas lamps; then came incandescent lamps, first carbon filament and then tungsten filament; and, finally, flourescent lamps. In the imaging industry, discontinuities occurred as development went from daguerreotype, to tintype, to wetplate and dryplate photography; then to rollfilm, electronic imaging, and, finally, to digital imaging. Similar progressions have been noted in the development of computer disc drives and, more recently, computer client/server products and internet appliances. Two important observations can be gleaned from the commentaries that surround these studies:

1. Discontinuous innovations that supersede and often destroy established core competencies in a given technology usually come from outside the industry.

2. Products that result from disruptive technologies usually have lower performance levels at first and, hence, are not attractive to existing customers, even though ultimately such products may become less expensive, simpler, smaller, etc.

Patent portfolio management recognizes these observations, looks beyond the mainstream research and development activities where most of the money is being spent, and focuses instead on emerging technologies. It is on this landscape that the potential players and their strategies are identified, as are the relative patent positions in the technologies that may become important in the future. Technological progress often provides more capability than a market needs at any given point in time. Yet, from a patent standpoint, one can look at future markets and seek advance patent coverage, which is market based, covering products of all of the following: (1) competitors and substitutors; (2) product complementors; (3) downstream customers' customers; and (4) upstream suppliers.[4]

The value of patents in this area is high, because they are likely to cover discontinuous or disruptive technologies that fall within the strategic product development path of the company in future years or that may cover developments of more nimble newcomers to the market. In the latter case, such patents become useful vehicles in negotiating rights in new technologies, through patent cross-licenses, for example.

OFFENSIVE USE OF PATENTS

Exhibit 11.2 shows that one of the steps in the overall patent coordination process involves assessing the offensive use of company patents. The offensive use of patents is both a business and legal issue and involves decision makers in all business functions that could be affected, including participants in the patent coordination process as well as others in marketing, manufacturing, and senior management. The patent coordinator meeting provides a forum for assessing whether offensive use of patents should be considered in any given situation. Since assertions of patent infringement could lead to litigation, there should first be efforts to conduct rigorous cost/benefit and risk/reward analyses before asserting a patent. Typically, this involves a multistep process, including characterization of the infringer, determination of company business objectives, evaluation of the particular patent involved, evaluation of the alleged infringers position and any counterclaims or defenses, and preparation of an action plan, followed by implementation. The business objectives may include stopping the infringer's sales or licensing the infringer for royalties.

A collateral aspect of offensive patent use is the establishment of an out-licensing activity to systematically identify company patents that have income generating potential and also to identify target companies that might want or need a license under particular patents. Typical considerations are whether to license core or non-core technologies in strategic or non-strategic markets. The scope of such an activity in terms of required staffing and skill-mix depends on overall corporate purpose.[5]

THE CHALLENGE IN A KNOWLEDGE-BASED COMPANY

In summary, success in the patent area is process intensive. At HP, there are three aspects to this: (1) getting information from the innovators through the use of incentives; (2) building the patent portfolio through the patent coordination process, strategic patenting initiatives, and patent portfolio management; and (3) extracting value from the patent portfolio through assessment of business purposes and the offensive use of patents. Superimposed on these activities is the realization that in a large enterprise, patents come with a cost which is not insubstantial. To maintain cost effectiveness and appropriate focus, there are oft-repeated messages to management emphasizing the need to aggressively file new patent applications on inventions relating to core technologies and key business strategies, and to avoid patents that may not be needed, for example, in some foreign countries. Also, to optimize and control the inexorable growth in expenses to maintain a worldwide patent portfolio that increases in size year by year, emphasis is placed on weeding out on a regular basis any patents that are no longer needed.

The processes described in this chapter did not come about simultaneously. Rather, they were developed over an extended period of time and then refined based on experiences. For companies just starting out in developing patent processes or for those seeking to revitalize existing processes, it is helpful to recognize that trial and error will likely succeed over the endless and careful planning of flawless intellects. Just talking about problems and solutions will not work. It is better to start with prototypes rather than spend too much time writing process specifications. Everyone can relate to a prototype and tell you what is wrong with it, and this in turn permits changes to be made in response to real-world issues.

NOTES

1 See Chapter 1 of this book.

2 Additional examples are provided by Peter Farb in his book *Man's Rise to Civilization As Shown by the Indians of North America* (New York: E. P. Dutton & Co., Inc. 1968).

3 See James M. Utterbach, *Mastering the Dynamics of Innovation* (Boston: Harvard Business School Press, 1994). Also see Clayton M. Christensen, *The Innovator's Dilemma* (Boston: Harvard Business School Press, 1997).

4 Market-based patent strategies are addressed in more detail in *Technology Licensing,* ed. Russell L. Parr and Patrick H. Sullivan (New York: John Wiley & Sons, Inc., 1996). See especially chap. 10, "Strategy for the Times: Intellectual Property Can Drive Corporate Profitability," by James P. O'Shaughnessy.

5 See chap 6, "Establishing an Out-Licensing Activity" by Patrick H. Sullivan and Stephen P Fox in *Technology Licensing,* ibid.

12

Intellectual Capital Development at a Spin-Off Company

Willy Manfroy

Fairfield Resources International, Inc.

Harry Gwinnell

Eastman Chemical Company

In this chapter, we describe how a spin-off company, namely Eastman Chemical Company, is developing its intellectual capital management (ICM) program.

BACKGROUND

Eastman Chemical is a $5 billion USD multinational chemical company. On January 1, 1994, it was spun off from Eastman Kodak as a completely independent company. Eastman Chemical's roots go back to 1920 as a source of raw materials for Kodak's photographic business. Its product line evolved as Kodak's needs for specific intermediates and raw materials grew and diversified. Over the decades, it ventured from methanol (the original product) into photographic intermediates, coating intermediates, chromophores, and polymers such as cellulose acetate derivatives and polyesters. The company's early dependence on Kodak was critical in shaping its intellectual property strategies. Because Eastman's primary goal was to be a reliable and cost effective source of critical components for Kodak's photographic needs, process development rather than product and application development was emphasized early on. Also, because of Kodak's dominance in the photographic area, Eastman minimized its efforts to protect and exploit its intellectual assets. Over the years and with the reduced importance of Kodak as a sole customer, this philosophy changed gradually; but, even in the early 1990s, Eastman had done little to protect its intellectual properties. At that time, Eastman was operating as a separate division (not a subsidiary), and realized that, over the long run, its ties with Kodak would be significantly altered and that the company should prepare for an eventual split.

Eastman revisited its vision and strategies. It reorganized its very structured and pyramidal organization, which was well suited for a diverse manufacturing entity, into a highly matrixed one, shifting its emphasis to globalization and markets (in fact, a hybrid between market and products). Until then, the company's patent strategy had been driven by the manufacturing process; it had little or no foreign coverage and almost no end-use application patents. Intellectual property (IP) management was done with minimal or no input from the different stakeholders within the company and was driven from the top down. In other words, patenting had been a relatively low-priority activity.

Eastman had been drafting, filing, and prosecuting all of its domestic patents in Kingsport, Tennessee. International filings were done by Kodak at its headquarters in Rochester, New York. Trademark activities were handled in Rochester as well. Copyright work was done in Kingsport but without all the required emphasis.

Except in the early 1950s, little or no out-licensing occurred. The major exception was for the process of making cellulose acetate filter tow, which was extensively licensed to Eastman's major competitors in the field. In-licensing was done to develop new manufacturing processes as required. No formal licensing process or licensing strategy was in place. The fewer licenses entered, the happier management was. Knowing this, the licensing and legal departments pursued a risk-avoidance culture.

First Steps

After Eastman adopted its new strategic vision, however, it became imperative to change the company's culture and put in place an intellectual asset management strategy. As a first step and over a period of two years, an IP management process was put in place, based on benchmarking with major chemical producers such as Dow Chemical, Rohm & Haas, and Du Pont. A multifunctional team including technology, patents, research and development, technical service, manufacturing, business, and licensing staff drove the process to completion. Acting in parallel, R&D in concert with the business organizations, as the primary drivers, developed an elaborate innovation process to speed up new product introduction, reduce cycle time, and align innovation with market needs.

Also, as part of the new vision, the company reorganized along four dimensions: business, geography, function, and core competency. Not all these dimensions were equally developed at the start. Core competencies are the few institutionalized competencies that give an organization a sustainable competitive advantage. At the onset, Eastman defined its core competencies rather broadly, including technical (e.g., organic synthesis) and managerial competencies (e.g., site management, customer interface). Most were too broad to be able to manage a strategy around them.

Simultaneously, because the new outward and global look of the company was leading to a mushrooming of outside opportunities, the need to develop or redevelop processes governing outside contacts became apparent. As a result, joint ventures and alliances (JVA), licensing, and confidentiality processes were developed, as well as thorough management training programs for handling alliances.

As all of this was happening, Kodak's board of directors decided to refocus the company on its core businesses. A decision was made early on to spin off the chemical business as a stand-alone company.

Spin-Off

Soon after the spin-off was successfully completed in January 1994, it became apparent that it was necessary to inventory the company's patent portfolio to align it with existing businesses and eliminate unused patents. It was also an excellent opportunity to evaluate the company's overall intellectual property assets. With several starts and stops, this evaluation took approximately two years. Simultaneously, the company probed deeper into its true core technical competencies to develop their strategic management. The resulting assessments led to the definition of the company's technical "engines," which are covered in more detail later.

The final phase of this journey was the integration of all of these efforts into a coherent, companywide intellectual capital management strategy, a process that continues today. The need for that IP management effort was exacerbated by the inability of the company to educate Wall Street and the investing public as to the true nature of its business and of its earning potential. Eastman's business is mostly as a supplier of intermediates that go into such diverse applications as additives for paints, coatings and inks, photographic chemicals, and plastic fabrication. Very few products are recognized by the public except for PET (polyethylene terephtalate), which goes into soft drink container bottles.

We now examine in more detail the key elements of some of the processes that compose the company's intellectual capital, starting with the intellectual property management process, followed with patent mapping, technology engine development, and the licensing, joint ventures, and alliances processes. These processes represent some of the founding blocks needed to establish a comprehensive strategy for intellectual capital management.

THE INTELLECTUAL PROPERTY MANAGEMENT PROCESS

The intellectual property management process was the result of approximately three years work by a patent process quality improvement team. This team had representatives from the company's internal business organizations—research, corporate development, and the legal department. Interestingly, the process that was eventually put in place reflected this same mix in its makeup.

Intellectual Property Management Process Teams

The patent process quality improvement team recommended the formation of intellectual property management teams for each business organization. Each new intellectual property management process team was given the charter to manage international filing, technology disclosure, sampling, priority, and cost strategies from a business organization perspective. Specifically, the team was asked to ensure that:

- The organization's patent strategy matched the organization business strategy
- The patent strategy was adequate
- The international filing recommendations and renewals were relevant and accurate

The team was also to facilitate the movement of ideas to patent assets. An additional benefit of the team was increased intellectual property education for all those involved in the process. Other features of the process were the strong involvement of the business people in the organization and the use of a patent facilitator to energize and oversee the process.

Each team is led by a business organization technology manager who has a technology background but is part of the business organization, a sort of go-between between the research organization and the business organization. The team also includes:

A manager from the research and development area
A technology engine team leader
A legal representative (usually the intellectual property attorney associated with the particular business organization)
A licensing representative
The intellectual property facilitator

A significant factor is the number and variety of people involved. At different points in the process, the participants include the inventor, the inventor's supervisor, the research and development manager, the business organization stakeholder, the intellectual property attorney, the intellectual property facilitator, and a patenting mentor (see Exhibit 12.1).

The patenting mentor is typically a retired Eastman scientist well versed in the patenting process, who assists the inventor with collecting his or her ideas and writing the invention disclosure. Business organization support for the invention is addressed very early on in the process (as can be seen in Exhibit 12.1). The research and development group is also treated as a business organization and given the opportunity to support an invention.

Very early in the process, a meeting is held between the inventor and the attorney who will be drafting the patent application. This meeting helps the inventor at an early stage determine what additional work may be necessary to support the patent application. It also allows the attorney to become more knowledgeable about the invention and to discuss the filing schedule with the inventor.

From that point on, the intellectual property team is involved in (see Exhibit 12.2):

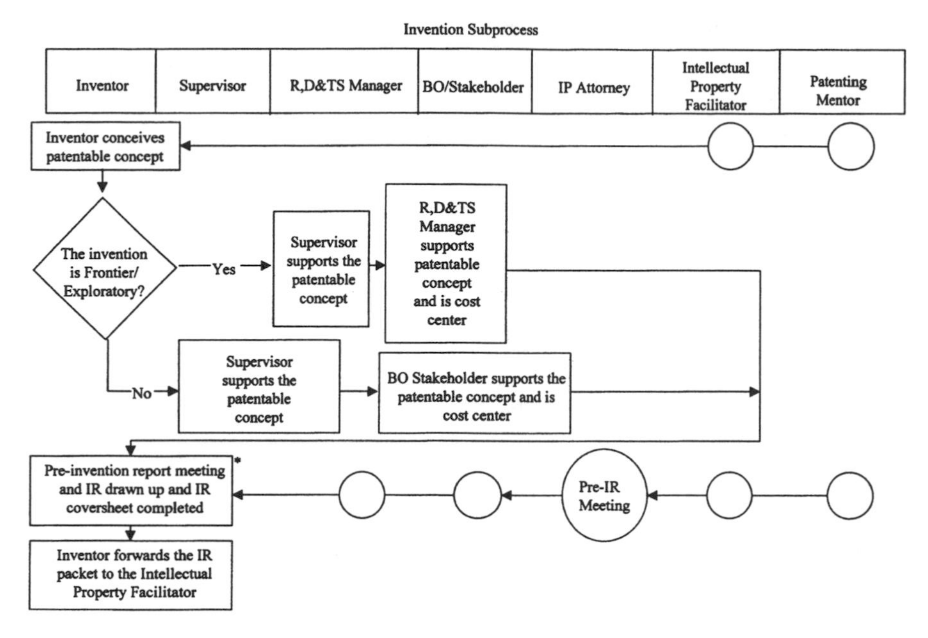

Exhibit 12.1 Overview of Eastman Intellectual Property Process

- Establishing priorities
- Making international filing recommendations
- Raising disclosure and sampling issues
- Reviewing subsequent intellectual property renewals
- Handling related copyright and trademark issues

Although the process was originally designed at a business organization level, it is now managed by the business units. Each of the original 13 teams has split into 2 or 3 teams within the business organization, resulting in approximately 37 business unit teams. Because each team has responsibility for a smaller number of intellectual properties, and there are fewer people on each team, the process is more manageable.

Patent Mapping

Another significant intellectual capital management tool used at Eastman is the patent mapping process introduced to Eastman by Pat Sullivan of the ICM Group. The process is used in the early stages of business development to analyze the strategic development possibilities for a new technology. In brief, it is an analysis tool with three elements:

- Developing a technology tree
- Developing a patent tree off the technology tree
- Analyzing the trees to develop:

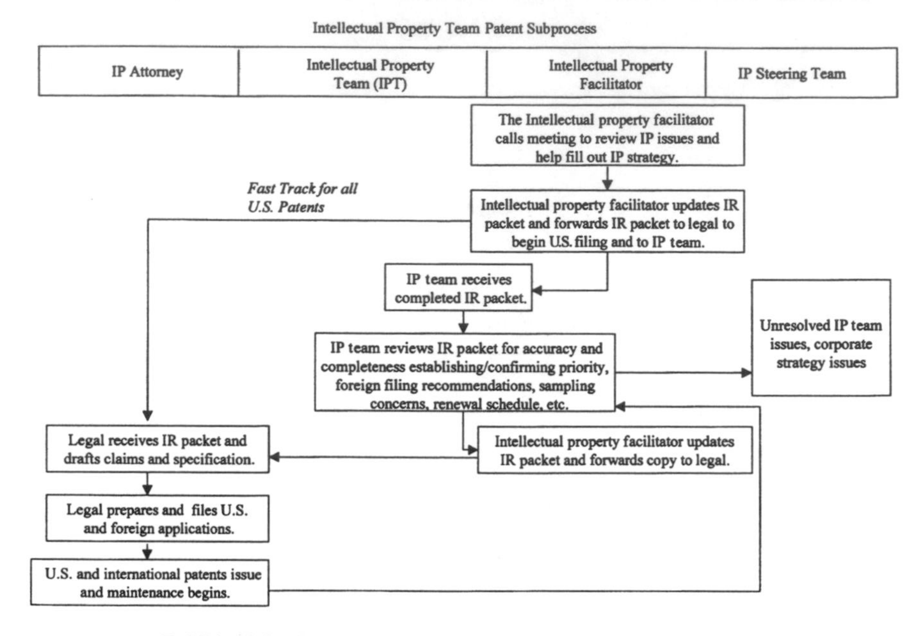

Exhibit 12.2 Overview of Eastman Intellectual Property Process

A business strategy
A patent strategy
An additional technology strategy where appropriate

While simple in its description, the process requires much in the way of preparation, especially ensuring that the appropriate people are involved. It is important to have both key business and technical people involved in commercialization of the technology. While the tree is being put together, it will be analyzed, expanded, and redone, in some instances many times. The result provides valuable technological information to the business people and business information to the technologists. At the same time, it clarifies goals and objectives for all parties. It identifies the necessary technology for the business, the complementary technology, and in some instances the competing technology. Once the technology tree is completed, patent searches are performed in the different areas of technology to put patent leaves on the technology tree.

Probably the most important benefit of patent mapping is to assemble in one place the thoughts, goals, and strategies of the business, technical, and legal areas, resulting in alignment, focus, and combined energy in a single direction. It is a very powerful analysis tool.

The Technology Engine Process

The technology engine process was developed as a management tool around the technology core competencies. The reasons for developing such a process were multiple, including the need to:

- Identify the key technical strengths (the technology engines) of the company
- Assess the strength and weakness of each of the competencies
- Define at which level the competencies can be managed strategically
- Identify interactions and interdependence and determine which ones are core
- Align product and service offered with these competencies and determine gaps and overlaps
- Identify the human capital associated with each of the competencies

A multifunctional team was set up to tackle the problem. Each major research division had a representative at the director level as well as representatives from development, technical service, business, strategic alliances, and legal. Initially, the team struggled with its mission and how to approach it. Every function came in with a different agenda. A high level of skepticism on the value and feasibility of the project was prevalent. The first task of the team was to define its mission in clear and actionable items (as previously defined). Once the team had reached consensus, it labored to define the technology groupings and engines and to classify the technologies by type (see Exhibit 12.3). The major issues it faced were first to identify all potential "engines," their relevance, and their interdependence. As an example, the team worked countless hours before it realized that by categorizing the technologies into where they fit into the value chain (raw material, product, process, applications), it could deal more easily with cross-functional expertise and reduce the number of engines to a manageable number.

Thereafter, the inventory of all technologies as well as their initial assessment was relatively simple. The team developed a complex flowchart that defines all engines for the company, their interaction, and their interdependence. Exhibit 12.4 shows how two technology groupings relate to two product groupings appli-

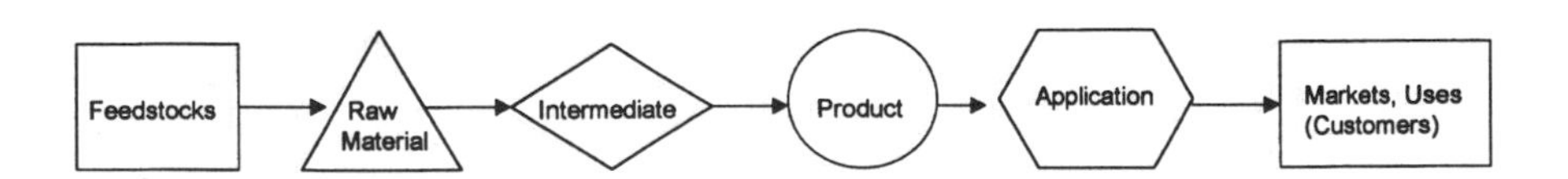

<u>Technology Engines</u>

- <u>Raw material engines</u>–Primary purpose is to provide basic chemical building blocks.
- <u>Intermediate engines</u>–Primary purpose is to provide intermediate products used by other engines. These products may or may not be sold externally.
- <u>Product engines</u>–Primary purpose is to produce products for external sales. These product(s) can be used by a company through its application engines.
- <u>Application engines</u>–Primary purpose is to: (1) Modify existing products through formulations, (2) use existing products in new markets, and (3) demonstrate new products in customer end-use applications.

Exhibit 12.3 Engine Classification

cations through multiple technology engines. It allows one to quickly grasp the interrelationship of those technologies and its effect on market and uses.

Over the next year, the team developed one of the engines as a test and an example. The resulting strategy was presented to upper management, which endorsed it. Over the next two years, an organization was put in place to take full advantage of this new developed management tool.

R&D management also uses the technology engine process to quickly assess the potential for new innovations. Exhibit 12.5 shows how the company's different functional groups interface—from the technology and innovative management teams (TIM teams), through the business unit managers and the technology engine teams, all the way to upper management (executive team).

A similar chart can be plotted showing market position and technology type (see Exhibit 12.6). In this figure, the markets are divided according to Eastman's knowledge fit and its novelty to the world. The technology is again classified by novelty. It allows management to see where its assets are positioned in the marketplace and to evaluate overall risk as well as risk by individual engine or project.

A fully developed technology engine assessment includes the following elements:

- A description of the technology
- The company's strategy for its use
- The linkage with other engines
- Key products and business units affected

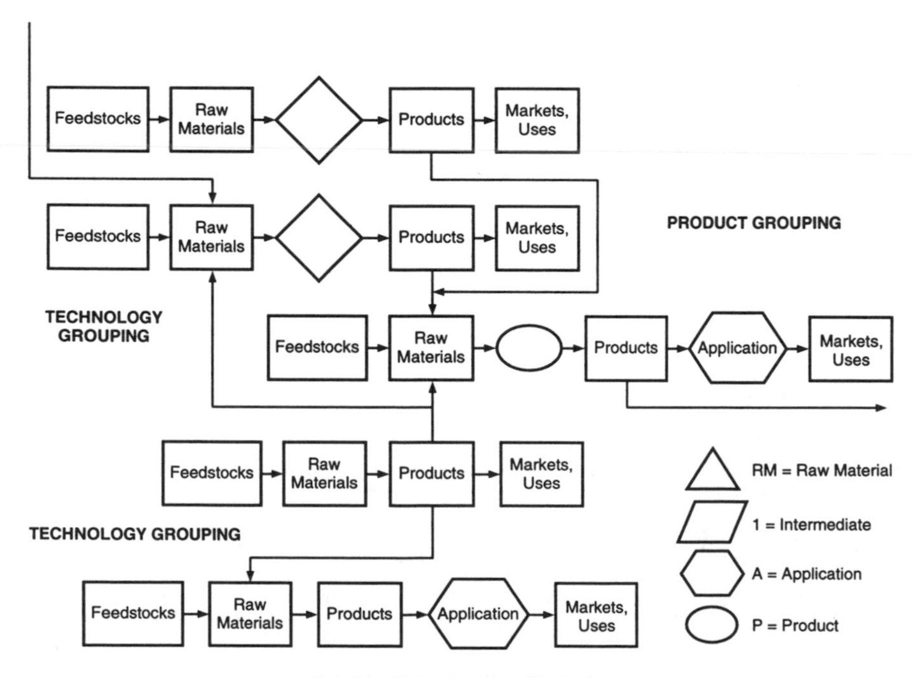

Exhibit 12.4 Product Grouping

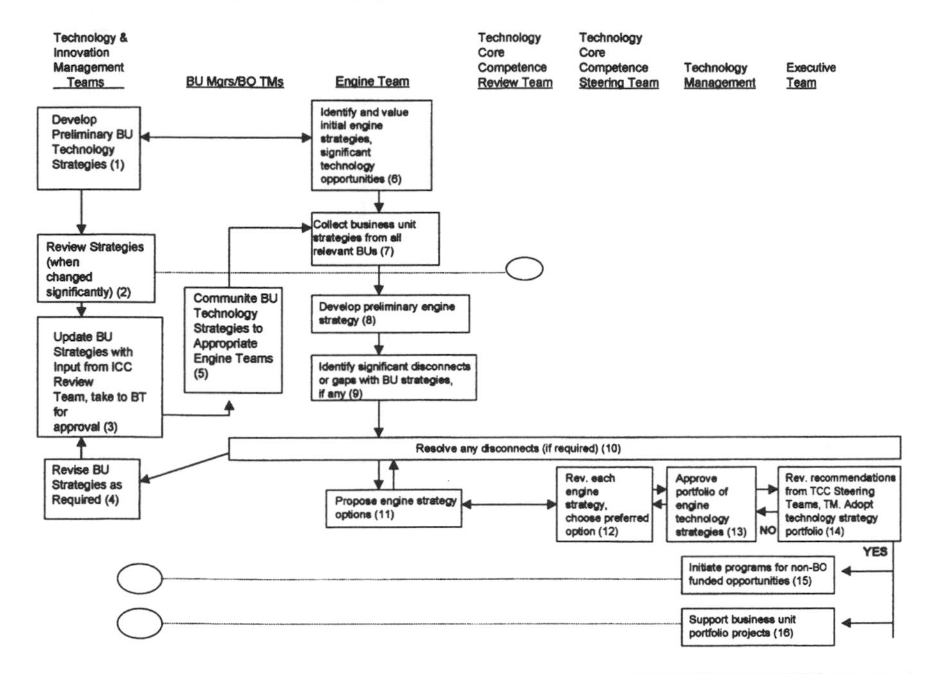

Exhibit 12.5 Technology Strategy Integration Process

- An analysis of how the other engines support the engine under discussion
- A summary of the proposed strategy, including current level of support and strategy options with key program linkage
- The expected value of the option selected
- An analysis of the human capital distribution supporting the engine

The Licensing Process

The development of the licensing process came in two phases: first, the licensing itself and, later, tying the IP process to the licensing process.

Eastman had two main concerns: (1) improving the efficiency of the licensing process to avoid the stress and frustration earlier licensing efforts had created, and (2) making sure that in- and out-licensing decisions were made in the best interest of the corporation.

The process needed to be: simple, easily understood, comprehensive, nonintrusive, and inclusive of, and accepted by, all stakeholders. A multifunctional team made up of senior managers of the R&D, legal, manufacturing, external technology evaluation, and strategic alliances and licensing departments was set up to accomplish this task. It took six months and more than 15 iterations to finalize the process.

Even then, a process to define how potential candidates for licensing would be brought into the process ("feed-in" phase) was missing. The "feed-in" phase needs to be completely integrated with the patent/IP management process as it becomes the responsibility of the technology and innovation management teams

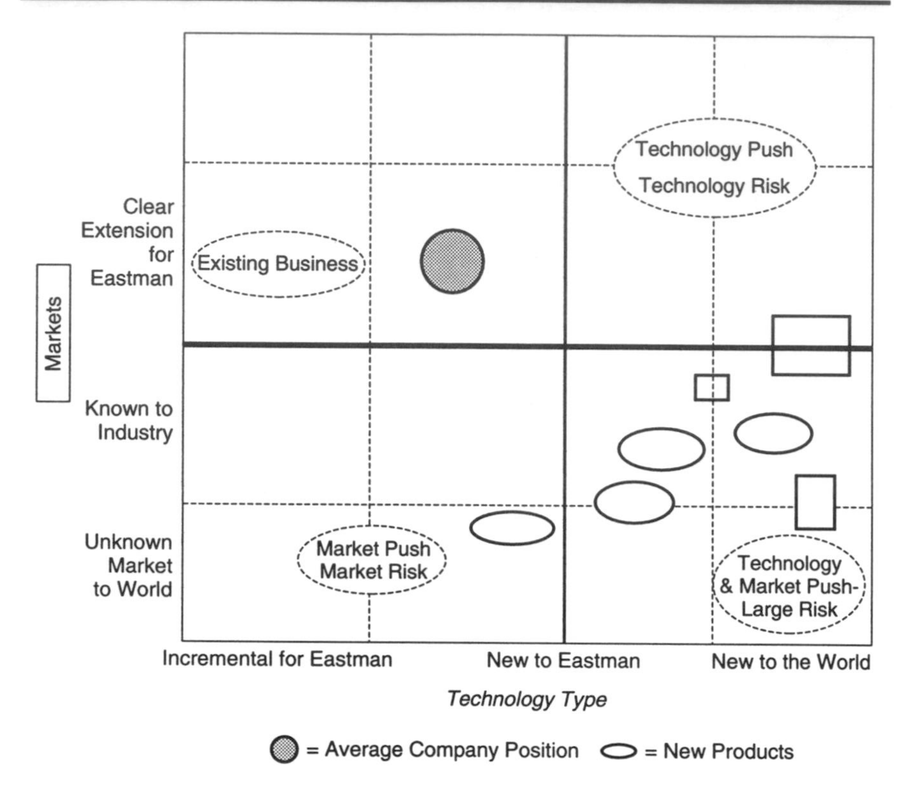

Exhibit 12.6 Positioning and Evaluating Assets

to screen all intellectual property (patents and know-how) for their appropriateness for licensing. This phase of the process is still being implemented, and its success will rely on the willingness of these teams to include licensing as a strategic option and on management support. It will require a significant change in the mindset of the corporation. The role of the IP attorney and the licensing manager will be to act as conscience and champion.

The key elements of the remainder of the process are to get preliminary and final stakeholder approval of the decision to license.

The final responsibility to go ahead with licensing lies with the primary stakeholder and is based on the input of the other functions. No veto power is given to any particular function, but it is expected that objections will be dealt with by the primary stakeholder before execution of the final contract. The principles and responsibilities of all those involved in the licensing decision are laid out in Exhibit 12.7.

The Joint Venture and Alliance Process

After Eastman made the decision to broaden its scope and globalize, management sponsored a major initiative to develop a process and a training course to give managers background and expertise in developing joint ventures and alliances. First, a multifunctional team outlined the principles and defined the curriculum.

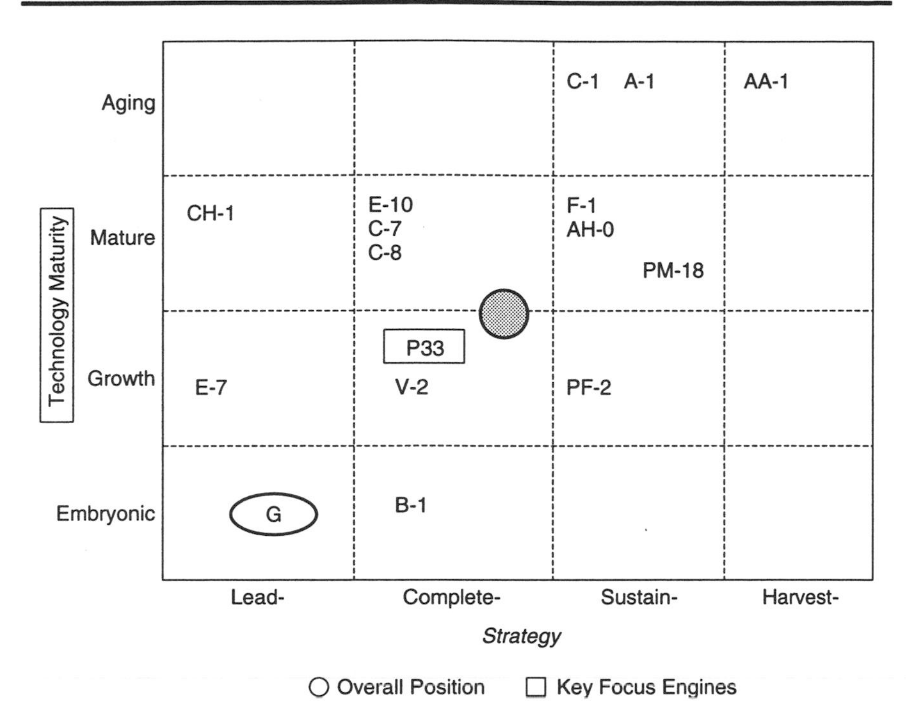

Exhibit 12.7 How Maturity Affects Strategy

Eastman's program uses exercises, case histories, and internal examples that are relevant to the participants. This focus is particularly important in Eastman's case because of the internal culture needed to evolve from a monolithic manufacturing style to one that emphasized diversity and conflict resolution. The resulting course has been integrated into the training curriculum for all management.

At the same time, the process for developing alliances and joint ventures was developed at two levels: an executive overview, and a more detailed overview, which covered specific tasks for each function at each stage of the project. Exhibit 12.8 shows the "gates" or decision points needed to progress from one stage to the next. The teaching of this process has been incorporated into the training course.

The major difficulties in developing the process were agreeing on the steps, authorizations, and reviews required to pass from one stage to the next. It was difficult to separate the need-to-know from the desire-to-know issues—that is, to make the required authorizations and reviews sufficient and comprehensive without being burdensome and superfluous. Exhibit 12.8 captures the increasing complexity and depth of the due diligence and negotiation phases and includes a description, by function, of the tasks to be completed at each stage.

Specifically, the JVA process covers the evaluation of business opportunities when the company takes an equity position through joint venture, merger, or acquisition. Other business alliances, such as divestitures, licensing, joint technology development, marketing alliances, and tolling arrangements, are not covered by this process.

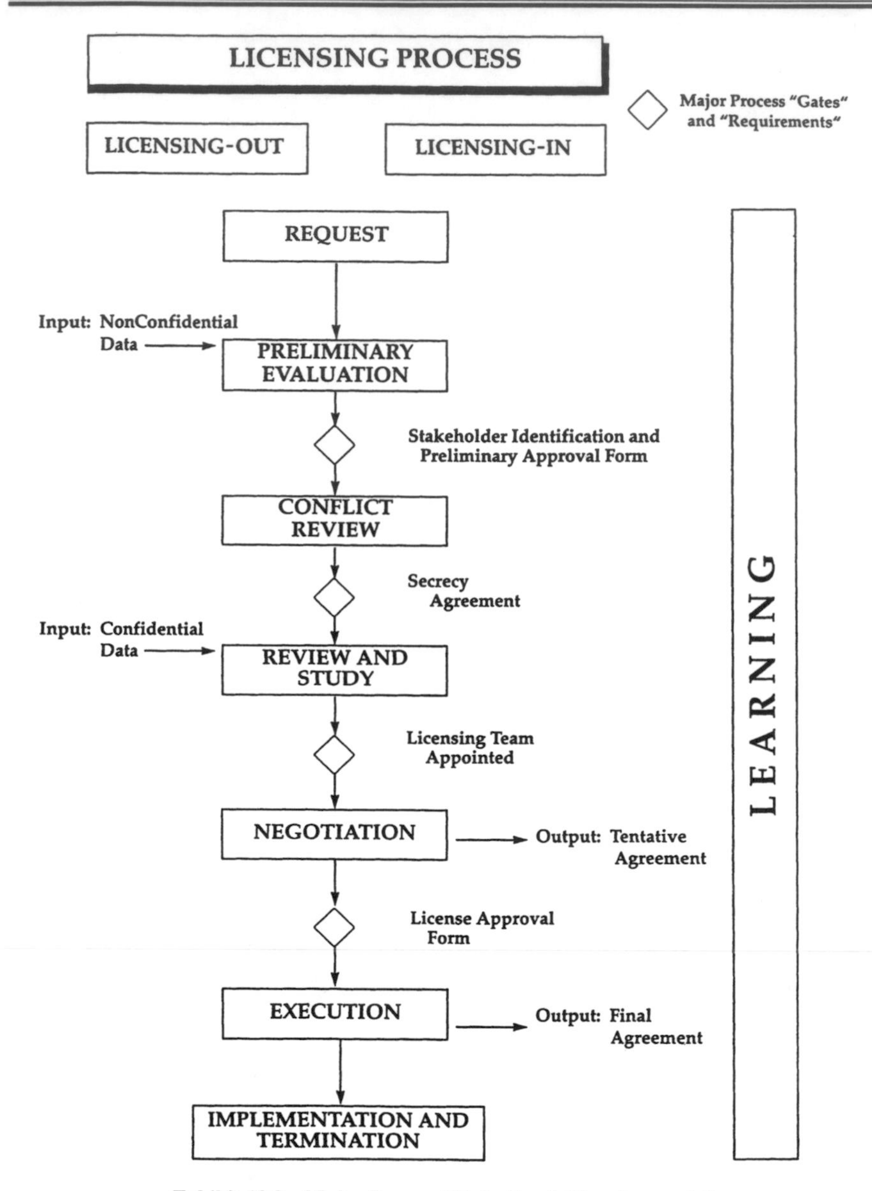

Exhibit 12.8 Major Process "Gates" and "Requirements"

The company pursues JVAs as a way to achieve strategic business objectives. Joint ventures can be:

1. *Resource-driven* when the prospective partner provides financing, key raw materials, underutilized physical plant facilities, or technology
2. *Market-driven* when the prospective partner provides local market access and knowledge or products that broaden or diversity the company's product line

3. *Risk-driven* when the inclusion of a prospective partner results in economies of scale, cost-sharing, or expedience

Acquisitions can provide assets at lower-than-replacement cost and expedite the attainment of the company's objectives. In evaluating JVA opportunities, the company's objective is to determine whether a JVA is the best way to achieve the strategy—not to "find a way to make the deal."

An efficient process for evaluating JVA opportunities is essential. Overseen by the corporate development unit, the company's JVA process:

- Involves few people in the early stages when confidentiality is important and the decision to proceed has not been made
- Addresses screening, evaluation, and implementation issues separately
- Proceeds step by step through each stage of the decision process
- Can be halted at any time if a project is determined to be infeasible

Input from many areas of the company is typically required to ensure proper evaluation of a JVA opportunity. Involvement of the internal business organizations likely to be responsible for managing a JVA is essential for successful implementation. Confidentiality is frequently critical to successful negotiation. Information should be shared only on a need-to-know basis.

Steering committees composed of members of management in the key business and functional organizations affected by a JVA are used to review the content and process of JVA evaluations. The steering committee approves movement of JVA projects from stage to stage.

Part III

Intellectual Asset Management

13

Extracting Value from Intellectual Assets

Patrick H. Sullivan

ICM Group, LLC

Extraction of value from intellectual assets, the company's codified knowledge (protected as well as not), builds on the system for extracting value from intellectual property. Intellectual asset management (IAM) is similar to intellectual property management (IPM) in that it uses the same conceptual basis that specifies that innovation and complementary assets as the primary sources of value for the firm. It also uses the same conversion mechanisms for converting value into profits. But IAM differs from IPM in at least three significant ways. First, the unprotected commercializable assets, when added to the protected commercializable assets, comprise a set of interactive intellectual assets that is significantly more complex to coordinate and manage. The second area of difference between the two concerns the time focus. Whereas IPM is focused on current extraction from assets currently or soon to be in the portfolio, IAM is concerned with assets that are less well defined and where it is their prospect for generating income that is of interest. Third, whereas extracting value from IP is *tactically* focused, and extracting value from IC is *strategically* focused, intellectual asset value extraction lies between the two, having both tactical and strategic implications.

This chapter discusses intellectual assets: What they are, the differences between commercializable and noncommercializable IAs, the differences between IAs that are managed for direct commercialization and IAs that become part of the firm's structural capital and, thereby, indirectly support commercialization. The chapter also discusses how intellectual assets are valued, how they are managed, and how profits may be extracted from them.

INTELLECTUAL ASSETS

Knowledge

Successful knowledge companies create sustainable value through the creation of knowledge and know-how. Some of that knowledge and know-how becomes codified and forms intellectual assets, the remainder stays as tacit knowledge that remains within the human capital. Knowledge firms know it is to their advantage to institutionalize much of the knowledge and know-how generated by their human capital. But what kind of knowledge is it that firms want to capture for themselves: A general list would include at least the following:

1. Values and culture
2. Mission, vision, objectives, and strategy
3. Customer relationships and know-how about customers
4. Technical knowledge and know-how
   a. Commercializable innovations
      (1) Strategic innovations (part of the firm's strategic thrust)
      (2) Nonstrategic (available for out-licensing or other value-capturing process)
   b. Other innovations bringing value to the firm
      (1) Innovations for internal operations (production/production processes)
      (2) Innovations protecting commercializable innovations
5. Organization and structure
6. Managerial methods
   a. Decision processes
   b. Databases
   c. Procedures
7. Work methods
8. Information providing access to company know-how and capabilities

Some of the above knowledge and know-how remains tacit and continues to reside within the human capital. The remainder, the portion that is codified, becomes the firm's intellectual assets.

Intellectual Assets

Intellectual assets are the *codified* knowledge and know-how of the firm's human capital. Exhibit 13.1, reprinted here from Chapter I, reminds us of the relationship between intellectual capital, human capital, and intellectual assets.

While the firm does not own its human capital, it does own the intellectual assets. Human capital, employees and stakeholders, may break their relationships with the firm at any time. Employees retire, are laid-off, are terminated, resign, or just leave. Whatever be their knowledge or know-how, regardless of whether they brought it with them when hired or learned it during their employ, it departs with them when they go. But any bits of their knowledge that have become codified remain with and are the property of the firm. Codified bits of knowledge add to the firm's storehouse and stock of intellectual capital. In addition, once committed to media, an idea can be shared with many others, can be discussed, improved, and expanded. It can be easily communicated to decision makers and actions or decisions made on its basis. In short, a codified bit of knowledge, an intellectual asset,

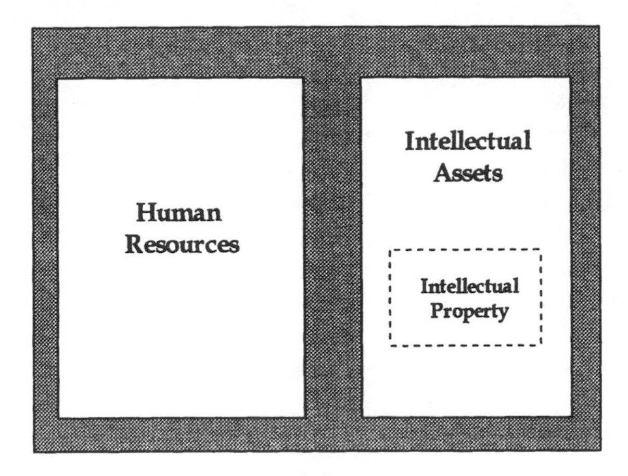

Exhibit 13.1 The Intellectual Capital of the Firm

can be leveraged by the firm. And, leveragable intellectual assets are what knowledge companies seek to develop.

It may be useful to describe examples of what the category intellectual assets contains. First, remember that intellectual assets are codified bits of knowledge and are comprised of two major sets: commercializable and structural as shown in Exhibit 13.2.

Commercializable Intellectual Assets

Commercializable intellectual assets are those that are capable of directly finding their way into either the business or the technology marketplace. Examples of commercializable intellectual assets for business use include trademarks, names, products, product features, manufacturing processes, and others.

There are two kinds of commercial intellectual assets, those that are legally protected and those that are not.

> *Legally protected:* The portion of the intellectual assets that is legally protected is collectively referred to as the firm's intellectual property.

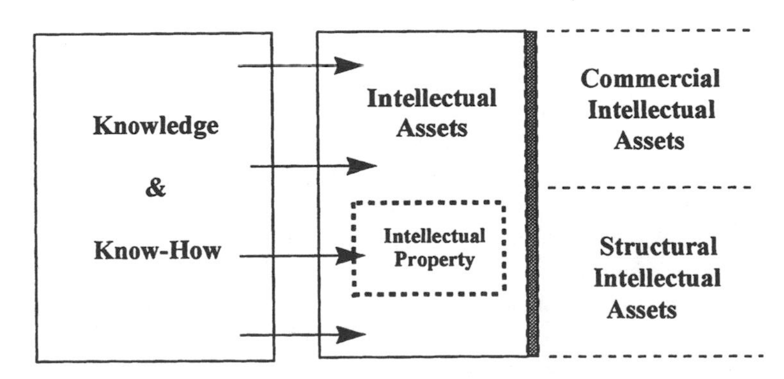

Exhibit 13.2 Intellectual Assets Comprised of Commercial & Structural Elements

- Patents
- Copyrights
- Trademarks
- Trade secrets
- Semiconductor masks

Legal protection means that the firm's rights of ownership are formally declared and that for each form of intellectual property there are different rights conferred. Exhibit 13.3 provides an overview of the rights associated with each form of legal protection.

Unprotected: The unprotected and commercializable intellectual assets of the knowledge firm are usually the firm's innovations that are still undergoing further development.

1. *Technical intellectual assets.* These include bits of know-how that are intended to be commercialized themselves or that will support a piece of commercialized technology in some way. In technological companies, the technical intellectual assets are of two kinds: design and operations.
2. *Design intellectual assets.* Innovations in this category are those relating to the technology processes involved with the firm's major activity. Examples here could be new production technologies or improved product features.
3. *Operations intellectual assets.* Different from design, which is largely a conceptual activity, operations deal with the day-to-day activity of the firm as it conducts business. Operational intellectual assets for a manufacturing company might include manufacturing methods, processes, and procedures. For other companies, these intellectual assets may be the documents, drawings, or otherwise codified bits of knowledge that define and guide the activities of employees. Documents that record operational activity are often of great commercial potential. For example, considerable business leverage may come from coordinating the information contained in a range of otherwise not correlated documents:
   - Licensing agreements
   - Confidential disclosure agreements
   - Joint venture agreements
   - Outsourcing contracts
   - Customer lists

Intellectual Assets and Structural Capital

Many of the firm's intellectual assets become part of the structural capital of the firm. They represent a portion of the firm's infrastructure, and, as such, it is appropriate that they be considered a portion of the structural capital. Items that become part of the structural capital include administrative and technical methods, processes, and procedures. In addition, the firm's organizational structure, the assigned roles, the reporting relationships, and the assignments of responsi-

Exhibit 13.3 Characteristics of Legal Forms of U.S. IP Protection

Consideration	Patent	Copyright	Trade Secret	Trademark	Mask Works	Trade Dress
Protected property	Invention	Expression of idea	Secret information	Goodwill	Semiconductors	Appearance
Scope of protection	Exclude others from making, using, selling	Exclusive right to reproduce, distribute, display, perform	Right to make, use, sell secret, & protect from use, disclosure	Protects misrepresentation of source	Exclusive right to produce chip	Presentation of product
Effective date	Patent application	Creation of work	Conception or receipt	Use or filing date	Registration, 1st commercial exploitation	General use
Requirements	Novel, nonobvious, useful	Original	Commercially valuable	Distinctive, nondescriptive	Original	Distinctive, nonuseful
Vulnerability	Invent around, improvements	Independent creation	Indep. creation, reverse engineer		Independent creation, reverse engineer	Independent creation
Duration	20 years (from application)	Author's life plus 50 years; or 75 years	Disclosure or independently developed	Perpetual if used correctly and policed	10 years	Perpetual if used correctly and policed
Cost	Moderate	Low	Low	Low	Low	Low
Maintenance cost	Moderate	Nil	Moderate	Moderate	Nil	Moderate
Enforcement cost	High	Moderate	High	Moderate	Moderate	Moderate

* Prior to 1994: US patent life was 17 years from grant date.

bility and authority all become part of the firm's infrastructure and its structural capital.

Up to this point, structural capital has been described as comprised of the physical assets (or tangibles) of the firm. The inclusion of intellectual assets (intangibles) with physical assets in the structural capital should not be confusing. It is done because the value extraction view finds it useful to consider the structural capital as the "owner" of the firm's infrastructure. This allows for the convenient (and useful) overlapping of intellectual assets into structural capital.

Originally, we had shown a model for a knowledge firm where intellectual capital and structural capital were related and separate from one another. Now we can show that the two forms of capital actually merge with one another, and the merging point is primarily around the intellectual assets that become part of the firm's structural capital infrastructure (see Exhibit 13.4).

Over time, as the firm grows, it adds more physical assets, resulting in a growth in structural capital. Equally, over time, there is growth in the intellectual capital as the firm hires more employees (human capital) and the employees codify their ideas into intellectual capital. One aspect of this set of growth activities is that the structural capital actually grows as more and more infrastructure-related intellectual assets are generated and used by the firm. This generates growth in the firm's structural capital, which becomes one of two locii of the firm's history, culture, and values (the other "residence," of course, is with the employees themselves, the human capital).

Whether diagrammed as part of the intellectual capital or the structural capital, the growth in intellectual assets over time adds to the firm's stock of intellectual capital as well as providing more methods, processes, and procedures for leveraging the commercializable intellectual assets in the marketplace. This adds to the firm's value. The degree to which the stock market sees or expects to see leveraging actually increasing the firm's revenues is the degree to which the stock market will add a premium to the firm's stock price.

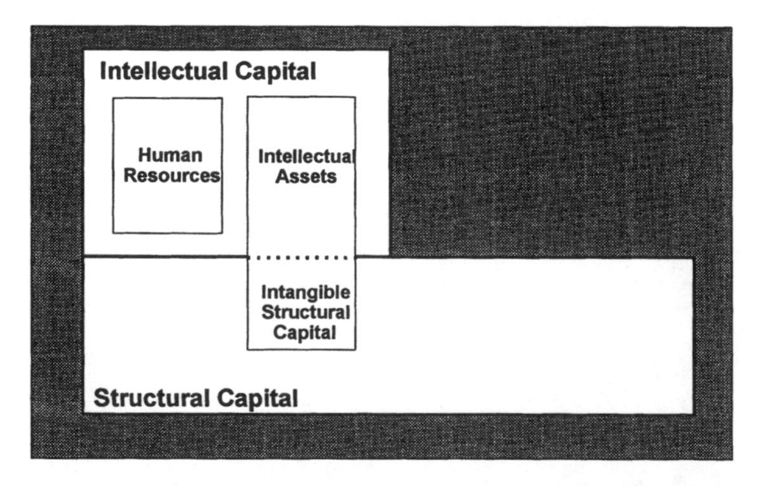

Exhibit 13.4 Model of a Knowledge Firm Showing Intangible Structural Capital

The structural intellectual assets, those that are not directly commercializable but that describe or define the ways in which the firm operates, include the following kinds of knowledge:

Organization & Structure: Definitions of roles, responsibilities, authority, hierarchical, and financial relationships.

Customer Capital: Whereas the relationship portion of customer capital resides within the human capital of the firm, the portion of the company's information on customers that can be codified into databases or otherwise systematized becomes a part of the firm's intangible structural capital.

Operational Methods and Procedures: Documents describing how the organization conducts itself, whether in a business or a technical sense, are called *operational methods and procedures.* These documents are important components of the firm's structural capital.

Managerial Methods and Analyses: Intellectual assets relating to the firm's managerial activities are also thought of as being in several categories:

1. *Strategic.* Intellectual assets categorized as strategic typically include the company's vision for the future, its strategy for how to get there, and any long-term or strategic plans for implementing the strategy.
2. *Administrative.* The bulk of the managerial intellectual assets are probably found in this category. Here are all of the firm's administrative processes, procedures, and methods. Typically included in the administrative category are intellectual assets associated with administrative or managerial methods, processes, and procedures. Also included in this category are organizational structures, organization charts, job descriptions, and assignments of responsibility and authority.

Collective: Some of the firm's intellectual assets may describe, define, or somehow involve themselves with the firm's collective ethos or way of doing business. Typically found in the collective intellectual assets under this category are know-how and knowledge relating to culture, values, and the firm's collective know-how.

Exhibit 13.5 shows an exploded view of a knowledge firm's intellectual assets to demonstrate that the intellectual asset category of intellectual capital contains more than just commercializable assets (intellectual properties).

MEASURING AND VALUING INTELLECTUAL ASSETS

Operational Value and the Knowledge Company

While the financial markets are interested in the current value of knowledge companies, the companies themselves are concerned about the value of their futures. Knowledge companies generally manage their IC to create a future income stream and to develop the intellectual wherewithal to enable the strategy to achieve the strategic vision. For this reason, the primary reference point for the measurement of the operational value of intellectual capital is the firm's vision and strategy. The pri-

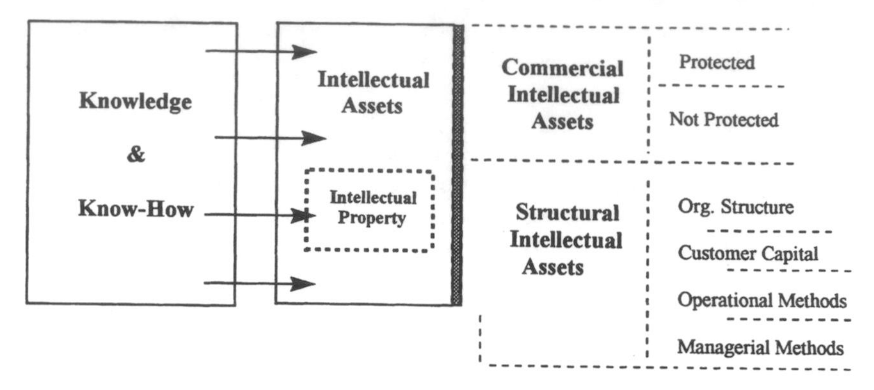

Exhibit 13.5 Intellectual Assets Component of Intellectual Capital

mary context for measuring value is the values of the firm. Economic value measurement may be done either qualitatively or quantitatively. Qualitative measures of economic value describe the manner in which an intangible brings utility to the firm. Quantitative measures of value, on the other hand, define the amount of a stock or flow or the rate of change of a stock or flow. Many quantitative measures of intellectual capital use money or currency as the primary dimension for measurement.

Measuring Operational Economic Value

Economic value may be expressed in two ways: quantitative and qualitative. We are used to expressing value in quantitative and currency terms. Value may be expressed directly, usually in terms of money; two such measures of value are price and cost. Price is the amount a purchaser will be willing to pay in exchange for the utility he or she will receive through ownership of an item. Cost is the amount of resources, expressed in money terms, that were required to create an item. Both cost and price are considered to be direct (and quantitative) measures of value But there are other, non-money or indirect measures of value as well.

Measures differ from measurements. Measures represent the dimensions or units to be quantified by measuring. Typical measures are: feet, miles, feet per second, miles per hour, and so forth. Measurements, on the other hand, are the amount or degree ascertained by measuring. The discussion that follows concerns measures of value, not measurements and not measuring. Of concern here are the dimensions or the terms of reference. In that regard, there are two kinds of measures used to value intellectual capital: qualitative and quantitative.

Qualitative Measures. Let's use an individual patent to develop or illustrate this issue of value. Suppose a company, Acme Widget, wants to know the value of one of its patents. One way of exploring value would be to ask "what value does this patent bring to the firm by its inclusion in the portfolio?" The answer may be qualitative. The value of this patent to the portfolio depends on several factors:

1. Intended Use of the Patent
   a. *Commercialization*—This patent is in the portfolio to be commercialized. Its measure and value may be expressed as its usefulness to the

firm in commercialization terms. For example, a patent that is by itself the complete technical basis for a business would be qualitatively valued higher than a patent that required other patented technologies to be added before there was a sufficient technical basis for a business.

b. *Protection*—This patent is not in the portfolio to be commercialized itself; it is there to protect another patent, one the firm does expect to commercialize. Its value is related to the amount of protection it provides to the patent(s) it is included to protect.

c. *Anticompetition*—This patent is in the portfolio as an anticompetitive measure:

(1) **Blocking.** This patent exists to block competitors from having free access to a predetermined field of technology.

(2) **Design freedom.** This patent is in the portfolio as a marker to demonstrate that our firm has done some research in a field and may feel free to do more in the future (for areas of new technology where the firm intends to continue its developmental efforts).

d. *Litigation Avoidance*—This patent is in the portfolio as a bargaining chip to be used against potential litigants to negotiate the settlement of differences rather than resort to a trial or an arbitration.

2. Ability to Exclude Others

a. This is the degree to which a patent can exclude others from infringing on the firm's rights to practice R&D as well as to exclusively use the patented technology in the marketplace. Patents that can exclude virtually all potential infringers have high value for a firm. Patents with a limited ability to exclude others from practicing in a field have lower value.

3. Ability to Detect Infringement

a. The degree to which infringement of a patented technology can be detected is another measure of the value the patent brings to its owner. It is difficult to detect infringement of a patented process because any infringing applications would likely be inside of a machine or system. Because of its location, infringement might be difficult to observe. By way of contrast, infringement of product patents is often easier to detect because the products may usually be seen in the marketplace. Infringing product technologies are often visible and easily detectable. Patents whose infringement is easy to detect are more valuable than those where infringement is difficult to collect.

Quantitative Measures of Value. There are a range of quantitative measures that are used with intellectual capital, both money-based and not. Things to be measured are often stocks (the total amount of something) or flows (the change or rate of change of something). Exhibit 13.6 shows examples of quantitative measures of intellectual capital value.

One final and important point concerning the quantification of value. There is a time dimension to value measurement. That is to say, some intellectual assets have current value to the firm while others represent value to be realized some time in the future. Intellectual capital management is the management of the firm's future. It largely deals with the processes for creating and commercializing innovations that will account for the firm's future income stream. Current intellectual capital, or the current stock of intellectual capital, is sometimes of interest to the financial markets. For this reason, there are several efforts afoot to create a reliable set of methods for capitalizing this set of intangibles in the form of an intellectual capital balance sheet. Knowledge companies themselves demonstrate little interest in managing or measuring the current stock of intellectual capital. Their interest, in contrast to the interests of the financial markets, is with the future. Knowledge companies are interested in measuring the results of their intellectual capital management activities. For this reason, they are interested with measures that tell them the vector of change for the company's stocks of intellectual capital, or they are interested in measuring the current value of the future income stream that innovations-in-progress are expected to generate.

When measuring intellectual capital, remember that the purpose of measuring has a significant effect on the measures that will be used. Measurements of the current stocks of intellectual capital are of interest outside of the firm. Of interest inside the firm are those measures that tell either of two things. First, are the innovations we are developing for our firm's future proceeding as planned? Second, as far as can be known, what can we expect each of these innovations to produce in the form of an income stream, and what is the net present value of that income stream?

Exhibit 13.6 Example of Quantitative Measures of Value

Identification	Management	Extraction	Alignment and Systemization
Definition of Assets: - # - Costs to Date - Forecast Costs - Subject/Techn. - Age - Remaining Life - Value Category - Rate of Addition - Rate of Deletion Categorization of Assets: - # of Categories - # of IA's in Category - # or % not in Category - Alignment with vision	General: - # Evals/Unit Time - # Techniques Avail. - # of Staff - Alignment with Vision - Skill Level of Staff - # Recc's Made - # Recc's Implemented - Quality of Evals - Backlog	For each: - # of Innovations - $ Invested - $ Received - Forecast Income - Alignment with Vision	Information Systems - % Coverage - % Complete - Accessibility - Completeness - Rate of Usage - Alignment Decision Systems - Age - Coverage - Purpose - Comprehensiveness - Connectivity - Alignment Managerial Systems - Satisfaction - Rate of Usage

Quantifying Value in Money Terms

When quantifying value in terms of money, there are a range of methods available for quantification. The particular method selected depends on the reasons for which the valuation is to be made and the degree of precision to which the resulting valuation will be held.

1. *Reasons for Valuation.* The situations most often requiring a knowledge company to produce a money-based valuation of an intangible asset are:
   - Litigation
   - Tax-related transactions
   - Joint ventures
   - Intracompany transfers
   - Business decision making
   - Out-license/Sale
   - In-license/Purchase
   - R&D investment
   - Portfolio management
   - In-kind contributions
   - Exploitation potential
   - Initial estimate of value
2. *Degree of Precision.* The precision required of a valuation may be measured by the relative importance of the result as well as the degree of scrutiny to which the resulting valuation number will be subjected. The amount of precision determines the amount of effort and resources necessary to expend on obtaining an answer to the question of how much is it worth (what is its dollar value)? Exhibit 13.7 suggests a relationship between reason for valuing, expected degree of scrutiny, and level of effort required to produce a valuation.
3. *Valuation Methods.* Value is quantified in money terms through any of the three classic methods:

Exhibit 13.7 Relation between Circumstance, Scrutiny, and Valuation Effort

Circumstance	Expected Degree of Scrutiny	Level of Effort Required
Litigation	Very High	Large
Tax-related Transactions	High	Large
Joint Ventures	High	Large
Intra-company Transfers	High	Large
Business Decision-making	Medium	Medium
Licensing (Sale & Purchase)	Medium	Medium
In-Kind Contributions	Medium	Medium
R&D Investment	Medium	Medium
Portfolio Management	Medium	Medium
Exploitation Potential	Medium	Medium
Initial Estimate	Low	Small

Exhibit 13.8 Table of Example Valuation Methods

Method	Description	Advantages	Disadvantages	When Used
Market (classic)	The economist's basic valuation method	Best match with Economist's definition of value	Difficult to find comparable Ips	Litigation Licensing Transaction
Income Approach (classic)	A basic technique on which many variations are based	Considers all factors associated with value Considered best alternative if market approach is unavailable	Difficult for layman to calculate	Litigation
Cost (classic)	A calculation of the cost to replicate or reproduce	A third approach used when the market income approach is not available Good method for brand-new technology	No measure of utility or market value Overhead allocations difficult to make/justify	Litigation
Technology Factor	Devised by Dow, a good method for internal valuation	Builds political consensus Methodical/systematic Good workbook	Requires assembly of many people Many assumptions underlying method	For internal use only
Probability Adjusted Expected Value	Method for valuation under uncertainty	Allows for quantification of elements of risk Models the development process	Can be costly if done to meet high precision standards	Where "strategicness" is important
Risk/Hurdle Rate	Financially focused method	Quantifies risk Mathematical analysis	Intensive calculation Not for the faint-at-heart	Financial Investment
Return on Sales	A calculation of royalty based on net sales	Quick Take advantage of industry norms	Difficult to allocate profits between 2 parties Value could be different from one company to another Requires agreed sales forecasts	N/A
Sullivan's Method	A quick method with a basis in theory *and* a coupling with judgment	Quick Based on business knowledge Order-of-magnitude results	Accurate to ±25% Requires some market knowledge Uses average exhibits	Initial Estimate
Make Me An Offer	Just what it says	Good approach when *no* valuation information is available	Leaves money on the table	All circumstances
25% Rule	A rule of thumb	Simple Provides an agreed (if not accurate) value Used only when nothing else is available	No basis in theory Not necessarily accurate or representative	Initial Estimate

- *Market method.* This method, probably the top choice of economists, uses the market price agreed on by willing buyer and seller as the best dollar measure of utility.
- *Income method.* This method, usually used when a market price is not available, involves calculating the future streams of income and cost and then discounting their sum back to present value.
- *Cost method.* Perhaps the least preferred by economists, the cost method calculates the costs required to duplicate (i.e., create an exact copy of) or to replicate (i.e., to create the functional equivalent of) an intangible.

Using these three methods as a basis, a range or methods have been created for specific purposes. Exhibit 13.8 lists some of these money-based valuation methods.

A comparison of Exhibits 13.6 and 13.7 reveals that for most managers, valuation requires a level of effort, training, and experience from the firm's financial staff. Nevertheless, for the "initial estimate," a simple method offering order-of-magnitude results will suffice. For an example of such a simple method, see the appendix.

14

The Intellectual Asset Manager

Joseph J. Daniele

Xerox Corporation

During the 1980s and 1990s, three things occurred to change the way that intellectual property and intellectual assets are viewed and managed. One was the creation of a specialized court for patent cases, the U.S. Court of Appeals for the Federal District, and its focus on patents and intellectual property enforcement. The second was the clear realization that the United States is part of a global economy, and its competitive position in that economy is as much dependent on its knowledge and know-how resources as it had been on its natural resources in the past. And third was the realization of the importance of purely knowledge-based works of all kinds (and their underlying knowledge assets) to the market value of corporations such as Microsoft, Intel, and others.[1]

Previous chapters of this book have introduced the definition of intellectual assets and showed that they include both *commercial* and *structural* intellectual assets. Commercializable intellectual assets are those that relate directly to the products and the business. Structural intellectual assets usually represent a portion of the firm's underlying infrastructure. The management of intellectual assets (IAM) includes the management of intellectual property, as well as management of all of the firm's codified knowledge assets. What has not yet been discussed is what the firm must do to ensure that its commercial intellectual assets are readily available for use, and that they are used in an effective and efficient way. This chapter discusses commercial intellectual assets from the management perspective (note: for the remainder of this chapter the term *intellectual assets* refers only to the commercial intellectual assets of the firm). This chapter describes how a knowledge firm selects its commercializable intellectual assets from the array of possibilities its human capital creates, and how it manages them. In particular, this chapter focuses on the work processes and systems that knowledge firms use to extract value from these intellectual assets, the databases used to provide information to these processes, and the work systems that are evolving for routinely ensuring that information is available where and when needed, so that decisions are made in a timely and structured manner.

This chapter draws on the author's knowledge of evolving IAM practices, primarily at Xerox along with information about other major firms.

BACKGROUND

The topic of IAM has received much attention lately. Sophisticated knowledge firms are realizing that much of their future (and present) value is determined by the innovations their employees develop and leverage. The financial markets that capitalize knowledge firms increasingly base their investment decisions on perceptions of these firms' intellectual assets rather than on the more traditional physical or financial assets represented on their balance sheets. Intellectual assets, the firm's codified knowledge, while including intellectual property, also include all of the firm's other knowledge assets and particularly the codified portion of the firm's differentiating know-how.

During the 1990s, firms have been seeking improvements in their overall operational effectiveness. They have implemented downsizing, right sizing, and reengineering to improve internal efficiencies. They have developed capabilities for outsourcing and joint venturing or partnering for those segments of the value chain of their businesses in which they are not world-class. This operational effectiveness approach, aimed at improving the firm's overall focus, efficiency, and cost structure, has been economically successful for most firms. As internal efficiencies have improved, however, and external extended webs of partners and suppliers have grown more and more complex, initial dramatic percentage-based improvements in the firm's overall performance have given way to ever smaller percentage improvements with ever larger amounts of effort involved. At this juncture, particularly for knowledge firms, management of the firm's portfolio of intellectual assets becomes increasingly important. Firms operating in extended networks of complex relationships are now finding that control is dictated less by financial capability than by the coverage and reach of a firm's intellectual assets, for example, patent rights, software, and know-how. These intellectual assets are key to negotiating access to another firm's intellectual assets, because intellectual assets are often available only in trade for the intellectual assets of the other party.

In firms with large complex portfolios of IA, the position of IA manager has been evolving and developing to address the modern internal and external business needs of an effective IA portfolio. In these firms, the IA manager usually manages transactions, including those associated with the patent, know-how, trademark, and software portfolios. Increasingly, the scope of this position extends to the internal generation, husbanding, and maintenance of an IA portfolio of the intangible assets of the firm. This can include the architecture, design, and operation of databases for the management of IA processes, the enforcement of patents, the infringement analyses of products, and corporate IA strategy. More important, the IA manager is often the process owner and manager of the corporate and divisional processes governing planning, creation, husbanding, maintenance, and utilization of the IA portfolio. Thus, the IA manager position is evolving from a legal staff position—in the past, primarily concerned with the filing and maintenance of patents, trademarks, and copyrights—to a corporate, line, process, and decision-making function associated with the development and use of a major corporate asset.

In this chapter, the full range of current and anticipated functions of the IA manager are discussed. How this person operates in an organizational environment, often with a small direct staff but with a large extended virtual organization, is reviewed. In addition, the role of the IA manager in creation and extraction of value from the IA portfolio throughout its life cycle is discussed, as well as the manager's activities at all segments of the IA value chain.

CONTEXT FOR IAM

IAM exists to some degree in all firms. The structure, scope, and importance of the IAM function is dependent on the tactical and strategic importance of the firm's IP and IA, and through this the firm's operation, growth, and long-term competitive performance. It is also dependent on senior management's understanding of the use and value of IA in operational and strategic contexts.

Moreover, the nature of the firm's IA and the way in which it is managed depends on the firm's IA basis for sustainable advantage. This basis may be training and agent relationships in an insurance firm, patents and trade secrets in a chemical manufacturing firm, software (source code), standards and know-how in a software or chip manufacturing firm, and know-how and customer relations in a consultancy. It might be a combination of all of the above in an equipment manufacturer, distributor, or service provider firm. Three elements of context are: What is the firm's basis for competitive rivalry, what IA does the firm hold and generate, and what is the role of this IA in providing a sustained competitive advantage?

In all of these environments, there are both constant elements and some differences in the assets, the management structure, and the processes appropriate to them. In the following sections, some of the processes used by major firms are described, as are several new concepts for managing intangibles: the IA life cycle, the IA value chain, and the knowledge management and databases that are needed for efficient operation of an IAM system. Later in this chapter, we discuss seven major subsystems of the IAM function in detail.

INTELLECTUAL ASSETS—WHAT ARE THEY? HOW ARE THEY USED?

As was described earlier in this book, intellectual assets comprise the codified knowledge of the firm. This includes both intellectual properties (reflected in documents, plans, procedures, blueprints, drawings, pictures, and code) and (at Xerox) the collective and codified know-how or proprietary knowledge of the firm.

This asset may be thought of as divided into two parts: One is largely public and legally protected; the other is private, usually proprietary, and closely held within the minds, processes, and communities of practice within the firm. The two forms of intellectual assets, when used together, form a powerful offensive as well as defensive asset for the firm. The intellectual property asset is primarily used as a defensive asset, to exclude others from practicing a specific process or making, using, or selling a product. The know-how or special knowledge asset is for active or offensive use, to enable an invention, process, or product. It is the basis for doing, rather than excluding. When intellectual properties are traded or licensed, these assets are often combined with know-how, so that along with the legal right to make, use, and sell, goes the know-how and knowledge needed to actually make the product.

For the IP portion of the IA portfolio, a primary purpose is protection and the need to guarantee the *right to use* and *design freedom* in product development both through one's own portfolio, and through access to the IP (and IA) of others by cross-licensing. IP can also be licensed for royalty alone or in combination with know-how. The know-how aspects of IA, when coordinated with specific IP, provide the means through which products and services are developed, delivered, and maintained. As such, they are usually proprietary and, when taken in aggregate, can provide a major specific competitive advantage to the firm.

THE IA VALUE CHAIN

All value-generating corporate processes operate in a value chain or sequence of operations. These operations can be inside or outside the firm, and the overall efficiency and effectiveness of value delivery is dependent on each element of the chain.

The IA value chain shown in Exhibit 14.1 consists of:

- IA strategic planning of the current and future state of the IA portfolio
- Creation, prioritization, codification, and securing of IA in legally protected IP, such as patents and trade secrets
- Valuing of IA for efficient allocation and usage

IA Strategy	IA Process for Generation Filing	Valuation Categorization Prioritization	Assessment Decision Making for IA Transfers	Competitive Analysis & Enforcement	Use of the Consolidated Portfolio - Arrangements - Joint Dev. - Licenses
	⇨	⇨	⇨	⇨	⇨

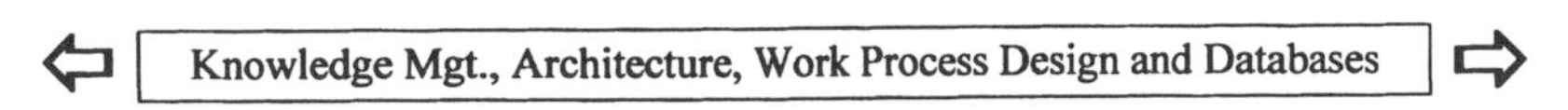

Exhibit 14.1 The IA Value Chain

- Maintenance and husbanding of IA across the firm
- Management of the decision processes associated with the utilization and transfer of IA
- Use of IA to mediate and direct partnering and supplier relationships
- Understanding of the aggregate IA value to the firm

The mission and objective of the IAM is to manage all aspects of the value chain and to design and enable processes and knowledge support systems for its efficient operation. The IA manager is often directly responsible for the quality of output of all of the stages shown.

THE INTELLECTUAL ASSET LIFE CYCLE

Another way to look at the IAM value chain in somewhat more detail is to see it in the perspective of the full IA life cycle. Like a firm's other assets, (or products), the IA of a firm has a life cycle from creation and use, to maintenance, primary value generation, and end of life/replacement. A life cycle for IA is illustrated in Exhibit 14.2. IA management is concerned with the full life cycle of intellectual assets, including the value creation activities of generation, husbanding, and alignment, and the value extraction activities of accessing outside IP and IA, establishing high ground in arrangements, internal and external strategic use, licensing, royalty setting and collection, and IP enforcement.

The interfaces between the stages of the life cycle are important in efficient IA management, and the IAM is often responsible for knowledge management and the overall architecture, design, and operation of the databases that support the various work processes. Some of the many databases and work processes that may be used in the management of IA are shown in Exhibit 14.3.

The IA manager works on all aspects of IA life cycle. The processes encompassing this and the related IA value chain constitute the primary areas of interest and responsibility for the IA manager. The efficient operation of this life cycle is

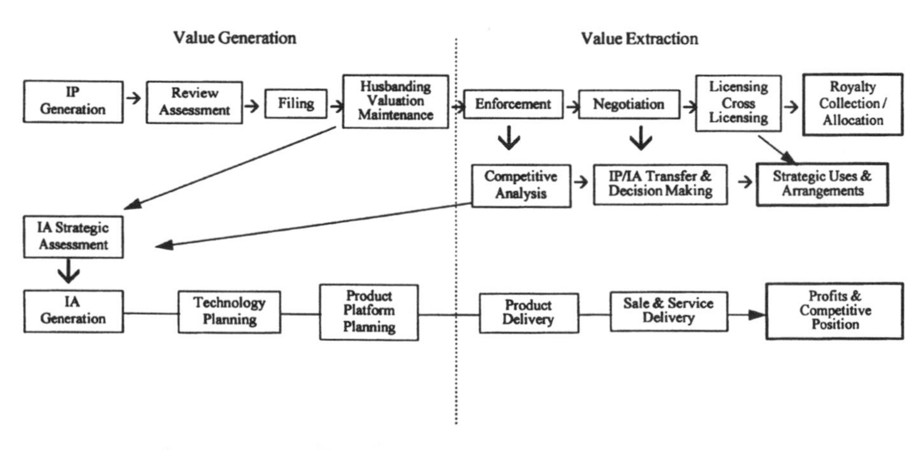

Exhibit 14.2 The IA Life Cycle

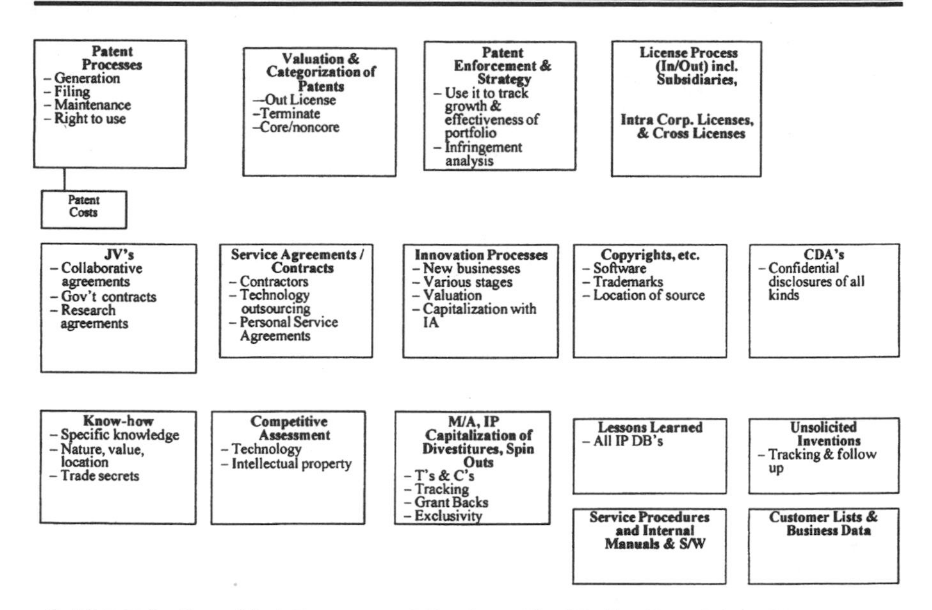

Exhibit 14.3 Some Work Processes and Databases Used for Intellectual Asset Management

crucially dependent on appropriate information being available at the right time and location. Here the knowledge and architectural aspects in the IAM are key, and the IA manager is usually responsible for the many databases and integration processes that allow the system to function.

By expanding and illustrating one of the work processes shown in Exhibit 14.4, we can better understand how databases enable the value creation at the interfaces. The use of knowledge databases at the interfaces of the IP enforcement process is illustrated in Exhibit 14.4.

WHAT DOES THE IA MANAGER ACTUALLY DO?

The IAM manages the higher order and more strategic aspects of both the IP and IA portfolios. Like the information manager of a company, the IA manager deals with the corporate architectural structure and work process aspects of IA. He or she usually operates in both centralized and decentralized contexts.

The IA Manager is often responsible for the following processes and functions:

Intellectual Property Management Processes & Functions

- Valuation and categorization of IP
- Processes for corporate decision making on the disposition or transfer of IP
- Processes for competitive analysis and enforcement of IP rights

Intellectual Asset Management Processes & Functions

- Architecture, design, and development of databases and supporting work processes for IA

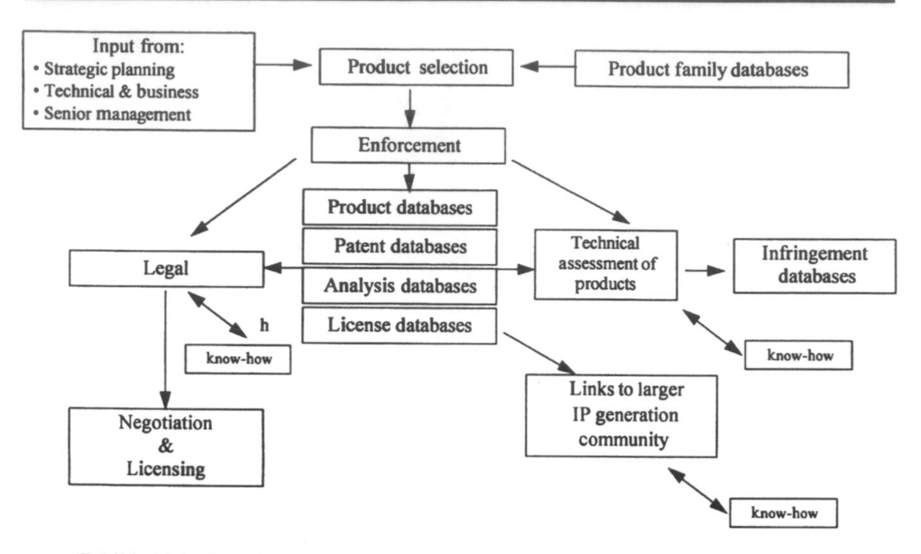

Exhibit 14.4 Interfaces and Knowledge Databases Supporting the IP Enforcement and Competitive Analysis Process

- Generation, assessment, filing, and maintenance of IP and IA
- Development and implementation of corporate IA strategy
- Knowledge management processes at key interfaces in the IA generation, evaluation, and enforcement interfaces
- Understanding, assessment, management, and utilization of the IP portfolio as a consolidated entity
- Management of licenses and royalty collection, forecasting, and allocation

Because the IAM must work across a large span of organizations and functions, he or she acts as a process designer, implementor, and monitor. In recent years, the strategic value of IA has been recognized by many firms; thus, the IAM often reports to senior management and sometimes has responsibility for senior management decision processes involving the IA transactions of the firm. He or she often also has both direct or indirect control of invention generation and review, IP assessment and valuation, and the IA strategy committees or functions.

THE IA MANAGER AND DATABASES

Because IA managers are responsible for work process efficiency, they sometimes have responsibility for the knowledge databases that enable all the underlying processes to function efficiently. Some of the databases and associated knowledge and work processes that may be encompassed by IAM are:

IP

Invention and patent analysis
Patent generation

Patent valuation/categorization
Patent enforcement and strategy
Licensing processes both external and to subsidiaries
Copyrights, trademarks
Source code

IA

Joint ventures, development, outsourcing contracts, and service agreements
IA aspects of innovation and new business development
IA aspects of mergers, acquisitions, spin outs, divestitures
Competitive assessment
Confidential disclosure and license agreements
Know-how assessment, inventory, demographics
Service procedures, manuals, and software
Customer lists and information

These databases are found in almost all large development and manufacturing, and to a lesser extent service, firms. In many cases, they are in paper form and may not be recognized and used as such. Exhibit 14.3 provides further description of these databases, which act at the interfaces between the various stages of the IAM life cycle and value chain. It is the responsibility of the IA manager to recognize and optimize the work process and action at these interfaces by providing ready access to accurate and appropriate information as well as a feedback loop for new information and knowledge as generated.

DISCUSSION OF MAJOR SUBSYSTEMS OF THE IA LIFE CYCLE

It is beyond the scope of this chapter to discuss in detail all the subsystems that constitute the IAM life cycle. (Processes for IP valuation and know-how/IA generation and assessment, for example, are covered in Chapter 15 on valuation processes at Dow.) Here we will review a few that are usually found in large multinational manufacturing and product development firms, including:

1. The patent generation and assessment process
2. The technology transfer/senior management decision-making processes
3. The patent enforcement and competitive analyses
4. Corporate license and royalty management process
5. Development and implementation of a corporate IAM strategy
6. Architecture, design, and development of databases and supporting work processes for IAM
7. The organizational structure of a corporate IAM office

1. *Patent Generation and Assessment for Filing.* In most technology-based firms, scientists and engineers are trained and encouraged to write patents to add to the IP portfolio of the firm. Many large firms have patent train-

ing seminars and collaterals for all new hires. Many firms also offer cash incentives both for writing an invention proposal and for filing a patent. These incentives can range from a few hundred to thousands of dollars per patent. For some inventions in government labs or at universities, the incentive can extend to a fraction (e.g., 25%) of licensing income that may accrue to the patent.

The invention is usually written on a form that asks for name of inventor, references to previous work, a description of the invention, and the reasons this invention is of significance to the firm. The form is signed, witnessed, and dated, and is usually submitted either to the firm's legal department or to an invention assessment committee for evaluation and processing. This process is illustrated in Exhibit 14.5.

Most firms that generate patents have invention assessment committees. These are either centralized in the corporate technical or patent departments or decentralized into the divisions. In almost all cases, the committees consist of experienced technical, business, and legal personnel. In large companies, there may be as many as 50 such committees, each associated with either a business, division, or technical specialty. These committees review all inventions for technical and business merit and fit. They usually assign a grade to each invention proposal designating the patent merit and the urgency of filing a patent. In some cases, inventions are recommended for publication (rather than patent) to protect future right to use, or they may be held as trade secrets.

The recommendations are then passed to the legal department for processing and filing of the patent. In some cases, the number of good inventions exceeds the available resources for patenting. Here, either centralized or decentralized patent committees perform periodic rank ordering to insure that the most important work is filed annually. In almost all cases, the assessment committees are run by patent coordina-

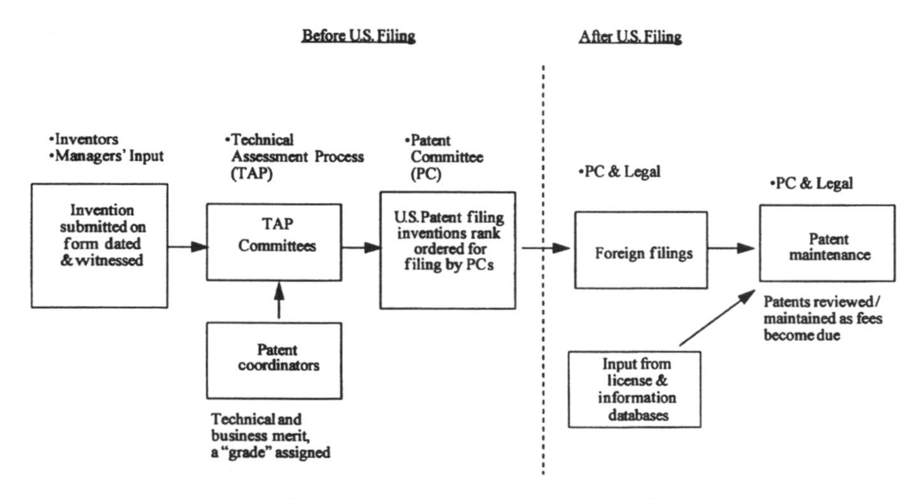

Exhibit 14.5 Invention Proposal/Patent Filing Process

tors who act in a full-time capacity organizing and chairing the committees. These coordinators usually report either directly or indirectly to the IAM group. In many cases, the overall assessment process is also the responsibility of the IAM manager.

2. *IA and Technology Transfer—Senior Management Decision-Making Process.* In firms with large IA portfolios, the transfer of IA into or out of the firm often involves transfer of very valuable corporate assets and is usually reserved to senior management decision rights either at the divisional or corporate levels. For firms with autonomous divisions, and with the IA portfolio broken up and in part associated and controlled by specific divisions, this decision making is done at the owning division. However, in firms where IA is considered a corporate asset shared across divisions, decisions on transfer are made at senior management and at office-of-the-president levels. At Xerox, this decision making is done centrally by the corporate office management of intellectual property (COMIP) committee consisting of the three senior vice presidents of corporate research and technology (chairman), corporate strategy, and the chief general counsel. The committee is managed by the corporate manager of intellectual property (the IAM).

   At Xerox, the decision process is based on two principles:

   - All IA (and IP) are corporate assets and all decisions concerning their transfer are office-of-the-president–level decisions.
   - Time is of the essence in this decision making.

   The COMIP committee meets monthly and reviews all transfers of IA (at Xerox, IP includes know-how) into or out of Xerox and to subsidiaries. The review process is outlined in Exhibit 14.6. A proposal for IP transfer must be sponsored at the division president level and submitted on a form. The form includes a description of the IP to be transferred, to whom, the business reason, the value of the IP, any issues or liabilities, and a summary of the terms and conditions of the arrangement.

   After preliminary review and revision for clarification, the proposals are distributed to a group of MIP champions reporting to all division presidents or their equivalent worldwide. These MIP champions are given ten days to review and comment on any of the cases up for review. If they have not commented within ten days, then by the rules of the process they have answered in the affirmative. A Lotus Notes database is used to provide these cases and background documents to the MIP champs and to collect their comments. After the ten-day review period is over, the comments are reviewed, and case briefs, including the background of the case, the proposal, issues, and the recommendation of the IAM, are drawn up. The committee meets monthly to review these briefs and make their decisions. The results are distributed electronically worldwide within hours of the close of the monthly meeting.

3. *The Patent Enforcement and Competitive Analysis Process.* Competitive assessment can focus in several different areas, from markets, services, and customers, to products' features and value, and to the underlying

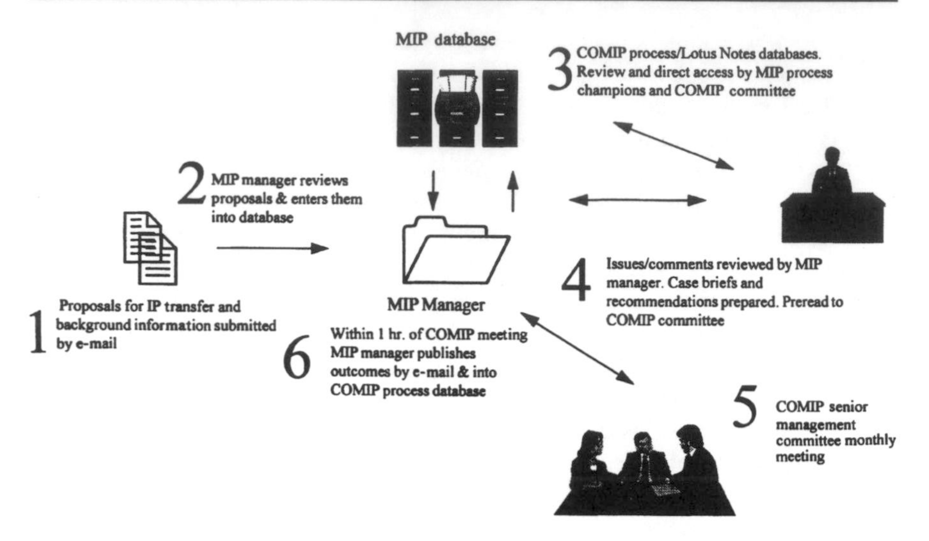

Exhibit 14.6 IA/IP Transfer—Senior Management Decision-Making High-Performance Work Process

technology and processes that comprise the product. Here we will focus on the products per se, the technology, the IP and IA embodied in them, and the enforcement of legal rights associated with this IP and IA.

Competitive assessment and enforcement is an essential element in the operational use of the IA Portfolio.

Competitive assessment of products and effective enforcement can enable:

- Acquisition of IP and IA not otherwise accessible (usually through cross-licensing)
- Establishment of a profit margin differential with competition through a royalty attached to specific infringing competitive products
- Generation of license revenue, per se
- In-depth knowledge of competitors' products and the design process behind them
- Ongoing awareness of specific competitive positions in the marketplace for use in strategic arrangements and outsourcing
- An essential input to strategic IA planning
- An understanding of the specific value of IP in your own portfolio in practical terms based on its effects on competitors, for example, infringements and design-arounds.

To be effective, competitive assessment must operate in the larger context of IA strategic planning, ongoing IA management, and, most important, knowledge management within the competitive and enforcement process. Of these, knowledge management is key. Competitive knowledge is context laden, and its acquisition and use require that knowledge of context is available and efficiently used in its generation. For example, to find a patent that is infringed, you must have organized access to your own patents. You should also have access to the infringer's product history and an understanding of product families and OEM arrangements. It is also important to know if the infringed patent has been licensed and to whom, as competitors may be outsourcing design and manufacture.

Moreover, information concerning previous patterns of infringement and design-arounds are very important to the technical and legal communities associated with IP generation, in that holes in the portfolio may be recognized and filled. Knowledge linkages to the larger technical, legal, and business communities are important as these can provide a large number of inputs and sources for leads on potential infringements worldwide.

The overall process for IP enforcement and competitive analysis is shown in Exhibit 14.4. The process begins with selection and acquisition of competitive products and collateral written materials, such as product brochures or manuals. Much preliminary competitive analysis can be done on paper. The selection process has inputs from strategic planning, technical and business competitive watches, and the senior management objectives. Once a product has been selected and acquired, the analysis occurs through joint technical and legal teams assigned by technical specialty, such as materials, mechanical, electronics, software, and systems.

The teams work through various stages, starting with product overview, comparison to previous products, analysis of written materials, and comparison to the portfolio. All of these processes are mediated and enabled by ready access to groupware, for example, a series of Lotus Notes databases containing on-line all of the needed information. These databases in turn keep a running record of the infringement process, including supporting evidence such as digital photos or materials analysis. From time to time, possible infringements of trademarks and copyrights may be found, and these are in turn entered into the database for future study.

After the portfolio has been fully reviewed and possible infringements have been identified and logged, the legal community takes over for final phases of infringement and patent validation studies, negotiation and licensing, and, if necessary, litigation.

At Xerox, knowledge management is an essential element of the infringement analysis processes. The Corporate Infringement Lab (reporting to the IAM) has a full-time knowledge manager. It is his responsibility to ensure that information is readily available and can be readily captured and reused as generated at each stage of the process. He is responsible for analysis and optimization of all work processes associated with this activity. He is the architect of, designs, and builds all supporting databases. He works closely with the corporate architect for IA databases who also reports to the IA manager.

As can be seen from Exhibit 14.4, know-how is both generated and used throughout the process. This know-how can take many forms. It might be a finding of common design patterns across competitors (use of the same suppliers or recent alliances among them), or it might be knowledge of the firm's own design processes and resulting patterns in the portfolio. It is the job of the knowledge manager to capture this know-how in a timely fashion, at the point of generation, and in a form that makes it readily available to the communities that may use it. Thus, with careful management, the enforcement and competitive analysis process can itself generate significant and important technical and business IA.

4. *Corporate License and Royalty Management Process.* All firms that license out their portfolios and licenses in IA for use in products and services have a function and process associated with the ongoing management of these licenses. This process often reports partially or wholly to the IAM, and execution of the process outputs (notifications, etc.) are usually shared with legal.

   This process, like others in IAM, is strongly dependent on databases for efficient operation. This process begins when a license agreement is signed. The license agreement, along with a key terms and conditions, is put into the license management database. Key elements of the license, such as expected royalties, key dates, provisions for exclusivity, change of control provisions, the specific IP or IA licensed, are extracted and cross-referenced to other databases as appropriate. For example, all licensed patents are noted for ongoing maintenance, as well as for infringement analyses. Using this database, royalty receipts are forecasted and tracked on a quarterly and annual basis.

   For licenses out, changes in receipts or missing payments are followed up each quarter. The status of the licenses are noted and followed up for changes in exclusivity provisions, changes in control of licensed parties, monitoring of grantbacks, and special tax provisions associated with foreign licenses.

   For licenses in, the terms and conditions are similarly tracked, and payments are calculated and made on a timely basis. The use of these licenses is similarly monitored to insure that IP has been received as agreed, and that the intended use has been carried out. It is not unusual for changes in product plans and delivery to affect the need for underlying licenses. These processes can be run either at the divisional or corporate levels, depending on the nature and distribution of the IA portfolio and the underlying organizational structure. When the process is run centrally, royalty receipts may be reallocated in whole or in part to the organization that generated the licensed IP. This may be done either as an incentive, or to enable and encourage any know-how transfer that may be associated with the license.

5. *Development and Implementation of a Corporate IAM Strategy.* Development of a corporate strategy for IA management can take many different forms depending on the business engaged in and the nature of the IA portfolio. There are several elements, however, that are clearly applicable to IP strategy for patents, copyrights, and trademarks, and

should hold across the know-how categories associated with IA. The process for IA strategy development usually reports to the IAM.

Several elements, common to almost any IA strategic planning activity, are:

- A competitive assessment of IA, both static and dynamic
- An understanding of the underlying business and technical strategy of the firm
- An understanding and assessment of the current IA portfolio and trends in its growth

Some objectives of an IA strategy include:

- Alignment of IP and IA generation with the current and future needs of the firm
- Categorization, valuation, and prioritization of IP
- Setting of targets for IP and IA generation in various categories
- Plans to access specific cross-licenses or specific outside IA by cross-license or acquisition
- Development of a distributed IA competency throughout the firm
- Development of processes and methods for valuation of know how and other intangibles.

Strategic planning is by its nature cross-organizational and cross-disciplinary work. A primary aim is alignment of the firm's IA strategy with the overall operational and business activities and plans of the firm. The output of strategic planning can affect the overall IP/IA output of a firm. It can redirect the technical planning and resource allocation from old to new areas, and it can result in new perspectives, processes, programs, and training.

Moreover, a strategic IA perspective can provide valuable new insights into the basis of value of the firm and open new possibilities for extracting value from IP, IA, and knowledge assets that may otherwise be taken for granted or go unnoticed.

6. *Architecture, Design, and Development of Databases and Supporting Work Processes for IAM.* As has been shown, a corporate IAM process involves the use of many interrelated databases. In companies that manage IA centrally, the architecture, design, and management of the IA databases fall under the scope of the IA Manager. At Xerox, this is the case, and the management of all corporate IA databases reports to the IA manager, and through him to the senior management IA governance (or COMIP) committee. At Xerox, IA database management is governed by five principles. The IA databases will be:
   - Architected
   - Integrated
   - Incremental
   - Accessed with restrictions
   - Services the work processes and users

   These principles are strictly adhered to and have resulted in a well-ordered, efficient, and useful system of corporate databases.

Prior to development of any database, the underlying work process is studied in detail, documented, and optimized. It is only when the human work processes are reasonably well understood that database design begins. At Xerox, the most recently designed databases are built around groupware such as Lotus Notes, and are designed for full user access through a web browser such as Netscape. As a result, widespread use is possible, and users do not need to have the client on their desktop to access, use, and input to the databases. The use of groupware also allows the databases to be integrated, enabling a database application in, for example, infringement analysis, to have seamless access to other database applications in license maintenance or patent filing. Thus, even though the databases are distributed and maintained locally, to the user they appear as one seamless database. The groupware also allows full text and context-sensitive search of all documents across all databases, as well as access to existing legacy systems and work processes.

In our recent use of these new accessible and searchable systems in the patent filing and enforcement areas, we have observed significant work process disintermediation, or removal of intermediate process steps. Steps in older work processes often involve requests for documents such as patents, license agreements, or other files, and hours or days of waiting for such paper documents. The almost instantaneous and near-simultaneous access to multiple documents through web browser access to databases has changed work processes dramatically. While not yet measured, the effects on productivity are likely to be real and substantial.

Another important role of the IAM in database development is the design and internal enforcement of an overall IA system and information architecture. One architectural finding has been that single sources of IA data (and especially purchased data) can and should be used by several communities. Prior to development of the architecture, communities would purchase and customize the data (e.g., patent data) to their needs. Now, a generic data set is purchased, and customized access, relevant to the specific work process, occurs instead.

Another finding is that there appears to be a natural evolution from the IAM role in work process–based architecture and groupware-based databases, to knowledge management, especially within the heavy IA user groups. In part as a result of this evolution, some of the groupware-based databases are being designed to be two way; that is, the user accesses them for information and is also allowed and encouraged to put information and codified knowledge back into the database at the time and point of generation. A very simple example of this is a patent database that allows annotation in the form of electronic notes to be added to any page of a patent.

7. *How a Firm May Be Organized for and Practice IAM—The Organizational Structure of an IAM Office.* An IAM office can be structured in many different ways in response to the underlying organization and busi-

ness needs of the firm. Here we discuss IAM at Xerox, a firm where IA is centrally owned and managed.

Exhibit 14.7 illustrates the organization of the IAM function at Xerox. The term *IP* is used at Xerox to cover all the areas defined as IA in this book. Here IAM is a corporate function, reporting to a corporate IP governance committee (the corporate office management of intellectual property or COMIP committee), consisting of the senior vice presidents of corporate strategy, corporate research and technology, and the office of general counsel. The functions presently under the COMIP office include:

- The process for review and approval of all IA transfers worldwide
- The process for the management of royalty bearing licenses, including royalty collection, forecasting, and allocation
- The IP enforcement process and the Corporate Infringement Lab
- The corporate IA architecture and database development process
- The corporate IA strategy process
- Processes for IP generation and assessment

MAKING IAM HAPPEN—SOME FIRST STEPS

The collective experience of the companies represented in this book is that successful construction and implementation of IAM is enhanced when some well recognized management process steps are followed:

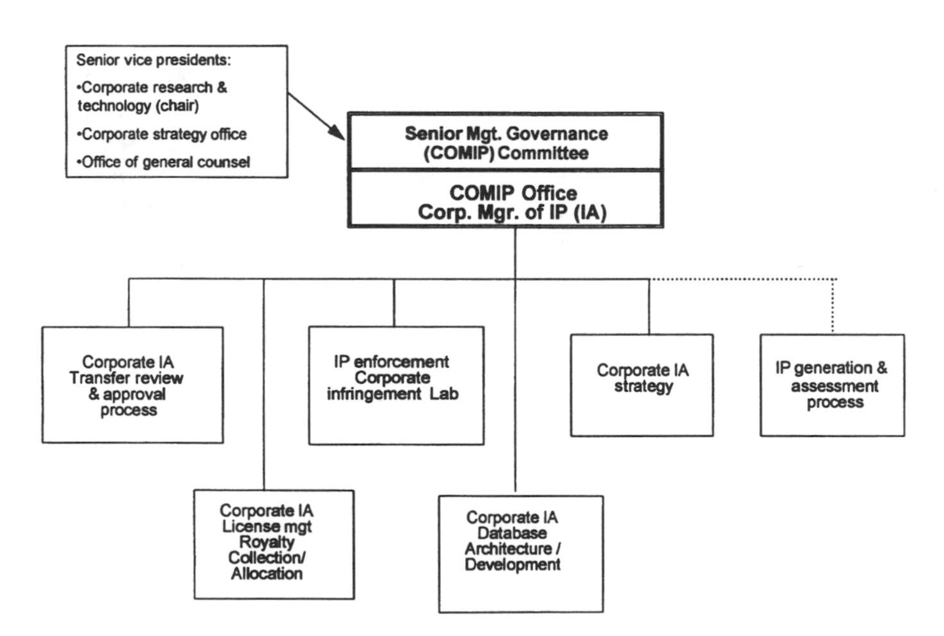

Exhibit 14.7 IAM Organization in a Centralized Environment (Xerox)

1. *Obtain the support of senior management:* One of the key enablers for initiation of an IAM process is senior management awareness of the utility and value of IA in corporate rivalry. It is important for senior management to see IA as a new currency in the knowledge-based worldwide environment of the 1990s and the coming century. A firm's IA portfolio can provide invaluable trading rights to the IA of other firms. In the environment of knowledge-based firms, few act alone; rather, they work through a web or network of relationships with other firms. An IA portfolio provides the table stakes that allow firms to play in the game and engage effective relationships with other similarly enabled firms. Moreover, a strong, well-managed IA portfolio allows a firm to have an advantage in all its relationships and arrangements. These can include OEM relationships, outsourcing of engineering, technology, design, and manufacturing services, as well as distribution and service relationships, and joint development and business relationships of all kinds. An IA portfolio can also be the basis for capitalization of new business start-ups.

   With senior management understanding and backing, IAM processes such as have been discussed here can be put in place, usually with continued management oversight and governance. The specific priorities and IAM activities focused on will depend on the business needs of the firm and the nature of the current and future IA portfolio.
2. *Develop an IA strategy:* The key to a successful IAM system is knowing the firm's corporate strategy and creating a tailored IA strategy aligned with it. A strong alignment of IAM with business needs and uses ensures its effectiveness, continued relevance, and healthy growth.
3. *Where relevant, build your IAM system on a strong IPM system:* Because intellectual properties (including know-how) are usually the basis for the current commercialization of innovations, a strong IPM system is fundamental to being able to successfully manage and exploit all of the firm's codified intellectual assets. This is less the case for service-based firms that depend almost exclusively on their human resources and knowledge-based IA for competitive differentiation.
4. *Expand the key elements of the IPM system—There are four elements of the IPM system that expand in an evolution toward IAM:*
   a. **The Portfolios of Assets to Be Managed.** In addition to a portfolio of patents and trademarks, etc., the IAM includes portfolios of other forms of codified knowledge, such as know-how and source code. These portfolios can be added to the "system" already in place for managing IP.
   b. **The Competitive Assessment Function.** In most firms, competitive assessment is largely tactically oriented around marketing, service, and sales issues, focusing on obtaining competitive advantage in the marketplace in the near term. IAM deals with longer-term issues and is associated with the strategic and competitive positioning of the intellectual assets of the firm.

c. **The IA Architecture and Database Design Function.** IA management is firmly grounded in the management of the knowledge and knowledge processes that constitute IA. Successful IAM is dependent on architecture and integrated IA databases that enable codified knowledge to be available when and where it is needed.

d. **The IA Strategy Function.** This function, for IAM firms, involves assessment of the IA portfolio life cycle and value chain with the strategic intentions and initiatives of the firm. It also involves the use of all of the information provided by the extended set of portfolios and databases under management. Thus, IAM-enabled firms can make better informed decisions about products, markets, litigation avoidance, access to needed intellectual assets under the control of others, and so forth.

5. *Apply Concepts, and Principles, but Tailor Techniques:* There has been some very creative work done by a number of companies around the world in managing their intellectual assets. It would be a mistake, however, to think that something developed by another company could be applied "as is" to your firm. When you find something that looks interesting or workable, determine its underlying concepts and principles, then apply those concepts at your company, not the details of someone else's technique.

SUMMARY

- For the first time, and with the author's practical experience as a basis, a model for the emerging field of intellectual asset management is defined and described. Managing IA means managing all of the firm's knowledge assets including IP and all codified knowledge.
- Sophisticated knowledge firms and the financial markets have realized that their portfolios of IA can have a great impact on the future of their businesses.
- Context is important; it defines much of what is done with IA, and how it is done.
- Managing IA involves learning and exploring new concepts, such as
  —The IA value chain
  —The IA life cycle
- The IA manager is often responsible for both IP and IA functions, such as
  —Valuation and categorization
  —Decision making and its support
  —Competitive analysis
  —Architecture and design of databases
  —Generation, assessment, filing, and maintenance of IP and IA
  —IA strategy
  —The interface with knowledge management processes
  —Managing IP income-producing activities

- An IAM system has known and definable subsystems
  —These can be built on similar subsystems in the firm's IPM system.
  —These involve an expansion in four of these subsystems.
    Portfolios of assets
    Competitive assessment
    IA architecture and database design
    Alignment with business strategy

NOTES

The author would like to gratefully acknowledge the work of Patrick H. Sullivan of the ICM Group for his contributions in discussion of the topic, and in reading, editing, and helping to structure this paper.

15

Intellectual Asset Management at Dow Chemical

Gordon Petrash

Dow Chemical Company

The following are insights in how The Dow Chemical Company created a vision for the management of its intellectual assets, and how it has successfully traveled down the path to getting there.[1] The processes that were developed and used, and the lessons learned along with future plans, are discussed.

Dow believes that in the future business environment, successful companies will be required to engage in more partnering and alliances, will do this globally, and will do it within legal boundaries. This is not to say that head-to-head competition will be minimized; in fact, it will most likely intensify. Dow is preparing itself for this future. It has recently reorganized itself around global business units and established strong business leadership reporting lines. Dow has implemented and is continuing to implement best practices. To do this effectively, it is benchmarking leaders in all industries. Dow believes that the better its competition understands their own intellectual assets and the process to manage them, the healthier the competition will be in the future. This could result in less litigation and misunderstanding. Dow sees other companies as potential customers and licensees for its technology. Raising the level of knowledge in this area will only benefit it in the future. Customers will understand and accurately value Dow's technology. This is important to Dow, because it expects to significantly increase licensing income by the end of the decade.

SETTING THE CONTEXT

Dow started in the United States in 1897 producing a few basic chemicals. It is now a large global company producing over 2,000 chemical-related products. The company is presently organized into 15 major business units along with over 40 joint ventures. Its 1995 sales were over $20 billion with about half of the revenues coming from European, Latin American, and Pacific area sales. Dow spends approximately one billion dollars a year in research and development and employs about 4,000 R&D people. Its present patent portfolio consists of about 25,000 patents globally. The company will spend over $30 million a year on maintaining and supporting this patent portfolio, which includes patent obtention, litigation, writing agreements, and so forth. Historically, Dow has been managed through a matrix-type organization. The matrix consists of functional, business, and geographical components. Throughout the company's history, deferent functions have taken on a leadership role. Presently, global businesses are in the leadership role. A quick profile of Dow and its culture would be best described as technology driven (we can do it better for less); a global player (think global, act on a national basis); and conservative (in true Midwest tradition).

Catalyst for Action

> Corporate intellectual properties will be more valuable than their physical assets in the 21st century.
>
> *Joel Barker, Futurist, Infinity Limited*

If I had to choose one idea that acted as a catalyst for action, probably more than any other, it is this quote from Joel Barker. The quote has floated around Dow for many years, resonating, but never resulting in action. The leveraged buyouts that took place in the 1980s are an indicators that what Joel Barker talked about had real creditability. This was further advanced by John Tobin, Yale University. Tobin addressed the differential between a corporation's book value and it's market value and called this difference *service value.* Much of this service value, I believe, incorporates intellectual capital and intellectual assets, both of which are defined later on. These ideas along with Dow's own experiences have contributed to building a framework for the future that will greatly value intellectual assets.

Some companies that were highly profitable only a few years ago are barely surviving today. Other companies that were not around ten years ago have leapfrogged the industry leaders. The ability of a company to manage and leverage intellectual assets has certainly played an important role in this repositioning of industry leaders. Dow must focus on the management of its intellectual assets and its intellectual capital not only to survive, but to prosper. It's certainly not to say that Dow or any other corporation has not managed its intellectual assets; in fact, I believe there is a direct correlation between how well the intellectual assets of a corporation have been managed and its financial success. The opportunity is in being able to visualize, better measure, and manage them.

The Vision

For the past three years, the intellectual asset management (IAM) function has had the responsibility to integrate Dow's intellectual assets into the business strategic thinking of the corporation.

Maximize the business value of Dow's intellectual assets and develop a management process that will help to maximize the creation of new valuable intellectual assets.

Intellectual Assets. Dow defines intellectual assets as knowledge or legal instruments (patents, trademarks, copyrights, and trade secrets) that have value or the potential for value. Intellectual assets are part of a larger body of intellectual property that does not necessarily have value. Dow also recognizes both of these to be part of an even more broadly defined body of knowledge called *intellectual capital.*

Intellectual Capital. I subscribe to the definition of intellectual capital being presently developed in collaboratives that include Leif Edvinsson, Skandia; Hubert Saint-Onge, Canadian Imperial Bank of Commerce (CIBC); Charles Armstrong, S.A. Armstrong Ltd; Patrick Sullivan, ICM Group; myself; and others.

Intellectual Capital = Human Capital + Organizational Capital
+ Customer Capital

where: *human capital* is that knowledge that each individual has and generates; *organizational capital* is that knowledge that has been captured/institutionalized within the structure, processes, and culture of an organization; and *customer capital* is the perception of value obtained by a customer from doing business with a supplier of goods and/or services.

Hubert Saint-Onge and Leif Edvinsson have both done an outstanding job of articulating these definitions and their relationships to each other. At a recent forum, a particularly interesting relationship diagram was developed with Hubert Saint-Onge facilitating (see Exhibit 15.1). It shows the interdependency of each of these elements and how "value" is created when knowledge flows between them.

This model is simple and exciting. It encompasses all of the basic concepts that ultimately capture and create value. I am sure you will be seeing it, as it further evolves, in many other discussions about knowledge management and intellectual capital management.

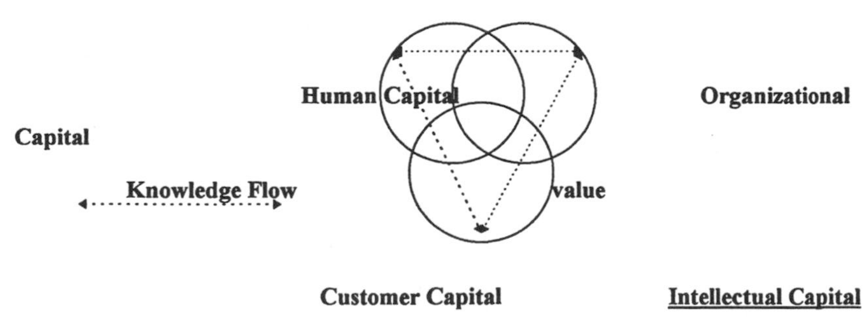

Exhibit 15.1 Relationship Diagram

STARTING WITH PATENTS

Evolving New Processes

So much for context and definition, though I think they are both necessary and critical to any discussion that deals with experiences and models. Where do we start? By recognizing that, within Dow, *evolving* new processes and opportunities is a much more sustainable approach to changing corporate culture and developing new business opportunities than a revolutionary one, recently better described as the "program of the month." It was understood that how and where this new effort was started would be critical to it succeeding. Therefore, it was decided to start in an area that was familiar to many within the corporation, had a high probability of success, would be an obvious value contributor, and could be implemented quickly. Within Dow, patents met this criteria.

Surveying Existing Processes

Starting with patents in no way means that we did not recognize the significant opportunities with other intellectual assets within Dow. Know-how is probably the largest and most valuable intellectual asset in Dow. If we could be successful in managing our patent portfolio, we felt strongly that we could follow that success with the management of our know-how, our copyrights, our trademarks, and trade secrets. The process changes were started by first surveying the way the existing processes were done—*current process*. This was done in a very detailed way for the intellectual asset management process. Getting the right people in a room together, which included all stakeholders in the patenting process, and literally mapping out all of the activities from cradle to grave and all the roles and relationships between stakeholders was completed.

Developing "Should" Processes

Having successfully completed this critical step, and revisiting the corporate vision, development of a *should process* was started. The development of these tools was no easy task. Critical to their success was having the right level of management that understood, in detail, the processes they were responsible for and could make commitments to support them. This careful mapping of the "is" and "should" processes has proven to be the cornerstone to our success in implementing many of the reengineered processes and tools that were developed. The process provided buy-in from all the key players. And it had enough complexity about it that higher management felt secure that all the right thinking went into it. It also limited those who would try to challenge it to truly interested parties.

To include the details of these maps in this forum is not possible. What is possible is to include the abbreviated model that we developed from the should process. This model has become the focus for all of our dialogue inside and outside the company (see Exhibit 15.2).

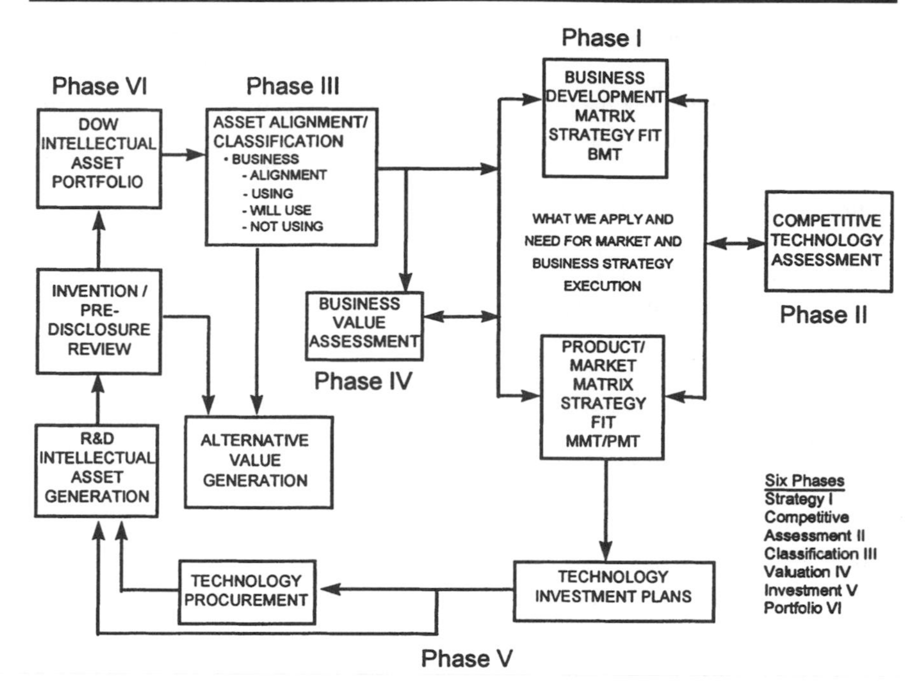

Exhibit 15.2 The Dow Intellectual Management Asset Model

THE INTELLECTUAL ASSET MANAGEMENT MODEL

Development Phases

Portfolio Phase. The best place to start is with the *portfolio phase* of the existing intellectual assets. In Dow we started, as previously indicated, with the existing patent portfolio. The model, in fact, will work for any of the intellectual assets in our company. This assembling of the patent portfolio was not easy. We had to identify all of the properties, determine if they were still active, and find an internal business or cost center that would take ownership and pay the costs appropriate with pursuing or maintaining the property. A lesson learned in this phase of aligning properties to a business was that identifying the business that benefited from the value of the property or that sponsored it made the process much simpler. Sounds like an obvious and easy task until you try it at a complex company like Dow, where there were over 29,000 patents that were not well organized for many years.

Classification Phase. With the portfolio in hand for every business segment within the company, we proceeded to the next *classification phase.* In this step, we determined the "use" of the property. Each business classified all of its properties into three major categories: the business is "using," the business will "use," and the business will "not use." Each of these classifications had additional detailed designations, for example, license, abandon.

Strategy Phase. The *strategy phase* is divided into two parts: (1) integrating the portfolio into the business strategy to fully leverage the properties for maximum value, and (2) identifying the intellectual property gaps to be filled in the portfolio to more effectively implement the business strategy.

Valuation and Competitive Assessment Phases. The *valuation phase* and the *competitive assessment phase* are necessary to accomplish with the strategy phase. Dow has developed a comprehensive intellectual (intangible) property valuation process for internal use in support of licensing, opportunity prioritization, and tax purposes. It is called the *Tech Factor Method* and was developed in close association with A.D. Little consultants. In short, it combines a number of industry-acceptable methodologies in such a way as to allow an abbreviated, low-cost, and self-facilitated estimation of the monetary value contribution from an intangible asset in terms of a percent of the total net present value of the business enterprise in which it resides. This methodology has been documented and is available on request (limited availability).

Obviously, no strategy is complete unless it is done in the context of a competitive environment. Competitive technology assessment tools are readily available, but the most valuable one to Dow in assessing patents is the *patent tree.* This tool has been used within the company for over 15 years. It is a valuable tool that allows you to visually organize your own patents along with any or all competitor patents and evaluate such things as dominance, breath of coverage, blocking, and opportunity openings. It has the flexibility to be organized in ways that can reveal the direction competitors are headed and which areas inventors are active in. Most of this information is available publicly. The Dow patent tree tool makes it easy to assemble, visualize, analyze, and explain. We are presently expanding this tool to include all intellectual assets, including know-how, so that it is evolving into a *knowledge tree.*

Investment Phase. With the intellectual assets integrated into the business strategic thinking, they can be leveraged for maximum value; and, with the strategic gaps identified, the next *investment phase* can proceed. This is simply the procurement of technology that will contribute to attaining the business objectives stated in the strategy. This procurement leads us to understand the external resources and the body of work that is available outside of the company. This survey acts as the first step to understanding what we would have to overcome if we were to develop this technology in-house. After this survey is completed, it must be determined whether to joint venture, license, purchase, do cooperative research with external sources, or develop the technology in-house. If we are successful in obtaining the needed technology and, where appropriate, securing a patent, the intellectual asset is incorporated into the portfolio and the process starts again.

Intellectual Asset Management Teams

There are over 75 multifunctional teams closely aligned with the businesses that are responsible for the management of the intellectual asset process and portfolio.

These teams are composed of front-line managers from the various functions within the businesses. They meet two to three times per year to review the portfolio and make recommendations to the business management regarding intellectual assets (initially, this only encompassed patents). The teams have operated in Dow for many years. Historically, they were little more than a forum for R&D and patent people to set priorities for which patents to file first and where to file them. Today, they are helping to integrate intellectual asset issues into the business strategy and implementing processes that will optimize the costs and gain maximum leverage.

Intellectual Asset Managers

The intellectual asset management teams (IAMTs) have been led by intellectual asset managers for the past four years. These managers report into both the intellectual asset management (IAM) function and into business R&D management. As part of the function, they have been the backbone for reengineering the many processes that were needed to make the intellectual asset management (IAM) model work. For the past four years, the focus of their job has been to identify best practices and reengineer or create the tools needed to do the IAM manager's job. Today the focus of their job is to take these tools from within their businesses and, through the IAMT's advocate for, implement the model and tools needed to make the vision of business ownership come true.

It is realized by the company that this vision will take time to accomplish, and that to do so, the culture of the company will have to change. And as I indicated before, the sustainable changes take place through an evolutionary process. The intellectual asset managers will be the focal points for this to happen. They will accomplish this by working within each of their individual businesses and through the intellectual asset network that has been created—The Intellectual Asset Management Tech Center.

The Intellectual Asset Tech Center

The Intellectual Asset Tech Center (see Exhibit 15.3) is the organizational structure that was designed to support the IAMTs and the IAMs. It refers to a similar organizational structure found within the manufacturing community at Dow. It's primary function within the intellectual asset management function is to directly manage those activities best managed from a central point and support the management of those activities best managed on a decentralized

The Tech Center responsibilities include:

- Maintaining the communications network (home page, staff meetings, workshops)
- Sharing best practices
- Continuous improvement of processes
- Database support
- Administrative support
- Leadership

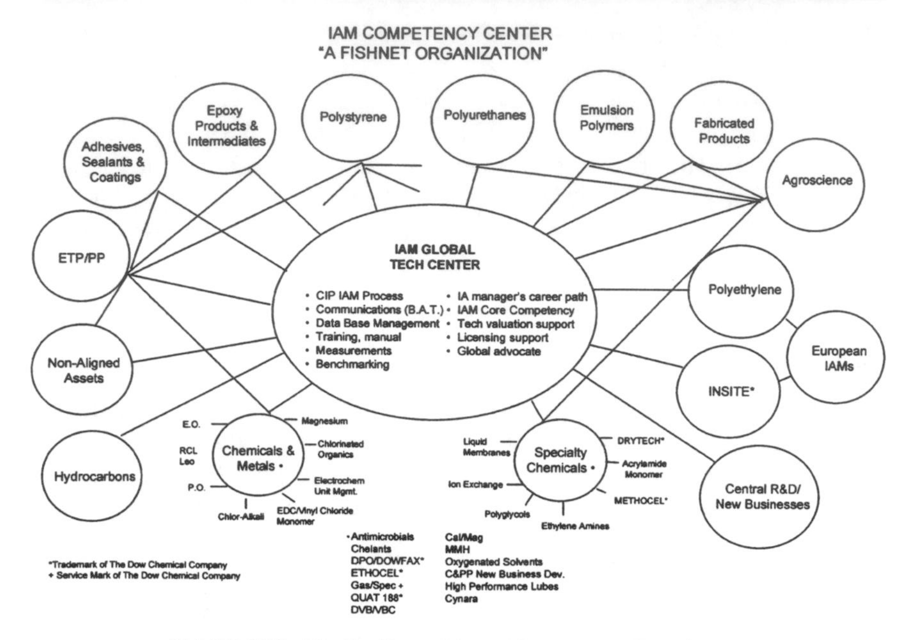

Exhibit 15.3 The Intellectual Asset Management Tech Center

- Career development of IAMs
- Training and training manual
- Measurements
- IAMT support

The intellectual asset managers, through their intellectual asset management teams, are responsible for the following (internally referred to as the IAMT minimum standards):

- Develop and maintain an intellectual asset plan aligned with the business strategy
- Review the intellectual asset portfolio at least once a year
- Identify key intellectual assets
- Classify intellectual assets by utilization
- Manage portfolio costs
- Where appropriate do a competitive technology and portfolio assessment
- Create and staff intellectual asset management teams and facilitate IAMT meetings
- Lead and advocate for the IAM vision and process implementation
- Make recommendations for licensing, abandonment, donation, and utilization of IAs

The Process and Tools

The process and tools that need to be developed or reengineered were many—from the development of a competency in and methodology for valuing intangible property to improving and simplifying the way we approve the release of technology for licensing. In all, over 60 processes, methods, and tools were developed, or reengineered. I will review a few of the more interesting tools that we developed in addition to the valuation and patent tree tools I described previously. I must emphasize the importance of having capable, dedicated, and focused people responsible for the completion of each of these goals. Having people unfamiliar with the subject and only able to work on IAM goals for 10 or 15 percent of their time would have caused this entire effort to die a slow death. The window of opportunity to focus resources was there and open for a limited time, we knew it and planned our projects accordingly. We also planned the completion of projects so as to allow us to use new tools that would make an immediate positive impact. This helped us maintain support for those projects that had importance but could not be accelerated.

Auditing and Classification

One of these initial projects was the *auditing and classification* of all of Dow's patents. This effort enabled the company to reduce its patent tax maintenance costs by $40 million over the life of the portfolio (about ten years) and about $1 MM in the year after it was completed. This was the function's first contribution and gained widespread recognition acting as a spring board for the many other process changes that would follow.

Key Patents

Another project recently completed was the identification of *key patents* in all of Dow's businesses. This effort proved to be more valuable than we had first envisioned. Not only did the company develop a database of all its key patents, it caused, for the first time in many businesses, an awareness of what the patent's contribution to the overall business really were and were not. It proved to be a vehicle in many businesses for debate and ultimately consensus building between the businesses, manufacturing, patent, IAM, and the R&D function. The businesses now have a solid understanding of their patents and can incorporate this understanding into their business strategies. We are seeing the results!

One result is the company's new licensing income target for the year 2000 of $125 million. This is a significant increase from the $25 million that we received in 1994. This can only be achieved when the business management understands what its intellectual property position is and develops plans to leverage it. In the past, we did not pursue licensing because we were not confident in knowing what impact it might have on our existing business. The only things that were licensed were those technologies that we were clearly not going to pursue.

Leveraging Approaches

The resulting reduction in Dow's patent portfolio (over 30%) challenged us to find a way to salvage some value from those properties that we decided to drop. We abandoned many patents that probably should not have been patented in the first place. Some of these might be better classified as vanity patents. The traditional way for technical people to advance and get promoted was to get a lot of patents and publish many papers. The emphasis was as much on "quantity" as "quality." This is changing quickly within Dow.

Out-License. Trying to out-license these properties proved to be unsuccessful. They did not justify the time and effort needed to market and support licensing opportunities. Utilizing brokers also proved to be unsuccessful.

Donations. We did develop an alternative leveraging approach that so far has proven to be successful, "donations." Simply put, we have given technology to universities and nonprofit institutions worth millions of dollars over the past few years. This has supported the overall corporate donation efforts and thus benefited the company. I might add this is not as simple as it sounds. There are many bureaucratic hurdles that must be cleared and liability concerns on both the giver's and donee's parts. If done correctly, there could be resulting tax benefits for the companies that make the donations in the United States.

Patents are where we started, but all of the tools and examples I have reviewed can be and will be used for trademarks, trade secrets, know-how, and copyrights. The company is presently building off the success it has had in managing the patent portfolio and is now focusing on probably the largest and most valuable body of intellectual assets "know-how".

THE NEXT STEPS

Know-How

Know-how is the next step on which Dow is focusing. As we start to adapt the processes and tools already developed for patents to know-how management, we will also be benefiting from a number of related corporate activities underway. Probably the most significant activity is the installation of a corporate-wide *standard workstation.* This workstation is presently being installed and before the end of the year will be fully operational. This new system will incorporate standard hardware and software, common networking, and database management systems that allow easy access and integration of data. The impact of this will be significant. It will get the company closer to being able to get *the right information in front of the right people at the right time!*

Know-how management is a more formidable challenge for Dow than the management of patents. First let me emphasize that managing intellectual assets is something all successful companies do well. The opportunity is in managing them better. The payback for doing this is significant. This is obvious and being recognized and acted on by companies all over the world. As obvious as the need to better manage know-how is, the "how" of doing it is not. Dow is utilizing its intellectual asset management model that has already been developed and tested with patents. The most difficult task is correctly identifying the know-how that you want to manage and "making it visible."

Making Know-How Visible

Making know-how visible is accomplished by first defining the limits. In Dow's case we have defined the limits to be *key technical know-how,* with "key" being defined as providing a competitive advantage. Building on previous approaches, as described earlier, the place to start is by focusing on one component of know-how that has the best chance of successfully being defined. Three questions need to be answered:

- What is the key technical know-how in a given business segment?
- Where does it reside?
- How is it articulated?

These are the questions now being asked in each of the intellectual asset management teams within the company. The debate that takes place between the different functions within each business and the coming to consensus will be invaluable. It will cause the technical community to take stake in what technology is truly a competitive advantage. It will begin to engage the business community and consequently lead them to greater understanding and ownership of the technology within their businesses.

Communicating Key Technical Know-How

The key technical know-how, once determined, will be documented in a common format that will fit easily into a retrievable database. An abstract that clearly and simply describes the know-how and the attributes that give it competitive advantage will be the most prominent aspect of the one-page data sheet. In addition to the abstract, information of the know-how origins, its ties to other know-how/patents, who is responsible for its maintenance, which business owns it, where additional or more in-depth information could be found and so forth, would be included. This know-how information tied together with Dow's newly created networking hardware and software will make the right knowledge accessible to more of the right people within the company. This will only lead to more knowledge creation that creates more value than before.

When thinking about key vantage points for a corporation, consider this:

> **An analogy of the human intelligence to corporate intelligence**—it is generally thought that humans utilize a very small portion of their brains. I have read that it could be as small as 10 percent. It is also thought that if this is the case, the difference between a genius and a remedial person may be only a few percentage points. The point is, that if a company can learn how to more effectively tie into its collective human capital and improve its corporate IQ even by small amounts, the rewards could be tremendous. For Dow, with about 30,000 employees, this is definitely worth focusing some effort on.

Measures

Measures are critical in the successful implementation of any corporate culture change, and intellectual asset management is no exception. It will be even more critical for intellectual capital management.

First some abbreviated philosophy of intellectual capital measurement.

1. The purpose target audience, or the context in which and how the measures will be utilized, must be understood (such as for broad strategic management use or tactical implementation).
2. Measures are necessary whether we like it or not; measures give more creditability to issues and inputs.
3. Everything can be measured (either qualitatively or quantitatively).
4. Intellectual capital must first be visualized it, then it can measured and managed for continuous improvement. The process of measuring has value in bringing the right people together to try to develop measures contributes to building a collective knowledge.
5. Measures are tools which "somebody" still must analyze and use to make decisions; this cannot be delegated to an expert measurement management system.
6. Only measures that are actionable should be taken.
7. Measures should be feedback to strategy adjustment and redirection.
8. Discipline to keep measures current and accurate is critical.
9. Measures of IC are highly context dependent.
10. Simplicity of measure contributes to its effectiveness.
11. Value measures are the end product of where the value is and process measures are indicators that predict achievement of value measure.
12. Range of values versus absolute values are usually sufficient for decisions.
13. Vector measures (directional and indicating a velocity) versus point measures (static and historical) are more useful.
14. Preponderance of evidence of measures is the only way to prove the value of knowledge management.
15. Quantitative measures are often developed from multiple qualitative inputs.
16. Graphic representation of measures is significantly more powerful than numbers and words only.
17. Strong insightful leadership requires less measurement and reduces opportunities for measures to become hurdles to delay or avoid decisions.
18. Diagnostic result, giving meaning to measures, is the most critical result of measuring.

Intellectual asset measures are still under development in Dow. This development is taking place in a corporate environment that is demanding simple and meaningful measures for every resource allocation. The need for measurement and alignment is becoming the corporate norm. Dow's measures are public knowledge. Each year the company develops an economic profit target. This, along with a number of other key measures, drives each of the 15 major business unit strategies. These strategies drive the functional plans, and this is where the bulk of the resources are deployed.

Every project must be aligned with its business strategy. An employee's personal goals must be aligned with functional plans and this business strategy as well. *Alignment* from the corporate objectives → to the business strategies → to the functions and, finally, → to every employee, is continuous and everyone's responsibility. In this kind of corporate environment the biggest dilemma is identifying the best measures of value contribution and process execution. This is not an easy task, though once completed, the resulting measures often look obvious and eloquently simple.

Within the IAM function, Carl Lucas (a Dow intellectual asset manager) has led the measures effort. We did not start with the measures but, rather, with the vision, the management system, and the questions that people managing the system must have answered to align intellectual asset management actions with business strategy and improve the related processes. The measurement system includes not only the measures (what and how) but also the "so what." The meaning of the measure must be communicated in terms of what is desired (e.g., "up is good"), as well as provide actions and/or tie existing actions together that will result in a desired (or undesired) change in the measure. The development of measures is a step, if not an iterative process, within the development of the management system.

Within Dow we started with The Intellectual Asset Management Model. There have been a number of measures developed over the past few years that supported this model. They started out being quite simple (e.g., the percent of unclassified IA) and were driven to zero over time. As the model became more established, the measures became more sophisticated (e.g., the percent of IA that are classified "business is using" within a business unit). This measure tracked over time can give strategic insights not only for an individual business unit, but for the entire company.

One cannot therefore simply look at a list of measures used by one company or business and wholesale adopt them unless the entire management system, philosophy, and support mechanisms are also adopted. Few functional systems can be easily or even preferably transplanted from one organism to another without rejection or chaos. Best practices, however, can, if selectively adapted and correctly transplanted (e.g., enforcement, benchmarking, product development).

The *key value measures* being considered are:

1. Percentage of sales protected by IA (Business is using)
2. Percentage of new business initiatives protected by IA (Business will use)
3. Percentage of technically relevant, competitive IA that require business response
4. Percentage of competitive samples analyzed that initiate business actions by purpose (e.g., enforcement, benchmarking, product development)
5. Value contributed to the business by significant/extraordinary IA management actions

The *key process execution measures/indicators* being considered are:

1. Notification of invention review time
2. Processing time

The I.A. *portfolio status indicators* being considered are:

1. Projected costs until expiration
2. Percent of "business using"
3. Qualitative value classification as a percent of projected costs
4. Classifications completed
5. Key patent cases as a percent of projected costs

Benchmarking

Bench marking has played and continues to play an important role in helping the company to both direct its future direction and determine best practices. Benchmarking has proved to be very helpful in reengineering the processes that went into the intellectual asset management effort. It provided needed perspective and confirmation of the need. It allowed the company to develop targets that not only would allow it to be a leader in the chemical industry, but in any industry. Dow has benchmarked with the leaders in many industry segments for both intellectual asset management and intellectual capital management (this includes knowledge management). We have found the companies in the computer hardware and software industries to be generally using processes and strategies that we feel are best practices. We have also found significant insights from companies in the insurance, banking, and consulting services. Within Dow, setting the competitive standard is an ongoing responsibility of each business and its functions. This leads me to the final discussion of "what is next," and allows me to give a glimpse of what is around the corner in Dow's ongoing journey to becoming a "knowledge value management company."

Visualizing Intellectual Capital

Teaching the corporation what this term means and about its components and how understanding them and their relationships to each other is in progress. The very powerful opportunity to tap into employees, customers, suppliers, competitors, and any sources of knowledge to create value is significant. Skandia Insurance, in Sweden, has produced a document that does this. This document, some encouragement from Leif Edvinsson, and a very powerful message that comes from the concept, has encouraged a small group of people to champion the effort in Dow. A prototype has been completed, and three members of the company's executive management have sponsored the development of a more thorough prototype that would be utilized to gain company-wide support. The objectives are:

- To enable all stakeholders to visualize and better understand the capabilities of the employees, the organization, and all the intellectual capital within Dow to achieve the corporate vision and objectives for the future

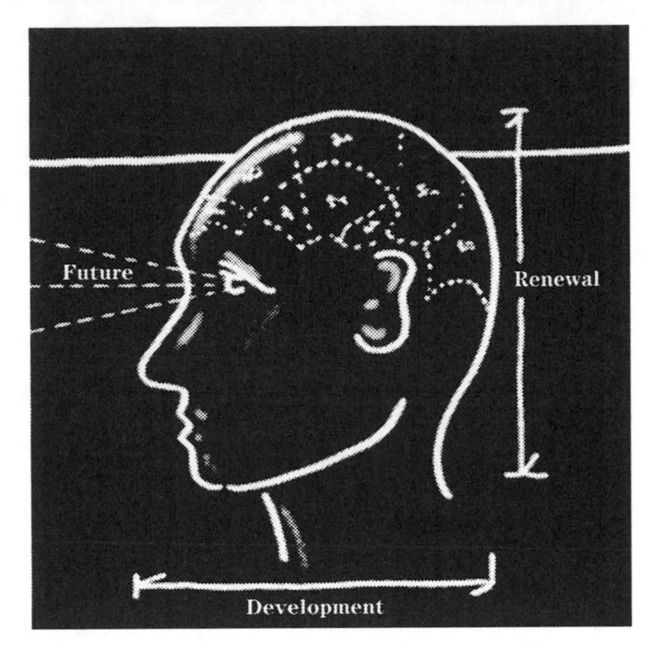

Exhibit 15.4 Visualizing Dow's Intellectual Capital

- To start a dialogue within Dow on the subject of intellectual capital and how to improve the management and measurement of it
- To use the process of developing and maintaining a document that addresses intellectual capital, human capital, its importance to the future of the company, and management's understanding of it, to reconnect the corporation back to the employees

This "visualizing Dow's intellectual capital" effort (see Exhibit 15.4) is planned to be ready for review this summer. If it is approved, it will be a major undertaking for the company. It will require top management involvement and contributions of people representing the breath of businesses in the company and its diversity.

It will not be the end of "Dow's Journey To A Knowledge Value Management Culture," but it could be an important milestone along the way, regardless of the outcome of this specific effort. As expected, the journey has no end but continually evolves with different more interesting venues and opportunities discovered as the road is traveled. Most importantly, Dow has started the journey and is willing to share some of the experiences, insights, and lessons learned along the way. I hope I have conveyed some that may have value for others.

NOTES

1 This journey started about five years ago, with the first step taken by a group of forward-thinking and creative individuals within The Dow Chemical Company. I'm not sure who the godfather of the vision was, but both Denny McKeever, vice president, North America R&D (retired), and Fred Corson, vice

president of Corporate R&D (Board member and my boss), were instrumental in placing me in my current position. They are avid supporters of the concept. Therefore, this distinction goes to both of them. Within Dow, this effort is viewed as very successful. The businesses that now compose the company have benefited and continue to benefit from the efforts of a small group of people who have applied creativity, knowledge, experience, and teamwork to reengineering systems and processes that contribute to the creation of value. The people who signed on to this journey have taken some career risks by jumping into a vehicle that was newly created, not complete, and only had a general direction to travel with no clear maps. This journey has been, and still is, through a territory of cultural change. It has been dangerous, difficult, exciting and rewarding. The people involved have been rewarded with the personal satisfaction of making real positive change and in their own career development and compensation. Sharon, Randy, Dick, Lori, Denise, Jim, Robert, Tina, Virginia, Sam, Bruce, Darryl, Charlie, Phil, Gordon, Cathy, Carl, Pat, Vicki, and Lori were, and will continue to be, instrumental in helping the company complete its journey successfully. I must also recognize the partnership and great support we have received from our Patent Department, Licensing Group, and R&D management.

16

Intellectual Asset Management at Avery Dennison

Lori Morrison and Paul Germeraad

Avery Dennison

INTRODUCTION

The purpose of this chapter is to share the learning and experiences of Avery Dennison's efforts to continuously improve the effectiveness of managing intangible assets. Avery Dennison is a 3.2-billion-dollar Fortune 500 company specializing in self-adhesive base materials, self-adhesive consumer and office products, and specialized label systems. The firm has enjoyed six years of improved profitability, with much of this success coming from focusing on global and new-product strategies designed to leverage the corporation's core businesses and markets. Strong, decisive management of the firm's intellectual capital has become increasingly more important for Avery Dennison, as the corporation implements its strategy to expand globally. Consistent communication of the corporate goals, methods, and value systems is desirable. The firm believes that its stakeholders need an understanding of the value of the firm's intellectual capital. The firm believes that this understanding is essential for maintaining its record of improved profitability and growth.

To continue its growth, Avery Dennison integrates its research and development strategic planning with intellectual property management. Higher value and maximized returns (as measured by a sustainable increase in earnings-per-share) occur when resources that select R&D projects and resources that create and protect innovation are combined. Avery Dennison believes that it has developed an approach to maximize its ability to turn knowledge into profits at a faster rate than in the past. This is achieved by building strong communication networks and encouraging collaborative sharing within the organization. One benefit of the convergence of R&D strategic planning with the management of intellectual capital has been an increased understanding of the intangible assets of the corporation. Another benefit has been the development of better measures to value these components of wealth.

DIMENSIONS OF THE INTELLECTUAL CAPITAL PORTFOLIO

Avery Dennison's corporate culture promotes an environment that recognizes and values each component of the value creation and extraction equation, from the interaction of the corporation's human capital complex to its technological contributions. Within its corporate culture, Avery Dennison defines the term *intellectual assets* as any or all marketable, value-adding tangible or intangible asset. Such assets include human networks, know-how, and expertise. The list also includes all forms of intellectual property, such as patents, trademarks, copyrights, and trade names. Other forms of intellectual assets include brand-name identity, customer databases, and market studies. The firm recognizes that each asset contributes to the overall market value of the corporation, as measured by increases in stock price. The value to the corporate stakeholder can be measured by higher earnings-per-share.

Brand-Name Identity

The firm's stakeholders recognize that brand-name identity is a core intellectual asset for Avery Dennison. The corporate image has been strengthened in the world market by the unification of its businesses under three powerful and leading brands: Avery, Fasson, and Avery Dennison. The firm continues to aggressively support and build on the common attributes that define its brands to leverage their growing value in the marketplace. Avery Dennison's brand names are viewed as competitive weapons, with equity as real as its manufacturing plants, or equipment, or people. The corporate brands are viewed as standing for quality, reliability, and value, features which enhance loyalty among the firm's current customers. The reputation the firm's brands carry also gives the corporation an edge when seeking out new customers as it grows and expands into new marketplaces.

Expanding Patent Portfolio

Another measure of the firm's growing intellectual capital is its expanding patent portfolio. Avery Dennison has approximately 500 U.S. patents covering a wide range of technologies, including pressure-sensitive adhesive compositions, tapes, and labels, fastening devices, variable imprinting, and office products. There is an increased emphasis on technology in manufacturing process improvements, to provide a basis for design and materials freedom.

Avery Dennison uses its portfolio in three ways. First, the firm uses its portfolio offensively, to establish its proprietary leadership position into emerging global markets and as a means to maintain and gain share with customers in its core businesses. Second, Avery Dennison uses its portfolio defensively, to protect its established markets. The portfolio is also used as a basis for conducting license negotiations.

Measuring and Communicating Value of Intellectual Assets

New ways of measuring and communicating the value of Avery Dennison's intellectual assets have recently been adopted. One of the guiding principles put in place was the utilization of economic value-added practices to identify, manage, and leverage the wealth creation of the corporation. Training the firm's human capital to recognize and understand that every decision is to be placed within a values-based context has been critical to the company's success in global expansion and new product commercialization. Additionally, for the latter, three types of new product development efforts were categorized and distinctly managed.

New Product Developments

These three categories of new product developments are line extensions, next-generation products, and game changers. *Line extensions* are defined as technology adoptions that meet the needs of current customers in the short term (1 to 12 months). They are defined as new products for current markets that include product refinements, improvements, and extensions, but not product substitutes. Next-generation products are the firm's answer to the needs of its customers in the near term (next one to two years). *Next-generation products* are defined as new products for current markets, newly designed product families with new materials, and processes that enhance marketplace value. Game changers are the firm's means to bring new-to-the-world features to the strategic pressure-sensitive materials, consumer, and converted products businesses. *Game changers* are defined as new products for new markets, or a step change in product features for current markets. In all cases, the introduction of technology developed as a line extension, next-generation product, or game changer is perceived by the firm's external customer as a new product.

New-product developments are aligned with divisional and corporate strategic intent. Identifying and selecting new projects to work on is accomplished by using internal processes. The processes include the use of strategic tools such as scenario planning and road-mapping to create a portfolio of projects that can drive the growth of the corporation. A fundamental component of each R&D project is to develop underlying technology that will result in distinct product features. Products and technologies are assessed for patentability at two stages in the project life cycle: feasibility and scale-up. The corporate goal is to commercialize and protect by patent an increasingly valuable stream of focused technologies for the firm. For key game-changer technologies, the project and patent portfolios are audited at the corporate level to assure that the corporate strategic intent is being safe-guarded.

Managing Intellectual Property Portfolios

Within Avery Dennison, central research or the originating division historically managed their own intellectual property portfolios, paying all patent filing and maintenance costs and making all filing decisions. Today, a global view to managing the corporation's patents has been implemented through the creation of three intellectual property teams covering the three sectors of the corporation's business interests. At commercialization, the costs of funding a technology are transferred from central research to the appropriate commercializing division or geographically based strategic business unit. Corporate R&D will take ownership of patents that have strategic value for the corporation but are no longer being utilized by the divisions that originated the patent. The intellectual property teams consist of senior business leaders, technical experts, R&D scientists, and patent counsel.

AN IMPROVED PROCESS FOR IDENTIFYING, MANAGING, AND VALUING INTANGIBLES

In 1994, the firm began a project to review its patent portfolio using known methodologies. The purpose of the project was to identify, manage, and then extract the value from the firm's intellectual property portfolio. At the time the corporation began this study, the firm's focus was limited solely to patents. The study now includes measuring and valuing the firm's entire intellectual capital.

To begin the process of valuing the corporate portfolio, the firm looked at emerging worldwide trends. One of the main trends that rapidly surfaced was a requirement to identify the firm's intellectual capital and utilize best-in-class practices to manage it for maximum shareholder value. Another trend identified was a need for better information. Within Avery Dennison, this included a need for better patent information that could be shared throughout the organization. A third trend was the need for rapid product development to keep pace in an arena of relentless competition.

As the first step in the process, the firm undertook a traditional, legal approach to analyzing its patent portfolio by a rather painful, slow review of each patent on a case-by-case basis. The preparation for this review took months. Nearly one man hour per patent was spent in these meetings. The reviewers were experts from the R&D organization and the Avery Dennison legal community. What the corporation found from this process was that it needed a good mechanism to share the knowledge gained. Another lesson learned was that the business element missing in these reviews was critical to the successful valuation of the patented technologies.

Considering this experience, an alternative approach to valuing the patent portfolio was desired. In 1995, the firm looked at the entire systems approach to patent valuation. First, a small group of individuals from the central R&D intellectual property team walked through the patent process. This involved mapping out each step in the intellectual property process. The first step identified was the actual concept of the invention by the inventor. The last step was the filing of the patent application by the firm's legal counsel. From this work, a document was created listing the 26 steps of the Avery Dennison patent process. For each step in the process, the firm identified the next actions to be taken. In addition, each step listed the business functions and roles that were to be involved in developing the intellectual property. Also featured for each step was the wait time or delay between steps. Finally, the work time or actual amount of time needed to complete the action was shown for each step. The process also included additional information for each step to give guidance on how to use the tool. Documented were the entire ideation, documentation, selection, and implementation processes for the firm.

As a second step, the firm worked on identifying where improvements could be made in the patent process. Again, the corporation searched for best-in-class methodologies to improve its practices.

In reviewing best-in-class efforts, members of the intellectual property team came across Thomas A. Stewart's seminal article, "Your Company's Most Valuable Asset: Intellectual Capital."[1] This article chronicled the efforts of Leif Edvinsson, of Skandia Assurance & Financial Services; Gordon Petrash, of Dow Chemical; and Hubert Saint-Onge, of the Canadian Imperial Bank of Commerce, in valuing a firm's intellectual capital. After reviewing this article, the firm came to two realizations. First, that its concentration on improving the patent process was too narrow in scope. Second, that the firm's real focus should be on valuing the corporation's entire stream of intangible assets, and not just it's patented technology.

As a next step, Avery Dennison met with Dow Chemical. From this meeting, the firm gained insight into the needed elements for building a methodology and systems approach to valuing its patents and other intangible assets. The goal was to develop a new methodology that would help the organization improve its communication on its strategic intent. At the same time, Avery Dennison also joined the Intellectual Capital Management (ICM) Gathering. The ICM Gathering is an informal information sharing organization cofounded by Gordon Petrash (Dow Chemical), Leif Edvinsson (Skandia), and Patrick Sullivan (The ICM Group). From these contacts, Avery Dennison gained a clearer understanding of what the firm's next steps should be in building its strategy to build and extract value from its intellectual capital.

Integration of the knowledge and understanding learned from these contacts was the next step. The firm reviewed the best-in-class practices and strategies learned from these organizations. Then, it created a comprehensive five-year plan and strategy for the effective management of its intellectual assets.

The first year's goal was to internalize a vision to be the best at identifying, managing, valuing, and capitalizing on the firm's intangible assets.

The second year's goal was to develop measures and track them across benchmarked organizations.

The third year's goal was to identify and/or build tools to communicate out the firm's shared knowledge and to identify the sources of variability and wait time.

The fourth year's goal is to reduce the variability and wait time by eliminating the known sources of variability and by improving the drivers of averages and work time.

Finally, the fifth year's goal is to stabilize on continuous improvement.

After creating the plan, the firm began the initial stage of implementation. First, it forged a vision to be the best at identifying, managing, valuing, and capitalizing on a new economy based on leveraging Avery Dennison's intellectual capital to maximize the firm's wealth. The firm's mission was to process and transfer knowledge more efficiently than benchmarked organizations, so that the corporation could continue to grow in economic value.

The second year's goal was to develop standard measures for assessing the rate of change within the organization. It was agreed that the metrics had to correlate to the firm's vision. The metrics were centered on the effective management of the firm's patent portfolio because of the relatively easy way of measuring the impact of change on the firm's patent strategy. The metrics were placed within an economic context, concentrating on measuring the effects of change in three areas: cost, quality, and service. In addition, a new-products metric was identified to ensure that the corporation was on the right strategic track. Reporting the sales and percentage of new products sold linked the firm's vision for effective management of its intellectual assets with its business impact.

The third year's goal was to identify and/or build tools to communicate out the firm's shared knowledge and to understand the sources of variability and wait time. Building an integrated, systems approach to managing intellectual capital for the future growth of the firm was the primary objective. To reach this goal, a reasonable amount of time was spent in defining a lexicography to fit the needs of the organization, taking into account Avery Dennison's existing corporate culture. One of the hurdles the firm faced was to define what "intellectual capital" meant to individuals within the organization. After some debate, a consensus was reached on the meaning and use of the term consistent with that used by others outside Avery Dennison. Another challenge was to train team members and have them use the new methodologies and tools developed.

Currently in the plan's fourth year, the firm is working on reducing the variability and wait time in its patent process. Much of the development in this area is centered on the application of fundamental statistical tools and on expert problem-solving methodologies to eliminate the known sources of variability. The firm's focus now is on improving the drivers of averages and work time. Avery Dennison continues to seek out robust tools that will provide the firm with a means for the effective management and valuation of intellectual assets.

INTEGRATION OF THE AVERY DENNISON INTELLECTUAL PROPERTY PORTFOLIO WITH BUSINESS STRATEGY

There is a strong nexus between strategic planning and extracting value from the firm's intellectual assets. Recognizing this link, Avery Dennison integrated its strategic planning process with the management of its intellectual capital five years ago. Exhibit 16.1 shows the relationship between business management and the tools, which will be described later in this chapter.

Assessing Current Position

The process of integrating the firm's business and intellectual asset management begins by looking at where the firm is currently positioned. The first step in the

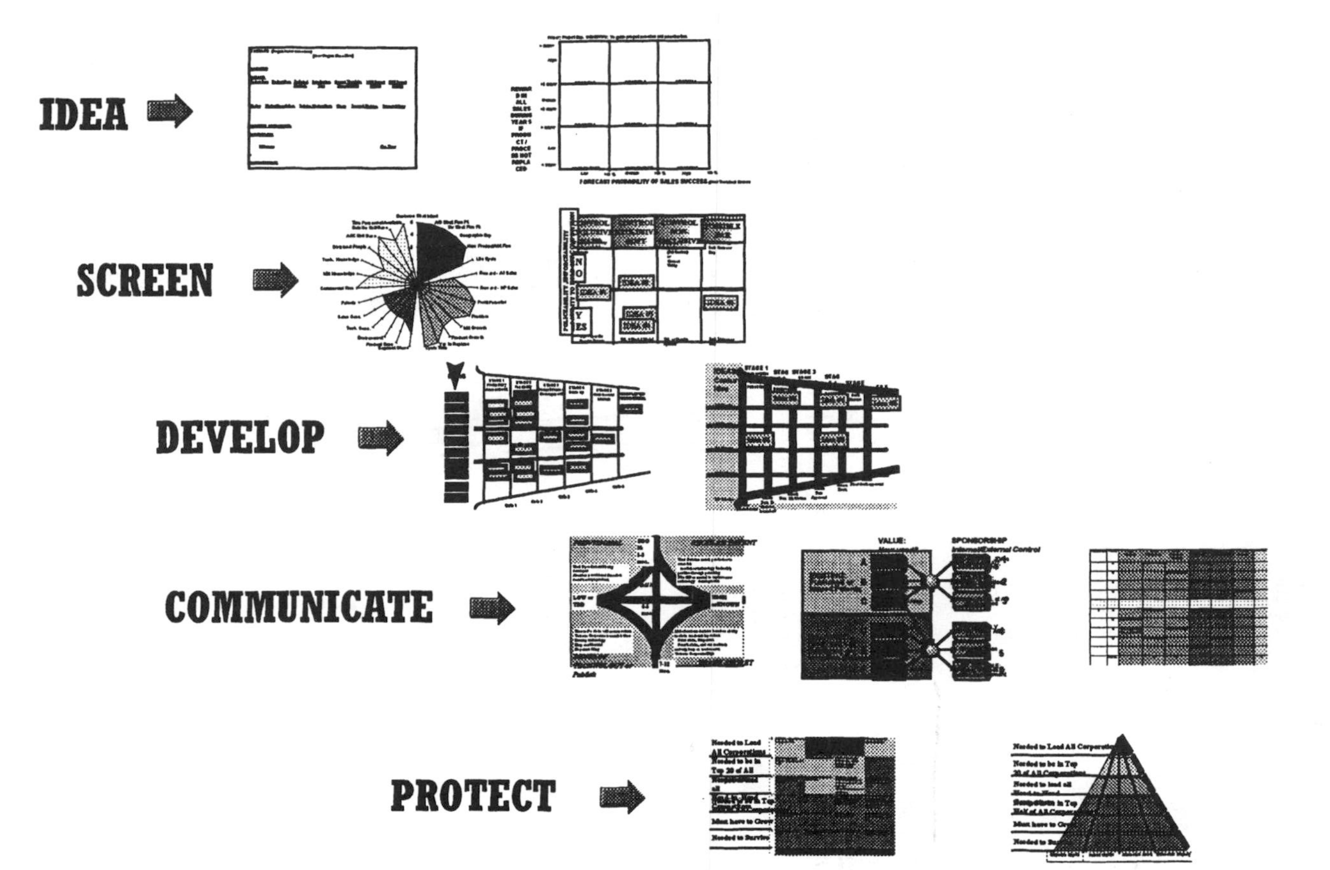

Exhibit 16.1 Relationship between Business and Intellectual Asset Management

process involves collecting and disseminating information on the pressure-sensitive and office products industries, the firm's competitors, and emerging markets. The firm then integrates this information with internal reports to generate a road map of technologies that graphically point out the firm's current strategic direction.

Scenario Planning

Scenario planning is used to describe possible future strategic directions. It expands the corporate perspective by capturing potentially powerful emergent strategies. This information is synthesized with the firm's understanding of its relative competitive position.

The 3 × 3 Matrix Map

To map out this position, a matrix map modeled after those shown in Philip Roussel's *Third Generation R&D: Managing the Link to Corporate Strategy*[2] is used. The 3 × 3 matrix shown in Exhibit 16.2 is used as a tool to identify and select critical projects. The tool identifies the forecast lead time the firm would have from its proprietary position versus the type of protected technology (core, new platform, breakthrough). In practical terms, the forecast lead time is that amount of time in which the corporation will have a proprietary advantage over its nearest competitor. In day-to-day operations, the firm uses this measure as a means of showing how successful the firm will be in obtaining an exclusionary position over newly introduced products or processes.

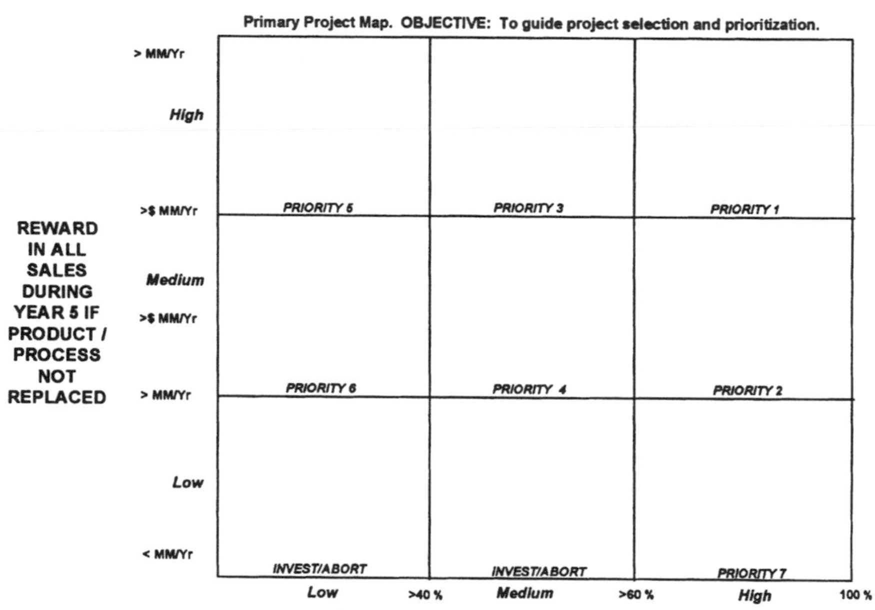

Exhibit 16.2 3 × 3 R&D Matrix Map

The Star Map

To visualize this information, a second "star map" tool is used to graphically illustrate and quickly compare the value of one intellectual asset to another. The star map is a model that makes visible what the firm believes are the four critical features of a single R&D project:

- Strategic fit
- Financial reward
- Risk
- Organizational capability to run the project

Each feature has from 4 to 6 attributes or elements, for a total of 18 attributes. A star map is shown in Exhibit 16.3. Each attribute on the map is designed to "tangibilize" the tacit and exploit the firm's understanding of the value of each R&D project. To use the map, the project is evaluated on the basis of each attribute. The project is given a value from 1 to 5 for each attribute, where a value of 5 indicates the optimum value. When each of the 18 attributes are plotted for the project, Exhibit 16.3 is created, which conveys strategic meaning to the viewer. An entire portfolio of R&D projects can be compared simply by laying each proposed star map side-by-side. By viewing the patterns created, the firm can quickly screen those projects with higher value from those with lower value. By moving the individual star maps around in two-dimensional space, emergent or potential shifts in strategies can be shared and communicated out effectively across the organization.

One of the eighteen attributes on the star map is specifically addressed to identifying the potential value of the intellectual asset within the firm. The "intellec-

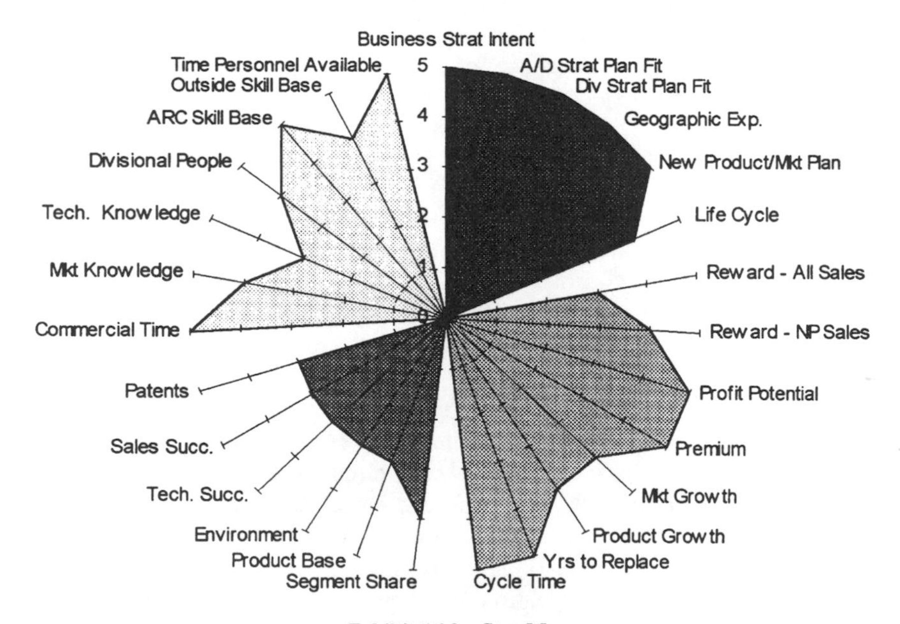

Exhibit 16.3 Star Map

tual property position" attribute is ranked from 5 to 1, with 5 being the desired value. A value of 5 indicates that the firm will "hold off competitive matching of product performance for >5 years [patent]." A value of 1 indicates that a "superior competitive product will be on the market when the firm's product is to go commercial [abandon/license]." The numerical ranking indicates the relative advantage the firm expects it will get from its proprietary position when the products springing from the project are introduced to the marketplace. A project having a rating of 1 for this attribute is considered a poor investment of corporate capital, as no distinct position will be possible.

Other star map attributes relate to corporate capability. These attributes highlight the human and financial capital Avery Dennison can bring to a program. The human capital attribute focuses on two features of the firm's human capital:

1. It looks at the capability of the firm to identify individuals with the right background to make an impact.
2. It looks at the availability of these individuals to participate in the project at the time needed.

The financial capital attribute focuses on the structural capital needed to run the project.

The Funnel Map

Exhibit 16.4 shows a third tool designed to track and communicate the current status of the firm's R&D projects. The funnel map combines the stage-gate process with the star map tool. It illustrates the developmental stage of an individual R&D project and its relationship to the entire R&D portfolio. The star maps for each R&D project are placed on a grid. The grid is designed to show where each project is in its developmental stage (idea, preliminary assessment, feasibility, development, scale-up, commercial launch, postcommercial review) and how long the project has been in that stage.

MANAGING THE FIRM'S INTELLECTUAL ASSETS

Avery Dennison has developed several tools that are used to manage and identify the value of the firm's intellectual assets. One tool is used to capture the intellectual asset, another to classify the asset by value and ownership, and third to help the firm communicate out business decisions related to the asset.

Strategic Planning Sheet. Exhibit 16.5 shows the first of these tools, the strategic planning sheet, which creates a methodology for capturing and sharing out information on a project or invention. Once captured, the R&D project is mapped out using the 3 × 3 matrix maps, star maps, and funnel maps previously described. Inventions are first captured on this tool. If the firm identifies the invention as having value, the high-level information on the strategic planning sheet is integrated with additional detail on the invention and then codified in a standard invention report.

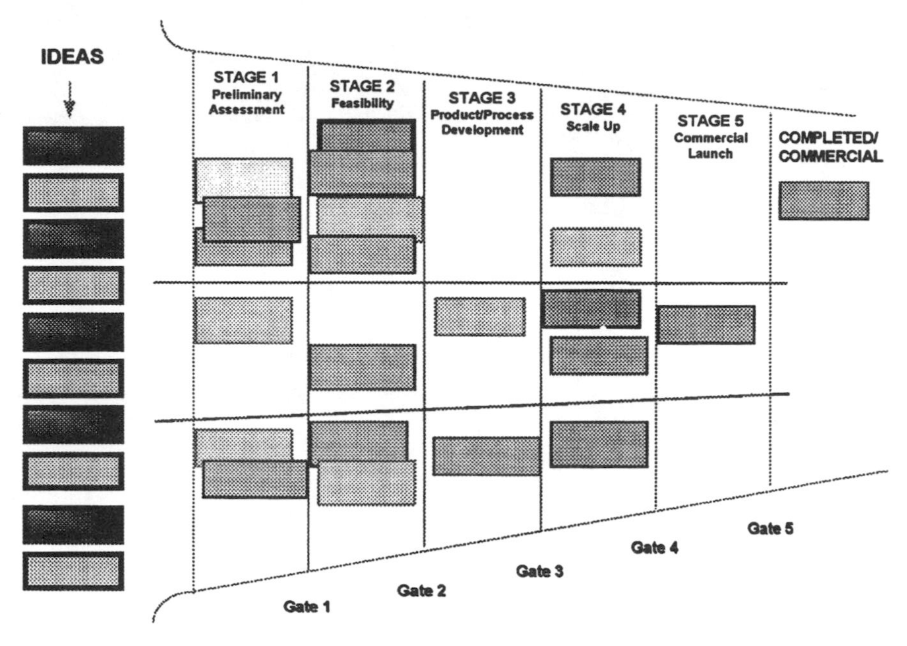

Exhibit 16.4 Project Funnel Map

Corporate Decision Model. A second tool, the corporate decision model for investing in intellectual property, shows how Avery Dennison ranks the potential opportunities made available by the intellectual asset, when the asset is compared to other forms of intellectual assets owned by the firm's competitors. This tool shown in Exhibit 16.6, provides additional insight on the firm's ability to gain exclusionary rights over the marketplace by introduction of a proprietary technology.

Exhibit 16.5 Strategic Planning Sheet

Contact: (Project leader name here)

[Your Project Name Here]

Concept:

Impact:

Project Type	Product Base	Technical Platform	Introduction Year	Current Year Sales Impact ($MM)	1997 Impact ($MM)	2002 Impact ($MM)

Market	Market Growth Rate	Relative Market Share	Group	Targeted Division	Interested Party

Business Objectives:

Milestones

Milestone	Qtr., Year

Expectations

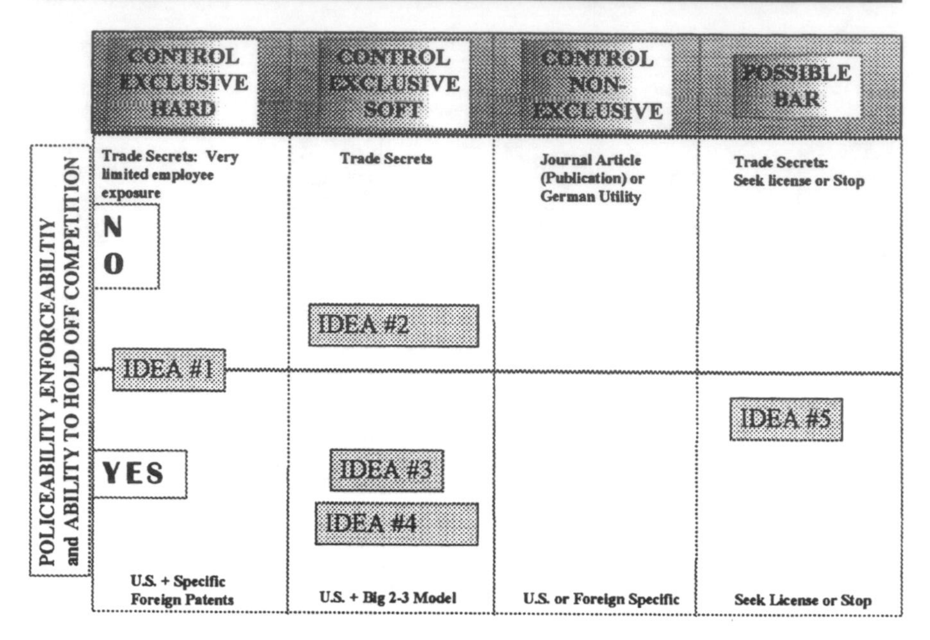

Exhibit 16.6 Corporate Decision Model for Investing in Intellectual Property

The Patent Map. The 2 × 2 intellectual asset (patent) map shown in Exhibit 16.7 provides the firm with a vector for managing its intellectual property. This tool gives some insight into how to classify and manage invention disclosures by requiring the firm to answer two critical questions:

1. What is the timing?
2. What is the technology value?

Four quadrants are created when technology value is mapped against timing. Each quadrant is a decision box on how to classify and manage the invention disclosure. Technology value looks at what opportunities are available to the firm if it goes ahead with developing the intellectual property. Timing (as measured in months) relates to the firm's urgency to leverage the opportunity made available by the intellectual property. Each quadrant directs the firm to a decision on what form the intellectual property will take. For example, one quadrant directs the firm to file a provisional patent application or continue development. A second quadrant directs the firm to publish the invention or continue development. The third and fourth quadrants recommend filing the invention as a regular patent or holding it as a trade secret.

The Patent Funnel Map. Exhibit 16.8 shows a funnel map that was created to track the development of the firm's intellectual property, including its patents, trade secrets, and printed publications. The patent funnel map tracks an idea from its inception to its outcome (for example, the issuance of a U.S. patent). The patent funnel map primarily is used to manage the firm's invention disclosures. It also helps to facilitate communication within Avery Dennison. The tool provides a global perspective on the status of each invention disclosure or family of disclosures within the organization. Using this tool, the inventor(s), the legal and technical communities, and the business units of the corporation are each made aware of the timing and developmental stage of the firm's intellectual property.

The Patent Value Model. The patent value model shown in Exhibit 16.9 is used to asses the value and control of the firm's patents and other intellectual assets. This model was originally developed by the Neste corporation. The original Neste corporation model has been modified by Avery Dennison and custom tailored to maximize the benefits for the firm in categorizing its portfolio of patents and related intellectual property. The patent value model is used to classify each of the firm's patents by one of five technology values:

- Key
- Base
- Spare
- Pacing
- Emerging

The critical question asked at this stage is: How is the asset used within the organization? *Key technologies* are those which grow the corporation; base technologies are those which protect core competencies, and spare technologies are those

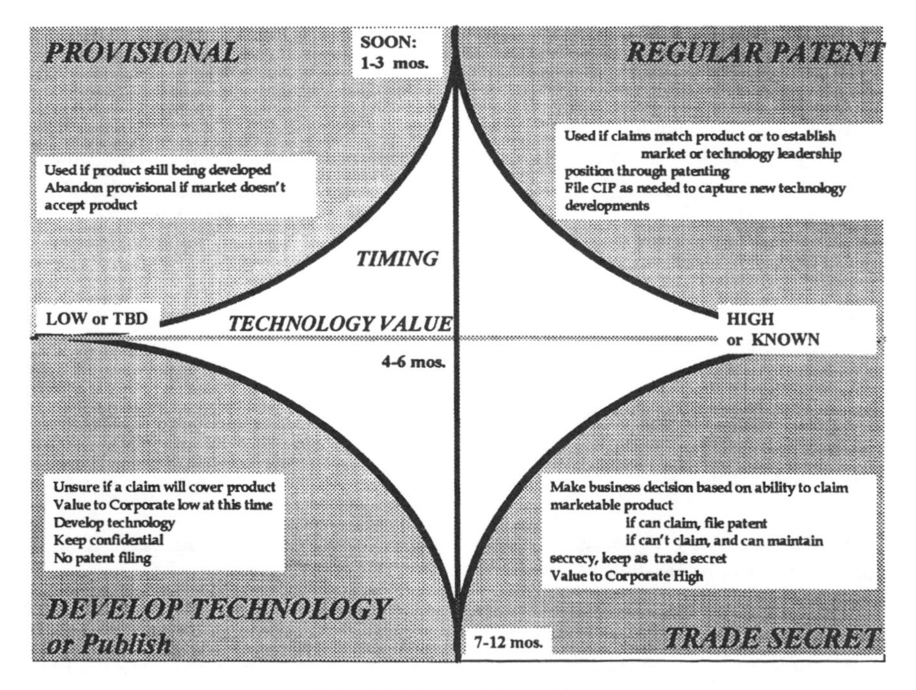

Exhibit 16.7 **2 × 2 Patent Map**

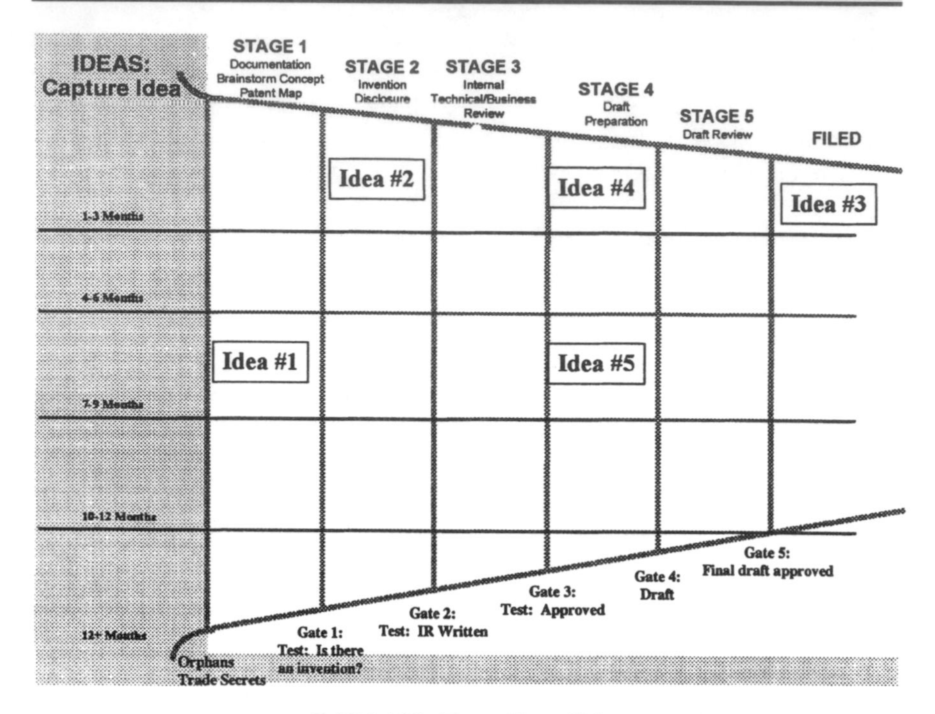

Exhibit 16.8 Patent Funnel Map

intellectual assets that the firm is not currently using. *Pacing technologies* are those which merely are keeping pace with the competition, and *emerging technologies* are those which will move the corporation ahead of the competition.

To use this tool, each patent (or other form of intellectual property) is first classified by its technology value. To make the model simple, an alphabetical index (A through F, as shown in Exhibit 16.9) is used to refer to the patent's technology value. Next, the sponsorship or control of the asset is identified. Sponsorship, which can be external or internal, is limited to one of six possibilities:

- Prohibited
- Strategic
- Commercial
- Potentially strategic
- Excess
- Not possible

Prohibited implies that the asset is not fully owned by the firm. *Strategic* implies that the asset is controlled by an internal strategic business unit and is currently not commercialized. *Commercial* means that the asset is fully owned by the firm and is on sale in at least one market. *Potentially strategic* means that the asset is currently supported by corporate R&D. *Excess* implies that the asset can be

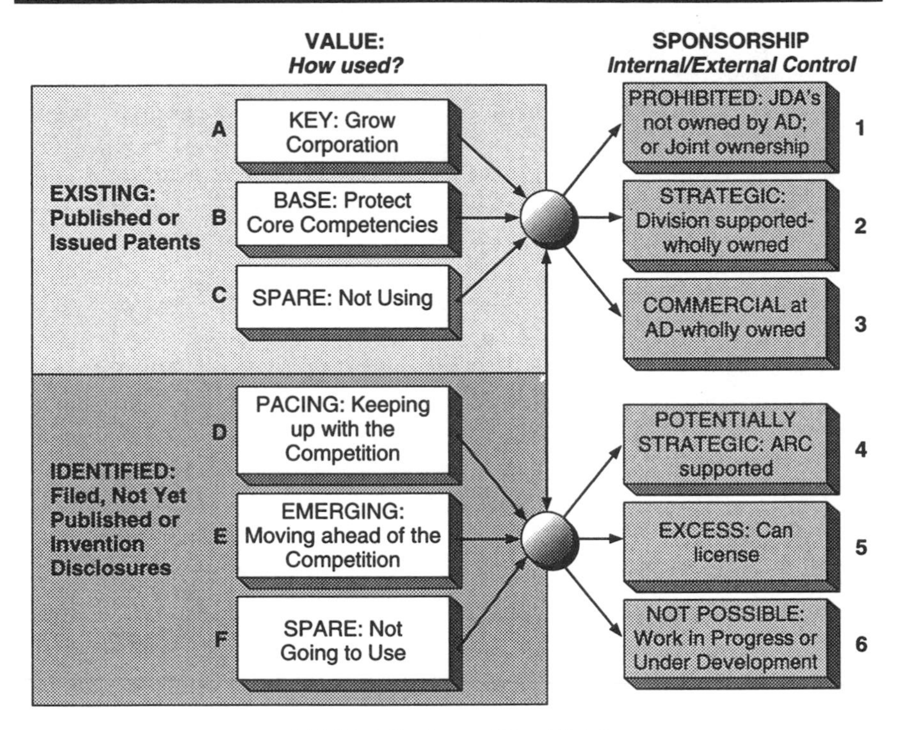

Exhibit 16.9 Patent Value Model

licensed, sold, or abandoned if no buyers are found. *Not possible* implies that further development work or competitive analysis must be done to determine if the asset will be of value to the firm. A numerical index (1 through 6, as shown in Exhibit 16.9) is used to refer to the sponsorship of the asset.

The primary advantage of the new model is in its simplicity. By assigning an alphabetical index to the technology value, and a numerical index to the utilization of the technology, the value of each patent is shown as the cross-product. Using this technique, the time spent in classifying each patent for value was substantially reduced from one man hour per patent to a mere five minutes per patent. Successful use of this tool relies on the knowledge embedded in the firm's human capital. An understanding of the asset's relationship to the firm's business is essential. Additionally, some ability to understand and analyze patent claims is helpful.

Matrix Map Showing Value of Intellectual Property. Using the patent value model, the firm's entire intellectual property portfolio can be categorized. For each of its technical areas, the firm created a tabular spreadsheet to show the number of patents for the technology, classified by the cross-product of technology value versus sponsorship. For each technology area, a further subdivision of the technology was necessary to help organize the data. A representative table is shown in Exhibit 16.10. In each data cell of the table, the patent number(s) are entered. The key to successfully designing the matrix and creating a useful tool was the expertise of the human capital within the firm. These experts had the needed technical background and knowledge to generate the matrix for each of Avery Dennison's technologies.

An advantage of the tool shown in Exhibit 16.10 is that it gives the firm a good perspective of its patent portfolio and its corresponding value by technology. Without adding a great deal of complexity or cost, it provides a way of quickly assessing the firm's strengths and weaknesses in its patent portfolio. The tool is useful for identifying individual patents that protect products or product lines that cover a stream of high-value core technology. It is also helpful in identifying patented technologies that are obsolete, unused, or underutilized. This tool is now being shared out to the entire corporation. One of its primary uses will be to identify residual value from unused or mature technology. Additionally, this approach provides information and guidance to Avery Dennison's business managers as they consider future patent-related decisions. With this new methodology, the firm believes it has identified a process to communicate more effectively to its senior management the value of the firm's intellectual property portfolio. The firm also believes that the tool will aid senior management in providing a clearer insight into potential value extraction from the firm's intellectual asset holdings.

INTELLECTUAL CAPITAL

Managing intellectual assets is more than leveraging a patent portfolio for its maximum return to the firm. Recognizing this, the firm turned its attention to finding a strategic tool that could be used to communicate to its senior management the current health of the firm's intellectual capital.

Corporate Hierarchy of Needs. Turning to an older model, the firm borrowed Maslow's concept[3] of a prioritized hierarchical triangle describing individual human behavior and survival mechanisms and applied it to the corporate entity. The new corporate hierarchy of needs is shown in Exhibit 16.11.

Enterprise Hierarchy Metrics. The corporate triangle was then segmented vertically by looking at the components that make up the firm's intellectual capital. In its current stage of development, the Avery Dennison model looks at the firm's structural capital, human capital, and intellectual assets (with a separate column for intellectual property). A metric for each component at every level of the corporate hierarchy was developed, as shown in Exhibit 16.12.

Mapping the Corporation's Health. The information in Exhibit 16.12 is made visual by color-coding the matrix to indicate the health of the firm's intellectual capital. Using a street light analogy, green is used to show that the firm is 100 percent healthy. Yellow is used to show the firm is weak in some areas, with its health somewhere between 50 and 75 per-

Technology	Family	Key: Strategic	Key: Commercial	Key: Potentially Strategic	Base: Strategic	Base: Commercial	Spare: Excess	TOTAL
1	A		U.S. X,XXX,XXX		U.S. X,XXX,XXX			
	B			U.S. X,XXX,XXX				
	C				U.S. X,XXX,XXX	U.S. X,XXX,XXX		
	D						U.S. X,XXX,XXX	
2	A		U.S. X,XXX,XXX		U.S. X,XXX,XXX			
	B	U.S. X,XXX,XXX						
	C	U.S. X,XXX,XXX U.S. X,XXX,XXX		U.S. X,XXX,XXX				
	D		U.S. X,XXX,XXX			U.S. X,XXX,XXX		
					U.S. X,XXX,XXX			
	TOTAL:	3	3	2	4	2	1	15

Exhibit 16.10 Matrix Map Showing Value of Intellectual Property

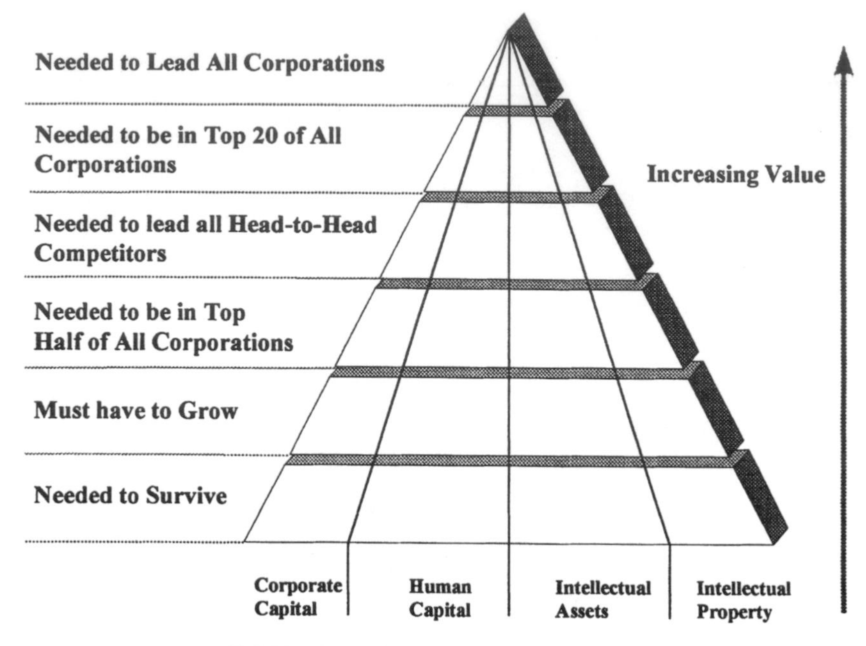

Exhibit 16.11 Corporate Hierarchy of Needs

cent. Red indicates that the skill and knowledge needed to support the firm operating at the particular level is nonexistent or minimal, with the firm's health in this area below 50 percent. An example of a color-coded model is shown in Exhibit 16.13. In this case, the firm has used the model to map out the health of a single technical area.

Triangle Showing Corporate Health. As a final step, the firm took the information shown in Exhibit 16.13 and overlaid it on the triangle showing the corporate hierarchy of needs. Exhibit 16.14 shows the results. The color-coded triangle is an effective communication tool that is used to share out the health of the organization to Avery Dennison's top management and the firm's stakeholders. Reaction to this particular model has been positive. In the next phase, the model will be expanded to capture key competitor information and other aspects of intellectual assets such as customer capital. The information captured in the corporate triangle map will be used to make informed decisions that will help grow the economic value of the firm.

SUMMARY AND CONCLUSIONS

Avery Dennison has found that traditional valuation methodologies are not entirely effective in communicating out the value of the corporation's intellectual assets to senior management and other stakeholders. The firm believes that active

	Hierarchy	Measurements	Corporate Capital (Physical Assets)	Human Capital	Intellectual Assets	Intellectual Property
6	Needed to lead all corporations	Creating and growing in new markets, dominating existing markets	ROE/ROTC > 20%. Market and sales grow > 20%	Global shared vision, planning and capability	Creativity & innovation (gamechangers) > 50% of total sales from new product introduction in last 3 years	IP is used successfully against competitors
5	Needed to be in Top 20 of all corporations	Gaining share-adding new markets	EPS, net income yearly increase > 20%, sales growth > 10%	Planning/strategic capability	Integrated link between business units, market research, competitive analysis and R&D	IP is found to be valid and enforceable
4	Needed to lead all head-to-head competitors	Gaining share in established market	R&D expense in the top 10% EVA in place, cash flow excellent	Communities of practice-shared vision	Competitive analysis; funnel map for tracking IP; other tools such as IP star map-risk/enforce-ability/benefits; stage gate process	Exploit IP; create patent maps & portfolio analysis; technology tracking and mapping
3	Needed to be in top half of all corporations	Maintaining share in established market	Systems management	Systems know-how	Market research; customer & supplier lists/surveys; shared communication means and tools	Procedures for separating out and protecting IP. Creating trade secrets, filing patents, registering TM, copyrights, etc.
2	Must have to grow	Growing at market segment rate	Credit, distribution, production and sales capacity	Education & value sharing	Standard agreed-on practices (SOP's)	Communicate out what is the IP of the entity, and its value
1	Needed to survive	In commerce	Financing, product, basic facility	People, skills and language (common jargon)	Know-how and practices	Capability to designate (separate out/identify) IP

Exhibit 16.12 Enterprise Hierarchy Metrics

	Level	Corporate Capital (Physical Assets)	Human Capital	Intellectual Assets	Intellectual Property
Needed to Lead All Corporations	6	ROE/ROTC > 20%: Market and sales growth > 20%	Global shared vision, planning and capability	Creativity & innovation (gamechangers) > 50% of total sales from new product introduction in last three years	IP is used successfully against competitors
Needed to Be in Top 20 of All Corporations	5	EPS, net income yearly increase > 20%, sales growth > 10%	Planning/strategic capability	Integrated link between business units, market research, competitive analysis and R&D	IP is found to be valid and enforceable
Needed to Lead All Head-to-Head Competitors	4	R&D expense in the top 10% EVA in place, cash flow excellent	Communities of practice-shared vision	Competitive analysis; funnel map for tracking IP; other tools such as IP star map-risk/enforceability/benefits; stage gate process	Exploit IP; create patent maps & portfolio analysis; technology tracking and mapping
Needed to Be in Top Half of All Corporations	3	Systems management	Systems know-how	Market research; customer & supplier lists/surveys; shared communication means and tools	Procedures for separating out and protecting IP. Creating trade secrets, filing patents, registering TM, copyrights, etc.
Must Have to Grow	2	Credit, distribution, production and sales capacity	Education & value sharing	Standard agreed-on practices (SOP's)	Communicate out what is the IP of the entity, and its value
Needed to Survive	1	Financing, product, basic facility	People, skills and language (common jargon)	Know-how and practices	Capability to designate (separate out/identify) IP

Exhibit 16.13 Mapping the Corporation's Health

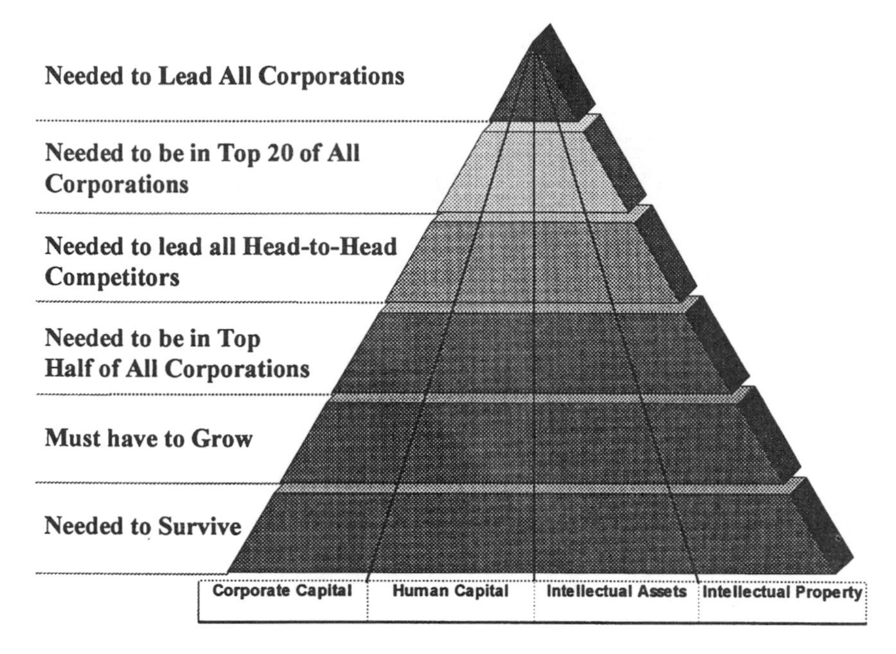

Exhibit 16.14 Triangle Showing Corporate Health

management of its intellectual capital is critical for the growth of the organization. Effective management requires a commitment to a plan developed with clarity, forethought, and creativity. As part of its plan, and in keeping with its corporate culture, Avery Dennison is committed to continuing to search for best-in-class methodologies to identify and extract value from its intellectual capital. This commitment includes the sharing out of the firm's best practices to benefit the corporation and its stakeholders.

NOTES

1 Thomas A. Stewart, "Your Company's Most Valuable Asset: Intellectual Capital," *Fortune* (Vol. 130, no. 7, October 3, 1994), pp. 68–74.

2 Philip J. Roussel et al., *Third Generation R&D: Managing the Link to Corporate Strategy* (Boston: Harvard Business School Press; Cambridge, M.A.: Arthur D. Little, Inc., 1991).

3 Abraham Maslow, "Maslow's Needs Theory," as first published in *Motivation and Personality,* cited in Chester L. Karrass, *Give & Take: The Complete Guide to Negotiating Strategies and Tactics* (New York: Thomas Y. Crowell Company, 1974), p. 110.

17

Intellectual Asset Management at Neste

Kari Laento

Neste

INTRODUCTION

Neste Oy corporation is a Finnish enterprise operating in the oil, energy, and chemicals industries. Founded in 1948, Neste is Finland's second largest enterprise, with annual net sales of approximately $8 billion. Neste was a state-owned enterprise until it was listed on the Helsinki Stock Exchange in the end of 1995.

The petrochemical industry was thrown into a global recession at the end of the Gulf War, reducing profitability for all global players. Neste in particular posted losses of $500 million in 1993 and 1994, the first losses ever reported in the history of the company. The downturn in the petrochemical industry led to a series of consolidations, joint ventures, and strategic alliances among and between most industry participants. In 1996, Neste and the Norwegian state-owned company Statoil decided to merge their petrochemical businesses into a jointly owned company called Borealis. Borealis became one of the four major global players in the petrochemical industry. Statoil's strong upstream positioning, combined with Neste's strengths in production, provided Borealis an excellent balance for the new highly competitive marketplace. The merger also helped Neste to reduce its dependence on the volatile petrochemical industry. Prior to the merger, Neste's petrochemical business had been the second largest business entity within Neste. The spin-off of Neste's petrochemical business had a dramatic impact on Neste's overall business portfolio.

This chapter explains how Neste, in anticipation of the merger, undertook a technology audit to help it better understand the contents of its existing portfolio; separate the petrochemical assets to better understand the effect the Borealis merger would have on Neste's profitability, extract more value from the company's existing intellectual assets; and, finally, determine the future direction of the company. It was my job to actually implement the Audit, and this chapter reflects my views and perceptions of both the process and outcomes of the project.

NESTE AS A COMPANY

Neste Oy is comprised of several large enterprises:

Neste Oil comprises all of the company's oil-related businesses which form an integrated oil chain. The Baltic Rim countries, all within a radius of just over 1,000 kilometers from Neste's refineries, constitute the core market area for Neste Oil. Neste is a significant exporter of petroleum products, base oils, and bitumen to northern European markets. Neste's fleet comprises 32 vessels totalling 964,268 dwt. Neste has also been an important player in international oil trading.

Neste Exploration and Production focuses on Norway and the Middle East. In Russia, Neste is engaged in joint ventures geared for eventual production start-up.

Neste Chemicals manufactures, develops, and markets forest industry adhesives and industrial coatings. Neste is the world's second largest manufacturer of adhesive resins used in the manufacture of wood boards and structures. The company also ranks second among the world gelcoat producers. Gelcoats are used in surfacing various reinforced plastics products such as boats.

Neste Energy Division comprises natural gas importation, transmission, and marketing in Finland. Neste Advanced Power Systems (NAPS) is engaged in the development, manufacture, and marketing of solar electricity, solar heat, and wind energy systems.

SETTING THE STAGE

In anticipation of the Borealis merger, the vice president of corporate technology within Neste proposed a technology asset auditing project in September 1994. The strategic intent of the project was described as follows: "To establish an Intellectual Property Rights (IPR) management group whose charter is to use corporate IPR as a strategic asset and to use technology transfer as a tool to achieve other corporate objectives."

The purpose of the project was to optimize the value of Neste's intellectual property (IP) by assuring the ability to use intellectual property where it has the highest long-term return for Neste—whether through internal use, licensing, partnering, or spin-offs—and by minimizing the costs associated with the acquisition, maintenance, and defence of IP rights. To achieve such monumental change, the project was divided into several subprojects, which included auditing technologies, establishing IP strategies and policies, creating a corporate IP organization and ownership structure, developing a trade secret identification and protection program, and, finally, designing a series of programs to educate employees and management about the IP and its new expanded role within Neste.

The original intent of the program was to audit the technology portfolio and determine its value based on three different criteria: technology transfer potential, management purposes, and increasing shareholder value.

At first glance, a program to redefine and expand the role of IP within Neste does not appear to be extremely challenging or complex. Neste, however, like most of the world's larger oil companies, is almost entirely technology driven. In fact, the company had no corporate language for these purposes. But the impending merger was a perfect opportunity to examine what was in the Neste portfolio, determine the role IP should play in Neste's future, and then determine how the Saltoil merger could strengthen the company.

Before undertaking the technology asset audit, as it was called, most Neste managers assumed that its businesses actively used the majority of their technologies for product research and development. At the same time, Neste managers believed most of the technologies were probably being underutilized and could generate additional cash flow by granting licences to other companies and by selling or exchanging rights of use.

THE BEGINNING

The first decision (and one of the most fortunate) that Neste made was to have the CEO and president of the corporation set up the project. This allowed the project immediate respect and cross-functional support along with enough momentum to get started.

The second fortunate decision was Neste management's determination that all technology assets were owned by the corporation. This meant that the divisions and business units had only the exclusive rights to use those technologies but not to make any final decisions regarding the disposition of them (sale, license, donate, cross-license, etc.).

According to an old Finnish saying: Even the highest tower grows from the ground. Likewise, before starting the actual auditing process, we knew that we needed a solid foundation for our project. We realized the need for a common language with clearly defined terms and meanings; without such clarifications it would be difficult to resolve misunderstandings later during the process. To minimize misunderstandings, we spent a lot of time and effort developing a clear, simple, and concise questionnaire to use in gathering information about each technology.

Our "gut instinct" was that, if we could not articulate our intentions to ourselves, we would be unable to explain it to the divisions; and without that, we would have no chance of succeeding. Also, if we could not define what we were about to audit and measure, we would not succeed in either effort. Therefore, we decided to be very pragmatic.

Until this time, Neste did not have any organization that resembled the technology asset management group. Understandably, people didn't know what to expect of the new organization, what it was supposed to do, nor how to incorporate it into their existing management processes. Exhibit 17.1 shows our first effort at "visualizing" the technology audit. Exhibit 17.2 is a more detailed visualization that highlights the information flow leading to a technology asset dispo-

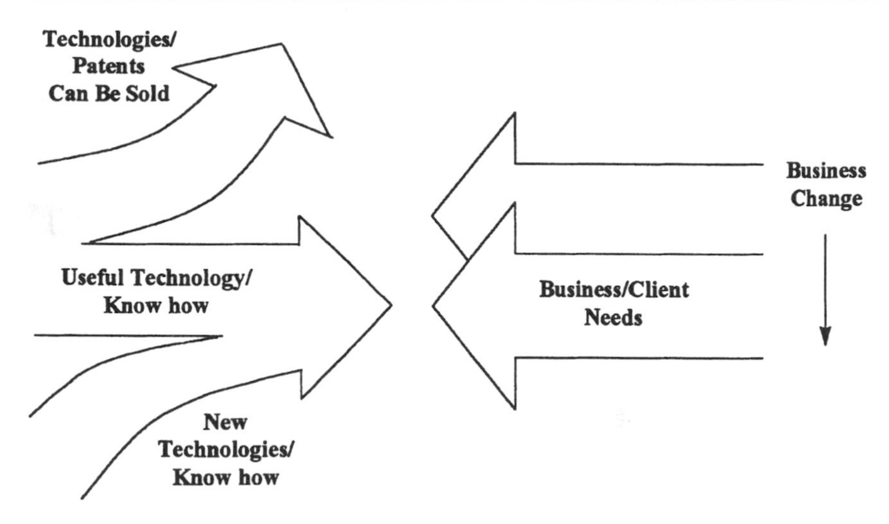

Exhibit 17.1 The Effect of Business Changes on Technology Assets

sition decision (i.e., what technologies and know-how did it have in its portfolio which enabled it to respond to a business change or a client need. Additionally, what excess technologies did the company have which could be sold or licensed to generate short-term profits).

Using Exhibits 17.1 and 17.2 to illustrate our goal and general workplan, allowed us to dispel a lot of questions and fear around the intent of the project. In fact, most managers were curious to see how much added value they could extract from their existing sets of assets.

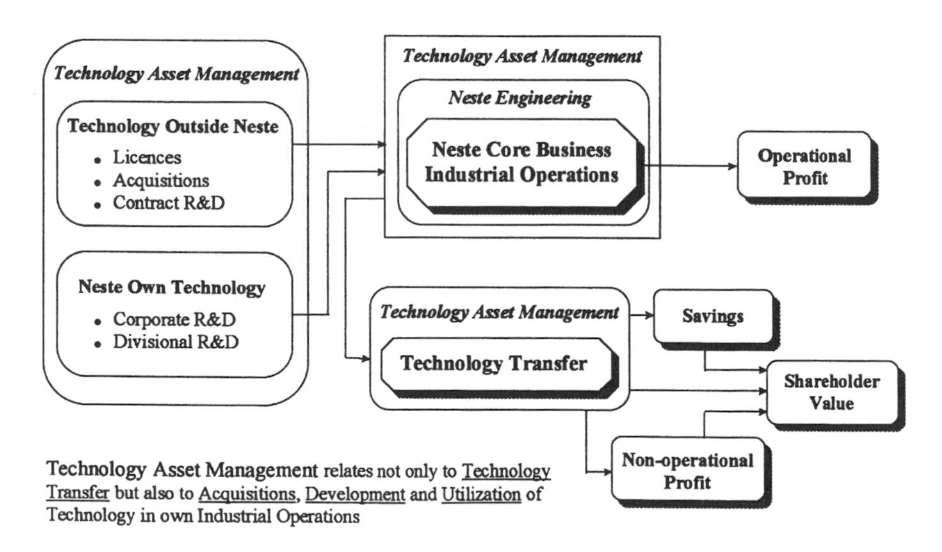

Exhibit 17.2 Value Optimization of Technology Assets

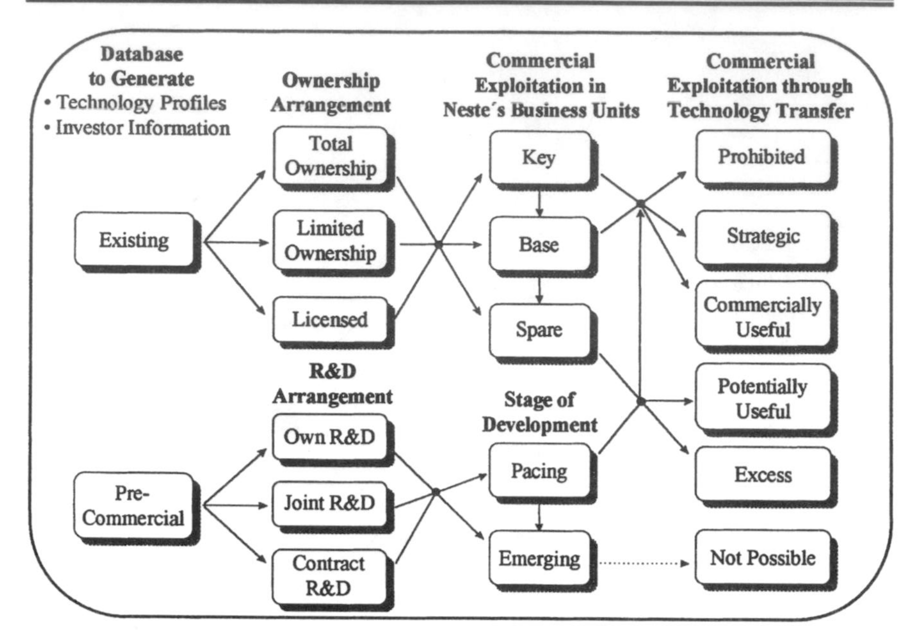

Exhibit 17.3 Neste Technology Audit—Classification of Technologies

CLASSIFICATION OF TECHNOLOGIES

Altogether, about 150 different technologies were audited jointly with division and business management. The evaluation team consisted of one representative from technology asset management group along with two to three from the business units. Initially we did not try to make any final decisions, but only to create a working hypothesis and a framework for each technology audit, recognizing that these definitions could change during the process if needed.

In the first phase of the auditing process, detailed information on all the technologies selected for the audit had to be collected. To simplify the process, we created a standardized questionnaire. It was also necessary to create a technology classification scheme (Exhibit 17.3).

There were four main questions that needed to be addressed for each technology: What stage of technology was it in; what was its legal ownership status; what type of technology was it; and what were the commercialization options for it?

Technology

In the first phase, we defined *technology* as an identifiable process that is or will be materially useful in either a commercial or precommercial product or service. A technology may be wholly or partly owned by Neste, or Neste may only have a right to utilize the technology. A technology may be based wholly or in part on Neste research, engineering, or development efforts or entirely acquired through a licence or other arrangement with someone outside Neste. A technology that has already been commercially exploited on an industrial scale was referred to as *exist-*

ing technology, and one that was in any stage of research or development was referred to as *precommercial technology.*

Ownership Status

We had to define the *status of ownership* of the technology; that is, the legal or contractual status or limitations of the technology. There was a fundamental assumption within the company that most of the technologies we were using in our processes were not our own.

Commercial Exploitation

Commercial exploitation status was the strategic importance of the technology to the Neste portfolio.

A *key technology* is a technology that provides competitive advantage to Neste. It is not widely used in the industry nor available to competitors.

A *base technology* is used and is readily available in the industry. It is necessary for Neste but not sufficient alone to achieve competitive advantage.

A *spare technology* is not currently in commercial use by Neste.

A *pacing technology* is a technology under development that has not yet been exploited on an industrial scale. Still, the development technology or research result has a monetary value and could be exploited through technology transfer.

An *emerging technology* is in an early stage of research or development and has not been and cannot be exploited internally or through technology transfer. Emerging technologies generally have not generated any patents or research results of monetary value so far.

AUDITING PROCESS

The audit was undertaken jointly with the business unit R&D management to ensure commitment for both the process and the results. The auditing team consisted of two representatives from the business unit and one from the technology asset management group. The audit was always conducted on the premises of business.

Each audit consisted of collecting the following types of information:

1. Description of technology
    - *a.* Title
    - *b.* Commercial readiness
    - *c.* Abstract
    - *d.* Technical nature, such as catalyst, unit process, or process configuration
    - *e.* Subtechnologies

   f. Related proprietary know-how that gives a competitive advantage
   g. Location and contacts, such as key personnel, technical contacts, or executive contacts
   h. Related technologies, including dependent and alternative technologies
2. Development and acquisition of technology
   a. Internal development
   b. Acquisition
   c. Commercialization
3. Rights to the technology with detailed description
   a. Patents
   b. Agreements
      (1) Rights granted to Neste
         (a.) Patent, know-how, or trade secret license agreement
         (b.) Confidential disclosure or restrictive agreement
         (c.) Joint-venture agreement, etc.
      (2) Rights granted by Neste
         (a.) Same classification as above
      (3) Technology transfer attempts
4. Disputes
   a. Adverse communication
      (1) Threat or assertion of patent infringement by someone
      (2) Claims of misappropriation of confidentially disclosed inform
      (3) Other adverse communications
   b. Legal proceedings
      (1) Court actions, including infringement suits and arbitration
      (2) Other actual disputes with respect either to the ownership or validity
5. Competing rights
   a. Third-party alternative technologies
   b. Competing rights
   c. Competing patents

As a next step, we tried to define the competitive significance and impact of each technology.

6. Potential for technology transfer
   a. Limitations of technology transfer potential—own, limited, prohibited
   b. Limitations on exploitation
      (1) Health, safety, or environmental hazard
      (2) Governmental or regulatory action–related reasons
      (3) Engineering or related technical concern
      (4) Economic concern
      (5) Other obstacles

After each audit, the information was entered into a relational database that could be queried and sorted by any number of different criteria. Corporate, division, and business level summaries of information were generated. The summaries were checked by the R&D management group of each division before they were considered to be final.

ACHIEVED GOALS

The successful completion of the technology asset audit program has helped Neste to achieve the following goals:

1. All Neste technologies are now classified by ownership and potential for commercial exploitation, both by Neste and by outside parties. The technology asset database contains all technologies of the corporation regardless of where they are located, and the intermediate results have been presented both to top management and to all division and business unit managements.
2. The creation of a common language around intellectual capital now makes it much easier to begin Phase II of this project, the creation of a common valuation process.
3. We were able to determine which technologies were excess and to start immediate action to capitalize on that revenue stream.
4. The following standardized processes were created within each of the businesses:
   - A systematic review of all patents within each business unit portfolio. Each patent is reviewed for relevance to the existing and future business, its commercialization potential, and ownership status. We have been able to save a significant amount of money by abandoning patents that no longer align with the business strategy.
   - A new corporate directive regarding innovation compensation was created to aid management to better focus the innovation process on the high-potential areas.
   - The integration of technology asset management into existing decision processes has increased significantly.
5. We created a technology transfer model, which is used whenever a technology transfer is considered (Exhibit 17.4).

This transfer model helped Neste management frame each technology decision based on its strategic importance to the company. The bottom left corner indicates those technologies in which Neste's investment is low and their ability to control the outcome is also low. In such cases, the technology is recommended for abandonment or out-licensing.

As a result of the audit, management is better able to discuss the possibilities of starting new businesses via JVs or spin-offs. Prior to the audit, most technologies were considered "strategic," and any discussion of out-licensing or selling them was like giving away the crown jewels. Some very promising spin-off businesses outside the excess classification have already started. So far so good. Def-

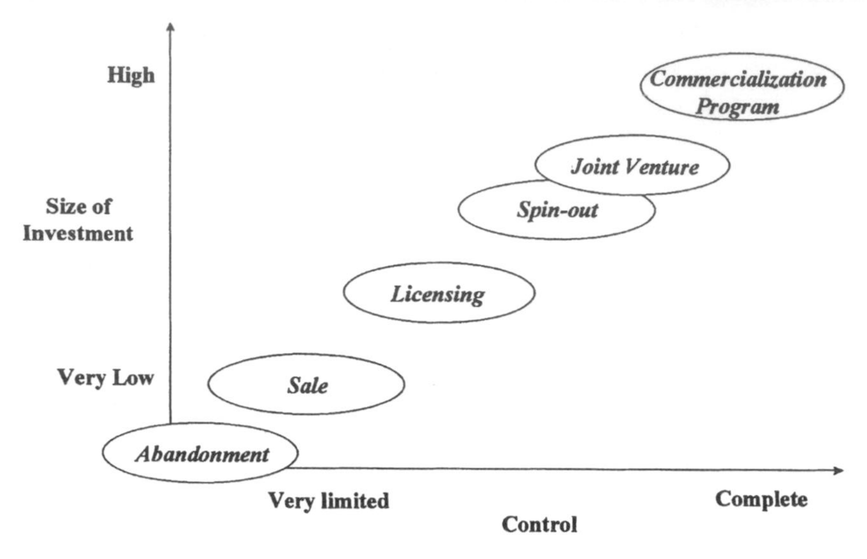

Exhibit 17.4 Forms of Technology Transfer

initions make it easier to decide what is what. Is it strategically problematic to out-license a specific technology to a refinery in South America if our home market is in northern Europe, even though the technology provides Neste a competitive advantage in our domestic market? The audit has provided a useful tool for having these kinds of conversations in a nonpassionate manner.

6. The final decision regarding all technology transfer issues is now made by corporate technology asset management, after getting permission from the corporate technology steering committee. In this way, we were able to double-check that anything of value in the longer perspective didn't vanish by accident. If one technology is classified as excess, it is automatically transferred to the corporate technology asset management's portfolio, along with all the expenses.

FINDINGS

Surprisingly, many technologies were not as well documented and protected as we had originally assumed, and therefore quite a lot of money and resources had to be invested in them before they could be transferred. Once this was completed, there were not as many limitations for technology transfers as had been expected, although quite a number of the processes in question were in-licensed, and not invented at Neste.

More than 50 percent of the patent portfolio was classified as excess. This allowed us to take immediate action and stop paying maintenance fees, as well as to initiate a series of out-licensing agreements, which generated short-term cashflow and budget savings. Also, we found lots of potential value in the excess technologies after we were able to reevaluate them in light of the audit results. Previously we would have viewed them as worthless.

We have successfully created several new business ideas utilizing some of the excess technologies—partly through continued R&D, MBOs, or by re-evaluating joint venture or our licensing opportunities.

The Microsoft Access database created for the audit serves as an excellent tool that can be used effectively as a database for annual planning and the budget process for different businesses. Using the database, business units can create technology leverage in their portfolios by having specific information about their own portfolio, by benchmarking what others are doing, and by determining what competitors are active in their businesses.

Some divisions and businesses are already using the information in this new database as a planning tool for their future activities, having initially reacted to the information as "dangerous," because it revealed that some businesses had over 40 percent of their patents in the excess category and a large portion of the rest in categories that were not in the businesses' future focus. Some are rethinking their patenting and licensing policies, questioning whether it was really necessary to their businesses to file patents, or whether they could build their businesses on know-how and trade secrets, etc.

We found that a large number of technologies were different from those normally understood to be transferable. The most valuable part of them relies on the know-how, expertise, and processes that cannot necessarily be patented or documented, but which could be used as an argument and reference when selling engineering consultant services.

We have found that the information in the database remains reliable, even if it is up-dated only once a year.

SELF-CRITICISM

When the project was started September 1994, we decided to name it the *technology audit* and called its organization *technology asset management* group. This was fine while we were conducting the audit. Now, as we implement the results, we find that many people misinterpret technology assets to mean only intellectual properties. In fact, the project involves all intellectual assets and, therefore, should have been named the *intellectual asset audit*. We have used this mistake to better educate people. To most, a technology asset is either a patent or license. Now, as we begin Phase II, and the valuation of each technology, we make sure that all employees understand technology assets include intellectual capital, intellectual assets, and intellectual properties.

The technology asset management group was organized as a part of Corporate Technology, which is responsible for long-term R&D in the corporation. We wonder now whether that structure sends an inaccurate message to the rest of the company, concerning the basic purpose of the group. Is it to develop new innovations and new technologies, or is it to add value to existing technologies by managing them differently than before?

We know, now, that if we were to begin the audit again from the beginning, with the same techniques and procedures, we would not evaluate all the technologies at once. Instead, we would draw conclusions in an earlier phase based on only a select few, from which we would make more courageous decisions and conclusions.

PHASE II—VALUATION PROCESS

Before valuing each technology, we plan to assign a strategic priority to each one. We believe that doing so will make the valuation process more efficient and flexible.

We are planning to use three different measurements: present value; potential value; and commercial value. In addition, we will define the exploited and unexploited value for each technology.

We are already developing a suitable tool box for these evaluation purposes and have decided on a process that is different from our audit process. We will subcontract the development of tools with contract partners and focus our concentration on businesses and technologies, as we try to improve evaluation and implementing processes.

LEGACY

When I first got involved with intellectual asset and capital management, I was somewhat skeptical. After having been in line management for 15 years, it was somewhat difficult to see that this was not just another fad, but, rather, provided a valuable new perspective and brought old beliefs into question and most important, provided new answers. Now, two years later, I am a strong believer. As I leave Neste after 16 interesting years, I am happy that in my new challenging position as a corporate vice president of Telecom Finland, I have as one of my the responsibilities the creation of an intellectual capital management system for the company, which will be a vital part of "normal" investment and procurement processes. Welcome on board, and try to remember this old Chinese proverb: To open a knot with your tongue, don't use your teeth.

18

Making It Happen

Patrick H. Sullivan

ICM Group, LLC

While worldwide there are only two or three dozen firms systematically extracting value from their intellectual capital, there are hundreds of firms that would like to do so. What stops companies in the second group from becoming like the first is knowing where and how to begin. Most companies wishing to develop the capability for managing their intellectual capital have little or no understanding of what it takes. Members of the ICM Gathering all report that they receive dozens if not hundreds of calls each year from companies asking to visit and to learn how ICM is done. Because we are all anxious to share what we've learned, we put aside time and agree to a visit. When the meeting begins, we all have found that as we describe the things necessary, in terms of knowledge-of-company context, decision processes, work processes, databases, and know-how, the visitors' eyes soon glaze, overwhelmed by what they are hearing. They thought that the "secret" to intellectual capital management was as complex as one or two "key" concepts and maybe two or three pieces of software they could acquire that would "do the job." Finding out that installing an ICM capability involves philosophy, the company's vision and values, decision processes involving senior executives. . . . it is just too much.

Managing intellectual capital is, like many worthwhile business activities, a commitment. It involves developing a capability that results from a logical and systematic set of activities, beginning with a crisp understanding of the firm's purpose and direction and the careful crafting of mechanisms to produce a desired set of results. This chapter discusses each step in the process and provides suggestions about how steps may be accomplished most successfully.

THE FOUNDATION

To begin with, it is necessary for the firm to know where it is going. What is its vision for itself in the future? What kind of firm does it aspire to become? Any journey without a destination may be interesting, it may be enriching, and it may be educational; but it will be neither direct nor without frustration. Remember Alice and the Cheshire Cat; when you don't know where you are going, then any path will do. The very first step is to define the company's long-term vision for itself.

It is often the case that firms do not have a statement of vision; or, even for those who do, the vision does not provide an adequate description of the business it wishes to become in the future. Most firms I deal with in my consulting practice fall into this category. Getting around this lack of a formal vision is actually reasonably simple. I usually bring together two or three knowledgeable senior employees and ask them to tell me what the "real" vision of the firm is. Based on their knowledge of the company and its business trajectory, I ask them to describe for me what they see as the target the firm seems to be moving toward in the future. In every case, the people asked have each been able to describe the company's real target for itself. Most often these descriptions are anecdotal and not necessarily complete. Nevertheless, each person's description of the "real vision" is complementary to that of the others. I typically take notes during each person's recital, then summarize what I understand them to have said. My summary takes the form of a bulleted set of descriptors of the company "in the future." We may modify the bulleted points, adding new ones that now become apparent or deleting some that now become unnecessary. From the bulleted points, the employees and I draft a "working vision" for the company.

With a company's formal vision statement available, or a working vision where a formal statement is not available, the next step is to know what the company's strategy is to achieve the vision. Many companies have a well-known and articulated strategy; others do not. For those lacking a formal strategy, a process similar the working vision process is used to define the "real" strategy of the firm. For purposes of the ICM capability-building "project," a working strategy is an adequate substitute for a formal one.

The final step in creating the foundation is to determine for a company with this vision and this strategy, the role(s) intellectual capital could or should play in helping to move toward achieving its vision and enabling its strategy. Roles should be listed under the two headings discussed several chapters earlier in this book: value creation and value extraction.

THE CONTEXT

Companies, like individuals, each exist in a world of their own. That is to say that each company exists within a unique set of aspirations, strengths, weaknesses, resources, culture, values, external realities, internal dynamics, personalities, politics, and worldviews. No two companies have the same context, even companies in the same or similar business or industry. Coke and Pepsi, both alike in many ways, have different contexts. They may share many of the same external realities, but they differ in their internal realities. No two firms are alike in context. And it is the firm's context that determines much of what is considered possible, achievable, or even valuable within a firm. Context is the reason why an idea that is rejected at one firm as silly or unworkable is seen by another as creative, insightful, or valuable. A firm wishing to create a capability for managing its intellectual capital does well to articulate its context, for it will be the context that will determine what kinds of capability the firm will support.

Context usually comprises three major elements: the business description, the external realities, and the internal realities. For each of these, few firms have a accurate (or politically acceptable) description of "what is." Most often, firms have a party line that describes the view it wishes people to accept as contrasted with a description of what is. The exercise of defining the firm's context is an exercise in defining "what is."

Business Description. Most firms have literature describing themselves, their products or services, and their markets. But often firms do not adequately acknowledge the business they are really in. For example, some time ago I was doing a consulting assignment of the chairman of the Southland Corporation, the parent for Seven-Eleven convenience stores. At the time, Seven-Eleven was the largest retailer of gasoline in the United States. In most states its convenience stores, in addition to their familiar food and home convenience products, sold gasoline at retail. The chairman was faced with internal pressure to purchase a gasoline refinery on the Gulf coast of the United States. Acquisition of the refinery, proponents argued, would integrate the company vertically and allow it to profit from refining as well as from retailing gasoline. The analyses presented to the chairman made persuasive arguments about enhanced profits, ability to sell the by-products of gasoline refining to industrial customers, and so forth. I remember clearly a conversation where the chairman said that his intuition was against the purchase, but he needed back-up data and analysis to buttress his intuition. My response to his comment was simple and direct. I told him that he and his firm had made a multi-billion-dollar success out of the convenience store business, one they understood and in which they had significant experience. But, I said, once you purchase that refinery, you will be in the petroleum business, and all of your convenience store know-how will not help you at all.

Within two weeks the chairman called to say that all of the purchase papers were prepared for his signature, and he needed my recommendations, even though he understood we had barely begun this complex financial analysis. I told him I could give him no better answer than what I had already told him: Purchasing the refinery will change the business Southland was really in. Southland will no longer be in the convenience store business. Despite my comments, and lacking any hard data to back up his intuition, he decided to bow to the internal analyses and purchase the refinery. Six months later he called to say, "Pat, you were right! I just thought you would like to know." He went on to say that he spent virtually all of his time tracking down tanker loads of crude oil to feed the refinery, as well as industrial customers to purchase the unexpected amounts of nongasoline output from the refinery, purchases that were necessary to make the refinery fully profitable. As a result, he was neglecting the convenience store aspect of the corporation's business. The lesson: Be sure you know the business you are really in, and be in that business.

The External Context. The forces extant in the external environment of the firm that drive change in the economy, the industry, and the business, make up the external context of the firm. Most firms can tell you of the forces that most immediately affect their business, changes in the price of raw materials, the general state of the economy, competing products or competitive thrusts. But few know or can define the forces that underlie these near-term forces for change. The external context of the firm includes the macroeconomic, legislative, regulatory, technological, and sociopolitical forces that drive the firm's business environment. These need to be defined, described, and the nature of their impact on the firm known. Once accomplished, these forces can be categorized into major and minor effects and into effects that are expected to be felt in the immediate, midterm, or long term. The key external forces for change, and their leading indicators, must be determined and monitored.

The Internal Context. The internal context is in many ways easier to determine because much of it is already known, if not yet fully gathered together. The internal context usually includes:

- The firm's vision, strategy, and business goals
- The firm's values and culture
- An assessment of the firm's strengths and weaknesses to perform in the business it is really in
- Strategies available to the firm, including those it is pursuing as well as alternate strategies it could pursue to achieve its vision
- Current performance against goals
- Potential usefulness of IC IA/IP in achieving the company's vision and strategy
- Current posture of the company on ICM (favorably disposed, strongly against, etc.)

Having defined the three major elements of context for the firm, it is particularly helpful to document what has been learned. Some firms have gone so far as to create a context document of internal report that captures this information. This report might contain information such as:

1. The strategic vision of the firm
2. Definition of the business the firm is in
3. Macroenvironmental forces
    a. Overview of macroenvironment
    b. Key forces for change
4. Definition of the firm's products and services
    a. Where each is in its product life cycle

5. Define the basis for competition
   a. Cost
   b. Differentiation
      (1) Dimensions of differentiation
6. Describe and define the technology strategy
7. Current firm performance
   a. Measures of performance
   b. Measurements of performance

DEFINING THE ROLE(S) FOR INTELLECTUAL CAPITAL

Once the firm's vision and strategy are known, the role(s) for intellectual capital can be defined. For many technology-based knowledge companies, the role of the human capital is to create patentable innovations that are consistent with the company's line of products and services. For these companies, the role for value extraction is constrained to defensive use: protection and exclusive exploitation of protected innovations. In addition to assuring exclusive use, defensive use of the firm's intellectual assets includes developing assurance of some freedom to practice a technology in the future as well as to avoid litigation.

But, increasingly, firms are realizing that there are offensive ways in which to use their intellectual capital. Firms may use their intellectual capital to generate new or otherwise unanticipated streams of revenue. Firms may use the portfolio to generate income they otherwise might have foregone. They may license core or strategic technologies into new markets that do not compete with their strategic or core markets. They may license or sell no-longer-strategic technologies into existing markets. They may license both core and noncore technologies into nonstrategic markets. Companies may also create de facto technology standards by cross-licensing with business or technology competitors to create a market for new or down-stream technologies yet to be developed. They may simply license out company technology because its widespread use may create a de facto standard, thereby forcing competitors to seek a license to produce products or services consistent with the newly established standard. Finally, many companies have learned that they cannot afford to maintain the range of competencies and skills required to sustain their product line. In this case, companies are creating strategic alliances with firms that have the capabilities needed. Successful negotiations with such alliance partners are often enabled by the presence of strong portfolios of intellectual assets and intellectual properties.

Still another role for intellectual capital may lie in its use to strategically position the firm. Making the outside world aware of the firm's capabilities, its stocks of IC, as well as its ability to leverage them, may position the firm in a marketplace, or it may equally provide access to capital in the financial markets which otherwise might either not be available or at least not available on favorable terms.

Whether the roles for intellectual capital are determined to be tactical or strategic, immediate or long-term, internally or externally oriented, it should be clear that there are many more roles for intellectual capital to play in firms who have carefully decided where they wish to go in the future. Such decisions make it easier to determine how intellectual capital, as well as other strategic assets of the firm, may be used to achieve the desired results.

DESIGNING THE SYSTEM

Once the roles for intellectual capital are determined, it becomes incumbent upon the managers of the firm's intellectual capital to develop the internal capabilities for exploiting the IC in meaningful ways. Beginning with the technology-based knowledge company, this section describes where and how to begin the process of creating the capability for managing intellectual capital.

Begin with the IP Portfolio

This section pertains to the companies having one or more portfolios of intellectual properties. For such companies the place to begin is with the best defined portfolio of intellectual properties. Typically this is the patent portfolio.

Define the portfolio. Managing intellectual properties means first defining the properties to be managed. For companies owning patents or the rights to patents, these constitute the company's portfolio. The first question to be asked is what does the portfolio contain? Are the patents known (surprisingly, there are many companies who cannot define the patents they own)?

Design the IPM system. Describe the IP management system the firm ultimately wishes to create. Include the basic functional elements as well as the decision processes and their supporting work processes and databases. The system design at this stage should be at the overview level. (Detailed design information is not necessary at this early stage, and could even be a nonproductive diversion.) The overview IPM system design developed here becomes the template the firm works toward implementing.

Define the portfolio database. In addition to hard copies of each patent, effective patent management demands that there be a computer file containing useful information on each patent. Useful means that it is information that is needed for decisions at several levels: portfolio management, tactical business decisions, and strategic business decisions. (See Chapters 10 and 14 for a discussion of how a portfolio database can be defined.)

Establish the competitive assessment activity. Fundamental to managing the firm's intellectual property is a knowledge of what the competition is about. This means that the firm needs to know, for both its business and its technology competitors, what they have produced, what their current position and capabilities are, what their strategies are, and what action can be expected from them in the future. Competitive assessment should be performed by people with business as well as technical analytical backgrounds. Many technology firms try to convert technologists into business analysts on the mistaken assumption that business analysis is relatively easy if one has a scientific or analysis background. Make no mistake, business analysis requires the kind of special training found in business or economics programs at universities. Anything less than this level of training is not recommended.

Create a patent policy for the firm. In an ideal world, businesses would only develop innovations that are in line with the strategy or that enable the vision. Our world is, unfortunately, less than ideal. Innovators produce what they produce, and these innovations are not all necessarily on target for the vision or the strategy. To make decision making easier, firms have found that a policy that establishes guidelines for what the firm wishes to patent is desirable. Patent policies span the range of possibilities. For example, a range of potential patenting policies might include the following:

- Patent in order to have a portfolio with which to negotiate business agreements (licenses, joint ventures, alliances, et al.) with other companies.
- Upon brief examination, patent most things which have a chance of technical success.
- After careful scrutiny, patent only those discoveries that have a strong chance of technical success regardless of potential business application or use.
- Patent only those discoveries that have a clear application to your own company's produces or processes.
- Patent discoveries that might block or delay similar discoveries by competitors.
- Patent most things that are patentable.
- Patent only the occasional discovery of quite exceptional importance.
- Do not patent anything.

Regularize the patent generation process. All technology firms have a process of some kind that produces innovations targeted for patenting. Not all of the innovations produced are of patentable quality; and even if they were, the firm might not wish to invest in patenting them. While the patenting policy provides one level of decision-making guidance, many more innovations clear the policy guideline hurdle than the firm may wish to patent. The decision to patent is best made in the context of the firm's business strategy, the dollar amount of budget it has reserved to cover the costs of patenting and the set of patentable innovations available for consideration.

Firms wishing to ensure an adequate flow of innovations into its patent decision process create information processes that highlight innovations under development. This makes it easier for firms to know whether sufficient numbers of innovations are in process to meet their strategic needs, whether too many are in progress in one technology area and not enough in another, or whether not enough innovations are in progress at all. The firm's existing processes for knowing what is in the pipeline and for making the patent decision should be regularized and perhaps made more efficient. Such a regularization will allow the firm to know that it has a sufficient number and quality of innovations to meet its needs.

Develop a valuation process. Create the capability for people within the organization to develop both qualitative and dollar-based estimates of the value of the firm's intellectual assets. The capability should provide a range of valuation methods providing dollar values ranging from coarse valuation to fine. The Appendix contains the Dow Chemical Company valuation process procedures, outlining a range of valuation methods for use by Dow people to accommodate a range of valuation needs.

Develop a value extraction analysis capability. For each technology with the potential for commercialization, several questions must be asked and answered before the company can decide to invest in commercialization. Among those questions will be which combination of conversion mechanisms should the firm use to extract the most value from the innovation? Should the firm: sell the innovation, license it, joint venture to obtain necessary complementary assets, enter into a strategic alliance to obtain access to markets, integrate everything, or donate the technology for a tax benefit? Each technology requires an analysis to determine how many of the conversion mechanisms the firm can use to obtain the best profit results from the innovation.

Create a licensing/joint venture/alliance capability. Once the firm has decided to commercialize an innovation, it needs the capability to make the commercialization happen. In many cases this means commercializing the innovation through licensing, joint venturing, or entering into a strategic alliance. Firms must develop an office or a capability that will be able to expeditiously develop license, joint venture, and strategic alliance agreements and execute them for the firm.

Moving Up to Managing Intellectual Assets

At this point, firms having created the foregoing capabilities have largely developed a systematic approach to managing their intellectual property.

Develop portfolios of nonprotected assets. Create defined portfolio (and databases) for intellectual assets with commercial use or interest. The list of portfolios of nonprotected assets might include licenses (both in- and out-licenses), nondisclosure agreements, joint venture agreements, outsourcing contracts and service agreements, IA aspects of mergers and acquisitions, and customer lists.

Develop IT linkages between portfolios. Identify linkages between the IA portfolio databases. These might include company names, individuals' names, technologies, and products or services.

Expand competitive assessment. Whereas the IP level of competitive assessment has already been developed, the IA level may involve information about the specific marketplace positions and long-term strategies of competitors for use in strategic arrangements and outsourcing, and an ability to determine the specific value of your own current and potential portfolio based on its effect on competitors (e.g., infringements and design-arounds, as well as predicted competitor response to your potential strategic thrusts).

Create litigation avoidance analytical capability. The ability to know when and how your company is at risk of infringement litigation is important. Perhaps of even greater importance is the degree to which potential litigants may be infringing on your own firm's intellectual property, or where the competitor has previously signed a nondisclosure agreement, or is party to a contract or supplier agreement. All of this information, when correlated, is part of the creation of a viable litigation avoidance capability.

Managing Intellectual Capital

Firms managing their intellectual capital are strategically focused in managing both the human and the "paper" assets of the firm. Here the emphasis is on strategy and strategic positioning; how to use the firm's intellectual capital to affect its ability to affect its position in its technology and business markets.

For the technology companies, the building block capabilities are already in place. But for nontechnology companies, they need to ensure that all of the following are in existence before proceeding:

Competitive assessment. Here the competitive assessment focuses on the business and technology competitors, but in addition to the assessment focus on technology of competitive products and services and markets, the ICM company competitive assessment capability focuses in particular on the competitors' human capital as well as on their technology.

With the foregoing capabilities in operation, nontechnology firms need to develop the following new capabilities:

Managing human capital. In the management of the firm's human capital, it is important to known the current and ideal use of the human resource. What is the ideal allocation or alignment of the firm's human capital for achieving near-term goals? Long-term goals? What is its actual current alignment? What is the value creation focus of the human capital? What is the know-how the human capital has created? How is this know-how defined? How may it be described? What is the firm's ability to access it? What is the firm's ability to commercialize it? How can or how has the firm developed systems to institutionalize the management of its human capital?

Measuring of human capital. How does the firm define, describe, and measure its intellectual capital? What kinds of knowledge does the firm's HC generate? What is the breadth and what are the levels depth of knowledge created?

Reporting on intellectual capital. What kinds of reports does the firm have or wish to have about its intellectual capital? Internal reports? Actual or potential external reports? Do these include measures of key IC activities? Do they include valuations of the firm's human capital?

COMMUNICATING THE VALUE OF IC TO THE FIRM

Every firm I have talked with about intellectual capital and ICM, including every member of the ICM Gathering, has expressed frustration about communicating the value of intellectual capital to their firms. This is a common problem that exists with any new idea or perspective. It is particularly important to be able to communicate the importance of IC within the firm if you wish to obtain the desired support from top management that is usually required to mount an ICM-capability creation effort. I have interviewed over two dozen companies and, from their experiences, distilled an approach to communicating an IC story. The following are the elements of an internal communication program.

Create the IC Story

The IC story is the message that is to be communicated. It should contain the information necessary to inform and to persuade the audience of the importance of IC to their own firms. The story should contain information about what intellectual capital is and how other companies have found it to be important, how it is (or could be) of value to their firms, and how the capability is (or could be) created at their firms. The following outline of an IC story is an approach drawn from the experiences of several companies:

The role of IC in company strategy. What is the company's strategy, and what is the potential role IC could play in that strategy? Is the company IC rich? Does it have unextracted value from its current stock of intellectual properties? From its stock of intellectual assets? From its stock of intellectual capital? What are the current roles IC plays in the company's strategy? What roles could it play?

Stories. Provide examples of the *success* some companies have had with the management of their intellectual capital. Try to show a range of kinds of success that companies have had. For example, one could detail successes in terms of income generation (Texas Instruments, IBM), stock price increase (Skandia), finding hidden value (Dow), creating a powerful portfolio (Hewlett-Packard, Xerox), creating new value (Swirl, Intel). Also provide examples of failures of companies who failed to grasp the basic concepts of ICM. Examples of some of the better known failures from not understanding basic IC value extraction concepts include: Xerox and the personal computer, Apple and software out-licensing, and EMI and the loss of its CAT-Scan business.

What some companies are doing. Using materials contained in their chapters in this book, you can discuss what Dow, Avery Dennison, Hewlett-Packard, Xerox, Rockwell, Skandia, Neste, and Eastman Chemical are doing to manage their intellectual capital.

The hook. Show "the hook." Using the company context as the basis, find the argument that compels the listener to agree that the concepts underlying the management of a firm's intellectual capital are of value to your company and that, indeed, the company should be leveraging its intellectual capital as part of its strategy and vision-achieving activities.

Outline the Capability-Building Process

It isn't enough to convince someone of the value IC could bring to the firm, you must at the same time demonstrate what is required to do so. This means that it is important to have developed a clear project plan for creating the capability. The plan should describe what capability is desired, what are the major steps (and milestones) involved in creating this capability, what is the "road map" and the timetable? A fairly detailed plan and schedule are an important follow-up to the "story" when one wishes to convince the company to invest in the capability.

Communicating the Value of IC

Obtaining consensus on the value of IC to the firm is an important step in the process of creating the capability. Where there is acceptance and interest in installing an IC capability, it is easier to obtain the top management support and the resources required to proceed. There are two directions in which communications should proceed: upward to the executive suite to obtain backing and resources and outward throughout the organization to gain awareness, interest, and general support.

Communicating upward typically involves personal visits with senior executives to make them aware, to garner backing, to obtain resources approval, and to obtain continuing interest and backing.

Communicating outward involves the use of multiple channels for communication. The channels might include traditional ones such as newsletters, group meetings, and speeches at local events. The channels might include new ones such as a company intranet or e-mail. Outward communications might extend beyond the firm's employees to some of the firm's stakeholders: vendors, suppliers, shareholders, customers, etc. For each communication channel, the messages or stories communicated should match the channel and the audience in terms of length, breadth, frequency, and style.

SUMMARY

This chapter has identified a series of steps for companies wishing to implement an ICM capability for managing their intellectual capital. While the chapter is focused on the issues facing technology companies, much of what is included relates to all knowledge companies, not just those commercializing technology. The areas of greatest importance are highlighted as defining the firm's vision and long-term strategy, describing the context within which the firm operates, defining the role(s) for intellectual capital, designing the IP and IA management systems, and describing and implementing the IC management capability desired by the firm. The steps outlined in this chapter are gleaned from the experiences of all of the firms in the ICM Gathering.

The importance of the building blocks cannot be stated too strongly. Firms without a clearly articulated vision and strategy will have difficulty implementing an effective ICM capability. Where a vision and a long-term strategy do not formally exist, create de facto working outlines for them. It is also vitally important to make explicit the firm's context, its internal and external realities. Without a thorough understanding of the context, it is impossible to create and utilize intellectual capital within the firm to its best advantage. With these two basic building blocks in place, it is possible to design, implement, and operate effective systems for managing and utilizing the firm's intellectual capital. Without them, the likelihood of success diminishes.

Part IV

Intellectual Capital Management

19

Measuring and Monitoring Intellectual Capital

Suzanne Harrison

ICM Group, LLC

Trent Walker

University of California at Berkeley

OVERVIEW

The importance of measuring and monitoring intellectual capital was best stated by Dow Chemical's Gordon Petrash: "If you can visualize it, you can manage it. If you can manage it, you can measure it." The previous chapters have helped the reader understand how to visualize intellectual capital in an organization and have emphasized the importance of creating decision processes for managing intellectual capital. This chapter focuses on measuring and monitoring intellectual capital.

For knowledge companies focusing on improving corporate performance, there is a concern that traditional financial performance measures are not adequate for measuring the firm's driving assets (i.e., intellectual capital). Whereas intellectual capital focuses largely on developing the future income and profits of the firm, present-day financial measures, such as stock price and quarterly profits, are focused on the short term and do not adequately address the firm's hidden value. Companies addressing the measurement and monitoring of hidden value usually discover several key questions that must be answered. This chapter discusses measuring and monitoring the firm's hidden value and answers questions that will aid in the development of capabilities for measuring and monitoring key intangible assets.

Measuring intellectual capital is really about measuring (or trying to predict) the future of the firm. Accounting provides a historical perspective of what the firm has accomplished. If accounting is used to tell you where you have been, can it be used to tell you where you are going? Furthermore, is this approach appropriate for measuring intellectual capital?

These are some of the fundamental questions currently being debated among accounting professionals, governmental agencies (such as the SEC), and companies themselves. While the wrangling continues, companies are actively measuring their intellectual capital. This chapter discusses *what* to measure and *how* to measure it.

MEASUREMENT

When developing a capability for managing intellectual capital, the firm must ask what business objectives it wishes to accomplish and how its intellectual capital supports the achievement of these objectives. Which pools of intellectual capital does management wish to change? How does it wish to change them? Over what time period should the change take place? The answers to these questions allow the firm to decide how to measure and monitor such changes.

The Relationships between Measures

Events occurring inside a company are not independent. By this we mean that different pieces of a firm's intellectual capital affect one another. Discovering and understanding these relationships is our final goal. For example, companies track annual expenditures such as advertising to understand the relationship between advertising dollars spent and increases in consumer awareness and, ultimately, increased sales revenue.

Our goal in measuring intellectual capital is to understand the relationships between and among IC components. Once the relationships are made explicit, then it is much easier to manage intellectual capital to obtain the corporate vision, strategy, and objectives.

Factors Affecting Measurement

There are a series of factors that determine what a firm wishes to measure and what measures it will select. For example, recall from Chapter 3 the discussion on aligning intellectual capital with the vision and strategy of the firm. In the course of such an alignment, the firm determines the various roles of intellectual capital. These roles are further subdivided into value creation and value extraction. In the case of value extraction, a further division may be required to elucidate what the firm wishes to accomplish through value extraction, thereby beginning the process of determining what it wishes to measure. Exhibit 19.1 is a visualization of this process.

Once the roles for value extraction are defined, you can develop a series of objectives for value extraction activities. Defining objectives allows the firm to make explicit what it wishes to accomplish through its management of IC. Further, the accomplishments, once defined in IC terms, allow IC goals and targets to be established. The creation of specific goals and targets for IC will determine what managers wish to see measured and what they will wish to monitor over time.

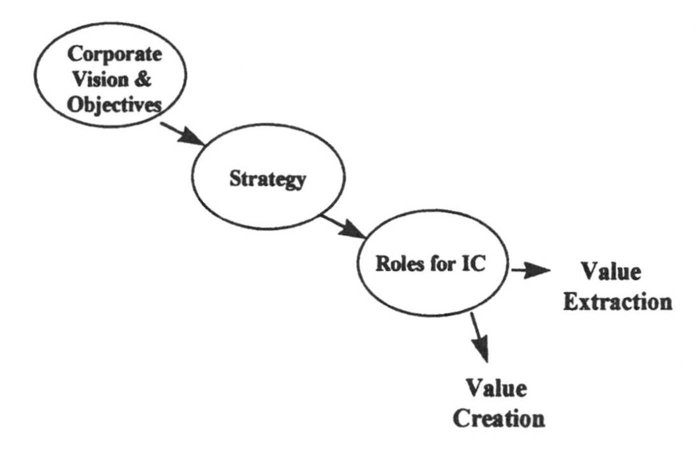

Exhibit 19.1 Strategic Alignment of Intellectual Capital

Dimensions of Measurement

Once the "what" of measurement has been determined, it then becomes necessary to decide how the measurement will be made. In making this determination there are several dimensions of measurement that need to be considered.

Qualitative versus Quantitative

Measures can be either qualitative or quantitative. Qualitative measures can be either value based (e.g., determining the quality) or vector based (are we moving forward or backward?). Quantitative measures can be either financial or nonfinancial. Again, all contain appropriate measures that depend on what you are measuring and why. Exhibit 19.2 highlights sample measures for each subheading.

For most of us, whenever we think of measurement, we immediately think of quantitative measures such as feet, time, weight, dollars, and so forth. These measures allow us to determine where we have been, where we are going (in terms of distance and time), and where we are today in a physical sense. For companies,

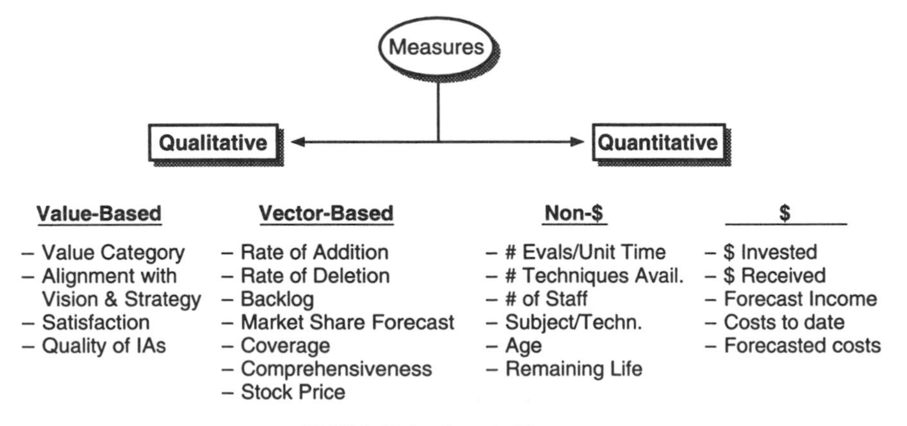

Exhibit 19.2 Sample Measures

measurement has traditionally been centered around quantitative output—in particular, dollars and time. Quantitative measures provide a numeric, and largely financial, snapshot of the firm. What has our net profit been for the past three quarters? How much have SG&A expenses grown as a percentage of revenues over the past three years? Here the emphasis has been largely on financial output, which was designed to provide accurate historical information.

Qualitative measures are measures that give us a sense of what is happening. Qualitative measures tell us the vector of change rather than the speed. Often when we work with companies to create an intellectual property management system, one of the first things they tell us is the number of patents in their portfolio. We are often more interested in the qualitative measures of the portfolio. For example, within a firm's patent portfolio, how many patents are of crown jewel quality? How many patents are really vanity patents with little value? Qualitative measures tend to be very context specific. Using the same example, Hewlett-Packard and Rockwell define *crown jewel–quality* patents in different ways. That is because the definitions are tied to the strategies of each firm, which are different.

The first step in the measurement process is to identify the result for which you are measuring.

The Past, the Present, or the Future

Intellectual capital that is the source of current profits for the firm is intellectual capital that existed in the past. Innovations on which an income stream is based must have been conceived in the past, codified, protected, and placed in an asset portfolio for commercialization. Looking at the assets that support current income streams is akin to looking into the IC past. Similarly, current innovations may be expected to produce future income; some of that income will be in the relatively near future, while other components of that income may take years to develop. Nevertheless, for most firms current intellectual capital management activity produces future income streams. Past intellectual capital management activity is the basis for current income streams.

When deciding what to manage, measure, monitor, and model, it is important to think in terms of two time dimensions. Firms wanting to measure and monitor the IC that is producing current income are talking about looking into the past. Firms wishing to measure and monitor current IC activity are talking about activity that will not produce income until sometime in the future.

Reasons for Measuring

When approaching the topic of measurement, there are several different viewpoints from which measurement can occur: internal and external, vector versus stock, qualitative versus quantitative, and more. An internal measurement focus deals largely with the operational tactics of the firm. Budgeting, TQM, cycle time, and staffing levels are all internal metrics designed to provide information to management regarding the day-to-day operation of the firm. The Dow Chemical Company is an example of an organization that is measuring intellectual capital for internal purposes. Dow is interested in finding intellectual assets within the firm to feed its extraction pipeline. With that in mind, Dow measures the number, type, quality, and commercializableness of its intellectual assets. An external focus is largely interested in explaining information to outside individuals or organizations that affect the firm: capital markets, stakeholders, fund managers, and so forth. Skandia's Annual Report Supplements on Intellectual Capital are a summation of measures designed for external reporting purposes. Skandia is interested in explaining its immense leverage capability and value drivers to its stockholders. Hence, Skandia measures include customer satisfaction metrics, process metrics, and renewal and development (the strategic/future orientation of the firm). Both Dow and Skandia are measuring their IC, and neither uses similar metrics.

Measuring the stock of intellectual capital does not always provide meaning. For example, many companies report the number of patents in their patent portfolio. This is a measure that is potentially interesting, but not very meaningful. Neste Oy, at the beginning of their Technology Audit program could have reported the number of patents in their portfolio. Neste subsequently abandoned close to half of those patents. Reporting the stock of patents in the portfolio turned out not to be a meaningful measure. Instead, reporting on the value of the patents in the portfolio (value can be measured in a variety of ways such as by enforceability, by financial contribution, or by technology classification) or the rate of addition to or deletion from the portfolio was much more actionable.

Don't mistake data for information. It is the understanding of how current (and extrapolated) data will affect the future that is important for intellectual capital. For example, a large company routinely profiled the average age of the employees within their organization. It wasn't until one of the executives noticed an unusual age cluster in one of the R&D labs and explored further that they realized key scientists in one technology area were all going to retire within the next five years—with no one to take their place. The firm immediately hired junior scientists and began an aggressive mentoring program to transfer knowledge from the key scientists prior to their retirement. Data is not information. Often, it is the interpretation of the data that provides information.

The measure must be something that can be managed against. More important, measure what is meaningful, not what is easy. One company found that patent filings were dramatically low in a key technology segment within the organization. They decided to pay engineers a fee for each new request for patent. Not surprisingly, patent submittals increased dramatically in the next several months. Unfortunately, the number of patent *filings* remained the same. When someone reviewed the patent submittals and created a quality scale (1 being low quality "not worth filing," 5 being high quality "will submit"), management realized that the increase was due to a rise in grades 1 and 2 patent submittals. The program was revised so that only grades 4 and 5 received the fee.

What Are the Questions to Ask?

Before we analyze the IC measurement currently in use, let us review the questions that matter:

1. Philosophically, is the firm more interested in knowledge management or value extraction?
2. What is the firm's context?
   a. What are the firm's vision, strategy, objectives, values, and culture?
   b. How well are these elements aligned together?
   c. What are the value drivers of the firm?
3. How will IC help the firm achieve its goals?
4. How does IC affect or interact with the value drivers of the firm?
5. Who are we measuring for?
   a. Internal or external focus?
6. What is the goal of the measurements?
   a. Are we interested in the vector or stock?
   b. Are we measuring to manage or managing to measure?
   c. Should information merely be reported, or should it be interpreted?
   d. Are we interested in gathering information or predicting the future based on the current information?
7. How do we define success?

Now that we know the questions that matter, let us review the existing measurement models and see whether they answer all of the questions.

Current Measurement Schemes

There are several measurement schemes that are often mentioned when discussions of IC measurement arise: the Skandia Navigator, the Balanced Scorecard, the Sveiby Model, the OECD Measures, and the Conference Board report. Each of these was reviewed to learn whether it contained measures useful to companies involved with value extraction. Each of these models and their capability for supporting value extraction measurement will be discussed.

1. *The Skandia Navigator* is a tool to help identify and report on corporate hidden value. It consists of five areas of focus. These are the areas on which an enterprise focuses its attention and from which comes the value of the firm's IC.[1] (See Exhibit 19.3.) The *financial focus* is the past history of the firm, a precise measure of where it was at a specific moment. This includes such measures as the balance sheet and other financial metrics. *Process focus* deals with the measure of structural capital. *Customer focus* is aimed at enhancing customer capital. *Renewal and development focus* largely contains the strategic, future-oriented measures of the firm. And finally, *human focus* consists of the competence and capabilities of employees and the continual enhancement of those skills through training and learning.
2. *The Balanced Scorecard* is designed to provide a comprehensive framework to translate a company's vision and strategy into a coherent set of performance measures organized according to four different perspectives:

Exhibit 19.3 Measurement Headings

• KE Sveiby	• Balanced Scorecard
- Growth and renewal,	- Learning and growth perspective
- Efficiency	- Postsale service
- Stability	- Customer perspective
	- Financial perspective
	- Innovation process
	- Operations process
• Skandia	**• Conference Board**
- Financial	- Customer satisfaction
- Human	- Workplace practices
- Customer	- Relationships with suppliers
- Process	- Environmental
- Renewal and development	- Innovation
• OECD	
- Cost of acquisition	
- Employee competence	
- Estimating productivity	

financial, customer, internal business processes, and *learning and growth.* "The scorecard provides a framework, a language, to communicate mission and strategy; it uses measures to inform employees about the drivers of current and future success. By articulating the outcomes the organization desires and the drivers of those outcomes, senior executives hope to channel the energies, the abilities, and the specific knowledge of people throughout the organization toward achieving the long-term goals."[2]

3. *Karl Eric Sveiby* tackles the problem of accounting for human capital. In particular, he attributes stock price premiums to visible equity (book value) plus intangible assets. Sveiby further refines intangible assets to include external structure, internal structure, and individual competence. External structure consists of brands and customer and supplier relationships. Internal structure models the organization: management, legal structure, manual systems, attitudes, R&D, and software. Individual competence is focused entirely on the employee and their education and experience. For each of the three intangible assets, Sveiby measures three things: renewal and development (in other words change), efficiency, and stability.[3]
4. *The Conference Board* surveyed approximately ten companies worldwide to determine new ways to track, value, enhance, and communicate the intangibles in their companies (including investments in intellectual capital and processes to improve customer satisfaction, workplace practices, and innovation). This report provides a summary of management techniques presently being used by a variety of companies.
5. *The OECD Report* attempts to develop a general conceptual model for assessing human capital information and decision-making systems, with

the goal of treating training and learning systems as we do investment under present-day accounting rules.

The measurement headings used in each model can be seen in Exhibit 19.3.

Results

Using the questions that matter as the dimensions of measurement, we analyzed each of the different models across the dimensions. Exhibit 19.4 highlights the results of that analysis.

The results outlined in Exhibit 19.4 were analyzed across a range of dimensions to better understand the results. The following dimensions for analysis are drawn from the table.

- Stocks versus flows
- Quantitative versus qualitative
- Predictive versus actual
- $-based versus non $-based
- Internal focus versus external focus
- Value creation focus versus value extraction focus
- Gathering versus interpretation
- Utilization versus allocation

Surprisingly, several themes emerged: Most of the schemes resulted in quantitative measures that were largely nondollar based; most measures are internally based; measuring the activities and stocks of value creation is a dominant theme; and most schemes report on current and historical utilization of intellectual assets.

There were also several noticeable gaps in the schemes reviewed. These include lack of qualitative measures, lack of predictive capability, lack of interpretative capability, no way to measure the tradeoffs of allocations of IAs, and no clearly defined link between intellectual capital and the net profits of the firm.

Exhibit 19.4 Results of the Analysis

Dimensions	Sveiby	Skandia	Bal Scorecard	Conf Board	OECD
Type of companies	Service	Service	Mixed	Mixed	Mixed
Conceptual basis	KM	KM	Fin/strategy	Fin/strategy	Fin/acc
Does model help					
Determine context?	No	No	Yes	No	No
Quantitative versus	90/10	Quant	Quant	Quant	Quant
$-based versus non-$ qualitative	20/80	25/75	30/70	Non	70/30
Internal versus external	Internal	External	55/45	70/30	External
VC versus VE	80/20	70/30	65/35	70/30	VC
Stock versus flow	60/40	40/60	Flow	Flow	Flow
Gather versus interpret	Gather	Gather	Gather	Gather	Gather
Report versus predict	Report	Report	Report	Report	Report
Asset utilization versus allocation	Utilize	Utilize	Utilize	Utilize	Utilize

Only one model (the Balanced Scorecard) highlighted the importance of context within the firm, particularly as a beginning to measurement. Also, there is presently a tremendous time lag between setting the measures and awaiting the results and then correcting or modifying the necessary inputs to help fine-tune the results. Wouldn't it be nice if there were an easier and quicker way to simulate the results?

MONITORING

Overview

Knowledge companies take it as an article of faith that there is a correlation, if not a link, between increased knowledge in the firm and downstream profits. Management activities center on increasing learning and knowledge in one portion of the firm, while activities associated with producing income streams and profits often reside in others. There is no current methodology for showing the effect that training or education activities have on firm profits. Indeed, there are no models to show the effect on profits of any intellectual capital management activity. We suggest that there are relationships between intellectual capital activities and financial results, that the relationships are dynamic, and that there is a way of modeling them to produce a tool for management.

Elements of the Solution

As we set out to design a model that relates intellectual capital to firm profitability, what is it that we would ask for? Such a model should at least describe or model a knowledge company in both business terms (i.e., a functional model) and intellectual capital terms. More important, it should identify the linkages between the two. For example, where do our intellectual capital strengths reside functionally? How does our firm think (or fail to think) about intellectual capital? Any model should incorporate the "futureness" of intellectual capital in its design. Based on the results of the current measurement model capabilities, we are looking for a predictive model. In particular, time frames for predicting the future can be divided into current, near-term future, and long-term future. Our model should incorporate these time dimensions, both functionally and financially. Our model should also incorporate the value-driving activities of the firm, described from a business perspective and as intellectual capital activities. Our model would enable conversations about intellectual capital and profits and aid managers to visualize intellectual capital within their firm. It should also help people understand how intellectual capital assets may be utilized. And finally, such a model should enable what-if analyses to explore the downstream effects of impending management decisions and understand the future tradeoffs associated with any course of action taken today. Exhibit 19.5 is a visualization of such a process.

Each company exists in its own reality (context) that is affected by external (outside) forces and by internal actions, some of which are intellectual capital–related (dials). Right now, we are faced with an incomplete list of dials, as

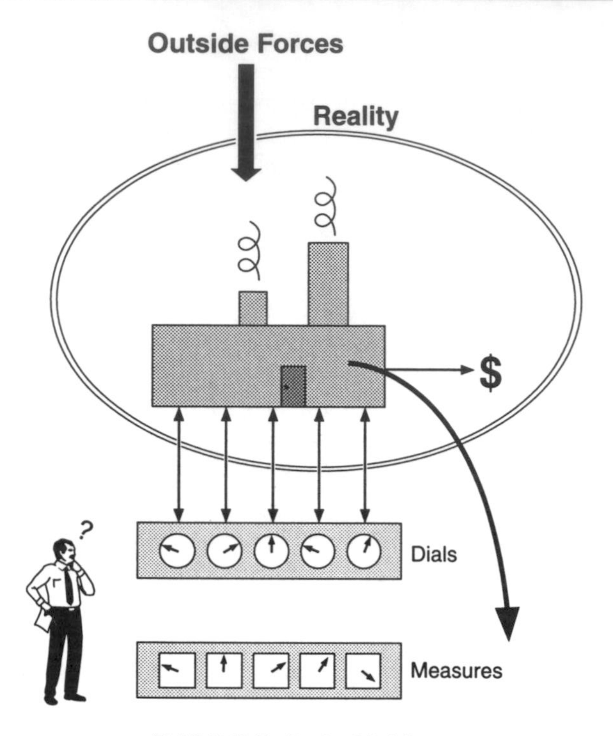

Exhibit 19.5 Design Model

well as an inability to predict how the measures and cash flow might respond over time to alterations in our intellectual capital (dials).

Framework

At its simplest, companies are comprised of people, tangible assets (stuff we can touch), and "other stuff." For the sake of discussion, we will refer to the other stuff as intellectual capital. Based on the earlier chapters of this book, the goal of knowledge companies should be to manage intellectual capital in order to develop a stream of products or internal processes (which we refer to generically as programs from now on), which can then be sold for cash. This statement lends itself to our next exhibit.

The arrows in Exhibit 19.6 crudely represent how intellectual capital can influence the program pipeline and the income stream of the company. We note that

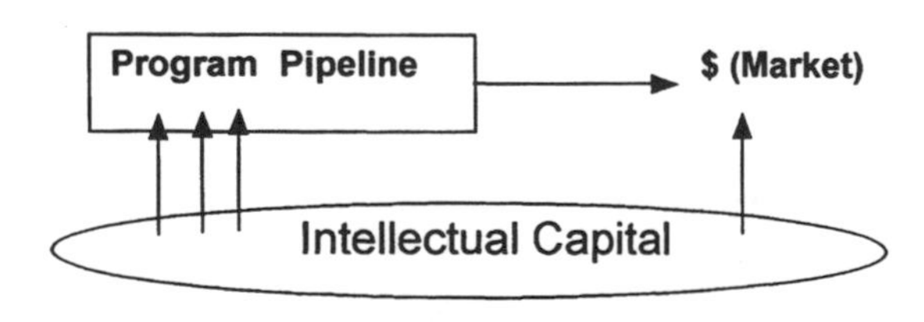

Exhibit 19.6 Company Framework

many nontraditional objects can be counted as intellectual capital under this model. For example, the outside market conditions affecting the company could be counted as part of the intellectual capital of a firm, albeit an external part.

We should note that Exhibit 19.6 is incomplete. Exhibit 19.7 more accurately represents the reality inside most companies.

The difference between Exhibits 19.6 and 19.7 is that Exhibit 19.7 symbolically represents the effects that the program pipeline and the external cash flow/market environment has on the company's intellectual capital.

We divide the diagram into two parts as depicted in Exhibit 19.8. One part becomes the *functional piece,* the other part becomes the *intellectual capital piece.*

To model a company, we must first construct our model of the functional piece in a way that allows for a natural addition of an intellectual capital plane later, as that is the final objective. (The intellectual capital plane is a reference map used to relate intellectual capital activities and business activities.)

In order to link intellectual capital to financial measures (see Exhibit 19.9) we need a basic way to classify company activities (we call these *programs*) and services, as well as a general set of measures that can adequately describe a program. These measures may be financial or not; we place no restrictions on their identification. Once we have a set of generalized measures, we then need a framework that will help us visualize and interpret these measures. Our long-term goal is the creation of a model that relates intellectual capital activity to profits. This model

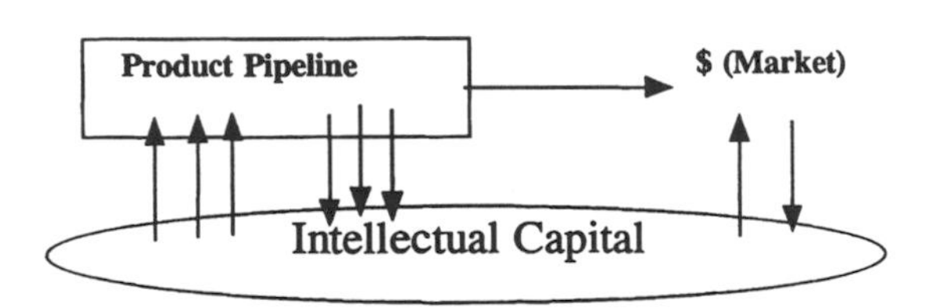

Exhibit 19.7 Company Reality

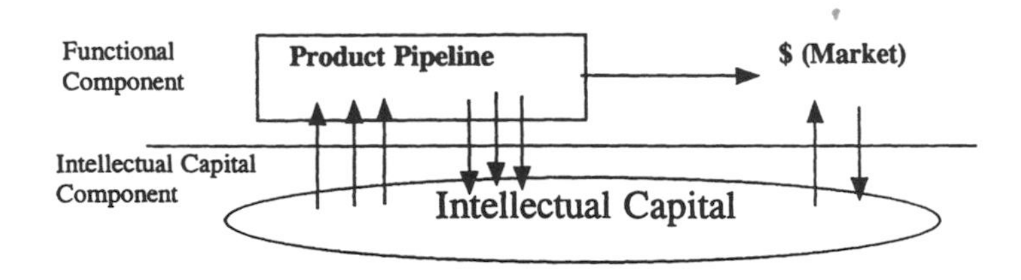

Exhibit 19.8 Functional versus Intellectual Components

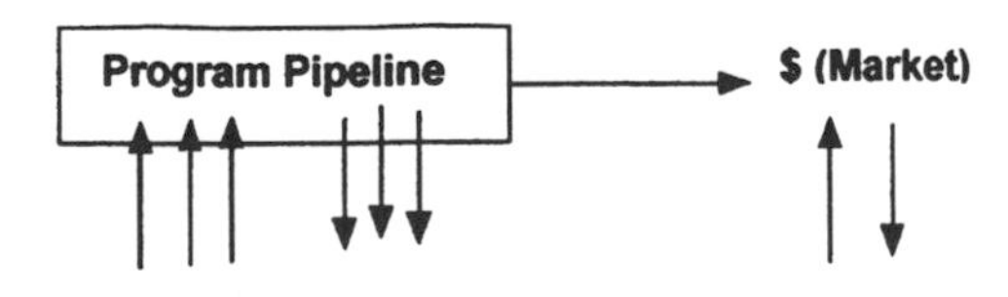

Exhibit 19.9 Program Pipeline

is to be created over a period of time, evolving and improving as it is created. As it progresses, we will be publishing results to elicit feedback and critiques.

CONCLUSION

The decisions of what to measure, how to measure, what to monitor, and what to model are obviously complex. To do this effectively, we need to understand our final objectives, the relationships between and among IC components and their effects on the enterprise, and our ability to measure and manage these various components.

It is important to realize that the process of deciding what to measure and how to measure it is constantly evolving. Moreover, understanding the relationship between and among the intellectual capital components will further crystallize as we continue to measure and explore.

NOTES

1 Leif Edvinsson and Michael Malone, *Intellectual Capital* (New York: Harper Collins, 1997).

2 Robert Kaplan and David Norton, "Why Does Business Need a Balanced Scorecard?" *Journal of Strategic Performance Measurement* (February/March 1997): 5–11.

3 Karl Eric Sveiby, *The New Organizational Wealth* (San Francisco: Berrett-Koehler Publishers, 1997).

20

Managing Intellectual Capital at Skandia

Leif Edvinsson

Skandia

Skandia, an insurance and finance company in Sweden, was an early entrant into the management of intellectual capital. In 1991 the company appointed a director of intellectual capital within one of its most dynamic global operating units, Skandia AFS (Assurance and Financial Services). Today the entire Skandia Group (a Fortune 500 company) is applying more and more of the intellectual capital management approaches pioneered by its AFS unit. These are approaches to managing the intangibles that underlie knowledge-intensive service companies; but they are applicable to most organizations as a model for creating and extracting value from their investments in knowledge and other intangibles.

The Skandia approach, begun before there was a literature about intellectual capital management (ICM), and before there was an ICM Gathering, is one that has been enormously effective for the company. Fundamentally, it involved us visualizing the company's hidden value, telling our shareholders and employees about it, and developing management methods and tools to make more effective use of it. Lacking books and articles to draw from, or the collective learning of the Gathering, Skandia created its own simple term for intellectual capital. Firstly, if something was tangible and "remained" after the employees went home, it was called *structural capital.* All else was called *intellectual capital.* For Skandia, intellectual capital included knowledge, relationships, know-how, and other such intangibles.

BACKGROUND

In 1969 the noted economist John Kenneth Galbraith described intellectual capital as both a process of value creation and an asset. That view, that IC was both a flow of activity as well as a stock of the activity's results, framed the way in which IC was viewed in its early years. Recently, ICM has been characterized by the ICM Gathering as involving creation, cultivation, and extraction. As Swedes with a long seafaring tradition, we at Skandia sometimes think of ICM in navigational terms, such as current position, course, and speed. One might also think of ICM in time-based terms, such as past, present, and future. Financial analysts and people concerned with the stock market might view it as a particularly key aspect of the future earnings capability of a company. From a management perspective, we at Skandia have come to believe that it is essential to focus ourselves not only on present company operations, but also on past and future operations. In viewing our operations from a three-part time perspective, we have found that we first visualize our intellectual capital, then we create multiplicative flows of it, then we futurize it. From roots to multiplicative future fruits, this kind of three–generational leadership perspective and capability is becoming essential for us.

THE HIDDEN CAPABILITIES FOR THE FUTURE

On the New York stock exchanges, the top five valued companies have a market value that is approximately 13 times their book value. The two leading companies on this score, Microsoft and Coca-Cola, have market values at 21 and 26 times book value, respectively (as of July, 1997). This difference between the value of a company's tangible assets (its book value) and its market value is the value the marketplace puts on the firm's intangible assets. By defining and "exploding" out these intangibles, a firm can identify the intangible capabilities of its organization that are not included in the accountant's calculation of book value. Further, the market value reflecting this hidden value may be thought of as the market's appreciation of the firm's future earnings potential. According to research by Professor Baruch Lev of the Stern School of Management at New York University, the gap between tangible and intangible value is widening, continuing a trend that has been escalating over the past 20 years.

Skandia, attempting to explain for its shareholders the hidden value represented by these intangibles created what we call the *Skandia Value Scheme.* This view of our intangible assets has been discussed in several Skandia publications and is further described in more detail in the recent book *Intellectual Capital—Finding the Hidden Roots of the Organization,* by Edvinsson and Malone. The Skandia view of its value scheme is as depicted in Exhibit 20.1.

The value scheme describes our view of the major building blocks of Skandia's intellectual capital. It starts by making the point that we view intellectual capital as more than just our human capital. It also includes what we call *structural capital:* organizational systems, trade marks, databases, and patents, as well as customer relations. It is the embodied or packaged human capabilities for recycling. We believe that our management focus should be on these components of the firm's hidden capabilities for future earnings potential, that is, the intellectual capital.

MAJOR STEPS IN THE FLOW OF IC DEVELOPMENT

The Skandia approach to developing its intellectual capital can be summarized into the following phases of activity:

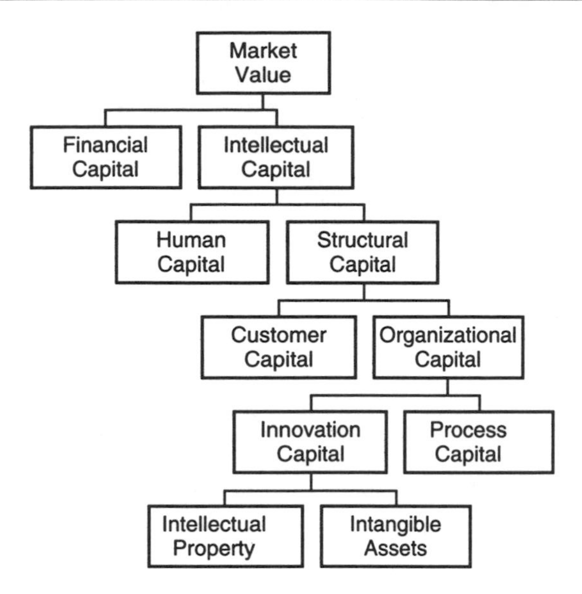

Exhibit 20.1 The Skandia Value Scheme

Missionary—to articulate a deeper understanding of the company's hidden capabilities and their contribution to a growing future value to shareholders and stakeholders. This is accomplished through a common language and a taxonomy that helps people visualize the intangibles. It is also accomplished through metaphors, such as the knowledge tree (see Exhibit 20.2), where the nourishment of the roots is more important for the future than the harvesting of today's fruits. The missionary phase is also accomplished through a quantification of measures of IC indicators.

Measurement—to develop the metrics as a quantitative language that describes the position, evolution, velocity, and direction of the hidden capabilities and the investment into knowledge and other intangibles. This is done by the balanced reporting format called the *Skandia Navigator,* which highlights four key focus areas for indicators that supplement financial indicators, thereby providing a broader and more balanced management perspective. The measurement phase produces an increased ability to visualize the firm's IC in quantitative terms, as well as providing an overview map for the IC leadership of the firm. This map, or Skandia Navigator, covers three time perspectives: past financial performance, present operations and relationships, as well as future renewal and development. Skandia has created a visualization of these quantitative measures in what it calls its *IC-index*™ to highlight the value evolution of IC that relates to our four focus areas as driving forces. The company now publishes semiannually a public IC-supplement to its annual financial report.

Leadership—to provide navigation of the organization and to nourish the firm's future earnings capabilities based on the map of IC-indicators.

Today, Skandia reports internally on its IC measures through an electronic PC and intranet-based model called *Dolphin.* Through this mechanism, we believe our leadership will become more balanced and focused on how to grow future earnings capabilities. It will also make it possible to align the knowledge development and reward schemes to this balanced quantitative reporting format.

Technology—to develop the structural capital component of Skandia's human capabilities. This is one of the most essential multipliers for productivity. Customer relations can be embodied by customer databases; organizational procedures can be summarized in computerized modules; back-up skills can become accessible over large global distances by communications technologies, internet technologies, global shopping, and knowledge delivery. Technology helps to package, recycle, distribute, and trade on human skill. Knowledge managers tend to limit this to data warehousing, but it is much more. It is the tool for participating in the global digital economy and multiplying the knowledge investments of the firm.

Capitalize—to look for the extraction as well as the creation of value in intangibles. This is often done within the intellectual property function, by extracting value from patents, copyrights, trademarks, and so forth. But it is also possible to package the firm's human capabilities into structural capital and to trade on it. This conversion of a firm's human capabilities into structural ones is said to be the fastest growing global trade today. Capitalization also means looking for alliances with others to

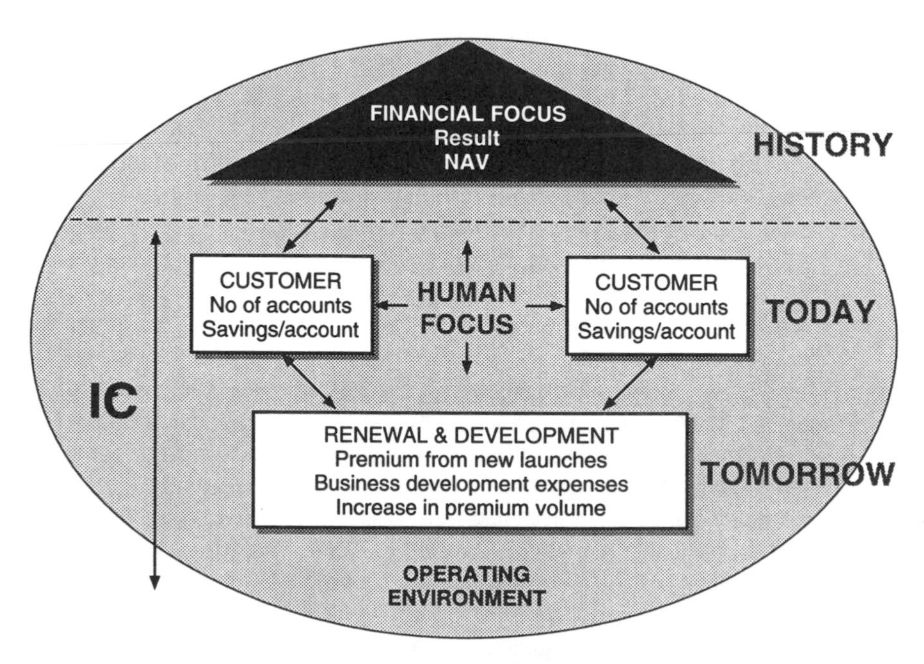

Exhibit 20.2 The Skandia Knowledge Tree

jointly leverage structural and human capital. This is becoming more and more essential as enterprises become virtual networking organizations.

Futurize—to amplify and focus the firm's IC leadership and management efforts toward the firm's future capabilities. Skandia's theme here is: Turn the future into an asset. This concept of futurization at Skandia is both a leadership development process and a gestalt approach for the renewal and development focus in our Navigator. It is a process to stretch the organization's current capabilities into future ones. This process is embodied in Skandia's concept of future teams whose purpose is to determine how we can better futurize our activities. Our future teams are comprised of employees from three different generations, with ages ranging from 25 to 45+ years. In parallel with the future teams, we also have implemented a gestalt approach to futurizing through our creation of a series of future centers, or locations where people meet to create prototypes of new developmental efforts. Our first future center was established in 1995 at Vaxholm in Sweden. Since its inauguration in May 1996, the Voxholm Center has had more than 5,000 visitors, both Skandia working team members and outside observers, during its first year of operation. Its success has prompted us to schedule other Skandia Future Centers to be opened at locations around the globe.

THREE GENERATIONS OF IC

Today the learning and development within Skandia of our firm's intellectual capital can be summarized by what we now realize were three evolving generations of approaches:

- First generation: Visualize the hidden capabilities of IC within the firm.
- Second generation: Measure and leverage investments in IC.
- Third generation: Futurize IC capabilities for value development.

The three generations of activity are being simultaneously refined and focused during their application within Skandia. They represent a work continuously in progress and an application of knowledge management in practice. The emphasis, however, is much more on stretching the known management practices of today into a learning about how to nourish our future earnings capabilities.

Intellectual capital is a concept that is broader than knowledge management. For Skandia, it is a process of knowledge navigation, a process into the unknown. Intellectual capital is necessary for our corporate competitiveness and survival. It is a quest to become a knowledgeable, as well as a more intelligent, enterprise.

21

The Role of Intellectual Capital in Valuing Knowledge Companies

James P. O'Shaughnessy

Rockwell International Corporation

Patrick H. Sullivan

ICM Group, LLC

INTRODUCTION

When purchasing or merging with a knowledge company, how does the dominant firm determine the value of the acquired or merged company? How does the potential purchaser make the calculation? Is the frame of reference an accounting or financial one? Or is it an intellectual capital one? Too often, companies being acquired are valued based on antiquated or passe methods.

The term *M&A* (for mergers and acquisitions) gained currency during the 1980s. That decade was viewed as the heyday of M&A deal making. Companies were bought and sold, often dismembered, because "values" favored the economic model. True values were rarely created; hidden values were uncovered and cashed to generate the income necessary to support the highly leveraged firm. One of the most stunning examples of that style of M&A is represented in the multibillion-dollar RJR-Nabisco transaction. Many financial wonks, in awe of the magnitude of the deal, found rationality in the transaction because of the independent values of several of the franchises in the acquired business. Repackaging the packaged goods company, spinning off individual businesses each supported by its own trademark and trade identity, was seen as the way to pay down the costs of the core business the acquirer really wanted.

Irrespective of one's view of the financial prudence of these acquisitions, the most common factor driving the M&A frenzy of the 1980s was this concept of finding hidden values—normally off balance sheet assets that could be cashed to pay the enormous cost for junk bonds and other creative financing. History shows that one of the more significant sources of unexploited value was to have been found in the intellectual assets of the acquired company.

The decade of the 1990s ushered in a different look at mergers and acquisitions. Business leaders were now thought to be better focused on growth rather than dismemberment, on creation rather than exploitation. Merger talk turned to expressions of "industry consolidation" and "strategic growth" through targeted acquisitions. The aerospace and defense industries exemplify this plan raised to an art form. Capital market dynamics also differentiate the mainstream acquisitions of the 1990s from those of the 1980s. The fantastic run-up in stock market values has given today's management equity as a vastly preferable tool of acquisition in comparison to the debt financing of the previous decade.

The purpose of this chapter is to acquaint readers with a new and potentially powerful approach to valuing knowledge companies for merger or acquisition; an approach that describes why a purchaser should pay more than the asset value (book value) for a knowledge company. This approach uses the intellectual capital framework as its conceptual basis for valuation.

When one looks at the acquisitions that occurred in the 1980s or in the 1990s to date, one factor seems to be consistently in place: Managers of purchasing firms paid premiums above the market value for the purchase of knowledge companies. Few if any transactions would have been consummated if the purchaser had not come forward with a price exceeding, sometimes considerably exceeding, the book value of the seller. Premium pricing in the form of cash or stock became a necessity of transactional life in the M&A lane.

What does a buyer see in a knowledge company to be acquired that can justify paying premiums over book value? Unless we are willing to believe these transactions are the work of compulsive gamblers hoping to win on the acquisition bet, there must be more to it than that. Indeed there is, and it appears to be rooted in the instincts of purchasers that intellectual capital is worth the premium.

We carefully characterize these actions as instinctual because the available valuation techniques are not focused on the value of intellectual capital as a quantifiable business asset either driving the transaction or justifying its seemingly high price. Even in those instances when intellectual capital—almost always intellectual property and then almost always patents—has been examined for value, we believe the examination to have been cursory and fairly myopic. But despite these shortcomings, the ultimate value of intellectual capital, both real and perceived, should not be underestimated for its ability to explain the final purchase price.

Acquisitions are typically inspired by the purchaser's conviction that it can derive so much value from the acquired company or the acquired portion thereof that premiums are warranted. The purchaser is convinced that its ability to maneuver the levers of control of the acquired assets will return leveraged value as a return on purchase price. These beliefs are often buttressed by the perceptions of decision makers and analysts concerning the implicit value of the firm's intellectual capital. However, because the concept of intellectual capital valuation is only approximated in the analysis, the results themselves are only approximate.

Our purpose here is to make explicit some of the actions or techniques appropriate to discern the value of intellectual capital in an acquisition, both the financial value and the intrinsic value. We do not suggest quantitative techniques for valuing intellectual capital. Of greater importance, our purpose is to identify the manner in which critical thinking on intellectual capital values can lead to a more thoroughgoing understanding of what is being purchased and, therefore, what it is that is to be valued or priced. The discussion here concerns the process of *qualification* of the asset base from the perspective of the intellectual capital manager.

PREMIUM PRICING

Once the term *premium* enters the transaction picture, those who must justify it invariably turn to "intangibles" to carry the load. The reason is obvious: The premium applies to some imperceptible value not found on the balance sheet. It must be accounted for by some factor not immediately apparent from even close inspection of the balance sheet or cash flow statement. In earliest times, these premium-satisfying intangibles were thought to be the value of a "going concern" and its "goodwill." These intangibles categories were seen as convenient and useful fictions whose legitimacy was sufficient to permit the transaction to move forward.

Going Concern Value

An analyst thinking about the value of a going concern values the ability of the operation to continue its business functions on the day after the transaction in much the same way they were conducted the days before. There is clearly defined value in the capacity to continue churning out the products or services that generate the income sought by the purchaser of the knowledge firm under examination. This value distinguishes the going concern from a start-up with a much smaller storehouse of knowledge and learning and less ability to demonstrate broad capabilities for designing, manufacturing, and delivering products to customers.

Going concern value, for a knowledge company, is largely composed of the value of the tacit knowledge of the workforce carrying out the operational functions of the business, thereby making it a going concern. Astute analysts today will seek more understanding of the elements underpinning company operations and "going concern-ness" than would their counterparts decades ago. Then going concern value was set at a number that felt good under the circumstances. Often it was based on a finger-in-the-wind estimate thought to be justifiable in the sense that it would pass the "red-face" test on presentation to the tax authorities or the financial community. Though it may be no easier today to ascribe a quantifiable valuation, simply understanding what underlies the recognizable value of being a going concern allows a more critical analysis of whether a purchase premium for going concern-ness is in the right order of magnitude.

What is the going concern value of a service company whose tacit knowledge could leave the company shortly after the company is purchased? What is the going concern value of a company producing a product having an unrefreshed life cycle measured in terms of a few months or a few years (at most) if the tacit knowledge necessary for continuous improvement departs postclosing? For purchases of knowledge companies under these conditions, what has the purchaser obtained beyond inventory, plant and equipment, and a distribution network? Of course, there is the explicit knowledge component of intellectual capital left behind in any of those scenarios, but will its value be sufficient to reimburse the purchaser for his or her going concern premium? These questions are far from rhetorical in the acquisition of knowledge-based companies or those whose livelihoods are predicated on the daily productivity of knowledge workers. And in today's marketplace, what companies not fitting into these dimensions are also worthwhile acquisition candidates?

The purchaser who recognizes the "fleeting" value of tacit knowledge would do well to launch a campaign to convert tacit know-how into more fungible forms of codified knowledge, here termed *intellectual assets.* Ultimately that codification becomes the hedge against complete loss of premium value.

Goodwill

The concept of "goodwill" has been a convenient category for the allocation of intangible value. Goodwill is often described as the corporate reputation of the acquired party; it might also be flagship value, customer relationships, and a range of equally difficult to describe, much less quantify, business intangibles. Using intellectual capital and its unique perspectives on the corporation provides ways of thinking about the business intangibles that subjects them to greater scrutiny than historically they have received. Although we may still be unable to determine a precise value for these intangibles, the more rigorous analysis may identify their components and allow us to define and understand them more rationally.

Goodwill is also thought of as the value of the company's trade identity. For companies where this is true, the goodwill value is almost always thought to reside in the trademarks and trade names by which the company is known. This view is often true, but at the same time, it is incomplete.

Of course, trademarks and trade names can have great value because of what they imply to the customer about quality and reliability of the product or services provided. But what else is there standing behind these market perceptions? A company's commercial reputation may be captured in a mark or name just the same as an individual's personal reputation is bound inextricably with his or her name. But the trade mark or name is a proxy: It captures the value of a reputation gained through the application of the firm's culture, know-how, and relationships, practiced in a way that the reputation is produced. The underlying value is both created by and reposes in the firm's intellectual capital.

There is a debate on whether trademark value is extinguished when the mark for a product (i.e., its "brand name") is separated from the tools of its production. This is the so-called "naked trademark" grant that many worry about in the acquisition arena. The underlying philosophy acknowledges that a trademark cannot exist apart from its goodwill and that both are bound up in the customer's perceptions linking branded products with expectations concerning their essential attributes. Were you to separate the brand from the tools to produce it—the complementary assets of production—the argument goes that the consumer association likewise is going to be altered. With it falls the goodwill that is the wellspring of trademark value. Thus, the grant of a trademark absent the tools of production is argued by many to destroy the legal value of the trademark.

It is understandable how such a principle found its way into medieval Anglo-Saxon jurisprudence, given the importance of guilds in that time. It is more difficult to rationalize the argument today. But it is not our intention to resolve trademark controversy, just draw the link between the origins of value for goodwill and the evaluation of knowledge company value. As the reader may expect, in our view the subject goes deeper than the raw value of names, whether trademarks or trade names. Something more intrinsic to reputation justifies the perception of value in a name by those impressed by the foundational reasons giving rise to the reputation associated with that name. Accordingly, the more important question becomes whether the acquirer can, following the transaction, perpetuate the reputation and realize value for it or suffer its dissipation and lose whatever value was allocated to this category of intangibles. There is more to it than simply maintaining signage or other visible reminders of what the reputation used to be when dependent on the characteristics of the now-departed seller.

The essence of any commercial transaction, such as the sale of a product or delivery of a service, is evident when one party parts with money or something of value to acquire from another party something that assists the first either in solving a problem or seizing an opportunity. This is true whether the problem is how to print a page or the opportunity is recreational.

The other essential feature of such a transaction is that there are many different people or commercial enterprises who can assume the role of either party to the transaction, whether seller or buyer. Once past this elemental view of the commercial world, the question on which the money rides is, "Why these two parties, at this time, for this purpose?" As often as not, the purchasing decision is accompanied or inspired by the buyer's view that the seller has a reputation for delivering something the buyer values.

This value issue is broader than quality or even mere price or convenience, and it is also different from the question of optimizing price, quality, convenience, and so on, along a dimension important to the purchaser. Beneath it all, there is usually a sense that this seller has the product or service this buyer wants or needs at that instant. This sense is bound inextricably with the seller's reputation despite whatever other considerations may enter the purchasing decision.

While reputation may be borne throughout a market by a corporate moniker, reputation stands for what the buyer believes about the company at the time of a purchasing transaction. Reputation is a marketplace projection of the company's values Brian Hall describes in Chapter 4. In turn, this reputation will be found to be a reflection of the intellectual capital of the firm. Looked at from a different perspective, every action of the enterprise affects the reputation it enjoys in its markets; what differs here is the attention brought to the enterprise because of its acquisition and the changes expected or imagined by the public. Reputational value thus further reflects the commitment of management to deploy its complementary assets in the future in a manner consistent with the reasons for the corporate reputation. All of the reputational components of goodwill can change post-closing, giving goodwill the same kind of fleeting form we touched on when considering the exodus of the tacit knowledge found to support going concern value.

For our purposes, we note the obvious importance of avoiding double counting when allocating premium costs between going concern values and goodwill values. They overlap.

It is also important to scratch the surface and examine the constituents that comprise both going concern and goodwill valuations. They both rest significantly on intellectual capital foundations, and intellectual capital principles will help the analyst and manager alike in gaining a better understanding of how these values play out in the contexts of both preclosing analyses and postclosing realizations.

SUSTAINABLE COMPETITIVE ADVANTAGE

We all know that every going concern enjoys that status because it has some demonstrable source of competitive advantage in the markets in which it competes. Michael Porter describes a few generic sources of competitive advantage when he distinguishes among those who are successful because they sell differentiated products or because they dominate the low-cost position in their industry or because they occupy a valuable niche in the marketplace.[1] These three sources of competitive advantage are recognized as the corporate bedrock that can sustain the enterprise and its market value. Treacy and Wiersema take a different tack when they describe the path to sustainable market success as that of product leadership, or operational excellence, or customer intimacy.[2] Other writers on business strategy abound. What they all have in common is a description of reasons why companies gain and maintain marketplace success. Each of these views of how and why companies develop and maintain sustainable competitive advantage is rich in intellectual capital implications.

Consider Porter's concepts concerning the value of product differentiation as a source of sustainable market success and compare it with Treacy's product leadership. The two are closely akin to one another. The product source of competitive advantage begs for an analysis calling on patents to protect the attributes of differentiation. Patents properly deployed have the capacity to safeguard the differentiation features, the market position of the differentiated product and, also, to control the marketplace opportunity for it by controlling product or feature substitution.

Think about Porter's views on the importance of cost leadership and its impact on the bottom line, and then compare those views with Treacy's thoughts on operational excellence. The two are particularly apt for an intellectual property analysis based on trade secret protection for the production attributes giving rise to low-cost production. Examine for a moment both niche marketing as recounted by Porter and customer intimacy as explicated by Treacy and Wiersema.[3] Then correlate those sources of competitive advantage with structural intellectual property such as patents or trade secrets along with the reputational value of trademarks.

There is a high degree of complementarity between the business strategist's analysis of sustainable competitive advantage and the intellectual property specialist's views of how to shelter and sustain those self-same sources of competitive advantage. Because the value of the source of competitive advantage can be measured by business analysts, we get the sense that the complementary value of the intellectual property also should be measurable. Some would argue that the values are the same and should be attributed mostly to intellectual property. After all, if it were not for the intellectual property protection, the value of the source of competitive advantage would be reduced in the cauldron of the marketplace itself—differentiated features would be copied, manufacturing techniques mimicked, and so forth.

INTELLECTUAL ASSETS

Analysts relied for decades in their premium allocations on the two categories of going concern and goodwill. During the 1980s, with the phenomenal rise in the strength of patents, intellectual property was added to the arsenal. It, too, represented a classifiable intangible that could carry some of the excess value over book. What made it even more attractive, is that intellectual property and particularly patents possess tangible characteristics not found when dealing with going concern or goodwill valuations. For example, patents have a physical manifestation; they can be counted, accumulated, viewed, handled; and, best of all, there are sound ways to account for value of these intangibles. Intellectual property thereby found a special niche in acquisition accounting.

At first, intellectual property was treated simply as another bucket for carrying premium value. Later in the evolution of premium analysis, intellectual property began to share more of the load. Because this is an intangible that can be counted, it was counted on to justify as much of the premium as could be allocated to this category. Its stature as an intangible of real value was promoted by the courts, which increasingly found patents valid and worth enormous sums of money in comparison to previous generations of these intellectual assets. This spawned a range of quasi-analytical approaches to quantify the value of these assets in the quest of closing the premium gap between book and purchase prices.[4] A few became widely popular.

Every enterprise must possess a source of competitive advantage if it is to remain viable, let alone command premium prices for its stock in trade.[5] To the extent this source of competitive advantage is preserved by a patent portfolio, that intangible asset can be viewed as a proxy for the revenue that otherwise would have been appropriated by competitors wishing to erode that source of competitive advantage. In turn, if the asset can be correlated with an income stream that can be cranked through a standard NPV macro now on everyone's PDA and *voilà,* value is quantified. The same kind of analysis can be performed based on the anticipated market position of the postacquisition successor. Predicting the emergent source of competitive advantage allows one to evaluate the robustness of the patent portfolio to safeguard it from appropriation by those who would desire to enter or move throughout the market or sector. A comparable analysis, then, could be undertaken and value found for the intellectual property protection bought for part of the purchase price representing barriers to entry or mobility created by blocking patents.

A few problems became apparent to those who anguished over intangibles valuation based on the NPV approach to predicted streams of income that would arise or be diverted depending on the power of patents to protect market position. Even once all the double counting problems are cured, it is sobering for those who undertake the analysis how few patents actually protect the products and/or services offered by the average company. Elsewhere we have written about our findings that the patent portfolios of even the best-managed companies are full of chaff.[6] By our estimates, it is often the case that no more than about 20 percent of the portfolios of even world-class companies are market strategic. The balance is nonstrategic or "junk." Moreover, of the 20 percent that could qualify as strategic to the markets of interest, perhaps half or less actually covers products or services offered by the enterprise into its markets. In other words, in some of the best companies, only a small percentage of their intellectual property assets have the capacity to afford shelter for their sources of competitive advantage. This percentage differs, skewing sharply upward for smaller companies and even more so for nascent ventures.

But as a matter of generalization, the "average" acquisition sees a premium that cannot fully be accounted for by a patent portfolio whose composition largely does not cover the sources of competitive advantage enjoyed or anticipated by the parties to the transaction.

This disconnect between the coverage of the portfolio and perceived sources of competitive advantage has hardly caused a pause. In fact, this disparity is the source of new-found value. Drawing from the "junk in the garage" metaphor, one man's junk can be another's treasure, made real through the process of the "garage sale." Though presented tongue-in-cheek, this process inspires a valuation analysis based on the projected streams of licensing income to be derived from those patents that are not strategic to the postacquisition company. The deft advantage of this approach is that the sale never needs to take place; it merely needs to be plausible. Though aggressive, this tool for value extraction from intangibles has found a place in the arsenal of those who are challenged to close the premium gap.

Another technique is now under consideration, promising utility in the quest of quantifying intangible valuation. Some have proposed over the past few years the broad concept of augmenting standard NPV analyses with an options valuation. Intellectual property has a natural fit in the analysis insofar as a patented position protects the future opportunity to enter a market and, thus, safeguards the option of waiting to do so until the company chooses to move. *However, some characteristics of intellectual properties, particularly their relatively short life, are inconsistent with the assumptions underlying the popular options-pricing formulas.*[7] Therefore, while we believe there is valuable insight in the options viewpoint, we urge great caution in applying any standard formula to value an intellectual property.

Thus, the tools presently used to gauge the reasonableness of a purchase premium rest heavily on the value of intellectual assets. Those assets actually used by the enterprise to shelter its market positions have demonstrable value that is subject to reasonable quantification. Those assets useful by others to achieve that selfsame position in their markets likewise have demonstrable value that is subject to reasonable quantification. And then, too, those assets that might be used in the future have a present options value that is subject to reasonable quantification.

All told, the intangible intellectual assets of an organization can carry a considerable load for those engaged in this form of gap analysis. But, as imaginative as some of these procedures may be, they overlook the full panoply of intellectual capital as the basis for an intangibles valuation. Next we turn to a few examples of intellectual capital valuation in action.

LOOKING FOR HIDDEN VALUE

Returning to the bedrock of this book's premise, intellectual capital management is the conversion of knowledge into profit. Beginning at the beginning, the knowledge base of the company is the first place to look. This is akin to the concept of finding value in a going concern. After all, what is that value but the value found in the ability to turn out tomorrow the same goods and services turned out today. That ability, to the extent it has value, is found in the ability of the existing workforce to deploy the complementary assets of the concern to a productive end. It is the knowledge, tacit and explicit, that lubricates the machinery of those complementary assets. Without the knowledge, there is no concern, going or otherwise.

Knowledge as an asset is readily likened to machinery as an asset, drawing out the obvious, fundamental distinction between the intangible and tangible. Some is sustaining, some is enabling, and some is core. Just as there are machines or devices that are fungible, for example a lathe, others are central to productivity, such as a programmed lathe. Likewise, the workforce of a going concern comprises workers whom some classify as agile, passive, and blocked learners. Despite the ability of most managers to agree with these distinctions and appreciate the intrinsic differences, we still see profoundly different reactions to the failure of a mission-critical machine and the departure of a key employee. The loss of knowledge is lamented; the anguish over the departure of an important contributor is palpable, but, in the end, it is viewed as the inevitable dynamics of the American workforce.

This book is not about human resources (as in the "HR department") but about human capital as a component of intellectual capital and, more to the point of this chapter, its valuation. In the context of M&A valuation and the category of going concern value, not all human capital is or should be valued equally. But, it should in some manner be valued and those key employees identified with at least a qualified or indexed value. It is these, the agile learners in particular, who are as mission-critical to the organization as are the core competencies they embody or represent, which valuation of intellectual capital should recognize. Yet it is too often these most valuable contributors to the preacquisition company who depart postacquisition.[8]

When key employees depart, there is a demonstrable loss in value. It can exceed the financial loss of a machine that breaks; likewise, its replacement cost can be as high or higher, especially for a true knowledge company. Reserves are taken for various contingencies, and postclosing adjustments are made once predicted facts or assumptions materialize or are confirmed. There is no more speculation in the quantification of loss resulting from departed key employees than is present in the valuation of patents in the manner described above. Human capital in its broadest sense needs to be included in the analysis of premiums paid. In many ways, this is one of the oldest recognized bases for doing so, once we understand explicitly the underpinnings of "going concern" value.[9]

Raw knowledge is worth little. Knowledge absent those complementary assets allowing it to be launched productively is of little commercial value. So, from an intellectual capital viewpoint, the examination of human capital and even the value of intellectual assets drawn from it, must take into account the role of a firm's complementary assets. This plays out in several ways.

On the broadest scale, knowledge in the form of human capital is a leveraging asset when it works with complementary assets of the firm. Foremost, if there are no adequate complementary assets, knowledge per se would be of little if any intrinsic value to its holder—there is no fulcrum for the lever. Likewise, different enterprises may be more or less adept in the manner in which they are able to use their complementary assets. Looking at the concept of contextual value examined in Chapter 2, it becomes apparent that there is no true extrinsic value of human capital but only that intrinsic to the enterprise when all of its complementary assets are taken into account.

Reexamining the technique of valuing intellectual assets, such as patents or other intellectual property, based on licensing streams of income, the necessity of including complementary assets in the equation becomes obvious. It is much too simplistic to assume that a potential licensee would pay a royalty unassociated with the status of the licensee's complementary assets related to the intellectual asset. Thus, we must be cautious not to trivialize the valuation analysis by failing to take into account all of the factors of leverage, and the characteristics of complementary assets constitute one of the most profound factors in the equation.

Other factors also warrant a place at the evaluation table, though the following tend to cloud our abilities seemingly to be objective in the admittedly murky process. We review them briefly.

Intellectual capital is the epitome of a deteriorating asset. First of all, few patents have real economic value for even a small portion of their legal lives. Most patents have more direct commercial value early in their patent lives than later. Also, few patents have value even for a small portion of their legal lives.

Long before the patent on a product expires, most products or the features of interest are obsolete. The same is equally true of the intellectual property protecting software. Though there are works of enduring value, all of these are as scarce as hen's teeth. Human capital is no different, though its demise takes a different path. We live in a time of "continual learning." Failure to keep current on trends in knowledge dooms the laggard while those who carve new areas for opportunity based on their creativity are increasingly rewarded. To the extent we wish to imagine the latent value in the acquired storehouse of human capital, it is as apropos to keep in mind the fleeting life of that value versus the investments necessary to preserve let alone enhance it.

VALUING THE PATENT PORTFOLIO

All of the foregoing has given rise to difficult calculations to determine the value of the intellectual property component of an acquisition. Here we are concerned with those intellectual assets that represent some component of the explicit knowledge base of the company's intellectual capital. The difficulties can be daunting, but for those who seek to rationalize or justify a qualitative evaluation decision, the process provides some comfort in the sensibility of the approach. We illustrate this approach using patents as the intellectual assets of interest, because their use is more straightforward and the techniques are as applicable to non-patented intellectual assets.

Market-Strategic Patents: The first step in the evaluation is identification of those patents underlying the firm's sources of competitive advantage. These are called *first-tier* patents. To accomplish this, three patent categories are created.

1. The first category comprises the most easily identified patents, those actually covering important products or features, or those sheltering the advantages of low-cost production. They also represent the smallest percentage of patents in the portfolios of the vast majority of companies.
2. The second category comprises those patents that more broadly protect the market for the goods of the company to be acquired. These could be patents that block or make more difficult the entry of product substitutes.

Categories one and two constitute the firm's strategic patents.

3. The third category contains all of the remainder of the patent portfolio.

When all of these patents are aggregated, strategic patents typically constitute about 5 to 10 percent of the portfolio of even the best-managed company.

Discounted Income Stream: For all of the patents that have been out-licensed, it is possible to calculate the discounted present value of their income stream. To accomplish this calculation, it is necessary to make several judgments or assumptions. For example, it is necessary to decide what the economic life of a licensed income stream would be, knowing that the economic life of a technology usually falls far short of the duration of the patent life. The focus must remain sharp on the longevity of the product or functionality in the market. In other words, the analysis as a function over time must be undertaken with a critical view of the time dimension.

One of the obvious reasons most patents have lives vastly exceeding their period of value is the advancement of technology and the progress of markets. Also, as much as 80 percent or more of the patents in most corporate portfolios can be classified as "junk" or nonstrategic. However, today's junk is most often yesterday's treasures, fallen on hard times. This presents both problems and opportunities for the valuation specialist. By far, the opportunity space is the larger.

If we adopt the "junk-in-the-garage" metaphor to describe the vast majority of patents in most portfolios, then the "one-man's-junk" analogy is particularly apropos. In modern times, we wring value from junk by selling it to someone who will treasure it or otherwise find a profitable use for it.

Thus, as the company moves up-market, it leaves in its wake opportunities for others to provide goods to the underserved portion of the departed market. Accordingly, the patents that no longer provide shelter for the sources of competitive advantages past, have the ability to generate funds when held by others who can operate in those arenas.

In sum, the ability to define the latent income represented by the portion of the portfolio that no longer supports the business plan harbors the latent source of value when analyzing the potential of the acquisition. The reality of the valuation then varies directly with whether the acquirer can locate a licensee willing to sell into a market the acquirer and his or her seller have rejected. Irrespective of the manner in which the analyst answers that question, this intellectual asset has the ability to support a portion of the premium valuation.

Future Value: There is another reason why a discernible element of the patent portfolio does not respond directly to products or services currently offered into the market however broadly defined. Sometimes the patent portfolio protects technology whose time has yet to come because it is simply off the mark or too futuristic. If it diverges from the normative view of the future (if ever one could exist), the value represented here is minimal to nil. However, if the trajectories are convergent in a reasonable time frame, there are sound reasons to associate value with these patents.

Disruptive Technology: One example of future value is found in the concept of disruptive technology. Disruptive technologies are known to overtake literally every market; the question is not whether, but when. In some markets the period of the cycle is long, while in others it is quite short; but the cycle always exists. Hence, if one reasonably can predict the wave of disruptive technology, the purchased company may have patents from which value can be captured.

It may be the case that the portfolio houses patents within the scope of the next or some successive wave of disruptive technology. If so, one can predict value and attempt to quantify it adopting either conservative or aggressive models. On the other hand, the portfolio may have patents important to the potentially disrupting technologist as it blossoms the market. Then, too, value may be observable. The point is to note the potential for value and treat it accordingly.

There is another way to look at value in a portfolio represented within the expanse of patents not directly or indirectly supporting today's source of competitive advantage. The acquirer may have a future interest in moving into a market but lacks the current resources or desire to do so. Patents that preserve that opportunity to enter the market at a more propitious or selected time in reality represent an option and are amenable to option-valuing methods. However, as mentioned earlier, great caution should be exercised to ensure that the underlying assumptions of the method used reasonably approximate the characteristics of the asset which the patent protects.

As we see, intellectual capital has a spirited role to play in the valuation of mergers or other acquisitions. Its role has been underplayed in the past. It will continue to grow as more mergers and acquisitions are driven by the intellectual capital considerations afoot whenever we seek to acquire a knowledge company or a company whose market position depends to any significant degree on technology. With greater use of the tools will come refinements that improve their quantitative reliability. For the immediate future, we will do well to apply these techniques at least qualitatively. The accuracy of this approach cannot be less than the finger-in-the-wind approach used in the past.

NOTES

1 Michal E. Porter, *Competitive Advantage Creating and Sustaining Superior Performance* (New York: The Free Press, 1985).

2 Treacy and Wiersema, *The Discipline of Market Leaders: Choose Your Customers, Narrow Your Focus, Dominate Your Market.*

3 F. Wiersema, Customer Intimacy (Santa Monica: Knowledge Exchange, 1997). Wiersema refines and expands on the concept of customer intimacy as an essential "value proposition."

4 Another interesting financial tool accompanied this insurgence of intellectual asset value. If the completed asset programs would have value, then the effort to create it, namely, research & development costs, could be written off immediately as the purchaser shut down those R&D activities.

5 Porter, *Competitive Advantage.*

6 See chapter 10, "Strategy for the Times: Intellectual Property Can Drive Corporate Profitability," in *Technology Licensing: Corporate Strategies for Maximizing Value,* eds. Russell Parr and Patrick Sullivan (New York: John Wiley & Sons, Inc., 1996).

7 To illustrate, the Black-Sholes formula, which is broadly used to value securities options, assumes that the value (i.e., price) of the underlying asset (security) behaves indefinitely as a continous geometric random walk. The value of a patentented technology, by contrast, is usually more complicated, falling over time as the patent expiration approaches and as replacement technologies become available.

8 This is an issue which admits of considerable wisdom to be drawn from Brian Hall's views on values. From our experiences, departures of key employees is as often a reflection of the change in values, or the perceived change in values, accompanying the acquisition. Proactively managing the values component of the satisfaction equation may well result in the retention of these highly prized assets.

9 This discussion begs the question of how to value, or even view the value, of employment contracts, both those designed to secure the continuing services of key employees or those noncompete covenants in jurisdictions where permissible. On the one hand, securing services is a vastly different objective from securing creativity, where the value is likely to be found. On the other hand, thwarting ready competition by employment restrictions at best is evanescent. In both events, we believe current valuation tools will not yield acceptable results.

22

Reporting on Intellectual Capital

Patrick H. Sullivan

ICM Group, LLC

Generally, three different groups are interested in information on intellectual capital. The first group consists of the companies themselves, whose primary concern is the measurement of activities and outcomes to determine the efficiency and effectiveness of their management and utilization of the firm's intellectual capital. A second group interested in intellectual capital information includes those involved in the capital markets, including regulators, major investors, academic accountants, accounting consultants, and legal scholars. The issues for members of this group are how to make measures of intellectual capital conform to methods and practices that have evolved over several hundred years to provide financial information to the capital markets. This group deals with both the capital markets' interests in information on intellectual capital and the countervailing set of interests on the appropriateness of disclosure: What is disclosed, its accuracy, timeliness, balance, and the degree to which it provides a whole picture of the firm's intellectual capital. The third group contains the academic macroeconomists and policy analysts. Their interest is in the effectiveness with which society's intellectual resources provide a return on society's investment in them, as well as on the national resource allocation and policy implications of society's investments in intellectual capital. To use a sports analogy, the macroeconomists are interested in analyzing the inputs and outputs of the ICM "game"; the capital market interests want to set the rules for the game; and the knowledge companies are the only group interested in the game itself.

In sophisticated companies—those that are aware of the importance of intellectual capital—managers are debating whether and to what degree their companies would benefit from releasing additional external reports on their IC. These debates center on how to use the firm's intellectual capital information to the company's advantage. In less sophisticated firms, many managers are averse to the idea of IC reporting, if they think it means releasing "secret" information to competitors. In fact, most companies already generate reports containing information about their use of intellectual capital. Most of what is contained in these reports is already public, just not all pulled together into a neat package. As a result, the "secrecy" concern about IC reporting is rarely supported by facts. The other often-stated concern about external reporting is less easy to dismiss. The argument here is that an external report on the firm's IC would not produce the promised results and, therefore, would waste money. Depending on the circumstances and the delivery, this could, of course, be true. Nevertheless, this argument may be circular in nature. If you report poorly, then you cannot expect to achieve the objective. If, on the other hand, you report well. . . .

The capital market and disclosure interests continue to view companies according to the old physical-assets model, in which companies make money by applying the traditional land, labor, and capital resources to the manufacture of a physical product. For manufacturing companies, the amount of physical and fiscal resources were excellent measures of the current wealth of a firm. The income statement was used largely as a short-term look into the firm's future. The capital markets group apply that same physical-assets model to the emerging knowledge company, whose physical and fiscal assets are significantly less important as measures of the company's current value and even less so as an indicator of future value. Their search for "reporting rules" for measures of intellectual capital bring to mind the old saw: "The nickel may not be in this corner, but the light's better over here!"

The topic of intellectual capital seems to have taken macroeconomists and policy analysts by surprise. It appeared suddenly, with little of the usual warning signals analysts have relied on to develop appropriate measurement tools, values, and standards. The field has little in the way of literature on how to analyze intangible assets, and there are no standards for evaluating the degree of goodness or not-goodness associated with any economic analyses that are attempted. This interest group will need to obtain data from companies to study the societal and national implications of intellectual capital ownership and management. A fear of government-mandated external reporting has triggered much of the discussion on intellectual capital reporting. Recent events suggest, however, that we are years, if not decades, away from mandated reporting. Securities and Exchange Commissioner Steven Wallman, the driving force behind virtually all of the SEC's efforts in this area, has stated that, aside from his own interest, there is very little SEC or other government-agency interest in the topic.

Recognizing its importance, however, the ICM Gathering has stated its intention to develop a set of measures of intellectual capital that its member companies might use. Further, the Gathering's intention is to learn whether and to what degree companies may be able to agree to standards involving these measures.

The existing literature on reporting deals largely with intangibles from an accounting perspective, either in terms of financial accounting or in terms of an "intangible balance sheet." This chapter reviews a broader range of interests and perspectives on the reporting of intellectual capital.

U.S. GOVERNMENT INTEREST IN INTELLECTUAL CAPITAL REPORTING

The U.S. government's interest in this topic is currently centered at the Securities and Exchange Commission, where one commissioner has expressed public concern that small investors are not privy to the same information about intangible assets as large investors. "Very large investors," says Commissioner Steven Wallman, "can call the CEO of a company like Microsoft and be able to obtain information on the company's intangible assets directly from the top, whereas there is no such channel available for the small investor to obtain access to the same kind of information."

Wallman's concern led him to host a symposium on the measurement of intangibles for financial reporting in 1996. Speakers included large investors, regulators, academics, consultants, and corporations. Some declared that intangibles were (by definition) not assets; others asserted that it was impossible to value intangibles accurately enough to capitalize them. The results of the symposium were inconclusive except to demonstrate that there was a great interest in seeking credible methods for valuing intangibles for inclusion on a knowledge firm's balance sheet and on the need for further discussion. Shortly thereafter, New York University's Stern School of Management established the Center for the Measurement of Intangibles. The Center's purpose is to research the management, valuation, and disclosure of intangibles.

REASONS FOR REPORTING ON INTELLECTUAL CAPITAL

From the perspective of corporations, the issue is not whether to report on intellectual capital, but how. Indeed, corporations already report internally on a number of measures of intellectual capital. The issue is what kind of reports of intellectual capital would be useful for what purposes. An informal survey of companies that already report internally on their intellectual capital reveals that the reasons for reporting are several fold.

Reasons for Internal Reporting

There are a range of reasons why firms invest resources in developing and operating systems for internal reporting on the management and use of the firm's intellectual capital.

Managing the firm's intellectual assets. Firms that actively manage their intellectual assets report to their management on the results of their efforts. These reports focus on management activity at several key junctions in the chain of activities producing commercial innovations.

Assessing effectiveness of the firm's IC utilization. Some CEOs and boards of directors ask managers to evaluate and report on the firm's effectiveness in utilizing its intellectual assets.

Reports of current and future income from IC. Some firms wish to know the amount of income generated by their intellectual assets, both current income (usually associated with IPs) and future or expected income (usually associated with IAs). Often the current income report deals with income from royalties on licensed IPs or know-how.

Relating employee contributions to IC to profits. Some firms report the linkages between employee activity, the intellectual capital it creates for the firm, and the profits that result from that intellectual capital. This kind of report is often issued as a morale builder, or as part of an attempt to link employee satisfaction more closely with company activity.

Alignment of IC resources with strategic vision. Some firms report on the degree to which a knowledge firm's intellectual capital is aligned with activities that will allow it to implement its business strategy and achieve its vision.

Reasons for External Reporting

Although there is only one firm currently making routine external reports on its intellectual capital, several other companies are actively considering doing so. The reasons for developing an external reporting capability include:

Stock price. Skandia, the first company to release an intellectual capital supplement to its annual financial report, found that its stock price rose by approximately 40 percent. Leif Edvinsson, vice president for intellectual capital, reports that Skandia considers 25 of those percentage points to be a direct response to the IC supplement.

Strategic positioning. Companies trying to change their strategic position may consider generating external reports about their intellectual capital to demonstrate that their knowledge is consistent with the new company direction and that their intellectual resources are aligned with their new vision. Examples of companies that might change strategic position include a pharmaceutical company that is becoming a biotechnology company, a military-industrial supplier that wants to shift into consumer products, or an aerospace company moving into the ground transportation business.

Effect on the cost of capital. Economists and capital market people say that, by producing a solid report for the external audience, knowledge firms can demonstrate that their intellectual capabilities are so substantial as to mitigate the normal risk inherent in developing and commercializing new products in an industry. With a reduction in risk comes a concomitant reduction in the cost of capital.

Some Implications of Reporting on Intellectual Capital

Safe harbor. Because major corporations are constantly being sued for one reason or another, companies may be concerned that reporting on intellectual capital will open the door to a fresh spate of lawsuits. For this reason, companies interested in external disclosure of information on intellectual capital are interested in the degree to which current law or regulatory practice will provide a safe harbor from law suits.

Predictive statements. Reporting on intellectual capital inevitably means discussing the firm's expected future for itself. Unfortunately, many senior executives of U.S. corporations grew up professionally in a world where predictive statements were at least frowned on and sometimes not allowed. For the period 1945 to 1976, the Securities and Exchange Commission specifically prohibited the inclusion of predictive information in prospectuses. Since 1977, the SEC has allowed companies to include predictive information in their annual financial reports as long as it is adequately identified as predictive and the usual cautions are made visible.

Level of detail. Some company executives are concerned that reporting on intellectual capital will provide too much detailed information to competitors. This belief is founded on the assumption that IC reports should contain mountains of key detailed information and, in so doing, would reveal too much. In fact, in the reports on intellectual capital that have appeared to date, the level of aggregation of the data is so high that little if any competitively useful information is revealed. In addition, since every company controls the nature and amount of information it releases, it can determine how closely it wishes to skate to the line bordering its cherished secrets.

Giving away inside *information.* Company executives mistakenly fear that in reporting on their intellectual capital, they might give away specific secret information. For most companies, the kind of information reported in an IC supplement would be information that has already been made public in other reports, speeches, or company publications. The IC report typically pulls together what has already been released.

INTELLECTUAL CAPITAL INFORMATION DESIRED BY AUDIENCES

Internal Audiences

Internal audiences are interested in a range of items of information, some of which are reported qualitatively and some quantitatively. There are generally considered to be three different audiences for internal reports:

Executive management. Executive management, typically the senior executives of the firm, as well as the members of the board, are interested in the strategic implications of intellectual capital for the firm. Their interests usually include strategic direction for the firm, profitability, stock price, litigation, and competitive position. Their interest in a report on the company's intellectual capital might include:

1. The degree of alignment of intellectual capital resources with the company's vision and strategy
2. Assessments of the company's competitive position on two fronts
   - Business: routine assessments of the competitiveness of the company's products, processes, or services in the business marketplace
   - Technology: routine assessments of the company's competitive position
3. Forecasts of company income based on innovations under development
4. Identification of the drivers of value and reports on value-driving activities and stocks

Employees. Also concerned with the current and prospective health and well-being of the company, employees nonetheless are usually more narrowly focused in their interests. Employees are interested in their own contributions to the firm's intellectual capital, where those contributions fit into the company's intellectual equation, and how their contributions will move the company forward. Many employees like the concept of themselves as the "hidden value" of the firm.

Whereas the employees working directly on the company's value-added activity can see their contributions to the bottom line, and the employees working in product R&D can see their contributions to the bottom line of the future, most employees provide indirect or infrastructure support. These employees, like the others, are interested in how and where their contributions matter. Internal reports to this audience should provide and explain an intellectual capital framework, point out where organizational units and even individuals fit in, and make clear the importance of all of the parts of the intellectual capital "machine" to the company and its future.

IC managers. For IC managers responsible for value creation or value extraction, internal reports provide information about the effectiveness of management actions and initiatives. This audience is the working audience. It is concerned with focusing the firm's intellectual capital onto its assigned tasks and then ensuring that the results are consistent with the goals. Internal reports to this audience tend to be long on data and short on explanatory materials.

External Audiences

External audiences are almost always looking for financial results. They are used to working with an accounting framework and find it difficult to think of externally reported information in terms other than financial ones.

Capital markets. The investment community has a long history of financial analysis and reporting for companies. From its perspective, virtually all of the company's key information can be reduced to financial or some quasifinancial information. Information that does not lend itself to quantification is covered in brief narrative statements.

As has been shown elsewhere in this book, many of the measures of intellectual capital of interest are qualitative, or not quantifiable in dollar terms. The capital markets require methods and procedures that will convert intellectual capital information into dollars and cents. Several organizations are working to develop credible methods for measuring the firm's intangibles.

Shareholders. As owners of the company, shareholders expect to receive from the company any information that will allow them to better evaluate the company's direction, management, and long-term potential. Although many of their interests in intellectual capital information are similar to those of the capital market representatives, because of their ownership status, shareholders believe they have a right to more. Intellectual capital statements designed for shareholders would explain the role of intellectual capital within the firm and how it is contributing to the creation of the firm's future. Such reports would be expected to contain little hard financial data and to focus on qualitative information.

Other stakeholders. Other stakeholders in the firm, such as vendors, suppliers, families, and collateral businesses, care about the implications of the firm's direction for their own business health. External reports of intellectual capital directed at these stakeholders could be expected to contain explanatory frameworks as well as information about the company's long-term business and employment prospects.

In summary, reporting on intellectual capital is in its infancy. Each potential audience has its own agenda and concerns. The company agenda is perhaps the simplest and most direct. To profit, knowledge companies must create sustainable value through innovation. To this end, they are learning of the importance not only of measuring but also of reporting on their intellectual capital.

Most of today's executives were trained in corporations that followed the old physical assets model, where the control of assets and their denial to the competition were keys to success. In the new model, control of information is key. Success requires disseminating information that is to the firm's advantage and protecting information that is the core of the firm's business. Advanced telecommunication technologies such as computing and the internet have made secrets harder to keep. The old model is crumbling. What will the new model for information reporting be?

23

Understanding and Managing Knowledge Assets for Competitive Advantage in Innovation and Product Development

Joseph J. Daniele

Xerox Corporation

INTRODUCTION[1]

Although the importance of human capital among the assets of a firm is commonly accepted, its intangibility and the absence of a common metric make it difficult to assess and quantify. Yet, as the pace of change in global markets continues to increase, the value of flexible human resources is advancing more quickly than that of static physical and financial assets. As more of the competitive advantage of a firm lies in its human assets, the necessity to understand the sources of the value of that asset becomes greater. Much of Japan's success in the 1980s and 1990s is the result of very efficient and effective use of its human capital, rather than any specific advantages in physical or investment assets. Today, we see this same highly effective use of human capital reflected in the high market valuation of knowledge-based firms like Microsoft and Intel.

The relative advantages of human and physical capital can be illustrated by comparing two hypothetical business investments. Both investments are in state-of-the-art microelectronics factories, but the investment choices differ. In one, a state-of-the-art Japanese factory is copied down to the last stepper and filtering system and duplicated in Europe, entailing a huge investment in physical capital. It is staffed by local engineers with substantial formal education, but with experience primarily limited to the previous generation of microelectronics technology. In the other, the dozen or so engineers and managers who designed, built, and operate the Japanese factory are sent to the new site to build and operate the new plant. Assuming that roughly equal amounts of financial capital were provided in both cases, one would expect the second factory to be much more successful than the first. Yet, the only difference between the two hypothetical situations is the quality and quantity of the knowledge held by the dozen or so Japanese engineers and managers and their European counterparts, both as individuals and as a group. This particular or *specific knowledge* is the central topic of this paper.

In the two alternatives just discussed, the two groups of engineers are assumed to have about the same formal education and background in basic microelectronic technology; the difference between them is in their hands-on know-how in the practice of the latest generation of technology. Their general knowledge, or the kind that can be obtained from books and literature in the public domain, is not the source of competitive advantage, except as it relates to the ease and cost with which the second type of knowledge, *specific knowledge,* can be obtained. The difference between the two groups is in the *know-how* or *specific knowledge* of the latest generation of equipment and technology. This specific knowledge is often in the form of tacit knowledge. It is frequently not written down, sometimes because the engineers know that a particular procedure or combination of procedures works but do not understand exactly how or why. This kind of knowledge is generally obtained through what is known as learning-by-doing, and its growth rate is dependent on how fast and efficient the underlying work processes are. Most important, because this knowledge is held by individuals, it is very costly to transfer from one to another. Thus issues of organization and location are important in managing this kind of knowledge.

In this chapter we will see that the corporation's aggregate specific knowledge is a key asset and factor in the value of the corporation, that a focus on this asset provides a theory and guiding principle for general management, and that this theory provides guidance for product development, engineering, human asset management, mergers and acquisitions, and corporate strategy. Also, we will see that a focus on transfer cost provides a useful management tool.

What Is Specific Knowledge and Why Is It a Useful Unifying Concept?

The information that an individual generates, collects, and processes into knowledge and decisions has value and cost. Like tangible assets in the physical world, knowledge, too, can be classified by type, cost, and value.

In the present study, we use the concept of specific knowledge. In a product-development context, specific knowledge is equivalent to what is sometimes called *design learning* or *know-how.* As such, it consists of the hundreds of tricks, shortcuts, and complex solutions discovered and developed by individuals practicing in a field. In a marketing or sales context, it is salesmanship, tricks of the trade, or the preferences or purchasing circumstances of a customer or group of customers. Specific knowledge generally resides in the minds of individuals at the point of knowledge production and can have high value. It sometimes is useful for only a short time, but often it has wide applicability. Engineering-specific knowledge consists of that knowledge gained and held by individuals through practice of a particular field at the state of the art in a specific product area. General knowledge, in contrast, is knowledge that can be found in books and literature in the public domain; it is widely available to anyone for the price of a library card (or the price of a consultant's public report).

Objectives and Key Messages

An understanding of the specific knowledge asset can have great utility in competitive rivalry. This utility may take several forms, for example:

- A simple recognition of the asset being managed-knowledge and information closely held by individuals
- Accurate assessment of the competitive capability and competitive disposition of the key assets of the firm now and in the future
- Identification of knowledge gaps, present and future, and relative rates of change in the growth of the knowledge asset base
- Identification and location of key or core knowledge assets; realization that these are corporate assets and may be imprisoned resources, as Prahalad and Hamel refer to those human and knowledge resources held by one business unit to the exclusion of others[2]
- Some rules of thumb and key considerations for active management of specific knowledge assets

At Xerox, the concept of specific knowledge has been used as a basis for developing the strategic "View of Xerox" and providing a present and future view of Xerox's core papermarking competence in 28 knowledge categories. Moreover, it has provided a language and consistent methodology for quantifying and assessing the engineering human asset base. This analysis has proven helpful in the Xerox 2000 strategic planning effort carried out in 1989 and 1990, and has helped to identify specific knowledge gaps and long-term remedial actions. Also, by focusing attention on the strategic importance of the specific knowledge asset base, it has increased the emphasis placed on active management of the human resource asset.

Specific knowledge is often the key variable and differentiator of competitive success or failure and is a major, if not the major, asset of many corporations. Yet, while much attention is paid to and effort expended on the management of physical and financial assets, relatively little attention is paid to the management of the specific knowledge asset base and to the human assets who hold it. This is in part because the value of knowledge is so obvious that it is often taken for granted, and in part because a methodology or science for conceptualizing and dealing with various types of knowledge has only recently been broadly developed or communicated.[3] Prior work and references to specific knowledge are found primarily in the specialized literature of the economics of innovation and technological change.[4] This paper attempts to bring the concept out of this specialized context and make it accessible to general management, engineering management, and corporate planning practitioners. The next section briefly reviews some of this literature.

PREVIOUS WORK AND REFERENCES

Tacit, Specific, and General Knowledge

While philosophers and economists through the centuries have recognized the various types of knowledge, not much emphasis has been placed on specific knowledge, or know-how, since by its nature it is difficult to describe and quantify. The Greeks recognized the difference between the unwritten, hands-on knowledge of the craftsman, or techne and scientific knowledge, or episteme. Masahiko Aoki, quoting from Stephan Marglin's essay "What Do Bosses Do Again?" writes:

> The Greeks looked down their noses at the craftsman because craftsmanship, the techne of production, was derived from tradition and dealt with approximation, to which "neither exact measure nor precise calculation applies" [quoting the French philosopher Jean Pierre Vernant]. Thus techne belonged to an entirely different realm from episteme, or science, which was based on logical deduction from self-evident first principles.

Aoki goes on to note that much of the success of the Japanese in product development and manufacture can be ascribed to delegating practical problem solving to the lowest possible level, "where knowledge of circumstance exists," and to focusing on "expanding in-house engineering knowledge—techne—with the aid of episteme and not vice versa."[5]

Much practical knowledge is not only unwritten but also not easily described in words. The late philosopher M. Polyani wrote extensively on the body of human knowledge that cannot be articulated—tacit knowledge. His philosophy is based on the simple observation: "We know more than we can tell."[6] He felt that it is common for a person to know how to do something without being able to explain how it is being done. These tacit skills and knowledge extend from the physical and the athletic to the skills of the businessman. Tacit knowledge as described by Polyani forms an end point for a wide range of specific knowledge. Most of the tacit dimensions of skills are unconscious, such as the skills in riding a bicycle, in the controlled breathing of a swimmer, or in the symbol manipulations of a mathematician.

One of the earliest attempts to define knowledge by type and cost was by the Nobel laureate economist F. A. Hayek in 1945. Hayek took an economic/societal view and was one of the first to make the distinction between general knowledge and particular knowledge, or "the knowledge of time and place."[7] His work argued for the decentralization of economic planning and controls because of the dispersed nature of particular knowledge and the very high cost of accurately collecting and analyzing it. Hayek's thesis was that decision making should be where the knowledge is. M. C. Jensen, in an unpublished work, pulled these concepts together in the context of corporations and organizational structure. Jensen made the distinction between general knowledge, or "knowledge that is transferred among people at low cost" and specific knowledge, or "knowledge that is transferred among people at high cost."[8]

A few economists, beginning with K. J. Arrow, have discussed learning, experience, and accumulation of knowledge as key sources of change in productivity and shifts in production functions. In retrospect, it is surprising that these thoughts were new and in some ways revolutionary as recently as 1962. Arrow's words follow:

> I advance the hypothesis here that technical change in general can be ascribed to experience, that it is the very activity of production which gives rise to problems for which favorable responses are selected over time. . . .
>
> I would like to suggest here an endogenous theory of the changes in knowledge which underlie intertemporal and international shifts in production functions. . . . Learning is the product of experience. Learning can only take place through the attempt to solve a problem and therefore only takes place during activity.[9]

Others discuss tacit knowledge as a key source of costs and entry barriers. In the context of analyzing contracting costs for R&D and the value of vertical integration, David J. Teece speaks of the high transfer costs associated with tacit or state-of-the-art know-how. As he puts it, "the less codified is the relevant know-how, and the closer it is to the state-of-the-art, the more costly it is to transfer."[10] In a thorough review of the economics of technology and innovation, Giovanni Dosi describes the distinction between specific and general knowledge: "In general, technological progress proceeds through the development and exploitation of both public elements of knowledge, shared by all actors involved in a certain activity, and private, local, partly tacit, firm-specific, cumulative forms of knowledge." In describing an economist's view of the solution to a technological problem, he refers to "scientific knowledge" and other knowledge, "specific to particular ways of doing things."

> The solution of most technological problems (e.g., designing a machine with certain performance characteristics, developing a new chemical compound with certain features, improving the efficiency of a production input, etc.) implies the use of pieces of knowledge of various sorts. Some elements represent widely applicable understanding: it might be direct scientific knowledge or knowledge related to well-known and pervasive applicative principles (e.g., on electricity, mechanics, more recently, informatics, etc.). Some other pieces of knowledge are specific to particular "ways of doing things", to the experience of the producer, the user, or both.
>
> Moreover, some aspects of this knowledge are well articulated, even written down in considerable detail in manuals and articles and taught in schools. Others are largely tacit, mainly learned through practice and practical examples (of course, "training" and "apprenticeship" relate also to this aspect of technology): there are elements of being a "good engineer," a

> "good designer," or even a "good mathematician" that cannot be entirely transmitted in an explicit algorithmic form.[11]

Finally, the concept of the experience curve and the effects of learning on product costs and business strategy are well known in the business literature.[12]

The Specific and Tacit Knowledge of the Business Person

According to H. Mintzberg,

> The value of tacit and specific knowledge will, upon reflection, be familiar to managers and business people. Much of the daily activity and decision making in business is oral, face-to-face, and based not on written analysis, but on a feel for the situation. Nelson and Winter[13] have elaborated on how day-to-day business decisions are often based upon an unconscious working knowledge of microeconomics.

Mintzberg has ascribed the highly intuitive nature of managerial work as a primary reason for his "dilemma of delegation." As he puts it: "The manager may simply be incapable of disseminating some relevant information because it is inaccessible to his or her consciousness."[14]

For the purposes of this chapter, rather than focus on the full range of tacit knowledge, we will focus on those areas commonly called *know-how* that are of particular value to the design and manufacture of products. Obviously, valuable specific knowledge also extends throughout the value chain to sales, distribution and service. Richard Hall[15] and Hiroyuki Itami[16] provide some discussion of the value of intellectual assets in those other links in the value chain.

Learning-By-Doing, Specific Knowledge Generation, and Organizational Memory

If specific knowledge cannot be articulated, then how is it stored and maintained? Several economists believe that specific knowledge is stored and maintained in the routines or accepted processes, both informal and formal, that an organization develops in the course of designing, manufacturing, and selling a product. For example, Richard Nelson and Sidney Winter describe routinization as the basis for organizational memory as follows: "But where and what is the memory of an organization? We propose that the routinization of activity in an organization constitutes the most important form of storage of the organization's specific operational knowledge. Basically, we claim that organizations remember by doing."[13]

Going a step further, Dosi describes firm-specific knowledge as related to both products and processes and generated through "learning by doing" and "learning-by-using." According to Dosi, these routines develop naturally through the day-to-day problem solving of business operations:

> A significant amount of innovations and improvements are originated through "learning-by-doing" and "learning-by-using" [Rosenberg, 1976,

> 1982]. That is, people and organizations, primarily firms, can learn how to use/improve/produce things by the very process of doing them, through their "informal" activities of solving production problems, meeting specific customers' requirements, overcoming various sorts of "bottlenecks," etc.[11]

While economists have long recognized the importance of various types of knowledge in bringing about progress and technological change, taken as a group, they have tended to undervalue the tacit and specific aspects of knowledge. Hall,[15] writing about general management of intellectual assets, laments the underutilization of intellectual assets, and especially know-how. Know-how takes time to accumulate; it forms the core knowledge areas of the firm; it cannot, in general, be bought; and thus, its lack can be a substantive entry barrier.

USE OF THE SPECIFIC KNOWLEDGE CONCEPT AND ITS CONSEQUENCES

Relationship of Specific Knowledge to the Engineering Asset Base

Two categories of specific knowledge that are useful for product development and engineering are knowledge of product and knowledge of process. Product knowledge refers to design and engineering knowledge of metals, chemicals, circuits, algorithms, tolerances, and complex materials interactions, and especially the knowledge that is specific to the state-of-the-art design of a product or group of products. The knowledge of process refers to knowledge of the design, work, and manufacturing processes embedded in the organization, and the extended organization, including suppliers, customers, and all outside knowledge sources. This is the knowledge of who knows and does what and when. These knowledge bases together provide what Teece calls the "learning domain of the firm," which he defines as "where the firm has been and what it has experienced."[10] This "learning domain" provides for knowledge accumulation and has important implications for the next round of products.

How Is Specific Knowledge Efficiently Generated, Maintained, and Disseminated?

In the context of appropriateness of technology, Teece speaks of process knowledge as being stored in routines; the constant practice of those routines is required to retain organizational competence and specific competencies.

> After first commercialization, a set of routines will develop which will lead to a deepening of competencies in certain areas. The skillful performance of organizational routines provides the underpinnings for what is commonly thought of as the distinctive competence of an enterprise.
>
> Routines, since they cannot be codified, must be constantly practiced to exhibit high performance. This in turn implies that the firm must remain in certain activities in which short-run considerations would indicate that aban-

donment is desirable. Put differently, core business skills need to be constantly exercised to retain corporate fitness.[10]

Hall has noted that intellectual assets, including know-how, build through each turn of the business cycle in a parallel path to business operations. As he puts it, "The operation of the business process should be not only cash positive but also information positive. Each turn of the business cycle should result in the organization having more skill, experience, information database, and reputation."[14] Ikujiro Nonaka has described the practice and methods of Japanese firms in the creation, development and dissemination of tacit and explicit or general knowledge in product development.[17]

Some characteristics of the dynamics of specific knowledge generation and growth are illustrated by examples in copier and duplicator product development. The rate of specific knowledge generation can be related to the product design and development cycle for low- and high-speed copier products. New specific knowledge, or the hundred or so tricks required to design and manufacture a specific product at the state of the art, is created with each new product turn or cycle. Since specific knowledge is generated in the course of active design and development, the shorter the development time per product, the greater the rate of specific knowledge generation and the more specific knowledge accumulated in a given time. Also, the total amount of specific knowledge per product may not be greatly different for a low-, mid-, or high-speed product. We expect that while the character of the knowledge may be different, the quantity is the same. Low-end products turn much more rapidly on a cycle time of 1 to 2 years, while mid- and high-end products turn every 3 to 7 years. Thus, the knowledge-generation rate in low-end product development may be 2 to 7 times higher than that in mid- or high-end products. As a result, participation in product areas with a high turn rate can be central to having a specific-knowledge growth rate sufficient to remain competitive in the other parts of the business. Also, it is apparent that shorter development times may contribute to a higher knowledge-generation rate across the board. Finally, an improved knowledge-generation rate alone, while necessary, is insufficient. Efficient maintenance and dissemination of knowledge is of equal importance.

Knowledge Gaps and Competitive Rivalry

Engineering-specific knowledge consists of that knowledge gained and held by individuals through practice of a particular field at the state of the art in a specific product area. Since specific knowledge is a continuously self-renewing resource and is valuable for only a limited time, when the knowledge chain is broken, the loss of this specific knowledge is irreversible or reversible only at high cost. Thus, when scientists and engineers do not practice in a specialty area, they do not keep up with the field and lose the specific knowledge base required to practice that field, even though they have the fundamental background and general knowledge. When a company chooses not to practice in segments of a business for many years, specific knowledge gaps open between it and practicing companies.

These gaps become the basis for competitive advantage or disadvantage. They occur when a company retreats from a field or product line. Common examples in the United States are the retreat from consumer electronics and television design and manufacture. During the years that a company does not practice, the state of the art moves forward, and the cost to a company in time and money of acquiring the new knowledge and closing the gap becomes prohibitively high.

Perez and Soete discussed the costs of closing these gaps as a function of the knowledge status of the firm. As shown in their graph, redrawn in Exhibit 23.1, a knowledge threshold or barrier can occur below which the costs of acquiring new knowledge are very high:

> The generation of new knowledge obviously has costs in time and personnel for design and experimentation as well as equipment and prototype expenses. The actual costs for the innovator will consequently include not only that of generating the new innovation-bound knowledge but also the cost of acquiring that part of "freely" available relevant knowledge which the innovating firm did not possess to begin with. . . .
>
> There is a threshold level below which costs to the firm would be infinitely high. This threshold cannot be defined a priori, but would depend on how science-based or how truly "new" the innovation is.[18]

Dosi also refers to the irreversibility of technological progress: "patterns of innovation tend to follow rather irreversible "trajectories" defined by specific sets of knowledge and expertise."[19] Moreover, according to Dosi this irreversibility tends to be reinforced by changes in internal and external infrastructures. Thus, the management of specific knowledge can be a very effective competitive weapon, especially when used to convince a competitor to withdraw from a field, even temporarily, since the withdrawal is often irreversible and the intellectual and specific knowledge ground, once taken, is nearly impenetrable to counterattack. Specific knowledge gaps can open in product, technology, and process areas. For example, in the 1980s a substantial gap in specific knowledge of process has been opened by the Japanese development and use of highly productive and flexible development and manufacturing processes. Kim Clarke et al. have written about this gap in the context of automobile design and manufacture.[20]

Reverse Engineering

In the context of product development, one way that a knowledge gap can be reduced at modest cost is to reverse-engineer an existing product. The process of reverse engineering or copying a product can release some of the specific knowledge captured in the design, convert it to general knowledge, and reduce the gap. For complex products such as copiers and printers, not all the specific knowledge can be extracted from the design, and a simple copy of the product often does not work because of some missing piece of specific knowledge. As in the initial design process, new knowledge must be generated. Nevertheless, the net cost of the knowledge is less than it would have been if all the specific knowledge had been generated rather than extracted. As shown in Exhibit 23.1, reverse engineering or imitation tends to move the knowledge acquisition cost curve down, without changing its shape. Although the cost of entry has been reduced, a threshold or minimum knowledge barrier still remains.

In a fast-moving field, reverse engineering can never fully close the knowledge gap, but it can reduce the cost of catching up to acceptable levels. Moreover, there is substantial specific knowledge of process in the art of converting the specific knowledge captured in a competitor's product design. State-of-the-art practice of this process with good general and specific knowledge bases can provide the basis for an effective follower strategy. This sort of strategy was practiced by the Japanese during the 1960s and 1970s before their specific knowledge base had matured sufficiently to take on leadership positions.

IMPLICATIONS FOR PERSONNEL POLICY AND HUMAN RESOURCE MANAGEMENT

Relationship Between Aptitudes and General and Specific Knowledge

Three knowledge factors are important in the assessment and management of the human resource asset base. At the individual level, the factors are talents and aptitudes, general knowledge, and specific knowledge. Talents tend to be very specific and to self-select individuals based on inherent aptitudes, such as mechanical, mathematical, artistic, or literary aptitude. General knowledge is that accumulated in the individual through schooling, training and self-teaching from books, and other generally available sources. Specific knowledge is generally obtained in the practice of a field and is often tacit knowledge of the work process. Specific knowl-

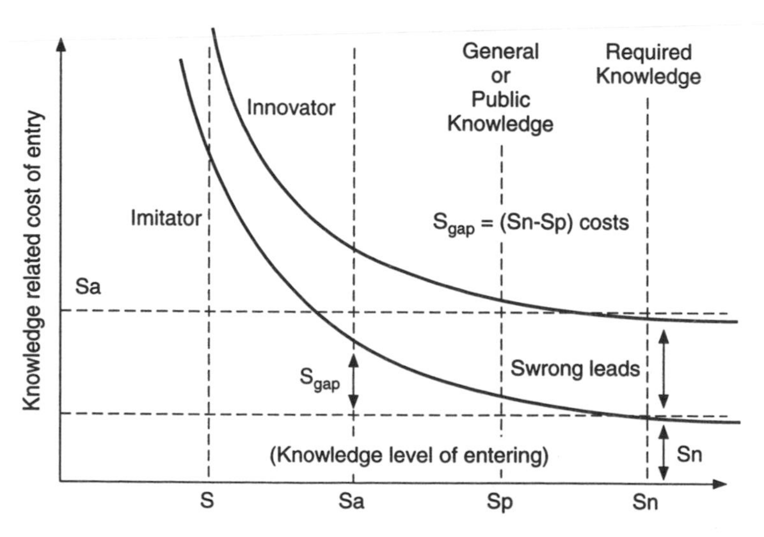

Exhibit 23.1 Knowledge-related Cost of Entry for Different Innovating and Initiating Firms[21]

edge includes playing musical instruments, solving mathematical problems, writing good prose, doing good mechanical or electrical design, and other physical and intellectual activities. While specific knowledge is the key human asset base differentiator, the level of general knowledge the individual or group has attained strongly affects the cost of obtaining new knowledge, either general or specific.

Skills, Knowledge, and Job Categories

Corporations usually categorize human assets by skill or job category. Here, skill categorization is based primarily on general knowledge. Thus, new graduates are lumped with old hands as mechanical engineers, chemists, accountants, or sales representatives. Job categories are based primarily on general knowledge, some information about experience is captured through grade level, assignment, or area of specialization such as xerographer or polymer chemist. However, the actual specific knowledge held by individuals is almost never addressed, quantified, or categorized. Skill names rarely reflect the complexity or scope of the behavior they represent. Moreover, much of this job behavior is difficult or impossible to articulate. According to Nelson and Winter, while names can communicate units of "purposeful behavior," they do not describe the "inner workings of a skill," or the relevant, often idiosyncratic specific knowledge associated with it.[12]

SOME IMPLICATIONS FOR CORPORATE STRATEGIC PLANNING AND GENERAL MANAGEMENT

Organizational Effects and Competitive Advantage—Core Competencies

Much attention has been paid to the competitive advantage derived from the active use of core competencies. Exactly what constitutes a core competence? The core competencies of a corporation are made up in part of the knowledge held by the management and employees of that corporation, and of the important physical and financial assets. The specific knowledge aspect of the core competence is the most important because it is the most difficult to acquire and replicate and is central to competitive differentiation. The knowledge piece of a core competence is made up of process and product knowledge and is present in at least two forms, specific and general knowledge. Specific knowledge is important, because while it may or may not be costly to generate, it is very costly to communicate or transfer to others. It is primarily accumulated through practice, by its nature closely held, and often the basis for competitive advantage in corporate rivalry. Thus, understanding the types and knowledge value, and the communications costs associated with knowledge is important in managing and building corporate core competencies. Moreover, the concept of specific knowledge provides a new way to measure human capital in strategically relevant dimensions. A focus on the generation and maintenance of specific knowledge can provide direction to active human resource management and to the planning and development of the core competencies.

Clearly, the core product development capability—the engineering human resource—is a critical corporate asset, which produces a basic source of value and competitive advantage. Therefore, the management and husbanding of this asset should be a critical corporate function. This asset consists primarily of the aggregate specific and general knowledge held by the individual employees of the corporation. As the competitive difference between corporations becomes more and more defined by human rather than physical or financial assets, knowledge development and management gain increasing importance. Many corporations, especially in fast-moving fields, already feel the consequences of effective knowledge management when used as a competitive weapon. Their competitors continuously develop better and better products, faster, and with fewer resources, by recognizing and taking advantage of effective management of specific knowledge.

Finally, in a corporate strategic planning context, a focus on specific knowledge allows managers to evaluate relative competitive strength and weakness, and appropriateness of fit with potential alliance partners. Also, a comparison of relative rates of growth in specific knowledge bases can signal dynamic changes in relative strength.

Mergers and Acquisitions

The high transfer or transaction cost associated with specific knowledge is the characteristic that enables corporations to use their specific knowledge resource to generate and sustain competitive advantage. It is clear that a corporate-specific knowledge base is a key source of value for any business, whether it is the specific knowledge of design and manufacture of a product or specific knowledge of customers for sales and service. Moreover, as corporations increasingly merge with and acquire others to gain the scale and scope needed to remain competitive, the ability to measure, gauge, and value the specific knowledge of a corporation grows in importance. The asset being merged or acquired is increasingly a specific knowledge asset, and its distribution among key individuals and the difficulty in transferring it to others is often a major source of risk and failure in mergers and acquisitions. J. L. Badaracco has written on this topic.[22]

SOME KEY CONSIDERATIONS FOR MANAGEMENT OF SPECIFIC KNOWLEDGE ASSETS IN PRODUCT DEVELOPMENT

If specific knowledge is crucial and fundamental to the competitive conduct of business, is closely held by individuals, and is costly to transfer from one person or group to another, then what organizational processes are most effective in managing this asset? A few important considerations for product development follow:

- Knowledge flows, and especially specific knowledge flows, are key enablers of most work processes. Efficiency in these flows leverages the effectiveness of the whole business. Thus, those process elements and interfaces that deal substantively with specific rather than general knowledge require special attention.
- Colocation of all personnel associated with critical transfers of specific knowledge is important.

- High-efficiency use of stored and general knowledge acquired from outside the enterprise is important and has been a cornerstone of Japanese strategy.
- Development of methods for sharing, coordinating, and communicating specific knowledge between teams is important, as are methods for its maintenance and storage.

SUMMARY

While the basic concept and consequences of specific knowledge are recognized in the economics literature, they have not seen much application in management or strategic planning. Moreover, no systematic approach has been available to derive utility from them in a practical business context. This chapter has attempted to systematize these concepts in the context of business applications primarily related to engineering and product development, but with clear implications for corporate strategic planning and general and human resource management.

Xerox has used the concept of specific knowledge in its strategic planning effort and to provide a present and future view of Xerox's core papermarking competence in 28 specific knowledge categories. It has provided a language and consistent methodology for quantifying and assessing the engineering human asset base. This analysis has proven central to strategic planning and has helped to identify specific knowledge gaps and long-term remedial actions. It has also increased the emphasis placed on active management of the human resource asset.

An understanding of the specific knowledge asset can have great utility in competitive rivalry. The corporation's aggregate specific knowledge is a key corporate asset and critical component in the value of the corporation. A focus on this asset can provide a theory for general management, which provides guidance for product development, engineering, human asset management, mergers and acquisitions, and corporate strategy.

NOTES

1 The author would like to gratefully acknowledge the work of Roger E. Levien, formerly of Xerox Corporation (currently of Strategy and Innovation Consulting), for supporting this work as part of the Xerox 2000 Strategy effort, for his insightful contributions in discussion and exploration of the topic, and for editing and helping to structure earlier versions of the paper.

2 C. K. Prahalad and G. Hamel, "The Core Competence of the Corporation," *Harvard Business Review* (May/June 1990).

3 See Ikujiro Nonaka and H. Takeuchi, *The Knowledge—Creating Company* (London and New York: Oxford University Press, 1995); K. E. Sveiby, *The New Organizational Wealth* (San Francisco: Bennett-Koehler Publishers, Inc., 1997); and Leif Edvinsson and M. S. Malone, *Intellectual Capital: Realizing Your Company's True Value* (New York: Harper Business, 1997).

4 N. Rosenberg, "Problems in the Economist's Conceptualization of Technological Innovation," in *Perspective on Technology* ed. N. Rosenberg (New York: Cambridge University Press, 1976): 61–84.

5 Masahiko Aoki, *Information, Incentives, and Bargaining in the Japanese Economy* (New York: Cambridge University Press, 1988): 239–240. From Stephen Marglin's essay "What Do Bosses Do

Again? An Essay on the Moral Economy of Work," (Mimeographed by the World Institute of Development Economic Research, June 1986): 12. The quotation from Vernant is from his *Mythe, et Pensée Chez les Grecs* (Paris: 1965).

6 M. Polyani, *The Tacit Dimension* (Garden City, N.Y.: Anchor/Doubleday, 1967).

7 F. A. Hayek, "The Use of Knowledge in Society," *American Economic Review* 35:4 (1945).

8 M. C. Jensen, "Organization Theory" (class notes. University of Rochester, March 1985).

9 K. J. Arrow, "The Economic Implications of Learning by Doing," *Review of Economic Studies:* 29 (1962), 155–173.

10 David J. Teece, "Technological Change and the Nature of the Firm," in *Technical Change and Economic Theory,* ed. Giovanni Dosi, et al. (London: Pinter Publishers, 1988).

11 Giovanni Dosi, "The Nature of the Innovative Process," in *Technical Change and Economic Theory,* ed. Giovanni Dosi, et al. (London: Pinter Publishers, 1988): 221–238.

12 Bruce Henderson, *The Logic of Business Strategy* (Cambridge, M.A.: Ballinger Publishing Company, 1984).

13 Richard R. Nelson and Sidney G. Winter, *An Evolutionary Theory of Economic Change* (Cambridge, M.A.: Harvard University Press, Belknap Press, 1982): 72–261.

14 H. Mintzberg, "Planning on the Left Side, Managing on the Right," in *Mintzberg on Management—Inside our Strange World of Organization* (New York: Free Press, 1989): 43–78.

15 Richard Hall, "The Management of Intellectual Assets: A New Corporate Perspective," *Journal of General Management* 15:1 (1989), 53–68.

16 Hiroyuki Itami with Thomas W. Roehl, *Mobilizing Invisible Assets* (Cambridge, M.A.: Harvard University Press, 1987).

17 Ikujiro Nonaka, "The Knowledge-Creating Company," *Harvard Business Review* (Nov./Dec., 1991): 17.

18 C. Perez, and L. Soete, "Catching Up in Technology: Entry Barriers and Windows of Opportunity," in *Technical Change and Economic Theory,* ed. G. Dosi et al. (London: Pinter Publishers, 1988): 458–479.

19 Giovanni Dosi, "Sources, Procedures, and Microeconomic Effects of Innovation," *Journal of Economic Literature* 26 (1988): 1120–1171.

20 Kim Clarke et al., *Product Development Performance: Strategy, Organization, and Management in the World Auto Industry* (Boston: Harvard Business School Press, 1991).

21 Perez and Soete, "Catching Up in Technology," p. 467.

22 J. L. Badaracco, *The Knowledge Link,* (Boston: Harvard Business School Press, 1991).

24

Maintaining the Stock of Intellectual Capital

Pamela Jajko

Roche Bioscience

Eugenie Prime

Hewlett-Packard Company

Until recently, the intellectual assets of a company were considered its legally protected intellectual property, such as patents and copyrights. Today, the concept of intellectual assets has dramatically expanded to include numerous types of information created by employees. Knowledge companies recognize that their competitive advantage is dependent on maximizing the access, retrieval, and utilization of these intellectual assets throughout the company in a way that provides some economic benefit.

This chapter discusses how central coordination of intellectual assets can dramatically expand the awareness of the firm's previously created knowledge, effectively increase access to this storehouse of knowledge, and substantially improve its timely retrieval by a variety of interested persons or organizations.

THE IMPORTANCE OF INFORMATION ORGANIZATION AND RETRIEVAL

Six years after the Gulf War, the CIA admitted that it had fumbled much of the information about the Iraqi chemical weapons depot at Khamisiyah. Robert Walpole acknowledged that the "agency was reluctant to share some of its most sensitive information with other top government officials"; had "problems with multiple databases" that contained multiple names for a single site; and conducted "incomplete searches of files."[1] This was a startling admission from the CIA. It recognized that the failure was one of basic information management. The erroneous decision to bomb the chemical weapons depot was a direct result of inadequately stored, poorly shared, and ineffectively accessed information.

Most organizations have problems similar to those admitted by the CIA and do not even know it. Consider a simplified example of information flow within a typical company. Information tends to move from an individual (level 1), to a department or team (level 2), to higher levels of management (level 3). As the information moves up, it is usually managed differently at each level. At level 1, individuals may know/learn/create information but retain most of that information in their heads or stored on their own personal computers, filed in desk drawers or stuffed into a briefcase. This kind of information is difficult for others to know about, difficult for others to locate, and difficult to retrieve or save by the author.

As individuals participate in department and team activities, a small part of what each individual knows is shared with a group (level 2). The department or team usually compiles the most relevant information from its members into some form of report. Any information not captured in the report is usually discarded unless it is needed for back-up documentation, in which case it may be stored in a central departmental location and the contents noted in some form of database. The report and back-up documentation are usually known to, and accessible only by, the department or team.

The report goes to management (level 3). The management team usually assumes that the department or team compiling the information is responsible for the report and for archiving it. Thus, the management team does not generally issue any directives on its retention or destruction. And as for the comments generated by the report, only the managers involved will have any knowledge of what was discussed.

In such a scenario, information is continually being created and utilized at each level but with little attention given to whether the information was used to its maximum value. How would this scenario be different if the information at each level were considered a valuable intellectual asset?

WHAT ARE INTELLECTUAL ASSETS?

Intellectual assets are created whenever employees commit to media any bit of knowledge, know-how, or learning. An intellectual asset is knowledge that has been captured and can be used to create profits. Intellectual assets tend to fall into two main categories. The first are commercializable assets such as patents and copyrights. These are the assets that have been traditionally identified as the intellectual property of an organization; some companies are focused on improving their management of these assets and increasing the value extracted from them, as discussed in other chapters of this book. Other intellectual assets may not be directly commercializable but capture the innovative ideas and processes that can sometimes differentiate a company from its competitors. These include strategic plans, administrative or operational procedures, blueprints, drawings, computer programs, and software code. Some high-tech companies, whose products change rapidly, are finding that little is to be gained by focusing on patents that are likely to become obsolete within a very short time.

Intellectual assets exist in many formats, and this diversity of media types presents significant challenges in storage, access, and retrieval. Paper continues to be an important medium, ranging from single pages to bound reports. Information is increasingly stored in electronic or digital formats, including data points from research instruments, documents, e-mail, CD-ROMs, images, videos, and even sound bites. However, the development of information technology to support the type of textual information integral to intellectual asset management has progressed much more slowly than the technology needed for data management.

THE IMPACT OF TECHNOLOGY AND THE INTERNET/INTRANET ON INFORMATION MANAGEMENT

Since the late 1980s, increasing capacity and decreasing cost of electronic information storage has substantially affected the management of data by financial and accounting systems. As noted above, the technology has had an important but less dramatic impact on document and text management because these require more complex and sophisticated systems. Development for this type of information was also slowed by the efforts to maintain all the characteristics of print as the information was converted to electronic formats. Reengineering processes, although often unsuccessful because they focused too much on the technology and not enough on the business, at least attempted to encourage users to think differently about the creation and management of information outside of the traditional constraints imposed by print. Even when such new concepts in information management were visualized, computer software could usually handle only one information format, resulting in very fragmented storage and retrieval of information. Information management was further complicated by the proliferation of different computer platforms throughout a company with differing and incompatible operating systems. Developing applications on a UNIX platform often required parallel development for the PC and/or the Mac.

When the Internet and then internal company intranets were developed in the mid-1990s, information management in companies was fundamentally altered. For the first time, it became possible to provide access to diverse types of information through one "system," independent of computer platform. And using the basic concept of hypertext, it also became possible to easily link different types of information from documents, to animated images, to real-time videos. What was significant and new is that these linkages could take place without affecting ownership, changing where the information resided, or requiring any type of organizational restructuring. All that was needed was permission to link. In corporations, intranets exploded, with a wild mixture of information mounted by individuals, departments, and central corporate groups. Most recently, project and program teams are increasingly using the World Wide Web to communicate globally and to keep everyone on the team up to date.

Almost everyone has now concluded that the Internet/intranet is so powerful that it is "the solution" for information management. And they are right. Internets/intranets excel in allowing access to a wide variety of information in a wide variety of formats. However, companies in which the use of corporate-wide intranets has become pervasive are now finding their Webs increasingly difficult to navigate, and more important, company-critical information can be lost in the huge volume of available information. Thus, the technology for providing and developing information is now readily available, but the need for better information management, including the management of intellectual assets, is more critical than ever, as illustrated by the CIA example. Better information management could be achieved through centralized coordination.

THE CASE FOR CENTRALIZED COORDINATION

What does centralized coordination mean? It is a coordinating role to facilitate access. It does not mean that ownership of information passes from an individual to central control; individuals must own their own information to be productive. It does not mean that departments and teams would pass control to a central authority; departments and teams must also control their own information to accomplish their goals and directives. It does not mean that information must be stored in the same location; it is not data warehousing. Centralized coordination focuses on the coordinating function, not on the centralizing one. "Centralized" simply suggests a single locus or point from which the coordination emanates. Centralized coordination offers many benefits.

1. *Centralized coordination allows clear definition of the valued intellectual assets of the company.* As mentioned at the beginning of this chapter, companies have historically defined intellectual assets very narrowly to include only patents and copyrights. Now that the concept is expanding, without this redefinition, it is very possible for intellectual assets that are critical to the corporation to be missed.
2. *Central coordination permits identification of intellectual assets throughout the organization based on this redefinition.* This may be done by conducting a survey and completing an inventory. The information assets may also be mapped to capture important dependencies and interrelationships and to provide an understanding of these assets within the broader values, goals, and vision of the company. The assets may then be evaluated for importance, frequency of use, and confidentiality so that decisions about location, security, and adequate back-up of the information could be made.
3. *Central coordination helps limit the adverse effects of suboptimization where local emphases take precedence over larger organizational concerns.* Some information may be inefficiently managed, lessening the value of the information to the total organization. Central coordination could recommend when information should be leveraged for more efficient management.
4. *Central coordination fosters an increase in the number of opportunities for creative integration.* This integration could take several forms. One

might be the bundling of different information sources or databases together for greater synergy; central coordination could facilitate discussion between the information owners. Another form of integration could be the development of powerful search engines with common query language for extracting information from multiple databases simultaneously. Another type of integration might incorporate relevant external information with internal information wherever possible. David Teece recently estimated that several billion dollars are spent annually reinventing what is already available. The value of proprietary information can often be substantially increased when it is integrated with external information. For example, an intellectual asset would be a database that might capture all of a company's efforts worldwide on the development of a new product. If employees could, from the same database, tap into information about similar products other companies have in development and their projected market shares, the employees would to be able to see not only how their work fits into their own organizations, but also its potential in the marketplace.

5. *Central coordination increases assurance that information was managed in the appropriate context.* Recently, the CEO of a successful Silicon Valley networking firm commented that his firm's total innovation was driven by talking with customers and understanding their needs. He then stated that this effort was far more difficult than it appeared. Often customers themselves did not really understand what they were looking for. Thus, it required an extensive effort for his company to translate what customers were saying into the actual problems that the customers were encountering, so that a solution could be found. The same is true in managing intellectual assets. Gathering information from departments and allowing company-wide access to it requires that the future users of the information understand the context in which it was developed to use it in any meaningful way. Otherwise, they risk making decisions based on misunderstood information.
6. *Central coordination can result in cost efficiencies if duplication throughout the organization is reduced.* If two groups are managing the same type of information, recommendations could be made for sharing the responsibility. At the same time, through internal interviews and benchmarking with other companies, central coordination could identify gaps and recommend ways of supplying information that appears to be missing.
7. *Central coordination allows for the development of a global thesaurus and apply appropriate indexing.* This is very important. Indexing forces the analysis of the intellectual asset to accurately place it within the conceptual framework of the database. As in the CIA example, searching for concepts across several databases where multiple names or terms exist for the same concept results in incomplete information. Both Merck and Glaxo are aggressively working on this problem, creating positions called *director, vocabulary,* and *information architecture* to establish enterprise-wide vocabularies as a critical component of a knowledge

network. Although automatic systems for indexing information have improved, Du Pont has found the following:

> Today, only a conceptual approach requiring human intellectual analysis will be successful when indexing proprietary technical documents for future retrieval. If analyzed at too high a level, the document cannot be retrieved when it is needed. On the other hand, if analyzed at too detailed a level, the document can be retrieved frequently, but will often be irrelevant. We hear repeatedly about computer systems which automatically index documents. Many of these systems simply represent one more tool that will help to bury us in information. The proliferation of image management systems and the difficulties involved in retrieving information from them present an as yet unsolved dilemma. Although documents can be scanned into databases with relative ease, retrieval is greatly complicated by the low level of indexing. More complex indexing and content analysis are required to ensure more precise recall.[2]

THE CHALLENGES OF CENTRAL COORDINATION

Not withstanding the obvious benefits of central coordination, there are challenges that must be addressed. Owners of information are generally reluctant to relinquish ownership to anyone else. Their reluctance is usually caused by a fear of loss of control over the information and a fear that the integrity of the information might be compromised. Part of this fear may originate from efforts pre-intranet or Web technology, when centralized efforts did require that the information actually be turned over to a central group. Today's owners need to be reassured and educated that the technology now exists to permit the sharing of information without this loss of control.

Another challenge is the heterogeneity of information sources within today's complex organizations. Different types of information are stored in different formats and require different retrieval protocols. This challenge is more technological than political. In addition to taking advantage of hypertext linkages, there are currently efforts to develop "translators" and other powerful descriptive, abstracting, and summarization tools that would take a query and reformat it to meet the structure of different databases. These tools coupled with good indexing could enhance the quality of retrieval and use.

Cost justification is also a challenge. Although the expense of managing the information may be absorbed by a department, additional costs may be incurred in a central coordination effort. In addition, once central coordination exists, the costs of information hidden within departmental budgets becomes immediately more visible and may be challenged by management in evaluating the allocation of resources. In reality, central coordination may be more cost-effective, particularly since it is one way to recognize duplication of efforts.

These challenges can be met and the benefits realized if centralized coordination is managed by individuals with the appropriate skills and knowledge.

WHAT ARE THE ATTRIBUTES NEEDED FOR CENTRAL COORDINATION?

Any person or function assuming the responsibility for this central coordination of intellectual assets should have the following skills and knowledge base.

Central coordination should be politically neutral and not represent any particular faction within the organization. Although the concept of intellectual assets is usually introduced into a company by a key group such as a patent or licensing department, intellectual assets are mined from multiple departments. Central coordination should be objective and collaborative. This is especially important in the prioritization of information: The most important and potentially most heavily utilized information assets should be addressed first. And, as central coordination would have interactions with employees in every department, it should be a group that already understands the types of information coming from each department or team and its interconnectability. All of these efforts help to ensure that intellectual asset management decisions are based on the needs of the business and not on the needs or the power base of a single group within the organization.

Central coordination requires experience in managing collections and databases that are used across the organization. Note that the first problem listed in the CIA example was the reluctance to share information. The old cliché that "information is power" is still true. But companies are increasingly realizing that it is only through the systematic sharing of information that they can leverage their knowledge and remain competitive. Smart technology minus an environment that nourishes and supports sharing information is not enough. Policies and procedures are needed to ensure that this does not happen just serendipitously, but routinely and continuously. Central coordination should override departmental boundaries and connect groups working on similar projects.

Central coordination requires experience in database design with a focus on what information needs to be extracted after the database is complete. This is not as easy as technologists would have us believe! There are no easy answers when it comes to good information management. Ease of use means that complexity is often hidden. Thus, more care is needed in the design. Throwing more technology at a problem does not solve it. This is further complicated by the fact that intellectual asset databases will be primarily text management systems, not data management systems, which are far simpler. Unfortunately, few technologists understand the difference.

Central coordination requires an extensive understanding of information-seeking behavior by employees. Regardless of how well databases are designed or how important the information contained in them, if access to and utilization of the information are not incorporated into employees' workflow, the information will not be used. If the database design does not take into consideration how employees will search for the information, the information will also not be used.

Central coordination requires the tracking and evaluating of rapid changes in the information industry. Substantial increases in computing power plus the impact of Internet/intranets are rapidly changing how companies handle their information. Thus, a design or solution that worked well yesterday may not be as effective today. Central coordination should monitor the changes in the information business as part of their core responsibilities. They should be actively comparing the systems and structures in place with those that are evolving and making appropriate recommendations to management.

ROLE OF THE CORPORATE LIBRARIAN

The benefits of central coordination have been clearly outlined. The set of attributes just identified is most closely matched by the corporate library function. Librarians are in a unique position to facilitate intellectual capital management because they already manage collections and databases used across the organization. And because they serve employees in almost every department, they understand the types of information coming from each department and its interconnectability.

Libraries are recognized in most corporations as a neutral zone in departmental turf wars and, thus, as logical centers for maintaining corporate-wide assets. Corporate librarians already are known for overriding departmental boundaries and connecting groups working on similar projects. This often occurs when a librarian recognizes the relationship of an information request by one group to the request of another; unless confidentiality issues are involved, the librarian usually alerts the two groups to the similarities and thus facilitates communication between them.

Librarians can also draw on this neutrality for the prioritization of intellectual assets. Each department may assume that its information is the most important to the organization. Librarians can facilitate discussions on the prioritization of information so that the most important and potentially most heavily utilized information is addressed first.

Librarians are skilled at soliciting information and placing it in context. As part of their everyday work of conducting reference interviews, librarians conceptualize requests and analyze them, looking for their relationship to established knowledge databases and controlled vocabularies. Bonnie Nardi, from the Knowledge Systems Lab in the Apple Research Laboratories, conducted an ethnographic study on the expertise in context building that librarians use in this process. She notes that librarians may conduct their interviews so skillfully that the client does not even realize the extent of their collaboration with the librarian or the librarian's expertise.[3]

Because librarians extensively search both internal and external databases, they are aware of the requirements for database construction. And because they understand the user's information-seeking behavior, they can provide insight into what works and what doesn't work in the design of user interfaces. Different disciplines have different expectations, and thus the way information is queried by different disciplines varies greatly as well. This needs to be taken into consideration in the design process for optimal retrieval.

In addition to database development, companies are now using intranets extensively to facilitate communication and information sharing among employees, no matter where they are located in the world. Librarians have not only been leaders in introducing the Internet and the intranet into their companies, but also in helping to manage this unwieldy resource, as the Microsoft example in a 1997 *Fortune* article describes.[4] The librarian's role was also discussed in an editorial entitled "Civilizing the Internet," in *Scientific American.* John Rennie wrote:

> ". . . Conan the Librarian?" . . . For taming this particular frontier [the Internet], the right people are librarians, not cowboys. The Internet is made of information, and nobody knows more about how to order information than librarians, who have been pondering that problem for thousands of years.[5]

CONCLUSION

Companies are recognizing that information management is the key to competitiveness in the global market and of critical importance in intellectual capital management. The critical part of intellectual capital management is the ability to gather disparate types of information from diverse sources throughout the organization, to organize that information in such a way that the it still has meaning and relevance, to then design systems and processes and establish policies, and to maximize the retrieval and thus the usefulness of the company's intellectual assets. This is a complex integration of knowledge, tools, retrieval, and process. These are the skills librarians have and use effectively in the corporate world. Corporations that recognize the unique skills and knowledge of their corporate librarians will be better positioned to manage their valuable intellectual assets.

NOTES

1 Susanne Schafer, "CIA Acknowledges Missteps in Assessing Data on Chemical Weapons Depot," *Associated Press* 18:27 (April 9, 1997).

2 Margaret T. Nichols et al. "Survival in Transition or Implementing Information Science Core Competencies," *Bulletin of the American Society for Information Science* (December/January 1996): 11–15.

3 See Bonnie A. Nardi and Vicki O'Day, "Intelligent Agents: What We Learned at the Library," *Libri* 4:2 (1966); and Bonnie A. Nardi, Vicki O'Day, and Ed Valauskas, "Put a Good Librarian, Not Software, in the Driver's Seat," *Christian Science Monitor* (June 4, 1996).

4 Mary J. Cronin, "Reinventing the Microsoft Intranet," *Fortune* (June 23, 1997): 142, 144.

5 John Rennie, "Civilizing the Internet," *Scientific American* (March 1997) Special Report, "The Internet: Fulfilling the Promise," 6.

25

The Future of Intellectual Capital

Patrick H. Sullivan

ICM Group, LLC

Attempting to predict the future of anything in the business world, much less intellectual capital, is an enterprise that brings to mind the caption used by medieval map makers to describe what could be found in unexplored waters: *There, there be dragons!* Nevertheless, both science and practice tell us there are degrees of reasonable predictability about the future, and within reasonable limits, one can discuss the trajectory of events and where those trajectories may take us.

Several years ago, I was approached by Sally Ride, then the planning director for NASA. She had been asked by NASA's administrator to tell him which course the agency should take: Should it orient itself toward colonizing the moon? Should it be focus on a manned mission to Mars? Should it be working toward a complex unmanned exploration of the moons of Jupiter? Sally confessed she had no idea how to answer the question. "I don't either," I replied. "But I know those are the wrong questions." The questions were unanswerable and "wrong" because they were asked without context and without being able to know enough about the future to make them answerable. NASA, of course, developed throughout its early years as a project-oriented agency and during Sally's tenure as planning director still thought of itself in project terms: Mercury—putting the first man into space; Gemini—men working in space; Apollo—men operating on the moon. The agency defined itself by the major project(s) it took on, so the administrator's question had particular significance to NASA. The real question, and one that was answerable, was what does NASA wish to become in the future. If they knew the answer to that question, then the choice among moon colonization, manned mission to Mars, and unmanned exploration of the moons of Jupiter, and others could be easily determined.

With intellectual capital, as in the case for NASA, the future is filled with too much ambiguity and chance to believe one could make specific predictions about the future. In the business world, we have seen an increasing degree of turbulence growing out of a stable and predictable business environment at the turn of the century to one of rapid and discontinuous change today. Igor Ansoff, in his book *Implanting Strategic Management,* describes five stages of increasing business turbulence: stable, reactive, anticipating, exploring, and creative.

Stable Phase—During the early twentieth century, the business environment was relatively stable. Events in this world were familiar and known, their change tended to be at a pace slower than firms could respond, and future events could be expected to be largely a recurrence of past or well-known events.

Reactive Phase—By the 1930s, with the severe stock market crash and the rapid changes in the U.S. social and political landscape, events were becoming newer and less familiar than had been the case heretofore. The rapidity of change was happening at a rate that was faster than a firm's ability to respond. The visibility of the future was no longer a recurring one; rather, it had become one where the future was expected to be different, although forecastable through extrapolation from past events.

Anticipating Phase—By the 1950s, the business world had become used to events in the future being different from those in the past, but skills at extrapolating from experience allowed firms to still feel that the future was not unfamiliar. The rapidity of change was at a rate that was comparable to the ability of firms to respond.

Exploring Phase—By the 1970s, the future was seen to be discontinuous with the past but nevertheless still related to a firm's experience from the past. The rapidity of change had increased to a pace where events were occurring faster than firms could fully respond. The visibility of the future had changed from recurring or forecastable to one which was predictable through probabilities and scenarios based on trends and trajectories, particularly as it related to threats and opportunities.

Creative Phase—By the 1990s, events in the future are no longer seen as necessarily familiar. They are now viewed as novel and usually discontinuous with the past. The rapidity of change is much faster, typically faster than a firm's ability to respond. The visibility of the future has shifted from one that is probabilistic to one that is only partially predictable because the signals about trends and trajectories are weak. The future is now considered unpredictable and filled with surprises.

In the time since Ansoff developed his ideas about business turbulence, we have seen the emergence of chaos theory as a paradigm that describes ways of viewing complex events, particularly when we wish to make predictions about future conditions based on information about the past. Chaos theory tells us that the farther into the future we wish to look, the less likely it is that we can make accurate point predictions based on information from the past. This is because individual activities or flows of events become discontinuous as the turbulence of environment has more time to effect them. The partial solution, say the chaos theorists, is to recognize that turbulence exists at the finest levels of definition of events and activities. There are levels of aggregation or generalization where the flows are more laminar and therefore more predictable. In the case of the business world, this is translated to mean that while individual companies or industries may operate in environments that are turbulent, the larger or more macroforces that shape them are operating at a slower pace and may be more predictable.

Chaos theorists often use the smoke rising from a cigarette as an illustrative example. It is difficult to predict from one second to the next the path an individual molecule of smoke will take, because of the turbulence of the flow within the plume of smoke that surrounds the molecule. Nevertheless, it is much more likely one can predict the movement of the envelope of the smoke plume as it rises from the cigarette. It is our belief here that we can discuss the envelope within which the expected business turbulence affecting intellectual capital can be expected to occur. We will leave predictions of individual events or activities to others more skilled than we.

INDICATORS OF THE FUTURE

There is an increasing awareness that Paul Romer's view may be the correct one. Romer, The Stanford University economist and proponent of what is called the *New Economics,* believes that innovation is the fundamental source of value in industrialized society. This simple thought has astounding implications for society and for those believing that intellectual capital is important. In the past, physical resources were deemed to be fundamental to value creation. This view spurred the great European waves of exploration to find new routes to the spices of the orient. That led to the desire to acquire the gold and silver of the new world. It fueled the colonization of the Americas, Africa, and Asia. The desire for control of physical resources was the underlying cause of the twentieth-century world wars involving Europe and Asia. If Romer is correct, and we believe he is, then what does his belief portend for our future?

Whereas in the past, the history of mankind was to use man's muscle to wrest physical resources from the environment and then to protect them, the future will involve the use of man's brain. The management of the past viewed the human resources as a source of physical strength, to be used and often discarded as strength declined with age. In light of Romer's thesis, the future looks quite different. Here, managements will view the human resource as a source of innovation, to be nurtured and developed. With increasing knowledge and experience, we can expect to see more innovation and creative production. Age, experience, and intellectual productivity will be encouraged and sought after. Our views of productivity can be expected to change from output measured in physical terms to output measured in innovation and quality terms. Indeed, Romer's view suggests that innovation and information can be expected to become the coin of the realm in the future and that the human resource in the future will be treated far differently from what has been the case in the past.

One can see this trend in operation around us today. We see the emergence of the information society, the explosive popularity of the internet, the emergence of service and information firms (software and information companies) as business juggernauts and the decline of physical commodity firms (steel and precious metals). We see the trend in transportation as well. Railroads went through their great expansion and use to move physical products, with passengers as a second priority. Airlines have evolved with passenger travel (human capital) as their primary mission with the movement of freight and physical items as secondary. Satellite communications, cellular telephones, HDTV, and digitalization of information are all technologies intended to increase communication for the world's human resource. The thrust of society's recent investment has been in the field of information movement, not in the movement of physical assets. Indeed, information is becoming an asset for society, and information is both an input and a result of the innovative process.

THE IMPLICATIONS FOR INTELLECTUAL CAPITAL

The implications of the foregoing for intellectual capital and its management are staggering. They suggest that intellectual capital is of such great importance to society and to business that we must develop more and better ways of nurturing its ability to innovate and create value. For those interested in ICM as a field of endeavor, it means many things. First, it encourages us to seek out the new paradigm and new models for management. It requires that we develop a common worldview of intellectual capital and its importance to business as well as to society. It further underscores the need for a language, terms, and definitions that allow us to speak a common language that is consistent with the new paradigm.

The innovation-as-value-creator view suggests that for large firms, systematic solutions that build on human-oriented processes will become increasingly important. It suggests that the individualistic home-run model of innovation so prevalent in small or entrepreneurial firms must give way to the team- and cooperation-oriented rugby team model for larger groups and businesses. It underscores our view that better processes for extracting value are necessary to create the profits necessary to fund the new methods and systems for managing the human resource.

The emerging view means we must develop new and better methods for dealing with know-how, that elusive bit of knowledge and lore that is not codified or written but that breathes life into otherwise sterile codified innovations. A patent without the know-how to manufacture or operate its imbedded knowledge is a patent without value. Whereas we have developed sophisticated knowledge about how to systematically extract value from the codified assets of the firm's innovators (that is what this book is all about), we have not yet understood how to do so for its uncodified assets, particularly its know-how.

THE IMPLICATIONS FOR INTELLECTUAL ASSETS

For intellectual assets, codified intellectual capital, we may be able to see a short way into the future. There are activities underway whose trajectories may be sufficiently apparent to suggest their near-term future. Turning first to the intellectual property component of intellectual assets. Recent history has seen an increase in the frequency with which the judiciary has upheld the rights of owners of intellectual property in the United States. The country's policy and practice has been shifting to an increased awareness of and interest in maintaining and upholding patent rights for its inventors. We note the fervor with which the United States has participated in the latest rounds of international treaty negotiations involving intellectual property and property rights as evidence of a trend of governmental support for the rights of inventors and for the importance of intellectual property. We see this trend increasing not only in the United States but in all of the world's industrialized countries. Further, we see several so-called Third World countries, notably India and China, coming to the realization that contrary to their former positions on IP rights, it is to their advantage to create and maintain a more rigorous system of intellectual property law to encourage indigenous inventors to create the innovations that will create value and jobs for their countries, forward over time.

Further on intellectual property, we see an increase in the breadth of innovations falling under the protection of intellectual property law. Recent discussions and practice suggest trends and trajectories in intellectual property breadth: The patenting of certain forms of biological life and the patenting of software are but two examples. Copyright law is being challenged by trends and trajectories. Copyrights for information that appears on the internet is an issue with enormous implications for intellectual property in the future. Recent discussions on anticircumvention of copyrights is yet another example of ways in which the legal protection for innovation can be expected to expand rather than to decline.

As more companies become aware of the value of their intellectual assets, we have already seen an expansion in the interest in managing and extracting value from them. The initial meeting of the ICM Gathering in 1995, targeted to include all the companies in the world actively managing their intellectual assets, contained eight companies. Now, in mid-1997, that group includes over 20 companies with more seeking to join. Companies are actively seeking to identify more commercializable intellectual assets. Or, in other words, companies are seeking to extract value from innovations already created and codified. Further, companies are seeking to develop methods for obtaining more information on what their intellectual assets are and how they may be located and leveraged (see Chapter 24 concerning the use of corporate libraries as a central clearing house for intellectual assets).

The role and definition of the intellectual asset manager is emerging as one of particular importance at knowledge firms. Companies can be expected to realize the power of better cross-coordination of information between and among the several portfolios of intellectual assets (see Chapter 14 on the intellectual asset manager). Further, as these assets increase in importance, yet another trend or trajectory is becoming clear. Executives no longer have the time nor are they always physically in the same place, to have the routine meetings still necessary to make decisions on the commercialization and management of the firm's intellectual assets. Increasingly, firms are developing the information systems capabilities to hold IA management committee meetings electronically so that key decisions may be made in a timely manner even in a world where key executives are traveling too frequently to meet in a face-to-face, decision-making environment. Finally, under the heading of intellectual asset management, firms are recognizing the importance of intellectual capital to their long-term viability and ability to reach their strategic goals. The trajectory many knowledge firms find themselves on is one in which the linkage between intellectual capital and profits, as well as between intellectual capital and strategic goals, is becoming more precisely known and more tightly linked.

THE FUTURE FOR IC REPORTING

Inside the firm, the future for the reporting of IC activities is dependent on the ability of firms to measure intellectual capital and their management of it. The field of measuring intangibles has developed rapidly, driven largely by the companies themselves. Increasingly, companies are finding more and better ways to define the intellectual capital activities they wish to influence, to manage those activities, and to find ways of measuring their inputs, processes, and results. These measures, both quantitative and qualitative, are becoming increasingly credible as firms practice and improve their use. Frameworks for defining intellectual capital within the firm, the division between IC stocks and flows, the willingness to accept fuzzy as contrasted with precise measures, all militate toward the emergence of new and better methods for measuring and managing this key intangible.

In some cases it is desirable for measures to be expressed in dollar terms. This often calls for the capability to value intellectual capital stocks or activities. Whereas the existing and classical methods for valuing intangibles—drawing on the economic, financial, and accounting literatures—are going through continual upgrading and improvement, the major trend in valuation is, again, occurring within companies as they struggle to find methods that will provide accurate enough valuations to meet company decision-making needs and yet still be accurate enough to be credible (see the Appendix for the Dow Chemical Company's internal paper concerning methods available for valuing intellectual assets).

The implications of the foregoing for external reporting suggest that companies will have a greater capability to create credible reports of their intellectual capital activities and that these reports can contain information that links their use of intellectual capital to the bottom line of the corporation. This capability will be seen as increasingly important to those knowledge firms for whom credibility in the capital markets is important. Parenthetically, for those firms whose financial credibility is already established, the thought of producing reports that expose their amount and management of intellectual capital are superfluous and perhaps in some cases threatening. Such firms view external reporting as an opportunity for investors to conduct critical reviews of company activities that might lead to a lowering of credibility in the capital markets. Yet for most knowledge companies, external reporting, and the promise of increased financial credibility, often opens the door to a lowering of their costs of capital, a prospect many would look on with a favorable eye.

THE IMPLICATIONS FOR LITIGATION

Intellectual property litigation is one of the fastest growing areas of litigation in the United States. Major corporations are often embroiled in several significant litigation cases at once, all requiring a significant expenditure of management time and company dollars. As the importance of intellectual property rights and governmental support for them increases, we can expect to see a continuation of the trend toward the judiciary upholding the rights of IP owners. Many knowledge companies are learning about the expense of litigation and, more important, that their expenditures are not investments in creating future value, but rather expenditures that reduce the amount of company financial capital available to invest in innovation.

A weak signal that is observable on the horizon suggests that firms are looking to find alternative methods, either for avoiding litigation in the first place, or for alternative forms of dispute resolution that require less "wasted" expenditure of company time and financial capital. In some industries, firms are increasing their cross-licensing activity as a way of ameliorating the effect of actual or potential infringement. In other industries, the "Mexican stand-off" strategy is practiced wherein each potential litigant recognizes that while he or she may be inadvertently infringing the patent of the other, neither will initiate legal action if the other doesn't. This weak signal suggests a trend toward fewer disputes being resolved in court and more litigation avoidance activity and discussions being held between companies.

The future for intellectual capital in industrialized society is difficult to comprehend. At this point in history we are only just becoming aware of the power and promise this new way of looking at business and its value creation activity. Value extraction, inevitably an outcome of value creation, is limited only by the amount of value firms can create and by our ability and creativity in thinking of new and more productive ways of obtaining and benefiting from the value created by innovation in firms. In thinking about the future for intellectual capital, the thoughts presented here barely scratch the surface of the possibilities. What will happen next? What new or exciting discoveries will management science and practice reveal tomorrow, next week, next year? The possibilities are, indeed, infinite.

APPENDIX

Valuing Intellectual Properties

Sam Khoury, Ph.D.

The Dow Chemical Company

INTRODUCTION TO VALUING INTELLECTUAL PROPERTIES

Introduction

One of the key value drivers of The Dow Chemical Company is the strategic assets that enable the company to achieve a sustainable competitive advantage. Strategic assets are a focal point for business management, and intellectual properties are one of those strategic assets. The following are examples of intellectual properties found within The Dow Chemical Company:

- Patents
- Trademarks
- Trade secrets
- Know-how
- Engineering drawings
- Computer software

Intellectual properties represent a foundation for building a business. A business strategy that leverages innovation and maximizes value to the corporation is essential. A thorough understanding of the following is required:

- Potential cash flows
- Complimentary assets
- Development costs needed to make a technology a commercial success
- Hurdles facing the commercial development

Technology-based intellectual properties have a "calculable value" based on the economic impact of the technology on the business enterprise in which it resides and the competitive environment. The challenge is to:

- Identify how the technologies contribute to a business enterprise's competitive advantage

- Differentiate the technological contribution from those attributed to other tangible and intangible assets
- Quantify the economic value of the technologies

Objectives of the Valuation Methodology

This document describes methodologies for valuing intellectual properties for purposes such as the buying or selling of technology. The results of the valuation could be used for:

- Internal decision making for Dow's profit centers
- External use such as out-licensing

It is also intended to familiarize the reader with the different methodologies available for the valuation of intellectual properties, their associated advantages and disadvantages, and guidance for using them.

Special emphasis is placed on explaining the Technology Factor (TF) method to value an intellectual property. The Technology Factor valuation method is an efficient technology valuation approach that allows a multifunctional business evaluation team to establish a first-pass estimation of the contribution of a specific technology (this could be a group of patents, individual patents, know-how, copyright, or trade secrets) within a defined business context and/or enterprise. The quality of the Technology Factor valuation is highly dependent on the quality of the assumptions and inputs. The composition of the team and the expertise of the individuals are critical to the accuracy of the valuation. In addition to a quantitative numerical result, one of the benefits of the Tech Factor methodology is to arrive at a consensus between the different functions within a business.

The value of the technology calculated by the Technology Factor method could be corroborated by applying at least one other methodology that fits the specific objectives of the valuation when needed. The course of action to leverage an intellectual property or technology, as recommended by the business, will guide the appraisal team to the appropriate methodology to value that technology. The American Society of Appraisers[1] and outside consultants recommend that valuation of technology be accomplished utilizing more than one valuation approach. This will help to narrow the numerical range for the technology being valued.

The Technology Factor method is a flexible tool that employs a uniform methodology from business to business. It also utilizes a consistent method for different stages of technology development from novel technology to established global businesses. The Technology Factor also incorporates an internal and/or external consensus of value in the form of:

- Internal business development (company experts)
- External business development—license, JV, JD, etc.

The Technology Factor method employs elements of other widely accepted valuation methods, such as:

- Market, industry standards, cash flow, and risk analysis
- A mix of qualitative and quantitative measures
- Team input (the technology is reviewed from commercial, technical, and legal strength)

[1]The American Society of Appraisers is a professional organization that works on standardizing the methodology and its appropriate implementation of business and intellectual asset valuation.

The Technology Factor method also employs a detailed and systematic qualitative assessment of the attributes of the technology and its impact on business which, when properly applied, can lead to a quantification of value that is usable for the outside (i.e., IRS, negotiations).

STRUCTURING THE CONTEXT FOR VALUATION

Introduction

Technology-based assets need not be valued in the abstract. The valuation of technology should, however, be calculated within a business context framework or enterprise, either actual or hypothetical. When the technology is in the early stage of development and a business team cannot identify an actual business enterprise that could exploit the technology, a model enterprise capable of capitalizing on all the products and applications stemming from the technology should be assumed by the team to serve as the basis for the most optimistic scenario ("best case"). The "best case" scenario represents the maximum potential value for the technology. Where there are known or identifiable limitations regarding the technology and its applications, the team must develop a "most probable" scenario within an assumed enterprise. If the technology has been developed to a point at which an existing business, within Dow or outside of Dow, shows or could show interest, then the valuation should be carried out within the framework of that real business.

The greater the extent to which actual, as opposed to assumed or hypothetical, data is available, the more certain and supportable the assumptions and the more accurate and realistic the calculated value of the technology will be.

Valuation within Company Context

Exhibit A.1 illustrates valuation within different company contexts. These companies can be actual or assumed. (Note: The same technology may be valued differently depending on the context.)

Example of Valuation within Company Context

The temporary vapor storage (TVS) technology is used as an example to explain the idea of valuation within company context as just illustrated. Researchers developed the TVS technology to reduce emissions and exposures to organic solvents. This technology is protected by patents that cover the process and the apparatus. The protected intellectual property can be valued within the different option enterprises mentioned in the previous model.

Model Enterprise: The valuation includes several organic solvents in any industry where there is a need to reduce emissions and worker exposures (dry-cleaning, metal cleaning, electronics, etc.)

Assumed Enterprise: The focus of the research effort is on chlorinated solvents and developing the apparatus for the dry-cleaning and metal cleaning industry.

Dow Business X: Dow Business X determines there is higher value added to the technology in the metal cleaning business. They have the contacts in the industry, and the commercialization strategy fits the overall business strategy. The dry-cleaning application does not meet the above criteria, and the business sanctioned its license.

Real Company X: Real Company X is an original equipment manufacturer (OEM) for the dry-cleaning industry interested in licensing the technology because it helps the customer to meet EPA regulations.

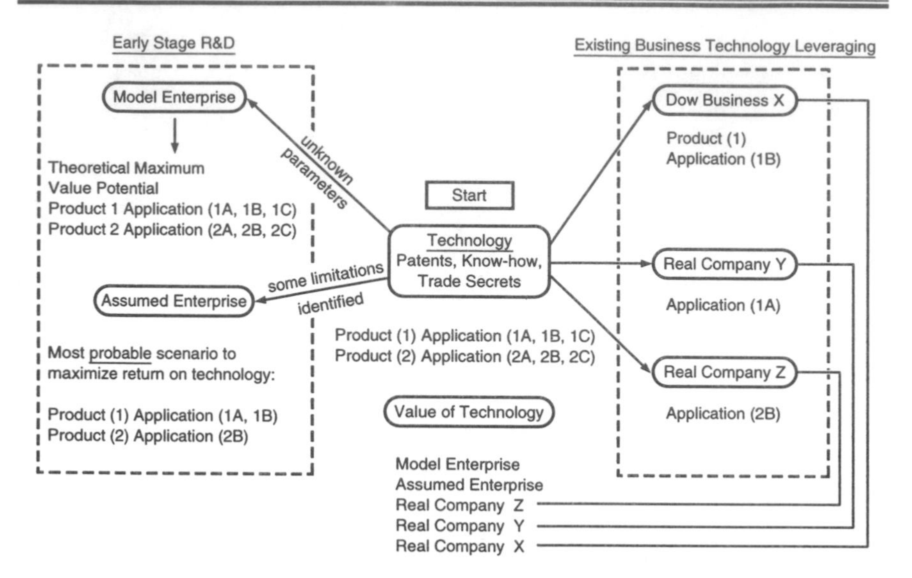

Exhibit A.1 Valuation within Company Context

Real Company Z: Real Company Z is an equipment manufacturer that focuses on the retrofit market. Owners of dry-cleaning machines that are currently in use and do not meet the EPA regulations can implement the technology without having to buy a new machine from an OEM.

The intellectual property protecting the technology will have different values depending on the context in which it is placed. The appraiser and/or facilitator should clarify the context to determine the value of the technology.

TECHNOLOGY FACTOR—INTRODUCTION

Method for Valuation of Technology

The Technology Factor method has been developed as one of the tools available for valuing the intellectual properties that may be applied to Dow's products and processes within Chemicals and Plastics. This methodology incorporates elements of two industry-accepted valuation methods. Those methods are:

- The Income Method, which ties in with Value Based Management (VBM)
- The Market Method, which is the most reliable technique used by independent outside evaluators

The value of technology is based on the cash flow generated by the utility and the competitive advantage that a company derives from ownership and/or use of the underlying intellectual property (patents, inventions, compositions, formulae, etc.). The Technology Factor is an expression of the expected incremental cash flow derived from the practice of a specific technology within a business. It is expressed as a percent of the expected incremental net present value (NPV) of the business as a whole. The resulting competitive advantage will manifest itself in one or more quantifiable ways. For example:

Market differentiation advantage resulting in:

- Volume—as increased market share (additional incremental volume)
- Price—as a premium over competitive technologies (incremental increased price)

Cost to serve advantage:

- Cost—as savings (incremental reduced cost to serve versus competitors)

For a technology which results in a net cost savings, the value of the technology is equal to the entire NPV of the incremental cash flow over time to a business due to the net cost savings from using, versus not using, that technology. Therefore, the Technology Factor in cost savings cases equals 100%.

For a technology which contributes to market differentiation, use of the Technology Factor methodology requires that the business team qualitatively assess how the practiced technology contributes (or could contribute) to the competitive advantage of the business practicing it. It also requires that the team differentiate the technological contribution from those attributed to other tangible and intangible assets.

Fair Market Value

The value of the intellectual property derived from the Technology Factor method is intended to represent the fair market value. Fair market value is defined as the amount of money at which property would change hands between a willing seller and a willing buyer when neither is under compulsion, and when both have reasonable knowledge of the relevant facts.

$$\textbf{Technology Value} = \textbf{TF} \times \textbf{Incremental Business NPV}$$
$$0 \leq \textbf{TF} \leq 100\%$$

Considering Attributes of a Technology

The Technology Factor is derived from a consideration of all the attributes of a technology that affect the potential for the technology to create value (e.g., incremental cash flow). These attributes can be organized into two general categories of "utility issues" and "competitive advantage issues." Additional detail regarding these categories will be provided in a subsequent section covering implementation of the Technology Factor methodology.

Technology Factor Ranges

According to Arthur D. Little, author of the Technology Factor method (see Exhibit A.2 for more detail), the following ranges represent the Technology Factor associated with each qualitative assessment of contribution to competitive advantage for technologies in the Chemicals and Plastics industry. The numbers are from public published reports and were checked internally with Dow's processes and products. These numbers fit the industry or market norms.

Qualitative Assessment		Technology Factor
Low	=	0–30%
Medium	=	30–50%
High	=	50–75%

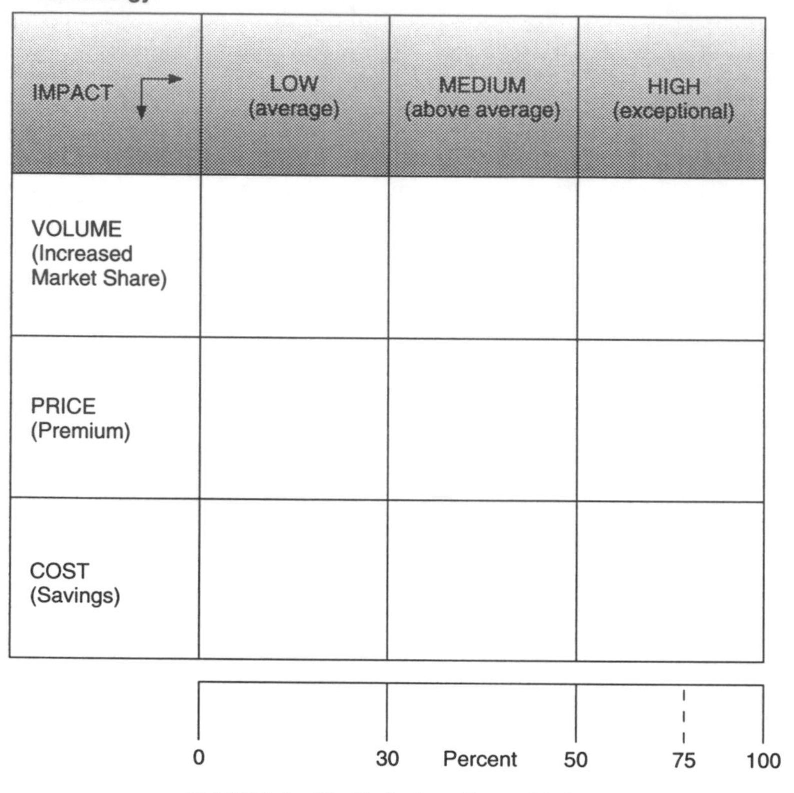

Exhibit A.2 The Technology Factor Method

Another part of the calculation is the NPV of future incremental cash flow attributed to the technology. The product of the Technology Factor and the NPV result in the fair market value of the technology.

Detailed discussion of the Technology Factor valuation process follows, focusing on:

- The process and its elements
- The mechanics of implementing the Technology Factor method

TECHNOLOGY FACTOR—THE PROCESS

Introduction

The following information provides an overview of the necessary participants for the valuation process, how a typical valuation process flows, and an explanation of the components of the process. An overview diagram is also provided as a complete picture of the process.

Participants and Their Roles

To begin the valuation process, an appraiser needs to determine the objective of the valuation of an intellectual property. If more than one scenario exists to leverage the intellectual property, it is essential to go through the valuation process for each one and/or to use different methods. **The evaluating team should not change the objective midstream or an incorrect value will be calculated.**

The makeup of the team significantly impacts the quality of the valuation. Getting the most knowledgeable people representing different functions in the business together is imperative. A team of experts (internal and/or external) assemble to define boundaries of the technology being evaluated and to determine its potential commercial, technical, and legal impact. The team also reviews the qualities and attributes of the technology. The patent attorney will determine the nature of the patent (i.e., process, product, or application) and through the claims, determine the boundaries of the intellectual property being evaluated, as well as its effective dates. The team will also analyze a business summary of the technology. This entails reviewing the economic impact on the value chain of the business utility and the nature of the patent. At the conclusion of the team's evaluation process, each member should be aware of the legal, technical, and economic impact of the technology.

Team Composition

The success of the valuation is highly dependent on the composition of the team and its contributions. It is recommended that the functions in Exhibit A.3 be represented:

Technology Factor

The same information used by the valuation team to determine the NPV of the incremental cash flow is also applied to determine the Technology Factor. The Technology Factor is composed of utility and competitive attributes. The determination of the impact of these attributes on the creation or destruction of value to the business will guide the team to the determination of the market value of the technology. The market value of the technology is expressed as a portion of the NPV of the incremental cash flow.

Cash Flow Analysis

The information derived from team analysis is then utilized to determine the net present value (NPV) of the business. The value of the technology should be tied to the life of the

Exhibit A.3 Function/Contribution Chart

Function	Contribution
Business	Strategic fit of technology with long-term business plan
Attorney	Defines the exact boundaries of the protected intellectual property
R&D	Competitive R&D and its impact on the obsolescence of the technology being evaluated
Technology Center	Scale-up hurdles and competitive manufacturing processes
Marketing/TS&D	Product attributes, market application, and competitive response
Business Analyst	Economic impact (profit/loss of market share or price). Calculates the incremental cash flow and NPV of the products relevant to the technology
Evaluator/Appraiser (if other than analyst)	Facilitates the generation of the technology factor and determines the value of the technology

patent if based on patents only. If technology is based on trade secrets and know-how, the calculation could cover a time frame of up to 15 to 20 years depending on eventual obsolescence of the technology.

Value of Technology

The value of the intellectual property is represented mathematically as:

Value of the technology = NPV of the incremental cash flow due to the technology × Technology Factor

Technology Factor and the Valuation Team

The valuation team, if composed of the recommended functions, would normally have available to it the information needed to establish the Technology Factor. Analyzing the technology with respect to economic issues (i.e., revenue and/or cost impact) is just part of the analysis. The remainder of the analysis can be divided into identifying "utility" issues and "competitive advantage" issues.

Determining the Technology Factor

Valuation team members become familiar with all aspects of the intellectual property on reviewing the patent or know-how, the technology, and the business summary. The business analyst can calculate the NPV of the products or processes that are directly tied to the intellectual property in question. At this stage, the team is ready to determine the Technology Factor. This is done by reviewing the "utility attributes," the "competitive attributes," and legal issues impacting the intellectual properties. These attributes are analyzed for their impact on the success of the business. The team needs to decide if a specific attribute creates, destroys, or has no impact on the business.

Assigning a Technology Factor Range

The next stage of the valuation process (see Exhibit A.4) requires the team to review all of the attributes associated with "utility" and "competitive" issues and to arrive at consensus. In addition, they will assign a low, medium, or high value for the Technology Factor range.

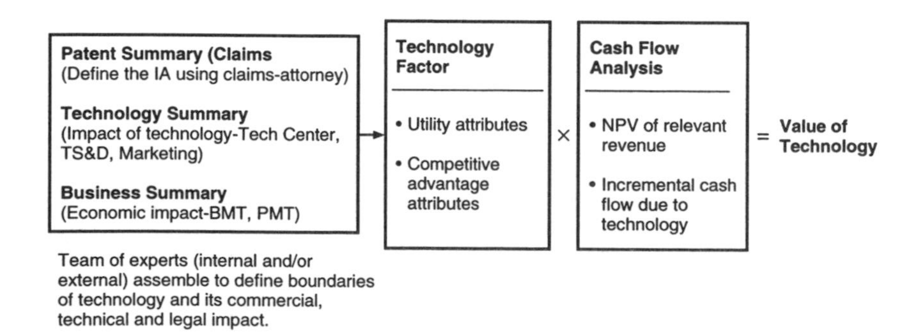

Exhibit A.4 Valuation Process

- Low (0–30%)
- Medium (30–50%)
- High (50–75%)

These numbers are specific for the Chemicals and Plastics industry, therefore, the appraiser should determine the Technology Factors that are specific for her/his industry. Intellectual properties in the pharmaceutical and software industries, where the basis of competition is almost entirely technology linked, can support much higher Technology Factors than, for example, the minerals or petroleum industries.

TECHNOLOGY FACTOR—MECHANICS OF IMPLEMENTATION

Introduction

The mechanics of valuation entail the calculation of the net present value (NPV) of the incremental cash flow and the Technology Factor determination (high, medium, or low). The product of those two variables gives the fair market value of the technology.

NPV Calculation

The net present value (NPV) of a business is the sum of several factors including tangible, intellectual, and complementary assets. One of the difficulties in valuing intellectual assets lies in their interdependence to complementary assets and tangible assets. Theoretically, the value of a technology can be determined by subtracting the value of the business without the technology, from the value of the business with the technology. The Technology Factor methodology is a direct approach to extract the value of the technology from the value of the business incorporating that technology.

Technology Factor Elements

The mechanics of the process include methodical review of the utility and competitive attributes. Team discussion of those attributes will lead to consensus on the contribution of intellectual property as low, medium, or high. The resulting contribution is converted to a percentage based on market data.

A comprehensive list of utility and competitive attributes is shown at the end of this Appendix. The appraiser and the team should review the list and discuss all the relevant questions. This process makes the Technology Factor flexible to accommodate different types of intellectual properties.

Assigning Values to the Utility Issue Work Sheet

Exhibit A.5 provides explanations for the different areas and blocks of the example work sheet (Exhibit A.6) for utility issues. It also helps to describe the major attribute, effect on value creation, and the function for the valuation process as it pertains to a utility issue.

Utility attributes of intellectual assets are reviewed, and their impact on value creation is determined. If the answer for a specific attribute is "creation of value," a (+) is placed in the column. Similarly, if it has no impact or a negative impact on value, a (0) or a (–) is placed in the table (as illustrated in Exhibit A.6).

It is important to note that one negative issue could alter or destroy all other positive issues determined by the team.

Exhibit A.5 Explanation Table

Attribute	Effect on Value	Function
Usefulness to Dow	Does the technology fit with current or future business strategy? Does the technology fit with vertical integration of the business?	Business
Usefulness to others	Is the intellectual property useful to other companies? How many competitors would use the technology? Are the competitors willing to pay to get the patents or spend money to invent around it?	Business/ Marketing/ TS&D
Capital required for implementation	This depends on the objective of valuation and type of business. Rule of thumb for Dow: If the figure is approximately $100 MM, then it might possibly destroy value because $ could be used in other higher-return projects with less risk. Rule of thumb for others: Determine the size of the company and their ability to spend the money for commercialization.	Tech Center
Time required for implementation of technology	This depends on the technology. Generally, it takes approximately 3 years to develop new technology or reinvent around existing intellectual property. If it takes >2 years, the risk factor increases for implementing the technology.	Tech Center/ R&D/ Marketing
Useful life of the technology	This depends on the industry in which the intellectual property resides. Will the technology have a useful life long enough to recover all the costs and the required return on capital?	R&D/TS&D/ Marketing
Other	The appraiser needs to determine if there are other attributes that are specific for the technology being evaluated.	Appraiser

Determining Impact of Utility

When all the attributes are discussed, the team needs to determine if the total impact of utility on the technology is low, medium, or high.

Example of Utility Mechanics

To illustrate the mechanics of the process, refer to the TVS example discussed earlier (Structuring the Context for Valuation). The selected team must review the attributes and see if any additional attributes are needed to better represent the intellectual property. For the temporary vapor storage (TVS) technology, one more attribute to utility, which is "meet EPA and governmental regulations," was added. The team filled in the utility attributes by answering the question for each issue as:

- Adding value (+)
- Destroying value (–)
- No impact (0)

The utility issues were highly positive for TVS. No negative issues were raised, so an assignment of "high" is appropriate (see utility issues table in Exhibit A.6).

Issue	Effect on Value Creation		
Utility	–	0	+
• Usefulness to Dow			+
• Usefulness to others – # of potential licenses			+
• Capital required for implementation of tech – Dow			+
– Others		0	
• Time required for implementation of tech			+
• Useful life of technology			+
• Other (Meets EPA Reg.)			+

(H)

Exhibit A.6 Intellectual Asset Valuation Utility Issues

Introduction

Exhibit A.7 provides explanations for the different areas and blocks of Exhibit A.8 entitled "Intellectual Asset Valuation—Competitive Advantage Issues." It also helps to describe the function, major attribute, and effect on value creation for the valuation process as it pertains to competitive advantage issues and legal issues.

Competitive Advantage Issue

Competitive issues are reviewed, and their impact on value creation or destruction is determined. The final result is not a mathematical summation of the negatives and positives of value creation. If the answer for a specific attribute is "creation of value," a (+) is placed in the column. Similarly, if it has no impact or a negative impact on value, a (0) or a (–) is placed in the table, as illustrated in Exhibit A.8. **It is important to note that one issue that destroys value could outweigh all the other positive issues that create value.**

Determining Impact of Competitive Advantages

When all the issues are discussed, the team needs to determine if the total impact on the technology is low, medium, or high.

Example of Competitive Mechanics

Continuing with the TVS example, the TVS team methodically reviewed the competitive attributes and their effect on value creation. Most of the issues were positive for the competitive attributes. The negative assignment, due to existence of alternative technologies of "in kind" and "not in kind," reduced the competitive advantage impact from high to medium (see Exhibit A.8).

Exhibit A.7 Explanation Table

Attribute	Effect on Value Creation	Function
Differentiation	Will the customer pay higher price for the product? Will the technology increase market share?	Marketing/ Business
Alternative technology	Do the same or similar products exist with different processes? Is there a different product and different process that could compete in the same market?	TS&D/ Marketing
Legal strength → defensibility	How difficult is it to engineer around the intellectual asset? What is the blocking power of the patent?	Attorney
→ scope of the claims	The broader the claim and the more novel an innovation is, the higher the probability to extract value.	
→ detection of infringement	Can infringement be detected by analysis of the product? Is the technology unique enough that the only process that could be used is covered by the patent?	
→ useful life of the patent	There is a tie between useful life of technology and useful life of the patent. Usually, if a patent has <2 years before expiration, the business is negatively impacted.	
Anticipated competitive response	Will the competition reduce price, add service, or fight for market positioning? Will competitors oppose and prove patent invalid?	Marketing/ TS&D
Teaching value of patent	This depends on the objective of the valuation (i.e., license, JV, or integration with Dow's business) and the resources available for the business. Currently, resources are scarce, and major engineering support to license a technology might be viewed as destroying value.	Attorney/ R&D
Right to use the technology	Are the intellectual properties totally free for the business to leverage its value? Is the technology tied to an exclusive agreement?	Attorney/ Business

The team reviewed the competitive and utility issues and evaluated their combined impact to arrive at a value for the Technology Factor. In the case of TVS technology, the options were at the high end of medium or the low end of high. The team decided the combined impact value was at the low end of high. The range for high is 50–75%, with 55% as the most appropriate number for the Technology Factor.

Technology Factor Determination (Implied)

Once the team determined and assigned a low, medium, or high range to the utility and competitive attributes, the evaluator or appraiser needed to determine the Technology Factor by combining the two dimensions of "utility" and "competitive." Exhibit A.9 helps to explain how this was done.

Technology Factor Determination (Integrated)

The Technology Factor can be determined qualitatively through consensus. This method is used when it is clear where the market range is for the technology. If the technology is on the borderline between high and medium, or medium and low, and the team cannot reach consensus, then the appraiser could apply any decision-making tool to reach a final decision on the Technology Factor.

Issue	Effect on Value Creation		
Competitive Advantage	–	0	+
• Differentiation			+
• Alternative Tech – In-kind	–		
– Not in-kind	–		
• Legal strength – Defensibility			+
– Scope of the claims			+
– Detection of infringement			+
• Useful life of patent			+
• Anticipated competitive response		0	
• Teaching value of patent			+
• Right to use the technology (Dow/Others)			+
		(M)	

Exhibit A.8 Intellectual Asset Valuation Competitive Advantage Issues

TVS Example

Technology Value Equation

Once the Technology Factor is determined and the net present value is supplied by the valuation team, multiplying the NPV by the Technology Factor equals the value of the technology.

NPV ($) X **TF (%)** = **Value of Technology ($)**

Final Valuation of TVS Example

The business manager, marketing person, and the economic planner forecast the future potential and discount the income stream to the present value. For the TVS technology, the incremental cash flow per machine was determined to be $1500/per machine. Market research on guideline retrofits helped determine the market value. A reasonable sales projection over the next ten years with reasonable market penetration on new machines gave a net present value after tax of $4.5 million. The value of the protected technology is about $2.5 million. This number is the result of the product of $4.5 million dollars of incremental cash flow and a 55% technology factor.

Value Analysis

Once the valuation team has calculated the value of the technology by using the Technology Factor method, it is prudent for the appraiser to calculate the value by using at least one

Exhibit A.9 Technology Factor Determination

Technology	Competitive	Utility	Tech Factor Implied	Tech Factor Integrated
Product or process name	Decide from competitive attributes whether the impact on value creation is: (low) (medium) (high)	Decide from utility attributes whether the impact on value creation is: (low) (medium) (high)	Place a weighted factor on competitive and utility attributes to evaluate how each could impact value and come to a decision whether: L = 0–30% M = 30–50% H = 50–75% From here one can bracket high and low end of value.	Revisit the attributes to see if technology is at the low, middle, or high end of the range and try to get an explicit number for the Technology Factor (i.e., 40%). This will give a $ value for the technology.

Technology Factor Range

L = 0–30%
M = 30–50%
H = 50–75%

(According to A.D. Little, these numbers represent the Technology Factors for technologies in the Chemicals and Plastics industry. The numbers are from public published reports and were checked internally with Dow's processes and products. Dow's numbers fit the industry or market norms.)

other relevant method (refer to Exhibits A.12–A.14). If the values are in close approximate ranges, then the data can be analyzed and a number determined with reasonable confidence. If a large discrepancy exists, then assumptions need to be reviewed, and the appraiser should reevaluate the technology. Exhibit A.11 represents TVS technology valued by several methods.

The appraiser may eliminate some methods that might not be representative. In this case the 25% Rule and cost methods are not appropriate. The appraiser can assess with confidence a range of $2–$2.7 million for the value of the technology.

OTHER METHODS FOR VALUATION OF INTELLECTUAL PROPERTIES

Introduction

Since the Technology Factor methodology uses elements from other existing and accepted valuation techniques, and since the use of two valuation techniques for corroboration is encouraged, it is appropriate to review the available range of valuation methodologies.

Valuation of intellectual assets is an inexact science. No single technique is accepted as "the best." Different valuation techniques can result in values which differ by as much as a factor of two. Accurate, useful, and defensible valuations require the selection of a methodology appropriate to the circumstances and applied with as much analytical rigor as the sources of input data will allow.

Technology	Competitive	Utility	Range of Tech Factor	Absolute Tech Factor
TVS	M	H	H (50–75)	55

Tech Factor Range:

L = 0–30%
M = 30–50%
H = 50–75%

Value of Technology:

\$4.5 Million × 55% = \$2.5 Million

Date:
Name:

Exhibit A.10 TVS Example

Alternate Methods of Valuing Technology

Exhibit A.12 illustrates methods other than the Technology Factor method for valuing technology. These methods are described by:

- The method type
- A description of the method
- The advantages of using the method
- The disadvantages of using the method
- When it is appropriate to use the method

Exhibit A.13, entitled "Recommendations for Valuation Method vs. Objective of Leveraging Technology," is a summary of the situations in which technology needs to be valued along with corresponding recommended valuation methods.

Exhibit A.14, entitled "Valuation Method vs. Technology Type," provides an overview of different valuation methods that are generally appropriate for the types of technology.

The methods suggested in Exhibits A.12 through A.14 are offered as alternate ways to value technology. One or more methods can be used, and the choice of the method will be based on the circumstance and objectives of the business in leveraging the technology. Discretion for use of the appropriate method is left to the valuation team.

Exhibit A.13 illustrates the different methods to value intellectual properties and the different objectives of the enterprise to extract value and leverage those properties. In valuation, every intellectual property is unique by nature. It is difficult to generalize on the proper tool for the objective. The process sets the basis for calculation using many other methods.

Exhibit A.11 TVS Technology Valued by Several Methods

Method	Value of Technology ($MM)
Tech factor	2.5
Risk hurdle	2.7
Cost	1.5
Market	1.9
25% rule	2.0

Exhibit A.12 Other Methods for Valuing Technology

Method	Advantages	Disadvantages	When
25% Rule[1] (method description below)	Simple	Does not consider: -potential profitability -risk/fair return on investment	Quick rough (ballpark) estimate—intellectual property is at commercial stage.
Market[1] (method description below)	Very credible technique	-Assumes current industry norms are correct -Existence of an active market with similar technologies -Companies with similar product (extrapolate) -Indirect approach of valuation[2] -High cost of obtaining accurate data from previous industry deals	If there is a comparable, this is the preferred method, as long as the disadvantages are addressed.
Return on Sales[1] (method description below)	-Quick -established industry norms exist	-Difficult to determine proper allocation of profits between two parties -Value could be different from company to company (may not consider value stream) -Does not consider investment risk associated with intellectual asset	-Established industry norms are present. -Sales projections are agreed on.
Cost[1] (method description below)	Quick/definable	-Revenue not related to value of intellectual asset -Imprecise/may under value technology -Viable for technology developed beyond semicommercial scale	A companion methodology used in negotiations
Auction[3] (method description below)	-Direct determination of willing buyer -No calculation is necessary	-Less control of the willing seller to set the price -Choice may not go to the buyer that is most compatible or may not commit to commercialization	-There are many interested buyers -Low negotiation resource commitment on seller's part is desired -Targeted at up-front payments
Income/Discounted Cash Flow[3] (method description below)	-Most accepted method in marketplace -Cash flow streams from all potential revenue -Takes into consideration competitive environment stage of project development	-Significant knowledge of competitive environment -Information usually needed from other parties on market dynamics -Detailed knowledge of business and market plan -Time consuming to get accurate data	-Unique technologies -Can be applied at any stage of development -Both parties have sophisticated licensing capabilities

Risk Hurdle Rate[3]	-Mathematical risk analysis -Easy to determine risk based on stage of development	-Intensive mathematical calculation -Fail to address the full potential of the technology within the business enterprise or the competitive environment	-An investment banker approach -Financial investment focus -Early stage project
Technology Factor[3] (method description below)	-Gains internal consensus -Isolates the incremental cash flow instead of total revenue -Incorporates theattributes from other methods[4] -Methodical/systematic -Easy to use -Tool considers business enterprise	-Requires assembly of a multifunctional team of experts -Significant knowledge of competitive environment -Detailed knowledge of business and market plan	-For internal valuations -Could be used for one patent or many related patents/technologies -Could be used for any circumstance -Used with any other valuation method

Method descriptions:

25% Rule: Calculates a royalty as 25% of the gross profit, before taxes, from the enterprise operations in which the licensed intellectual property is used.

Market: Measures the present value of future benefits by obtaining a consensus of what others in the marketplace have judged it to be. There are two requisites: (1) an active, public market and (2) an exchange of comparable properties.

Return on Sales: A royalty that is based on net profits as a percentage of revenues.

Cost: Cost approach seeks to measure the future benefits of ownership by qualifying the amount of money that would be required to replace the future service capability of the subject property.

Auction: Discloses intellectual asset information to broad potential customers and accepts sealed bids.

Income/Discounted Cash Flow: The value of property can be measured by the present worth of the net economic benefit (cash receipts less cash outlays) to be received over the life of the property.

Risk Hurdle Rate: Discounted Cash by $\text{NPV} = \frac{\$ \text{ in year } n}{(1+k)^n}$ where k is risk factor

Technology Factor: A measure of the extent to which the cash flow derived from the practice of technology is based on the technology asset itself.

[1] *See* Gordon V. Smith and Russell L. Parr, *Valuation of Intellectual Property and Intangible Assets, Second Edition* (New York: John Wiley & Sons, Inc., 1994).

[2] Value of enterprise – working capital – tangible asset = intangible assets (trademarks, distribution, work force, patents, etc.)

[3] *See* Gordon V. Smith and Russell L. Parr, *Valuation of Intellectual Property and Intangible Assets, Second Edition* (New York: John Wiley & Sons, Inc., 1994).

[4] Gross margins incorporate market method, NPV incorporates income/DCF method, review of attributes covers risk hurdle rates

This Exhibit is intended to provide general guidelines. Individuals involved in valuing technology should always be cognizant of existing exceptions and adjust accordingly. The objective of the valuation should be made very clear and remain fixed throughout the valuation process. Changing the objectives midstream will result in wrong assumptions. A business can, however, elect to value two or three different objectives separately and use the information to choose the option that maximizes the economic profit. **It is recommended that the team of experts use the Technology Factor methodology as the initial method to calculate the contribution of the technology.**

Exhibit A.14 outlines the different types of intellectual properties, their stages of development, and methods for valuation. The shaded areas represent the best methodologies to determine the value of an intellectual property. It is the responsibility of the facilitator to determine if a special case exists and adjust the valuation accordingly. **It is recommended that the team of experts use the Technology Factor methodology as the initial method to calculate the contribution of the technology.**

SUMMARY AND CONCLUSIONS

Summary

It should be clear to the reader that valuation is not an exact science. Valuation of intellectual properties requires an understanding of the general concepts involved in the development of the detailed methods described in this document.

Objective	**Tech Factor**	Market	Risk Hurdle Rate	Cost	Return on Sale	25% Rule	Discounted Cash Flow	Auction
Internal Business Valuation (Decisions to expand, maintain or reduce effort)								
Litigation Infringement (Business Using)								
Litigations Infringement (Business License)								
R&D Investment								
Out License/Sell								
In License/Purchase								
Collateral for Financing								
Joint Ventures & Minority Equity Position								
Taxation IRC (482/936/1253)								

Shaded areas are the recommended valuation method

Exhibit A.13 Recommendations for Valuation Method vs. Objective of Leveraging Technology

Chemicals & Plastics	**Tech Factor**	Market	Risk Hurdle	Cost	Return on Sale	25% Rule	Discounted Cash Flow	Auction
Process Production Plant	√							
Process Pilot Plant								
Basic Research Revolutionary								
Cost Saving								
Product Commodity								
Specialty								
High Performance								
Application Established								
New/Product Extension								
New/Revolutionary								
Intermediate Chemicals Pharmaceutical	√							
Intermediate Chemicals Agricultural	√							
Instrumentation	√							
Process Control								

Shaded areas are the recommended valuation method

Exhibit A.14 Valuation Method vs. Technology Type

Exhibit A.15 Asset Examples

Tangible Assets	Intangible Assets	Complementary Intangible Assets
• Working capital • Buildings • Land • Office equipment • Production machinery • Vehicles	• Copyrights • Patents, proprietary know-how, and technology • Service marks • Trademarks • Computer software	• Assembled workforce • Backlog (a source of future from sales that have already been closed, but not yet fulfilled) • Captive parts annuity (represents the continued purchase of replacement parts for capital equipment already sold to customers) • Culture and management practices • Customer lists • Distribution networks • Experience, insight, and understanding • Favorable contracts (i.e., distribution agreements, raw materials supplies) • Regulatory approvals

Exhibit A.16 Comprehensive List of Utility and Competitive Attributes

Attribute	Effect on Value Creation
Usefulness to Dow	Does the technology fit with current or future business strategy? Does the technology fit with vertical integration of the business?
Usefulness to others	Is the intellectual property useful to other companies? How many competitors use the technology? Are the competitors willing to pay to get the patents or spend money to invent around it?
Capital required for implementation	It depends on the objective of valuation and type of business. Rule of thumb for Dow: If the figure is approx. $100 MM, then it might possibly destroy value because $$ could be used in other higher return projects with less risk. Rule of thumb for others: Determine the size of the company and their ability to spend more for commercialization.
Time required for implementation of technology	It depends on the technology. Generally, it takes approx. 3 years to develop new technology or reinvent around existing intellectual property. If it takes >2 years, the risk factor increases for implementing the technology.
Useful life of the technology	It depends on the industry in which the intellectual property resides. Will the technology have a useful life long enough to recover all the costs and the required return on capital?
Anticipated competitive response	Will the competition reduce price, add service, or fight for market positioning? Will competitors oppose and prove patent invalid?
Teaching value of patent	Depends on the objective of the valuation (i.e., license, JV, or integration with Dow's business) and the resources available for the business. Currently, resources are scarce and major engineering support to license a technology might be viewed as destroying value.
Right to use the technology	Are the intellectual properties totally free for the business to leverage its value? Is the technology tied to an exclusive agreement?
Differentiation	Will the customer pay a higher price for the product? Will the technology increase market share?
Alternative technology	Do the same or similar products exist with different processes? Is there a different product and different process that could compete in the same market?
Legal strength	How difficult is it to engineer around the intellectual asset?
defensibility	What is the blocking power of the patent?
scope of the claims	The broader the claim and the more novel an innovation is, the higher the probability to extract value.
detection of infringement	Can infringement be detected by analysis of the product? Is the technology unique enough that the only process that could be used is covered by the patent?
useful life of the patent	There is a tie between useful life of technology and useful life of the patent. Usually, if a patent has >2 years before expiration, the business is negatively impacted.
Strategic positioning	Does the technology give leadership position for the company? Will the company's competitive position deteriorate if the technology is not protected?
Pioneering/new chemistry	Does the intellectual property represent a pioneering/new chemistry? Is it an incremental improvement?
Insurance value	How strong is the defensive position of the intellectual property?
Complexity of technology	How high is the barrier to entry due to the complexity of the technology? Are there any product liability risks involved?
Expected revenue	Steady stream, cyclical, or seasonal?
Breakdown of revenue	How much revenue is due to the technology? Products offered? Services rendered?

Exhibit A.16 (*Continued*)

Attribute	Effect on Value Creation
Customer willingness to pay for intellectual property	Is the customer willing and able to pay?
Geographic area	Is the interest in leveraging the technology regional or global?
Impact of intellectual property on other products within the company or with customers	Will the technology render other intellectual properties and products obsolete?
Ongoing technology	Is the research continuing, and are future developments expected? Is the research terminated and no additional support expected?
Other costs of maintaining and supporting the intellectual property	Policing strategy, competitive monitoring, warrantees, tax maintenance of patent, security measures to protect trade secrets
Company expectations	High, medium, or low
Other derivative or tag-along sales	Significant, acceptable, negligible
Customer impact	Which customers are impacted by the technology? What market share do they represent?
Competitor impact	Which competitors are impacted by the technology? What market share do they represent?
Stage of the technology	Growth/mature/decline
Credential technology	Will the technology mark you as the leader in the industry?
Royalty rates	What are the traditional market royalty rates for similar technology in the industry? Is it high, medium, or low?

The technology factor method is another tool that combines the market and discount cash flow concepts. The final value represents the fair market value of the intellectual property.

The other methods of valuation are used in determining the different types of value, in addition to the fair market value. The references provided at the bottom of Exhibits A.12 through A.14 should help the reader in developing the needed expertise.

Conclusion

In conclusion, the Technology Factor offers The Dow Chemical Company the flexibility of using one tool to value intellectual properties in all areas of Chemicals and Plastics. The "team of experts approach" expedites the valuation process by having all functions (e.g., business, marketing, R&D, manufacturing, legal counsel, economic evaluator) involved in the valuation. It offers the benefits of:

- Consensus
- Objective evaluation
- A system of checks and balances

Exhibit A.16 represents a comprehensive list of attributes that the appraisal team needs to check and build for the list of attributes required for the Utility and Competitive tables. This table should help steer the team in the proper assignment of the Technology Factor.

These attributes will not be classified under separate categories of "utility" and "competitive" headings. In some cases, one issue could be placed under "utility attributes." In other cases, the same issue could be placed under "competitive attributes." The process should be flexible enough to allow the individuals most familiar with the technology to determine the appropriate placement of the relevant issues.

Author Index

Subject Index